ANARCHY!

Also by Peter Glassgold

AUTHOR (FICTION)

The Angel Max (1998)

∞

EDITOR

James Laughlin, *Byways: A Memoir* (2005)

Living Space: Poems of the Dutch Fifties (1979; rev. ed., with Douglas Messerli, 2005)

New Directions in Prose & Poetry, joint editor with James Laughlin,
nos. 25–55 (1972–91)

∞

EDITOR/TRANSLATOR

*Boethius: The Poems from On the Consolation of Philosophy, Translated out of the
original Latin into diverse historical Englishings diligently collaged* (1994)

Hwaet! A Little Old English Anthology of American Modernist Poetry
(1985; rev. ed., 2012)

∞

TRANSLATOR

Hans Deichmann, *Objects: A Chronicle of Subversion in Nazi Germany and Fascist
Italy*, translated with Peter Constantine, from the German (1997)

Stijn Streuvels, *The Flaxfield*, translated, with André Lefevere,
from the Dutch (1989)

ANARCHY!

An Anthology of Emma Goldman's

MOTHER EARTH

NEW AND EXPANDED EDITION

edited and with commentary by

Peter Glassgold

COUNTERPOINT

CALIFORNIA

Library of Congress Cataloging-in-Publication data is available.

ISBN 978-1-61902-021-4

Cover design by Domini Dragoon
Interior design by Amy Evans McClure
Printed in the United States of America

COUNTERPOINT

Los Angeles and San Francisco, California
www.counterpointpress.com

Printed in the United States of America

For Suzanne
and to the memory of
Paul Avrich

CONTENTS

PART SIX: WAR AND PEACE

Illustrations follow page 220.

This new, expanded edition of *Anarchy! An Anthology of Emma Goldman's* MOTHER EARTH was conceived in an uneasy time, while the earlier edition, published before the attacks of 9/11, was born out of plain curiosity and a writer's need. Let's first consider the nearer anxieties and then how they relate to American anarchism of a previous troubling era.

The year 2012 found America struggling to recover from the greatest financial collapse since the Great Depression, following its engagement in two lengthy, expensive wars, amid protest on the right and left, political dissension and near paralysis, all under the generally dawning realization that the country was experiencing a dangerous imbalance of national wealth not seen since the turn of the last century, the time when anarchism and other revolutionary causes were at their prime. What, if anything, did the conservative and progressive protesters have in common with each other? The answer, it seems to me, is clear. Both movements were loosely organized and drew from the ranks of a disaffected middle class that saw its prospects steadily diminishing, and both were libertarian in the Jeffersonian sense of "that government is best that governs least." Beyond that, the gulf between them was immense, with the conservative, largely middle-aged Tea Partiers, insofar as they had a uniform agenda, being antitax, anti-union, antiabortion, vocally patriotic and promilitary, largely secular but in rapport with a determined religious minority, as well as increasingly nativist and disbelieving in global warming and other environmental concerns—

positions familiar and generally agreeable to the contemporary American far right.

On the progressive left stood Occupy Wall Street (OWS) and its independent offshoots nationwide, whose direct action brought to public consciousness that one percent of the American population controlled more than one third of the wealth, hence the rallying cry, "We are the 99%!" What, if anything, did Occupiers have in common with their dissident forebears of yesteryear? Their prolonged sit-ins certainly evoked the evolving methods, generally peaceful, of civil disobedience and protest begun in the days of Abolition and continued onward through Emma Goldman's time to the era of Vietnam, the nonviolent civil rights movement, and beyond, which called into question existing state institutions and the legitimacy of the legal system itself. Occupiers, mostly young, organized themselves as miniature communal societies based on the self-regulating counsel of direct democracy, as if to announce that such social harmony as theirs was an example to the world. It was a model of the leftwing libertarianism argued for in the pages of *Mother Earth*, but was it, in fact, in line with anarchist tradition? Here, a capsule historical survey is helpful.

The modern idea of political revolution resonates back to the American and French revolutions, which replaced monarchical and imperial rule and its attendant aristocracy with republican government. To this was added over the course of the nineteenth century the concept of nationalism; revolutions often became, in effect, unifying wars of liberation. However, a third idea had also begun to accrue to the idea of revolution, that of radical social and economic change brought on by an international upheaval of workers and peasants. A hundred years ago, when someone referred to the coming revolution, this last was the one that was meant, and it remains at the heart of anarchism then and now. The anarchist movement in America, initially shattered by the red scare of 1919–20 and depleted by defections to the Communist Party in consequence of the Bolshevik ascendance in Russia, nevertheless survived the century, though fragmented as always, drawing back from the expectation of imminent revolution and instead preparing the way to the future social order, with the main emphases on education and the environment in the here and now.

In the light of such history, what then of the Occupy movement? It was, as I've said, loosely organized, with no central coordination of any kind. But let's consider one "unofficial" OWS website, which displayed on its home page the traditional revolutionary worker's clenched fist, with the catchword, "The revolution continues worldwide!" Below that was a list of typical demands, among them a guaranteed living wage, a single-payer health care system, free college education, accelerated development of a green economy free of fossil fuels, an equal rights amendment respecting race and gender, open borders, debt forgiveness and the outlawing of collection agencies, and eased restrictions on unionization and collective bargaining. For sympathizers on the left, of which I count myself one, these are familiar and agreeable positions, none of them new, some more radical than others, but not essentially revolutionary—many have been tried successfully before—nor even socialist. The fact is, we are not living in an era of working-class and peasant revolt. Present-day revolutions are against authoritarian rule of whatever stripe, calling for regime change, not the end of capitalism itself. In relation to anarchism, OWS demands strike me as strictly reformist, which, to my mind, is by no means a bad thing. However, in the stateless society envisioned in *Mother Earth*, one with not less government but no government at all, and in which, by definition, essential services are free, a constitutional amendment would be no more relevant than a single-payer health care system. OWS was surely a descendant of anarchism, its strategies taken enthusiastically from the social libertarian playbook, but calling it anarchist as such seems to me a forgivable misapprehension of the word for which, perhaps, this book may stand as a corrective. For looking at matters from the long-term anarchist perspective, the course of history and true revolution never did run smooth.

Turning now to the first edition of *Anarchy!* (2001), it was, as I noted earlier, born of curiosity and need, a set of circumstances that has not changed much in the ensuing years. References to *Mother Earth* abound in written histories of American radicalism, and its publisher, Emma Goldman, has become an almost mythical figure, the archetypal woman activist. Yet until the initial publication of this book, scarcely any material from her magazine was easily available. Except for a few pieces in such collections as Goldman's own *Anarchism and Other Essays*, Alix Kates Shulman's *Red Emma Speaks*, and Emile Capouya and Keitha Tomkins's *The Essential Kropotkin*, little else had been in print at an affordable price. Then as now, few libraries held complete sets of the original printings. Interested readers still must search out collections that hold the magazine in bound facsimile, microfilm, or microfiche, without recourse to a published index of any kind. Even today, on the Internet, what articles are available are in digitized format devoid of context and historical commentary of any kind. As a result, a highly influential and provocative monthly that was intended for the widest possible readership remains a province for scholars.

I myself could have used a book such as this one some years ago when I was researching a novel, *The Angel Max* (1998), that was set against the background of the American anarchist movement at the turn of the last century. I needed to know not simply who wrote for the magazine, but what they wrote. There were other questions as well. What did it look like? How was it funded? What was its circulation? Where was the office, and who worked there? It was possible to pick up this information in bits and pieces, but bringing it all together between two covers seemed to be a useful task that would save other curious readers the search I had to make.

However, distilling over 5,000 pages of printed matter to roughly 400 pages requires clear criteria for selection. I used five: the pieces I chose had to be relatively short, so that the collection could offer the greatest possible variety of themes; they had to be interestingly written; they had to be unavailable elsewhere; they had to have had their first American publication in *Mother Earth*; and, as far as was practical, they had to be both relevant historically and representative of the magazine, while speaking as well to the issues of our day. With a few exceptions, I was able to stay within these strictures. Nevertheless, the choices were difficult, and this book could easily have been double its size. Reluctantly, I omitted selections from the monthly reports that Goldman published while on her annual lecture tours, which could make a book by themselves; they would also require heavy annotation far beyond the scope on this volume.

Length and availability proved to be the most worrisome concerns. To my mind, Voltairine de Cleyre was the most literarily gift of *Mother Earth*'s regular contributors. Her elegant but grand style needs room, and I allowed it for "Anarchism and American Traditions," "The Dominant Idea," and "The Mexican Revolution," all of which were originally published serially. I included Goldman's "The White Slave Traffic," which is an early and often substantially different version of what later became "The Traffic in Women," published in both *Anarchism and Other Essays* and *Red Emma Speaks*. Another essay of Goldman's I included is "The Philosophy of Atheism," which is also found in Shulman's book but not in Goldman's.

In June and July of 1917, Goldman and Alexander Berkman, her longtime principal editor and lifetime companion-in arms, were tried in federal court under the newly signed Espionage Act for conspiring against the institution of a wartime draft. Their eloquent self-defense was appreciated by the judge. They were found guilty nevertheless, sent to prison immediately, and afterward deported. To this new, expanded edition of *Anarchy!* I have been able to add as an appendix the summary and partial transcript of their trial published in the July 1917 issue of *Mother Earth* (see page 413).

The people who put out Goldman's magazine were themselves activists and, I suspect, had little time for rigorous copyediting and proofreading. In any case, typographical errors were not uncommon, and it is clear there was no house style sheet. Spelling varied between American and British usages from article to article, as did punctuation, and the rendering of proper names, especially those transliterated from Russian and Yiddish, was inconsistent. I felt free to do some light silent editing, no more than what I would have dared to do if, in my imagination, I had been working with Goldman and her inner circle at *Mother Earth*.

Many people had a hand in bringing about both editions of this book, and I am deeply grateful for the time, advice, and encouragement they gave—first and foremost among them, my best and closest editor, my wife, Suzanne Thibodeau, who makes all things possible and worthwhile. My thanks, as always, to Jack Shoemaker of Counterpoint Press; to my cousin Susan E. Wilson, for her ever spirited support; to Tony Outhwaite, my agent and invisible right hand; to Lars Meyers, Director of Preservation, the Columbia University Libraries; to the Tamiment Library of New York University; to the staff of the Emma Goldman Papers, University of California at Berkeley, most especially to its director, Candace Falk, and administrative editor, Barry Pateman; to Karen Karin Rosenberg, for our invaluable discussions, subsequent to the first edition, apropos the kaleidoscope of social revolutionary history; and above all, to the late Paul Avrich, Distinguished Professor of History, City University of New York, who graciously shared his vast knowledge of the field of anarchism, and to whom this second edition is dedicated.

Peter Glassgold

The Life and Death of *Mother Earth*

In March 1906, Emma Goldman published the first issue of *Mother Earth*, a "Monthly Magazine Devoted to Social Science and Literature." *Mother Earth*—"The nourisher of man," she later wrote in her autobiography, "man freed and unhindered in his access to the free earth!" The message of the name was not environmental but libertarian. The magazine was to be a forum for anarchism of every school and variety. It appeared without interruption until August 1917, when it was killed by the wartime postal censorship and succeeded by an abbreviated *Mother Earth Bulletin,* which lasted until April 1918. By then, Goldman and Alexander Berkman, her principal editor and closest comrade-in-arms, were each serving two-year sentences in federal prisons for their public protests against conscription. Both were subsequently deported to Bolshevik Russia in December 1919, victims of America's first "red scare."

Mother Earth was born in the early, optimistic years of what is sometimes called the era of the Lyrical Left. During the twelve years of its life, the magazine did more than report and comment on the contemporary scene—it was an essential part of the action. The decade that preceded World War I saw the rise in America of the birth control movement, industrial unions, modernism in literature and the arts; the fights for women's rights, free speech, civil liberties, education and prison reform; and a growing concern over poverty and homelessness in the cities' slums. But it was also a time of increasing public fear of revolutionary violence, which led to militant vigilantism and a governmental paranoia that labeled most radical activities "foreign" and "anarchist." *Mother Earth* died in one of the most repressive periods of America's history.

Among the hundreds of anarchist magazines and newspapers that have been published in the United States, *Mother Earth* ranks among the longer lived, best written, and best produced. This was due in large measure to Alexander Berkman, the editor from 1907 to 1915, who was an experienced professional typesetter, but also to Goldman's resolve, expressed in a 1915 editorial, "to keep *Mother Earth* untrammelled by party policies, free from sectarian favoritism and from every outside influence, however well-intentioned." This allowed it to develop a broad readership beyond anarchist circles and appeal to socialists, single-taxers, militant Wobblies, social reformers, and even parlor liberals. The idea for the magazine was Goldman's own. In early 1906, she was beginning to emerge from a period of relative inactivity, having assumed the pseudonym of Mrs. E. G. Smith amid the antianarchist hysteria that came in the wake of the 1901 assassination of President William McKinley by a man alleged—falsely—to be one of her followers. She made her living by practical nursing and in December 1904 opened a "Vienna scalp and facial massage" parlor in New York City, at Broadway and 17th Street, until a chance meeting the following year with a troupe of Russian actors led by Pavel Orleneff became the catalyst that brought her back into the public eye as "Red Emma" Goldman. She became the troupe's manager and interpreter, and in gratitude Orleneff put on a benefit performance in her behalf to raise the money she needed to launch the magazine she had long been contemplating, which would, she wrote, "combine my social ideas with the young strivings in the various art forms in America." The box-office take was small, only $250, but it was enough to start the enterprise.

Goldman and a group of friends gathered in her apartment at 210 East 13th Street to discuss her plans, and by the evening's end the name for the magazine was chosen: *The Open Road,* invoking the title of a poem by Walt Whitman, a favorite poet of American anarchists. However, according to Goldman, a general appeal for funds elicited the threat of a lawsuit from another publication with the same name. What to do? One Sunday in early February, during a buggy ride in the countryside near the city, Goldman noticed the early signs of spring, "indicating life was germinating in the womb of Mother Earth," and there and then determined the new name of her magazine-to-be. The first issue of *Mother Earth* appeared on March 1, 1906. It was sixty-four pages long, measured 5 inches by 8 inches, and had a price of ten cents. On the cover was a drawing, more New Age than anarchist, of naked Adam and Eve figures under a blossoming tree, with broken chains nearby, facing the rising sun (see Illustration 4, following page 220). For surprised subscribers expecting *The Open Road,* there was a short note of explanation inside. An initial printing of 3,000 sold out within a week, a second run of 1,000 followed, and Goldman closed the doors of her scalp and facial massage business.

The Adam and Eve motif was continued for six issues and was replaced by a pastoral triptych showing a figure in the central panel of a young woman, naked, gazing out at the landscape; this drawing was on the cover through July of the following year. After that, cover artwork on a regular basis was discontinued, very likely to hold down production costs, and the table of contents was usually displayed instead. From August 1907 through the final issue exactly ten years later, only twenty-eight covers were illustrated with photographs, drawings, or special graphics, and none was repeated. In all its years of publication, *Mother Earth* printed inside the magazine only one political cartoon (October 1912), by Ludovico Caminita, who later turned informer for J. Edgar Hoover during the 1919–20 red scare, and reproduced only two photographs (February 1911; see Hippolyte Havel, "Long Live Anarchy!" pages 50 and 51). Most of the cover drawings were by Robert Minor; others were by Jules-Félix Grand-jouan, Adolf Wolff, Man Ray, and Manuel Komroff; some were unsigned. The work of Minor and Grandjouan also appeared in the socialist *The Masses,* edited by Max Eastman. But while *The Masses* pointedly cultivated the political cartoon both for its covers and inside pages, *Mother Earth* immediately established itself as a magazine strictly for serious readers.

The typography and format changed little over the years. Articles were printed in their entirety, to be read straight through as in a book, without being continued in the back pages. Following or preceding the table of contents in most issues was an editorial or a poem, and then the contributions appeared in sequence. A regular feature was "Comments and Observations," consisting of brief, occasionally humorous news items, miniature editorials, and follow-ups relating to previous issues of the magazine—a kind of anarchist "Talk of the Town." Another feature, begun in April 1907, was Goldman's monthly reports while on her annual nation-wide lecture tours.

The roster of contributors remains impressive. Here is a partial listing, besides Goldman, Berkman, and Max Baginski, the magazine's first editor: Maxim Gorky,[*] John R. Coryell,[*] Sadakichi Hartmann,[*] Peter Kropotkin,[*] Voltairine de Cleyre,[*] Georg Brandes,[*] Bolton Hall, Hippolyte Havel,[*] Ben L. Reitman,[*] Leo Tolstoy,[*] Lola Ridge,[*] C. L. James, Floyd Dell,[*] Francisco Ferrer,[*] Harry Kelly, Don Marquis,[*] Eugene O'Neill,[*] Theodore Schroeder, Leonard D. Abbott, Ricardo Flores Magón, Will Durant, Bayard Boyesen,[*] Harry Kemp, Mabel Dodge,[*] Morris Rosenfeld, Elisée Reclus, Max

Nettlau,[*] Errico Malatesta,[*] William Z. Foster, Margaret Anderson,[*] Robert Henri, Margaret Sanger,[*] Louise Bryant,[*] Rudolf Rocker, Padraic Colum,[*] C. E. S. Wood, Ben Hecht,[*] Maxwell Bodenheim.

The inside and back covers, and sometimes the last couple of pages—and on occasion even the opening page below the masthead, instead of an editorial, poem, or the contents—were given over to advertisements. Some of them were paid for; most announced various publications of the Mother Earth Publishing Association, *Mother Earth* annual and seasonal balls or similar gatherings, upcoming lectures by Emma Goldman and other radical activists, and the like. The advertisements themselves make for interesting, even at times lively, reading. Here is a brief sampling from 1906 to 1918.

An announcement on page 62, in April 1906, placed by Benjamin Tucker, the publisher of the individual anarchist magazine *Liberty* (1881–1908), reads:

BENJ. R. TUCKER
Publisher and Bookseller
has opened a Book Store at
225 Fourth Ave., Room 13, New York City
Here will be carried, ultimately, the most complete line of advanced literature to be found anywhere in the world. More than one thousand titles in the English language already in stock. A still larger stock, in foreign languages, will be put in gradually. A full catalogue will be ready soon of the greatest interest to all those in search of literature.
Which, in morals, leads away from superstition,
Which, in politics, leads away from government, and
Which, in art, leads away from Tradition.

The back cover for November 1906 reads:

Mother Earth
Invites Her Children to
joyous Forgetfulness of the Troubles of Life
FRIDAY, NOVEMBER 23d, 1906
At 8 p.m.
. . . At . . .
Webster Hall
119–125 East 11th Street, New York
At the
Masquerade Ball
Tickets, 35 Cents
Through Our Office

[*]A contributor to *Mother Earth* whose work is included in the present volume.

At the back of the issue for November 1907, on facing pages, are two notices. On the left-hand page is an announcement for a mass meeting on November 11, at the Manhattan Lyceum, 66–68 East 4th Street, to commemorate the twentieth anniversary of the hanging of the Haymarket martyrs. Opposite, on the right, are the names and addresses of agent-sellers of *Mother Earth* in thirteen U.S. cities, as well as Toronto and Winnipeg in Canada and London, England.

The inside cover for August 1909 announces that a "Mid Summer Dance and Ice Cream Party" will be given by *Mother Earth* on the evening of Saturday, September 18, at the Terrace Lyceum, at 206 East Broadway. "Tickets, 20 cents"—"Hat Check, 10 cents."

In May 1911 is a complete of list of pamphlets, the "*Mother Earth* Series," brought out to date by the Mother Earth Publishing Association, available at five or ten cents each, except for a bound set of *Mother Earth* itself, going for two dollars.

In August 1917, for the final issue of *Mother Earth*—which was confiscated by the U.S. Post Office—is a full-page advertisement on the back cover for the "Trial and Speeches of Alexander Berkman and Emma Goldman": "The complete account of the arrest, trial and conviction for their activities in the Anti-Conscription agitation, with their remarkable speeches in the United States District Court in New York, July, 1917."

On the last page of the final issue of the *Mother Earth Bulletin,* April 1918, is an illustrated display for the short-lived Mother Earth Book Shop at 4 Jones Street in Greenwich Village, managed by Stella Comyn, Goldman's niece: a place "For Lovers of Art and Liberty."

Although the magazine was "Devoted to Social Science and Literature," the pages given to topical pieces and essays on anarchism and related matters far outnumbered those reserved for poetry, fiction, and other literary writings; but the latter were never used as fillers and were always given equal prominence with the rest. Perhaps if Goldman and her editors had more personal leisure in their very activist lives there would have been less of social science and more of literature in *Mother Earth*, as was the original intention. But unfortunately we will never know how editorial decisions were made or to what extent and how manuscripts were solicited (although Sadakichi Hartmann was reported to have said about the poetry, "We make decisions, but we don't abide by them"). On June 15, 1917, federal agents raided the office of *Mother Earth,* arresting Goldman and Berkman and seizing correspondence, subscription lists, and other files relating to the magazine's everyday workings over eleven years. A second raid was made a year later at the New York City apartment of M. Eleanor Fitzgerald, Berkman's companion, who, with Stella Comyn, had been running the *Mother Earth Bulletin* until it was forced to close. All of the confiscated material was subsequently lost, never to be recovered, and with it most of the internal history of *Mother Earth,* along with an invaluable record of anarchism in America during the peak years of its influence, before its suppression and decline.

Mother Earth had several homes during its lifetime, but the first and longest was in Goldman's three-room walk-up at 210 East 13th Street, where she had moved in 1904. By all accounts it was a lively place, with always an extra plate in the kitchen, and a spot somewhere for an unexpected guest to sleep. Mabel Dodge, about to be introduced to Goldman by their mutual friend Hutchins Hapgood, and not knowing much about anarchism except what the press reported concerning assassination, dreaded the visit—"But what a warm, jolly atmosphere," she wrote, "with a homely supper on the table, and Emma herself like a homely, motherly sort of person giving everyone generous platefuls of beefsteak (they were great meat eaters) and fried potatoes! She didn't look wild or frightening. She looked to me, from the very first, rather like a severe but warm-hearted school teacher and I am sure that that was, essentially, what she was: a teacher, with a very prognathous jaw."

Goldman recalled: "My room was the living-room, dining-room, and *Mother Earth* office, all in one. I slept in a little alcove behind my bookcase. There was always someone sleeping in front, someone who had stayed too late and lived too far away or was too shaky on his feet and needing cold compresses or who had no home to go to."

For two months, January and February 1907, the magazine gave its official address as 308 East 27th Street, and from January 1911 through September 1913, 55 West 28th Street—but Goldman's apartment remained the editorial hearth. She thought of the *Mother Earth* group as a family, and apparently the office, wherever it moved, remained very much a ragtag household, attracting strays as well as young people who put their eager energy into the magazine and to the causes it supported. We know the names of some of them: Rebecca Edelsohn, Frank Tannenbaum, Anna Baron, Pauline Turkel, Carl Newlander, Walter Merchant, William Bales. What gave the magazine stability was the determination of its inner circle, composed largely, though not exclusively, of men, whose members felt a deep loyalty both to the magazine and its tenacious publisher, if not always to one another. Some were Goldman's former or present lovers, such as Max Baginski, Alexander Berkman, Hippolyte Havel, and Ben L. Reitman; others, like Leonard D. Abbott, Sadakichi Hartmann, and Harry Kelly, were not. In later years, much of the work of the magazine was taken on by M. Eleanor Fitzgerald and by Goldman's niece and nephew, Stella Comyn and Saxe Commins. On the periphery of the inner circle, until her death in 1912, was Voltairine de Cleyre, whose strong but ascetic personality clashed with Goldman's, which was equally strong but—as Mabel Dodge observed—motherly inclined, schoolmarmish, and sometimes even jolly. Like any family, that of *Mother Earth* had its share of unhappiness and rivalries.

Mother Earth's first editor was Max Baginski, with whom Goldman had once had a brief affair. He was an experienced editor in both German and English and took up, almost simultaneously, the reins of *Mother Earth* and *Freiheit,* following the death of Johann Most in March 1906 (see Max Baginski, "The Pioneer of Communist Anarchism in America," page 53). Immediately after the first issue of *Mother Earth* was published, Goldman and Baginski left New York on a fund-raising lecture tour for the magazine to Toronto, Cleveland, and Buffalo—the last the city where McKinley had been assassinated four and a half years earlier. It was there that they learned of Most's death and where they encountered the kind of police censorship that would dog Goldman on her national lecture tours for the next twelve years. An edict demanding that they address the audience at their first meeting only in English effectively silenced Baginski, whose spoken English was poor. For the second meeting, the next evening, the tactics of the police were less subtle: they simply closed the hall before the speakers could enter.

On May 18, the man who would become *Mother Earth*'s second editor, Alexander Berkman, was released from a Pennsylvania prison after serving fourteen years for his attempted assassination of Henry Clay Frick (see Emma Goldman, "Alexander Berkman," page 14). Goldman had been awaiting his freedom with intense anticipation. She and Berkman had been lovers in their youth, almost from the day she arrived in New York in 1889 and joined the anarchist movement. They even had pooled their money to purchase his railroad ticket to Pittsburgh for the assassination and the handgun he used to shoot Frick. The idea of his prolonged suffering while she was free was a continuing torture for her, and she longed for the approaching time when they could be again as they once had been, intimate both as lovers and as comrades in the great social revolutionary cause. But after fourteen years of forced separation, only the latter proved possible, the gulf between them had grown so wide.

Berkman remained emotionally fragile, haunted by his prison memories, sometimes near suicide, and in a state of shock at the physical world beyond the penitentiary walls (he had never seen an automobile before). He resumed his anarchist agitation, but the movement, too, had changed, with a wider liberal support and Goldman, his "Sailor Girl" of earlier years, now its leading figure. His analytical mind, however, was as sharp as ever, and he immediately began writing for *Mother Earth*. He also announced in its pages his intention of setting up a printing business of his own; but the venture failed, and in April 1907 he posted the following notice in the magazine:

TO MY FRIENDS

I have quit my business.

Perhaps I owe you an explanation; I am sure I owe it to myself.

My original plan did not include exploitation. I intended to do all the necessary work myself, wishing neither to be exploiter nor exploited. The intense competition in the printing trade, however, plus union conditions, which do not permit the compositor to perform pressman's work, soon convinced me that my plan was not feasible.

The employment of a pressman at union wages necessitated the enlargement of the business, involving the usual business methods, etc. In short, I stood before the alternative of sacrificing either my principles or my business.

I quit the business.

I feel as if I were released from prison again.

ALEXANDER BERKMAN.

Box 47, Station D, New York.

There was another reason as well why Berkman closed the shop. Goldman was deeply troubled by his continuing malaise. About to leave on an extended lecture tour in March, she determined to turn over the running of *Mother Earth* to him in her absence, apparently with no resistance or resentment on Baginski's part, "to help release him from his cramped feeling and enable him to find freer expression," and he "readily accepted." Her instincts were sound. Berkman remained the magazine's editor until early 1915, after which he moved to San Francisco and started his own newspaper, *The Blast*. His preference was for timely and provocative articles on labor and economic questions—Baginski inclined more to the theoretical—and under his editorship, *Mother Earth*'s circulation rose as high as 10,000.

But by March 1907, after a year in existence, *Mother Earth* already had an established presence and a well-earned reputation as a gadfly publication, even without Berkman's strong editorial hand. For example, Goldman, going against the advice of some of her comrades, chose to commemorate the fifth anniversary of the death of Leon Czolgosz, McKinley's assassin, with several articles in the October 1906 issue. A public meeting followed on October 27—Goldman not was not there—to discuss the baffling question of Czolgosz's possible ties to anarchism, and three of the young speakers were arrested. Goldman and members of the *Mother Earth* group organized a free-speech protest three days later. Attendance was small, but ten minutes into the program the police charged the platform and cleared the hall, assaulting the speakers, pulling chairs out from under people seated in the audience, even dragging women by the hair. Goldman was arrested for inciting to riot and for publishing articles on Czolgosz in *Mother Earth* that in fact were in no way incendiary. Nine others were arrested with her. The charges were dismissed in January.

The *Mother Earth* fund-raising "Masquerade Ball" on November 23 at Webster Hall gave the enforcers of the law another opportunity to show their disregard of the First Amendment "right of the people peaceably to assemble." The police, fifty strong, raided the celebration, tearing off people's masks, and forced the owner to close the hall. Goldman tersely commented: "It was a great financial loss."

Such incidents as these were typical of the police harassment of Goldman and her associates and served in the end to enhance the growing mystique, or notoriety (depending on one's point of view), surrounding the magazine. For Goldman, arrest followed arrest with numbing predictability, but for a full ten years none resulted in conviction, and then it was the issue of birth control, not revolutionary anarchism, that finally landed her in prison.

Year two of *Mother Earth* was a period of travel for its publisher. Goldman's three-month lecture tour from March into June took her to cities in the Midwest, California, and the Pacific Northwest, as well as to Winnipeg and Calgary in Canada. In August, she and Baginski sailed for Amsterdam to attend an International Anarchist Congress. Goldman remained in Europe until mid-October and then slipped back into the United States unnoticed by way of Montreal, eluding American immigration authorities, who were investigating the validity of her citizenship. (Goldman was in fact an American citizen, as a result of an early marriage to a man named Jacob Kershner, from whom she had been estranged for over twenty years.) *Mother Earth* published reports of her activities and her speech to the Anarchist Congress, but it was her three-part "On the Road" that inaugurated a new, regular feature in the magazine, the journal of her annual fund-raising tours. The first installment, in April 1907, opened with a deliberate invocation of the long-abandoned original title of the magazine and the poem it was named after:

> The road, the open road! What grand inspiration it gave to the "gray poet,"
> what wonderful vistas it disclosed to him, of space, color, beauty, opportu-
> nity, wisdom. . . . But what of society's outcasts, the tramps, the homeless,
> shelterless, worn and weary. Does the road mean to them what it meant to
> the great Walt? Does it not mean to them a desert, cold, dreary, aimless? . . .
> And the workingman, tramping from town to town in search of a master,
> can he rejoice in the beauties of the open road?

This was followed by what came to be her signature monthly report: observations of the cities and towns where she lectured—or was kept from lecturing—comments on regional issues, anecdotes, sometimes tart, about the people she met along the way, with thanks by name to local supporters of *Mother Earth* for their hospitality, all interspersed with philosophical ruminations and impassioned outbursts. The title she gave to these pieces changed periodically: "On the Road," "The Joys of Touring," "En Route," "Adventures in the Desert of American Liberty," "Light and Shadows in the Life of an Avant-Guard," "On the Trail," "The Power of the Ideal," "The Ups and Downs of an Anarchist Propagandist," "Agitation en Voyage," "Stray Thoughts." As Goldman's tours lengthened and became more successful, the number of monthly installments increased to as many as seven a year, and in them she began to develop the informal and personal narrative style that would eventually reach its fullness in her 1931 memoirs, *Living My Life*. Taken together, they constitute an important chronicle of everyday radical activity in the United States and Canada from an anarchist perspective and are testimony to Goldman's extraordinary stamina at a time when roads were still primitive, many better suited to the horse and buggy than the automobile, and traveling long distances was by railway coach. A few excerpts give something of the flavor of her articles from on the road.

[January 1909]

Some years ago, when I first visited the State of Washington, I was informed that it rains thirteen months in the year on Puget Sound. I wonder if that accounts for the muddy state of mind of some of its people. At any rate, everything looked muddy, felt muddy, and was muddy in the State of Washington.

. . . Seattle seems to have muddled up the judgment and discretion of several comrades. At any rate, every meeting was a muddle, excepting one, which was saved by our getting to the city two days earlier than expected. It was held at the Labor Temple, Sunday, December 13th. Unfortunately, the proceeds of that meeting had to cover the loss of the other meetings. The crowning episode of the Seattle visit was the arrest of Dr. Reitman and myself, which, though not of grave importance for the moment, caused no end of trouble in other places.

. . . It was only when we reached Everett and Bellingham that we were made to feel the full consequences of the Seattle experience. In Everett the Chief of Police so frightened the city fathers with ghost stories of danger that they decreed I should not speak. Of course, the Chief meant only "my safety," bless his mud-soul. He informed me that I would be thrown into the river, tarred and feathered, lynched and quartered. I assured him that I should enjoy such gracious treatment, but he would not listen to me. Of course the meeting could not take place.

[May 1910]

Spacious, beautifully laid out, and spotlessly clean, Salt Lake City has much more the appearance of a European than an American city, where every inch of ground is mutilated for business purposes. As regards public buildings, the Mormons are almost as extravagant as in the number of wives. Quite a variety of them, each one a joy to the eye.

[April 1911]

Lincoln, Neb.

. . . The miracle of miracles happened there. The law students, usually among the most conservative, invited me to speak before them and showed genuine interest in the question of law, crime, punishment, etc. I am not optimistic enough to believe that any of the men will give up a career of lawyer. It's too good a business, this juggling with legal phrases. But that law students will stand for Anarchistic ideas is a significant sign of the times.

[July 1912]

Butte, Montana, proved a great treat. It brought us back to the warm, tender friends of old days, Annie and Abe Edelstadt. When I look back upon the human panorama that passed my gaze during the last twenty-three years, the Edelstadts stand out as among the few, the very few, who have remained pure and true in their idealism, in spite of the economic grind, poor health, and all sorts of adversities. Which merely proves that character is stronger than environment, stronger than external forces.

. . . Our three indoor meetings made up in quality what they lacked in quantity, but the street meeting in behalf of San Diego surpassed anything we had ever before experienced in Butte. As a rule, I do not relish outdoor propaganda, because it is next to impossible to concentrate on a subject with the thousand noises of the street to combat, nor does it seem that a street audience can be interested for more than a brief moment. But our experiences in Butte proved an unusual and most fascinating event. Fifteen hundred people glued to the spot for nearly two hours, with an attentiveness and earnestness I have rarely found in a hall. It was a wonderfully inspiring occasion, not easily forgotten.

[June 1915]

Six cities, twenty meetings, 7,000 people, all crowded into three weeks. What a panorama life is for him who lives intensely and dangerously. Certainly such a life leaves no room for monotony, nor yet for mental and physical repose for who's who are in the mad whirl.

For the observer who can sit back and watch the picture, it seems so easy, so effortless, such an envious occupation. Poor public! Poor agitators! Will they ever understand each other?

Because Goldman's tours were for the benefit of *Mother Earth,* she published her itinerary and an accounting of the funds taken in. She was an accomplished, charismatic, and courageous speaker, able to entrance friendly audiences and cow hostile ones that threatened physical violence. Her reputation alone drew considerable crowds, but their size and number increased dramatically starting in mid-1908, when Dr. Ben L. Reitman joined the *Mother Earth* group as her manager and publicist. The numbers speak for themselves:

Los Angeles, May 1908: for two weeks, nightly audiences of 350 people, with hundreds of others standing. San Francisco, January 1909: for two weeks, nightly audiences of 2,000 people. 1910: 120 lectures in 37 cities in 25 states, before a total of 40,000 people, selling 10,000 pieces of literature, distributing 5,000 free, netting over $5,300 in sales, magazine subscriptions, and paid admissions. 1911: 150 lectures in 50 cities in 18 states, before audiences of up to 1,500 people, a total of 50,000 to 60,000 at the tour's end. 1915: 321 lectures. By her own accounting, Goldman spoke before 50,000 to 75,000 people a year.

Goldman and Reitman met in early 1908 during her free-speech fight in Chicago, where the police thwarted all her efforts to secure a public meeting place (see Ben L. Reitman, "The Fight for Free Speech," page 243). They quickly became lovers, and he gave up his medical practice to join her on her tour. Their affair, Goldman recalled in later years, was the most sexually intense she had ever experienced, and also the most emotionally harrowing. Reitman was a flamboyant character, nine years her junior (she was thirty-eight), a former street kid from the Chicago slums who in his youth had ridden the rails as a migrant worker—a hobo—before getting his medical degree without the benefit of a high school education, as was possible in those days. His specialty was gynecology and venereal disease, and he worked among the migrant worker population in Chicago, which dubbed him "King of the Hobos." He was also loud, ignorant, and vulgar—everything Goldman and her friends were not. For Margaret Anderson, the editor of *The Little Review,* he was "the fantastic Dr. Reitman (who wasn't so bad if you could hastily drop all your ideas as to how human beings should look and act)." Berkman detested him, belittling his intelligence and his writing ability, and only grudgingly came to appreciate his qualities as a publicist and manager. (He also allowed Reitman to perform an abortion, in 1911, on Rebecca Edelsohn, his companion at the time.) Reitman on at least one occasion tampered with the magazine's financial records, skimming off money for himself. And he was a compulsive, blatant womanizer, which tested Goldman's well-known advocacy of free love to its limits. Nevertheless, he remained a member of *Mother Earth*'s inner circle for nine years, tolerated, however uncomfortably, for Goldman's sake.

Yet Reitman, for all his weaknesses of character, did carry a heavy share of *Mother Earth*'s burdens and faced the physical dangers they sometimes entailed. In May 1912, despite warnings, he and Goldman arrived in San Diego from Los Angeles on her scheduled tour, where they were confronted by murderous vigilantes working in collusion with the police. Reitman was kidnapped, tortured, and left half-naked in the desert to find his way back to Los Angeles, and Goldman, alone (see Ben L. Reitman, "The Respectable Mob," page 269). And if his grasp of anarchism was poor, when it came to the birth-control campaign of 1915–16, he was in his element, as a specialist in sexual hygiene among the migrant poor. In 1916, he served a prison term in the Queens County Jail, in New York— as did Goldman—for distributing literature on "family limitation" (he for sixty days, she for fifteen), and another for six months, in 1918, at Ohio's Warrensville Correction Farm, the longest sentence received in the United States by a birth-control advocate.

Margaret Sanger is rightly considered the preeminent pioneer of the birth-control movement in America, but she was not the first and, in fact, took up the banner only in 1912 after summering with her family among the anarchist community on Cape Cod, from whom she learned about contraceptive techniques. Goldman, long a proponent of contraception (in 1900, she attended a Neo-Malthusian conference in Paris), supported Sanger's efforts and distributed her writings through *Mother Earth* and at lectures. After Sanger was arrested in 1914, Goldman became even more outspoken and eventually, in April 1916, published a special "Birth Control Number" of the magazine. Reitman the publicist made the most of the circumstances, and Goldman's lectures on the subject drew some of her largest audiences. But where Goldman saw birth control as one of many causes central to the coming social revolution (of which the true emancipation of women was an essential part), for Sanger it came to be the single cure for all the ills of humankind. The two women did not get along well, and Sanger before long broke her ties with anarchism. (See Margaret Sanger, "Three Letters and a Vindication," page 126, and Emma Goldman, "The Social Aspects of Birth Control," page 134).

In addition to his talents for publicity and organization, Reitman brought to the magazine M. Eleanor Fitzgerald. They had once had a brief affair, and Goldman remembered her from the 1908 free-speech fight in Chicago. Fitzgerald came East in September 1913 to join the *Mother Earth* family as secretary at its new quarters at 74 West 119th Street. At Reitman's urging, Goldman had given up her East 13th Street apartment as well as the *Mother Earth* office on West 28th Street and rented the ten-room house in Harlem, big enough for the magazine, a bookstore, meetings and social gatherings for a hundred people or more, and multiple living arrangements. Besides Reitman and Goldman there were Fitzgerald, Berkman and Edelsohn, a French housekeeper with the improbable name of Rhoda Smith and, important above all for Reitman, his mother.

The ménage was a disaster. Ida Reitman became homesick for Chicago and, moreover, disliked Goldman and was jealous of her. Reitman read D. H. Lawrence's *Sons and Lovers* and had an emotional crisis. Berkman took up with Fitzgerald. And the house itself, Goldman later recalled, "turned into a free-for-all lodging- and feeding-place." By September 1914, she had found new and smaller lodgings for herself and the magazine in a two-room loft at 20 East 125th Street. Reitman had returned to Chicago with his mother and would join Goldman later on the road. Meanwhile, Berkman and Fitzgerald had found an apartment for themselves and Rebecca Edelsohn, prompting Goldman to remark in a letter to Reitman: "Life is certainly strange but I don't have time to philosophize now."

Throughout its life, *Mother Earth* was troubled by two pressing realities that kept its continued existence in doubt: the threat of insolvency and hounding by government authorities. For all Goldman's fund-raising— lecture tours, balls, sales of anarchist books and pamphlets under the Mother Earth Publishing Association imprint, and even published reminders to delinquent subscribers—most of the time the magazine was never more than a few thousand dollars in the black at best. Berkman was apparently inattentive to money matters, and more than once Goldman returned from the road to find the finances in shambles. One way to contain expenses was periodically, and then permanently, to reduce the size of the magazine. *Mother Earth,* which entered the world at 64 pages, was down to half that by the beginning of 1909, and so it remained, except for a special double-length "Souvenir Number" in March 1915 to mark the beginning of its tenth year.

Government harassment could have the effect of losing the magazine its subscribers if whole printings were delayed by the Post Office too often and too long, while outright confiscation would destroy circulation altogether. Whenever and wherever Goldman and her comrades spoke, there was always the possibility of the police seizing copies of the magazine and other radical literature that was for sale. It was the U.S. Post Office, however, that remained the most insidious danger. In 1908, for example, Postmaster General George von L. Meyer ordered local midwestern post office officials to supply the Department of Justice with the names and addresses of the magazine's subscribers. *Mother Earth* was also under the monthly scrutiny of Anthony B. Comstock and his agents, whose quasi-official censorial powers made them America's guardians of morality. On Comstock's orders, the issue for January 1910 was held until the end of the month because of his objections to Goldman's article "White Slave Traffic," which led to a direct confrontation between him and Berkman (see pages 113 and 183). (Even Canadian officials, in October 1910, banned subscribers from receiving orders from the Mother Earth Publishing Association, because of the books' "treasonable nature.") In the end, it was the Post Office that dealt the deathblows to *Mother Earth,* confiscating both the June and August 1917 issues for their stand against conscription, which was defined as "espionage" under wartime legislation, and depriving the magazine of its mailing privileges for refusing to comply with wartime restrictions on content. The *Mother Earth Bulletin* in the end fared no better.

Mother Earth was never a silent sufferer. What humor there was in its pages was often directed at Comstock (see Don Marquis, "Comstock Soliloquizes," page 183, and "Three Portraits of St. Anthony," page 229), while every arrest, confiscation, mailing delay, and free-speech fight was recorded. Reitman's ordeal in San Diego was covered thoroughly, complete with a list of his abductors' names and occupations, in the June 1912 "San Diego Edition" (see Illustration 7, following page 220). Topics that were also well reported in the general press brought the magazine into wider prominence in its last years; as, for example, in 1914, the campaign for the unemployed and the July 4th bomb explosion on Lexington Avenue in which three young anarchists were killed (which resulted in a memorial issue of *Mother Earth* that so dismayed Goldman with its calls for violence that she tried in vain from on tour to have it destroyed). (See Berkman, "Tannenbaum before Pilate," page 277, and "The Movement of the Unemployed," page 338, and Charles Robert Plunkett, "Dynamite!" page 75, and Adolf Wolff, "To Our Martyred Dead," page 212.) However, it was the birth-control movement and opposition to World War I that gained *Mother Earth* its greatest attention.

It is no accident that in its final years of 1914 to 1917, most of *Mother Earth*'s illustrated covers appeared. Aside from attracting new readers who had heard of but not yet read the magazine, a good cover could make good propaganda, as in the case of Man Ray's two contributions in August and September 1914 (see Illustrations 11 and 12, following page 220), and good satire, as in Robert Minor's "Billy Sunday Tango" for May 1915, skewering the hypocrisy of America's most famous tent evangelist (see Illustration 13, following page 220)—religion being one of the bêtes noires of *Mother Earth*'s revolutionary atheism. All of the artists were associated with the anarchist Ferrer Center nearby, at 63 East 107th Street, and were active in its educational programs, as were the members of the *Mother Earth* family. It was in fact at the Ferrer Center—and not in *Mother Earth*—that the full confluence of the arts and social sciences that Goldman had envisioned took place. Relations between the magazine and the center were so close that after classes the children at the day school would sometimes run over to the *Mother Earth* office, where they always met a warm welcome from Berkman, who would play with them and throw them up into the air. (But Goldman frightened them. They found her formidable and cold. Despite her motherly tendencies, she was uncomfortable with children.)

By 1916, important changes had taken place in the life of *Mother Earth*. Berkman had stepped down as editor in March of the previous year and moved to California with Fitzgerald, where they started a newspaper, *The Blast*. It was launched in January 1916 as a weekly, but turned biweekly two months later. Berkman continued to write for *Mother Earth,* however, taking up the cases of David Caplan and Matthew Schmidt, who had been indicted with the McNamara brothers in the 1910 bombing of the Los Angeles Times Building (see Goldman, "Donald Vose: The Accursed," page 347), and after July 1916, the frame-up of Thomas Mooney and Warren Billings for the Preparedness Day parade explosion in San Francisco, in which Berkman himself was falsely implicated (see "The Case of Mooney and Billings," page 285). The masthead of *Mother Earth* now indicated: "Emma Goldman, Publisher and Editor," but she had in fact placed the everyday work in the hands of Max Baginski and her nephew Saxe Commins.

The passion between Goldman and Reitman was cooling as well, after one explosive argument too many over his obnoxious behavior, his infidelities, and his mother. He also was carrying on an affair with Anna Martindale, a labor activist he had met at the *Mother Earth* office (and whom he would marry in February 1917). Nevertheless, he continued as Goldman's manager and remained deeply committed to the birth-control campaign. In 1916 alone, he was arrested three times for distributing "obscene" literature on contraception, in New York City, in Rochester, and in Cleveland. For the first, he served his sixty-day sentence in May to June. For the second, he was tried and acquitted. And for the third, after appeals and delays, he served his six-month term in February to August 1918, a year after his break with Goldman, with the magazine, and with anarchism.

Readers of *Mother Earth* had no indication of the emotional and physical strains these changes at the magazine had on Goldman, let alone the toll taken by the unrelenting pace of her scheduled tours and speeches and agitation on behalf of such causes as—to name only three—justice for Caplan and Schmidt, for Mooney and Billings, and for the jailed Mexican anarchist revolutionaries, the brothers Ricardo Flores and Enrique Flores Magón. To these would soon be added the campaign against universal military conscription, as the United States edged ever closer to joining the European war. Significantly, the last of the *Mother Earth* fund-raising celebrations took place in 1915. The "Red Revel Ball" on February 20, the biggest ever, drew 800 people, and Goldman—who always liked a good party—came dressed as a nun and danced a waltz called the "Anarchist's Slide." The *Mother Earth* "Autumn Festival" on October 16 was a quieter affair, with Goldman, near exhaustion, reporting on her recent tour of over 300 lectures, by Reitman's count.

By January 1917, Berkman and Fitzgerald were back in New York, after months of harassment by San Francisco's district attorney, Charles Fickert, who was determined to find evidence linking Berkman to the Preparedness Day bombing and had their office raided twice. The new quarters of *The Blast* were above those of *Mother Earth* at 20 East 125th Street. In February, President Woodrow Wilson signed the Alien Immigration Act, which permitted the deportation of undesirable aliens "any time after their entry." (Both Berkman and Goldman were now resident aliens; he because he had never tried to become a citizen of the United States, she because her former status had been revoked on the technicality that her estranged husband, Jacob Kershner—whose whereabouts were unknown—might have lied on his citizenship application.) On March 2, Nicholas Romanov abdicated the Russian throne. On April 6, the United States declared war on the Central Powers and prepared to institute universal military conscription. On May 9, at the office of *Mother Earth,* the No-Conscription League was organized. Between then and June 5, when the Selective Service Act went into effect, Goldman and Berkman spoke at four anticonscription demonstrations. On June 15, the day the new Espionage Act was signed that made agitation against the draft illegal, the offices of *Mother Earth* and *The Blast* were raided and Goldman and Berkman arrested. (See "The War at Home," page 391.)

The Blast died immediately, and Fitzgerald joined Goldman's niece Stella Comyn in keeping *Mother Earth* going through August, after which it was no more. In October, it was resurrected as the *Mother Earth Bulletin,* an eight-page newsletter with the same dimensions as the magazine but set in double columns in minuscule type. The price was still "10¢ a copy." With its limited space, the main areas of attention were the war, the Bolshevik Revolution in Russia, and news of Goldman and Berkman's legal battles. Under orders from federal agents, Fitzgerald and Comyn were forced to vacate the office at 125th Street in July, but found a new one downtown, at 226 Lafayette Street, in Little Italy.

The trial of Goldman and Berkman was almost immediate, running from June 27 to July 9, and the outcome seemed certain from the start, with laws and circumstances coming together to set the stage for the imprisonment and eventual deportation of America's two most undesirable aliens. With the counsel of their lawyer, Harry Weinberger, they argued their own case and did it very well, with all the aplomb of two seasoned public speakers. The July issue of *Mother Earth* was devoted to a summary and partial transcript of the proceedings (see Appendix, page 413), and the full account was published by the Mother Earth Publishing Association in October. Here are two passages from their summings-up, first in Berkman's and then in Goldman's words:

> And now to the case. The charge against us, as you know from the indictment, is that we conspired to advise and urge men of conscriptionable age not to register. Remember, gentlemen, the indictment is in regard to a conspiracy to urge people not to register. If you look through the indictment you will find not a single word about conscription. I want you gentlemen to bear it in mind that the indictment sets forth a conspiracy and overt acts alleged to be connected, in order to induce young men not to register. The question now is, Did the prosecution prove the alleged conspiracy? Did the prosecution prove that we urged people not to register? Did it prove any overt acts in furtherance of that alleged conspiracy? Did it even attempt to prove or to demonstrate that we are guilty as charged? Oh no. The prosecution felt its case so weak that it had to drag in a thousand and one issues that have nothing to do with the charge in question. It had to drag in the question of Anarchism, of violence, of the Ferrer Modern School, of mass meetings held three years ago under some special circumstances, of protest meetings held in the city about four years ago with regard to the Colorado miners' strike, of protest meetings held in connection with the Rockefeller treatment of the Ludlow miners. It had to drag in a thousand and one questions that had as much relation to this case as a lion is related to a jackass.

> . . . We simply insist, regardless of all protests to the contrary, that this war is not a war for democracy. If it were a war for the purpose of making democracy safe for the world, we would say that democracy must first be safe for America before it can be safe for the world. So in a measure I say,

gentlemen, that we are greater patriots than those who shoot off firecrackers and say that democracy should be given to the world. By all means let us give democracy to the world. But for the present we are very poor in democracy. Free speech is suppressed. Free assemblies are broken up by uniformed gangsters, one after another. Women and girls at meetings are insulted by soldiers under this "democracy." And therefore we say that we are woefully poor in democracy at home. How can we be generous in giving democracy to the world? So we say, gentlemen of the jury, our crime, if crime there be, is not having in any way conspired to tell young men not to register, or having committed overt acts. Our crime, if crime there be, consists in pointing out the real cause of the present war.

Even the presiding judge, Julius Mayer, grudgingly commended them: "In the conduct of this case, the defendants have shown remarkable ability. An ability which might have been utilized for the great benefit of this country, had they seen fit to employ themselves in behalf of it rather than against it." The jury nevertheless chose to ignore the heart of their argument and the evidence to prove it: that they never advised young men not to register for the draft, considering it a matter of personal conscience; that their anti-conscription activities ceased on June 5; that these activities in any event antedated the law that made them treasonable. They were each sentenced to two years in prison and fined $10,000. Judge Mayer recommended deportation to follow; Goldman's request that their sentences be deferred for a few days was rejected; and they were whisked away by federal guards.

Goldman was taken to the Missouri State Penitentiary in Jefferson City and Berkman to the Federal Penitentiary in Atlanta, Georgia. However, before the summer's end they had been released on bail, pending their appeal to the U.S. Supreme Court, and were back in New York, helping Comyn and Fitzgerald launch the *Mother Earth Bulletin* while they fought their case (and Berkman successfully fended off extradition to California on murder charges connected with the Preparedness Day incident). Goldman's dedication appeared on the front page:

This is the wee babe of *Mother Earth*. It was conceived during the greatest human crisis—born into a tragic, disintegrating world. To give it life, *Mother Earth* had to choose death, yet out of Death must come Life again. The Babe is frail of body, but it comes with a heritage of strength, determination, and idealism to be worthy of her who gave it birth.

To bring a child into the world these days is almost an unpardonable luxury. But the child of *Mother Earth* comes to you for a share of the beautiful love and devotion you gave its mother. Assured of that, it will make a brave effort to Live and to Do.—E. G.

The *Bulletin* had its own battles from the start. Circulation was small, mostly sales of individual copies. The issue for December 1917 was confiscated for printing a report of the lynching of thirteen black soldiers at a U.S. army base in Texas, the Post Office remaining vigilant for articles that might compromise the war effort and undermine morale. Yet Goldman in this period managed a short lecture tour, to Chicago, Detroit, and Rochester, on matters concerning the Bolshevik Revolution, in which she and Berkman put great hope—and against which they would later turn in bitter disillusionment (see "The Russian Revolution," page 405).

Their freedom ended on January 28, 1918, when the Supreme Court rejected their appeal. Goldman was returned to Jefferson City and Berkman to Atlanta. The front page of the *Bulletin* bore the headline, "Farewell, Friends and Comrades!" and beneath it a letter signed by both of them, which ended:

> The BULLETIN will continue, with your help, even in our absence. It will have a thorny path, but we know we may depend on your interest and cooperation as generously and faithfully as you have helped in the past. By means of the BULLETIN we shall keep in touch with you, while we are in retirement, and you shall hear the voices that cannot be stifled by stone walls.
>
> Au revoir, some day,
EMMA GOLDMAN
ALEXANDER BERKMAN

In February, the *Bulletin* featured Goldman's open letter, "On the Way to Golgotha," to her "Dear Faithful Friends," with these concluding instructions:

> You will want to help me while I am in prison, I know. You can do so in various ways. First, take care of my love child, *Mother Earth Bulletin*. I leave her to your sympathetic care. I know that you will look after her tenderly, so that I may find her bigger, stronger, and more worthwhile when I return from Jefferson. Secondly, spread my Boylsheviki pamphlet [*The Truth About the Boylsheviki*] in tribute to their great courage and marvelous vision and for the enlightenment of the American people. Thirdly, join the League for the Amnesty of Political Prisoners, which is working for the release of all Political Prisoners. And finally, write to Berkman and myself. Always address us as Political Prisoners. Always sign your full name.
>
> Goodbye, dear friends, but not for long—if the spirit of the Boylsheviki prevails.

Long live the Boylsheviki! May their flames spread over the world and redeem humanity from its bondage!

Affectionately,

EMMA GOLDMAN

U.S. Political Prisoner

Jefferson Prison

Jefferson City, Mo.

In March appeared two messages, one from Goldman (. . ."My thoughts are with you always and with our fighter, *Mother Earth Bulletin.* I can do nothing for it now, but I depend on all of you. Keep the child, *Mother Earth,* alive and growing.". . .) and one from Berkman, conveyed by Harry Weinberger:

> Berkman felt that absolutely no relaxation in the efforts in Mooney's behalf and of the other defendants in the California frame-up should be allowed to take place, as the entire battle in their behalf may be lost if there is the least cessation of fighting and the arousing of public opinion.
>
> Jails are civilization's confession of failure; and prisoners are prisoners only if they believe they are prisoners.

The front page of the final issue, in April 1918, was devoted to Goldman's swan song as publisher and editor, a letter "To All My Dear Ones," with news of her assigned work ("I now make 36 jackets a day. It's 'going some.' It means incessant grind for nine hours a day without letup.") and prison conditions in America generally ("How stupid of those who prate of criminal tendencies. Not one of my fellow prisoners is inherently criminal. The circumstances and a cruel lack of understanding for the human, the all too human, bring them here; nor are they likely to return to society with a more kindly spirit when their time is up."). Invoking the courage of two other women revolutionaries whom she admired, Ekaterina Breshkovskaya ("Babushka") and Louise Michel, she bid her last farewell:

> But I am fortunate in having the Babushkas, the Louise Michels, and the other great ones to draw from. I am rich after all. Then there is your friendship, my dear ones, and my faith in your comradeship. Nothing can shake that. May I hope that you feel the same about me? This hope is giving me the strength and will keep my spirit alive until I may again see you all and clasp you by the hand. This is the month of the [Paris] Commune. They said it was dead when they slaughtered thirty thousand, but it lives forever.

Thus ended the life of the *Mother Earth Bulletin*—but not without an aftermath. In June, Comyn briefly attempted an underground successor, a mimeographed newsletter entitled *Instead of a Magazine,* and Fitzgerald's apartment in Greenwich Village was raided by federal agents, who seized correspondence and mailing lists. In July, the Mother Earth Book Shop closed its doors, and a list of the names and addresses of *Mother Earth*'s nearly 8,000 subscribers was circulated among federal intelligence agencies.

Between November 1919 and February 1920, federal agents of the Department of Justice, with the help of local police, made a series of nationwide sweeps, arresting some 5,000 suspected radicals in 33 cities in 23 states. They seized people, often without a warrant, at work, at social clubs and other places of leisure, and at home, holding them incommunicado for weeks. Charges were vague, and there were few convictions. Most of those arrested had no criminal record, even the 800 aliens who were eventually deported.

Meanwhile, Goldman and Berkman were released from prison in the fall of 1919, and preparations were made for their deportation. At dawn on the morning of December 21, they boarded the S.S. *Buford,* along with 247 other undesirable aliens, and were shipped off to Russia, arriving on January 19. Their disillusionment with the Bolsheviks was painful and unrelenting. In December 1921, after less than two years in Russia, they once again went into exile and eventually settled in the south of France. (Goldman was allowed to return to the United States for a three-month visit, from February through March of 1934, on condition that she confine her talks to drama and literature.) They never gave up their belief in revolutionary anarchism and continued to write, lecture, and agitate to the end. Berkman, suffering from prostate cancer, died a suicide on June 28, 1936, and was buried in Nice. Goldman succumbed to a stroke on May 14, 1940, in Toronto and was laid to rest near the memorial to the Haymarket martyrs in Chicago's Waldheim Cemetery—a repatriate at last.

PART ONE

ANARCHISM

Mother Earth provided a forum for anarchism in its many varieties: collectivist, communist, individualist, philosophical, syndicalist, and, as some proponents would say, anarchism "without an adjective." Emma Goldman's own anarchism was very much a personal synthesis that reflected her passionate ideals. Its base was largely the communist anarchism developed by Kropotkin combined with an individualism that found its roots in the libertarian traditions of Jefferson, Emerson, and Whitman, as well as in the active civil disobedience of the abolitionists. This mixture of European and American radicalism, when couched in a revolutionary vocabulary shared with socialism, allowed for the characteristic openness of views that distinguished *Mother Earth* from other, shorter-lived English-language anarchist publications of the time. This section, entitled "Anarchism," contains contributions that address four essential aspects of the broader movement: its theoretical underpinnings; its self-mythologizing, which created an annual calendar of anarchist holidays and a gallery of heroes and martyrs; its uncompromising and principled atheism; and its relation to revolutionary violence, a minor question within the movement that nevertheless dogged its reputation and alarmed its opponents on the political right as well as the left, beyond measure.

VOL. V, NO. 2, APRIL 1910
VOL. VII, NO. 10, DECEMBER 1912

Some Definitions

The following definitions, stressing the cooperative aspects of anarchism, helped to establish a framework for the issues discussed in *Mother Earth*. The first three were displayed on the masthead of the April 1910 issue, and the fourth and fifth in the middle of the December 1912 issue. All were reprinted regularly after their initial appearance, singly or in groups, in successive issues. The now familiar formulation for "free communism" was one that both anarchists and Marxists could agree upon. It was appropriated by the Bolsheviks after the Russian Revolution and popularized as a wholly Marxist concept. "Direct action," the principal strategy of union-based syndicalists to bypass the political process, included such tactics as boycotts, slowdowns, and the general strike.

ANARCHISM—The philosophy of a new social order based on liberty unrestricted by man-made law; the theory that all forms of government rest on violence and are therefore wrong and harmful, as well as unnecessary.

ANARCHY—Absence of government; disbelief in, and disregard of, invasion and authority based on coercion and force; a condition of society regulated by voluntary agreement instead of government.

ANARCHIST—A believer in Anarchism; one opposed to all forms of coercive government and invasive authority; an advocate of Anarchy, or absence of government, as the ideal of political liberty and social harmony.

FREE COMMUNISM—Voluntary economic co-operation of all towards the needs of each. A social arrangement based on the principle: To each according to his needs; from each according to his ability.

DIRECT ACTION—Conscious individual or collective effort to protest against, or remedy, social conditions through the systematic assertion of the economic power of the workers.

VOL. I, NO. 10, 1906

The "Criminal Anarchy" Law

"The anarchist is the enemy of humanity," Theodore Roosevelt declared in a speech to Congress in December 1901, "the enemy of all mankind, and his is a deeper degree of criminality than any other." He demanded the enactment of laws to limit the activities of anarchists and the dissemination of their ideas. The president's views were widely held and had been hardened three months earlier by the assassination in Buffalo, New York, of William McKinley, Roosevelt's predecessor in the White House, by a self-proclaimed anarchist named Leon Czolgosz. New York State was among the first to respond to the new president's call with the Criminal Anarchy Act of 1902. The penalty for violation of paragraph 2—the printing, editing, publishing, distributing, or displaying of anarchist literature—was a $5,000 fine and ten years' imprisonment. *Mother Earth*, in a rare show of irony, reprinted the full text of the law, without introductory comment, in its December 1906 issue.

SEC. 468-a. CRIMINAL ANARCHY DEFINED:
Criminal Anarchy is the doctrine that organized government should be overthrown by force or violence, or by assassination of the executive head or of any of the executive officials of government, or by any unlawful means. The advocacy of such doctrine either by word of mouth or writing is a felony.

SEC. 468-b. ADVOCACY OF CRIMINAL ANARCHY:
(1) By word of mouth or writing advocates, advises or teaches the duty, necessity or propriety of overthrowing or overturning organized government by force or violence, or by assassination of the executive head or of any of the executive officials of government, or by any unlawful means; or

(2) Prints, publishes, edits, issues or knowingly circulates, sells, distributes or publically displays any book, paper, document or written or printed matter in any form, containing or advocating, advising or teaching the doctrine that organized government should be overthrown by force, violence or any unlawful means; or

(3) Openly, wilfully and deliberately justifies by word of mouth or writing the assassination or unlawful killing or assaulting of any executive or other officer of the United States or any state or of any civilized nation having an organized government because of his official character, or any other crime, with intent to teach, spread or advocate the propriety of the doctrines of criminal anarchy; or

(4) Organizes or helps to organize or becomes a member of or voluntarily assembles with any society, group or assembly of persons formed to teach or advocate such doctrine: is guilty of a felony and punishable by imprisonment for not more than 10 years, or by a fine of not more than $5,000, or both.

SEC. 468-c. LIABILITY OF EDITORS AND OTHERS:
Every editor or proprietor of a book, newspaper or serial, and every manager of a partnership or incorporated association by which a book, newspaper or serial is issued, is chargeable with the publication of any matter contained in such book, newspaper or serial. But in every prosecution therefor the defendant may show in his defense that the matter complained of was published without his knowledge or fault and against his wishes by another who had no authority from him to make the publication and whose act was disavowed by him as soon as known.

SEC. 468-d. ASSEMBLAGES OF ANARCHISTS:
Whenever two or more persons assemble for the purpose of advocating or teaching the doctrines of criminal anarchy, as defined in section 468 of this

title, such an assembly is unlawful, and every person voluntarily participating therein by his presence, aid or instigation is guilty of a felony and punishable by imprisonment for not more than 10 years, or by a fine of not more than $5,000, or both.

SEC. 468-e. PERMITTING PREMISES TO BE USED FOR ASSEMBLAGES OF ANARCHISTS:

The owner, agent, superintendent, janitor, caretaker or occupant of any place, building or room, who wilfully and knowingly permits therein any assemblage of persons prohibited by section 468 of this title, or who, after notification that the premises are so used permits such use to be continued, is guilty of a misdemeanor and punishable by imprisonment for not more than 2 years, or by a fine of not more than $2,000 or both.

SEC. 469. WITNESS' PRIVILEGE:

No person shall be excused from giving evidence upon an investigation or prosecution for any of the offenses specified in this title, upon the ground that the evidence might tend to convict him of a crime. But such evidence shall not be received against him upon any criminal proceeding.

VOL. I, NO. I, MARCH 1906

Without Government

By Max Baginski

Max Baginski, a German immigrant never completely at home in English, was *Mother Earth*'s first editor, and afterward he remained a regular contributor. His articles were often written in German and then translated for publication by Emma Goldman. "Without Government," which appeared in the inaugural issue of the magazine, is his concise, idealistic, and characteristically literary presentation of the basic anarchist argument: that government is intrinsically violent, relying on organized force for its existence, and repressive of humankind's natural instincts toward freedom and cooperation.

THE GIST OF THE ANARCHISTIC IDEA IS THIS, that there are qualities present in man which permit the possibilities of social life, organization, and co-operative work without the application of force. Such qualities are solidarity, common action, and love of justice. Today they are either crippled or made ineffective through the influence of compulsion; they can hardly be fully unfolded in a society in which groups, classes, and individuals are placed in hostile, irreconcilable opposition to one another. In human nature today such traits are fostered and developed which separate instead of combining, call forth hatred instead of a common feeling, destroy the humane instead of building it up. The cultivation of these traits could not be so successful if it did not find the best nourishment in the foundations and institutions of the present social order.

On close inspection of these institutions, which are based upon the power of the State that maintains them, mankind shows itself as a huge menagerie, in which the captive beasts seek to tear the morsels from each other's greedy jaws. The sharpest teeth, the strongest claws and paws vanquish the weaker competitors. Malice and underhand dealing are victorious over frankness and confidence. The struggle for the means of existence and for the maintenance of achieved power fill the entire space of the menagerie with an infernal noise. Among the methods which are used to secure this organized bestiality the most prominent ones are the hangman, the judge with his mechanical: "In the name of the king," or his more hypocritical: "In the name of the people I pass sentence"; the soldier with his training for murder; and the priest with his: "Authority comes from God."

The exteriors of prisons, armories, and churches show that they are institutions in which the body and soul are subdued. He whose thoughts reach beyond this philosophy of the menagerie sees in them the strongest expression of the view that it is not possible to make life worth living the more with the help of reason, love, justice, solidarity. The family and school take care to prepare man for these institutions. They deliver him up to the State, so to speak, blindfolded and with fettered limbs. Force, force. It echoes through all history. The first law which subjected man to man was based upon force. The private right of the individual to land was built up by force; force took way the claims upon homesteads from the majority and made them unsettled and transitory. It was force that spoke to mankind thus: "Come to me, humble yourself before me, serve me, bring the treasures and riches of the earth under MY roof. You are destined by Providence to always be in want. You shall be allowed just enough to maintain strength with which to enrich me infinitely by your exertions and to load me down with superfluity and luxury."

What maintains the material and intellectual slavery of the masses and the insanity of the autocracy of the few? Force. Workingmen produce in the factories and workshops the most varied things for the use of man. What is it that drives them to yield up these products for speculation's sake to those who produce nothing and to content themselves with only a fractional part of the values which they produce? It is force.

What is it that makes the brain worker just as dependent in the intellectual realm as the artisan in the material world? Force. The artist and the writer being compelled to gain a livelihood dare not dream of giving the best of their individuality. No, they must scan the market in order to find out what is demanded just then. Not any different than the dealer in clothes who must study the style of the season before he places his merchandise before the public. Thus art and literature sink to the level of bad taste and speculation. The artistic individuality shrinks before the calculating reckoner. Not that which moves the artist or the writer most receives expression; the vacillating demands of mediocrity of everyday people must be satisfied. The artist becomes the helper of the dealer and the average men, who trot along in the tracks of dull habit.

The State Socialists love to assert that at present we live in the age of individualism; the truth, however, is that individuality was never valued at so low a rate as today. Individual thinking and feeling are incumbrances and not recommendations on the paths of life. Wherever they are found on the market they meet with the word "adaptation." Adapt yourself to the demands of the reigning social powers, act the obedient servant before them, and if you produce something be sure that it does not run against the grain of your "superiors," or say adieu to success, reputation, and recompense. Amuse the people, be their clown, give them platitudes about which they can laugh, prejudices which they hold as righteousness, and falsehoods which they hold as truths. Paint the whole, crown it with regard for good manners, for society does not like to hear the truth about itself. Praise the men in power as fathers of the people, have the devourers of the common wealth parade along as benefactors of mankind.

Of course, the force which humbles humanity in this manner is far from openly declaring itself as force. It is masked, and in the course of time it has learned to step forward with the least possible noise. That diminishes the danger of being recognized.

The modern republic is a good example. In it tyranny is veiled so correctly that there are really great numbers of people who are deceived by this masquerade and who maintain that what they perceive is a true face with honest eyes.

No czar, no king. But right in line with these are the landowners, the merchants, manufacturers, landlords, monopolists. They all are in possession, which is as strong a guarantee for the continuance of their power as a castle surrounded by thick walls. Whoever possesses can rob him who possesses nothing of his independence. If I am dependent for a living on work, for which I need contrivances and machines which I myself cannot procure, because I am without means, I must sacrifice my independence to him who possesses these contrivances and machines. You may work here, he will tell me, but only under the condition that you will deliver up the products of your labor to me, that I may trade with and make profit on them.

The one without possessions has no choice. He may appeal to the declaration of human rights; he may point to his political rights, the equality before the law, before God and the archangels—if he wants to eat, drink, dress, and have a home he must choose such work as the conditions of the industrial mercantile or agricultural plants impose upon him.

Through organized opposition the workingmen can somewhat improve this condition; by the help of trade unions they can regulate the hours of work and hinder the reduction of wages to a level too low for mere living. The trade unions are a necessity for the workingmen, a bulwark against which the most unbearable demands of the class of possessors rebound; but a complete freeing of labor—be it of an intellectual or of a physical nature—can be brought about only through the abolition of wage work and the right of private ownership of land and the sources of maintenance and nourishment of mankind. There are heartrending cries over the blasphemous opinion that property is not as holy a thing as its possessors would like to make it. They declare that possessions must not be less protected than human life, for they are necessary foundations of society. The case is represented as though everybody were highly interested in the maintenance of the right of private property, whereas conditions are such that nonpossession is the normal condition of most people.

Because few possess everything, therefore the many possess nothing. So far as possession can be considered as an oppressive measure in the hands of a few, it is a monopoly. Set in a paradox it would read: The abolition of property will free the people from homelessness and nonpossession. In fact, this will happen when the earth with its treasures shall cease to be an object of trade for usurers; when it shall vouchsafe to all a home and a livelihood. Then not only the bent bodies will straighten; the intellect free itself as might the bound Prometheus rid himself of his fetters and leave the rock to which he is chained, but we shall look back on the institutions of force, the State, the hangman, et al., as ghosts of an anxious fantasy.

In free unions the trades will organize themselves and will produce the means of livelihood. Things will not be produced for profit's sake, but for the sake of need. The profit-grabber has grown superfluous just as his patron, the State, which at present serves by means of its taxes and revenues his antihumanitarian purposes and hinders the reasonable consumption of goods. From the governing mania the foundation will be withdrawn; for those strata in society will be lacking which therefore had grown rich and fat by monopolizing the earth and its production. They alone needed legislatures to make laws against the disinherited. They needed courts of justice to condemn; they needed the police to carry out practically the terrible social injustice, the cause of which lay in their existence and manner of living. And now the political corruptionists are lacking who served the above-mentioned classes as helpers and therefore had to be supported as smaller drones.

What a pleasant surprise! We see now that the production and distribution of means of livelihood are a much simpler matter without government than with government. And people now realize that the governments never promoted their welfare, but rather made it impossible, since with the help of force they only allowed the right of possession to the minority.

Life is really worth living now. It ceases to be an endless, mad drudgery, a repugnant struggle for a mere existence.

Truth and beauty are enthroned upon the necessity of procuring the means of existence in a co-operative organized manner. The social motives which today make man ambitious, hypocritical, stealthy, are ineffective. One need not sell his individuality for a mess of pottage, as Esau sold his primogeniture.

At last the individuality of man has struck a solid social foundation on which it can prosper. The individual originality in man is valued; it fructifies art, literature, science which now, insofar as they are dependent upon the State and ownership—which is far-reaching—must take the direction of prescribed models that are acknowledged and must not be directed against the continuance of the leisure classes.

Love will be free. Love's favor is a free granting, a giving and taking without speculation. No prostitution; for the economic and social power of one person over another exists no longer, and with the falling off of external oppression many an internal serfdom of feeling will be done away with, which often is only the reflex of hard external compulsion. Then the longing of large hearts may take tangible shape. Utopias are arrows aimed into the future, harbingers of a new reality.

Rabelais, in his description of life in the "Thelemite Abbey," wrote:

"All their life was spent not in laws, statutes, or rules, but according to their own free will and pleasure. They rose out of their beds when they thought good; they did eat, drink, labor, sleep, when they had a mind to it, and were disposed for it. None did awake them, none did offer to constrain them to eat, drink, nor do any other thing. In all their rule and strictest tie of their order, there was but this one clause to be observed: 'Do What Thou Wilt.'

"Because men that are free, well-born, well-bred, and conversant in honest companies, have naturally an instinct and spur that prompteth them unto virtuous actions, and withdraws them from vice, which is called honor. Those same men, when by base subjection and constraint they are brought under and kept down, turn aside from that noble disposition, by which they formerly were inclined to virtue, to shake off that bond of servitude, wherein they are so tyrannously enslaved; for it is agreeable to the nature of man to long after things forbidden, and to desire what is denied us. By this liberty they entered into a very laudable emulation, to do all of them what they saw did please one. If any of the gallants or ladies should say, 'Let us drink,' they would all drink. If any one of them said, 'Let us play,' they all played. If one said, 'Let us go a walking into the fields,' they went all. If it were to go a-hawking, or a-hunting, the ladies mounted upon dainty well-paced nags, seated in a stately palfrey saddle, carried on their lovely fists either a sparhawk, or a laneret, or a marlin, and the young gallants carried the other kinds of hawks. So nobly were they taught, that there was neither he nor she amongst them, but could read, write, sing, play upon several musical instruments, speak five or six several languages, and compose in them all very quaintly, both in verse and prose. Never were seen so valiant knights, so noble and worthy, so dexterous and skilful both on foot and horseback, more brisk and lively, more nimble and quick, or better handling all manner of weapons, than were there. Never were seen ladies so proper and handsome, so miniard and dainty, less forward, or more ready with their hand, and with their needle, in every honest and free action belonging to that sex, than were there."

VOL. I, NO. 3, MAY 1906

Alexander Berkman

By Emma Goldman

In *Mother Earth*'s anarchist pantheon, Alexander Berkman was both hero
and martyr, the man who had survived fourteen years in prison, nearly
half of them in solitary confinement, for his failed assassination of Henry
Clay Frick during the bloody Homestead strike of 1892. He was twenty-
one years old at the time of his *Attentat* and a recent immigrant from
what is now Lithuania. Speaking in German at his trial, he insisted on
arguing in his own defense and was summarily convicted and sentenced
to twenty-two years in the Western Penitentiary of Pennsylvania in
Allegheny City. He was, however, released early, in May 1906, his term
unintentionally commuted by a law enacted for the benefit of some former government officials imprisoned for corruption. Emma Goldman
marked the end of Berkman's "Calvary," as she sometimes called it, with
an emotional paean in *Mother Earth* to her former lover and closest companion of her early years in the anarchist movement. He replaced Max
Baginski as the editor of the magazine in March 1907. (See Bayard
Boyesen, "Prison Memoirs," page 202.)

ON THE 18TH OF THIS MONTH THE WORKHOUSE at Hoboken,
Pa., will open its iron gates for Alexander Berkman. One buried alive
for fourteen years will emerge from his tomb. That was not the intention of
those who indicted Berkman. In the kindness of their Christian hearts they
saw to it that he be sentenced to twenty-one years in the penitentiary and
one year in the workhouse, hoping that that would equal a death penalty,
only with a slow, refined execution. To achieve the feat of sending a man to

a gradual death, the authorities of Pittsburgh at the command of Mammon trampled upon their much-beloved laws and the legality of court proceedings. These laws in Pennsylvania called for seven years imprisonment for the attempt to kill, but that did not satisfy the law-abiding citizen H. C. Frick. He saw to it that one indictment was multiplied into six. He knew full well that he would meet with no opposition from petrified injustice and the servile stupidity of the judge and jury before whom Alexander Berkman was tried.

In looking over the events of 1892 and the causes that led up to the act of Alexander Berkman, one beholds Mammon seated upon a throne built of human bodies, without a trace of sympathy on its Gorgon brow for the creatures it controls. These victims, bent and worn, with the reflex of the glow of the steel and iron furnaces in their haggard faces, carry their sacrificial offerings to the ever-insatiable monster, capitalism. In its greed, however, it reaches out for more; it neither sees the gleam of hate in the sunken eyes of its slaves, nor can it hear the murmurs of discontent and rebellion coming forth from their heaving breasts. Yet, discontent continues until one day it raises its mighty voice and demands to be heard:

Human conditions! higher pay! fewer hours in the inferno at Homestead, the stronghold of the "philanthropist" Carnegie!

He was far away, however, enjoying a much-needed rest from hard labor, in Scotland, his native country. Besides he knew he had left a worthy representative in H. C. Frick, who could take care that the voice of discontent was strangled in a fitting manner—and Mr. Carnegie had judged rightly.

Frick, who was quite experienced in the art of disposing of rebellious spirits (he had had a number of them shot in the coke regions in 1890), immediately issued an order for Pinkerton men, the vilest creatures in the human family, who are engaged in the trade of murder for $2 per day.

The strikers declared that they would not permit these men to land, but money and power walk shrewd and cunning paths. The Pinkerton bloodhounds were packed into a boat and were to be smuggled into Homestead by way of water in the stillness of night. The amalgamated steel workers learned of this contemptible trick and prepared to meet the foe. They gathered by the shores of the Monongahela River armed with sticks and stones, but ere they had time for an attack a violent fire was opened from the boat that neared the shore, and within an hour eleven strikers lay dead from the bullets of Frick's hirelings.

Every beast is satisfied when it has devoured its prey—not so the human beast. After the killing of the strikers H. C. Frick had the families of the dead evicted from their homes, which had been sold to the workingmen on the instalment plan and at the exorbitant prices usual in such cases.

Out of these homes the wives and children of the men struggling for a living wage were thrown into the street and left without shelter. There was one exception only. A woman who had given birth to a baby two days previous and who, regardless of her delicate condition, defended her home and succeeded in driving the sheriff from the house with a poker.

Everyone stood aghast at such brutality, at such inhumanity to man, in this great free republic of ours. It seemed as if the cup of human endurance had been filled to the brim, as if out of the ranks of the outraged masses someone would rise to call those to account who had caused it all.

And someone rose in mighty indignation against the horrors of wealth and power. It was Alexander Berkman!

A youth with a vision of a grand and beautiful world based upon freedom and harmony, and with boundless sympathy for the suffering of the masses. One whose deep, sensitive nature could not endure the barbarisms of our times. Such was the personality of the man who staked his life as a protest against tyranny and iniquity; and such has Alexander Berkman remained all these long, dreary fourteen years.

Nothing was left undone to crush the body and spirit of this man; but sorrow and suffering make for sacred force, and those who have never felt it will fail to realize how it is that Alexander Berkman will return to those who loved and esteemed him, to those whom he loved so well, and still loves so well—the oppressed and downtrodden millions—with the same intense, sweet spirit and with a clearer and grander vision of a world of human justice and equality.

VOL. I, NO. 8, OCTOBER 1906

Leon Czolgosz

By Max Baginski

Leon Czolgosz's association with anarchism was brief and tragic. Emma Goldman recalled in her memoirs first meeting him in May 1901, at a lecture she was giving in Cleveland. He approached her during the intermission and, without giving his name, asked her advice about what anarchist literature to read. Two months later, at the end of a stay in Chicago, as she was leaving the house of Abe and Mary Isaak, editors of the journal *Free Society,* she again encountered the young man. He now gave his name as Nieman and rode with her on the El all the way to the railway station. There she commended him to friends—among them Max Baginski—who were seeing her off. On September 1, however, *Free Society* labeled Nieman a police spy, and on September 6, perhaps to disprove the charge, he assassinated President McKinley at the Pan-American Exposition in Buffalo. In the ensuing weeks, during the anti-anarchist hysteria that followed Czolgosz's arrest, trial, and execution on October 29, many anarchists distanced themselves from him, while Emma Goldman, writing in the pages of *Free Society,* courageously came to the defense of the hapless young man, if not his act. The October 1906 issue of *Mother Earth* was largely devoted to Leon Czolgosz, and Max Baginski contributed a regretful reminiscence of events five years earlier.

WHEN I THINK OF LEON CZOLGOSZ I reproach myself for having indifferently passed by, without a kind and tender word, an outraged and deeply wounded soul.

It happened thus.

On the 12th of July, 1901, a party of friends met at the Chicago railroad station to bid adieu to our departing comrade Emma Goldman.

As the train left, a friend remarked to me, "There is a fellow from Cleveland here who asks very peculiar questions. If we do not wish to be bored by him, we must make our escape." We went our way without taking leave of the rest.

The man from Cleveland was Leon Czolgosz. He had just arrived in Chicago and called upon the publishers of *Free Society* at the very moment when they were leaving for the railroad station. Czolgosz was invited to accompany them.

I had but a casual glance at the man. His picture, however, revealed to me a soul out of harmony with the world about it, shrinking from the coarse touch of life and finding shelter in its own seclusion.

His was a face with childlike eyes, full of eager questioning. Confronted with the cruel complexities of life they would express shyness and helplessness. It was a face that indicated a singular combination of tenderness and extreme daring. His was a composite character that reminded me of Souvarin in Zola's *Germinal.*

The latter shed tears of anguish over the death of his beloved squirrel; but the sight of slavish submission of the striking miners, driven back to work by hunger, exasperates him. He is so infuriated by the cowardly spirit of these slaves that he dooms them to perish in the mines. At night he descends into the shafts and, at the risk of his own life, he saws through the supporting pillars. He goes about his work coolly and without hesitation. In the morning he indifferently suffers the miners to go down to certain death.

The official history of revolutionary acts of violence is absolutely bare of psychological data. It pictures Ravachol, for instance, as an extremely cruel and heartless man; yet there are numerous incidents which prove him to have been unusually kind and tender.

This combination of extreme tenderness and cruelty is only an apparent contradiction. Supersensitiveness to suffering and injustice often is the richest soil that fertilizes hatred of the forces that cause human suffering.

The act of Czolgosz was the explosion of inner rebellion; it was directed against the savage authority of the money power and against the government that aids its mammonistic crimes.

But few characteristic incidents of the personality and life of Leon Czolgosz are known.

Reared under the lash of poverty and the tyranny of the home, he passed a wretched and joyless childhood. This misery soon forced the tender youth upon the block of modern slavery. Driven and kicked about in the industrial treadmill, unable to adjust himself to the demands of commonplace existence, he was often the target for the brutality and scorn of his colleagues.

It were too much to demand that the psychological keenness of the manufacturers of public opinion should concern itself with the motives and feelings of such an unimportant individual. Their wonderful ingenuity was exhausted by the blood-curdling portrayal of the man in dime novel style. These scribblers, as well as the mentally stagnated mass, considered the Czolgosz problem solved when the Auburn executioner had completed his horrible work.

Even the revolutionists and anarchists of this country have added nothing that would serve to silhouette the personality and act of the man upon the background of those black days. He was unknown to them; he seldom frequented their gatherings. Unaided he meditated upon our terrible social contrasts. Inevitably, his reflections crystallized in the conviction that the social hell in which the majority of mankind endured the agony of the damned must be abolished. His soul craved freedom and he longed to hear the trumpet of the liberating battle.

His naive questions about the existence of secret revolutionary societies merely proved his belief in the necessity of an uncompromising fighting organization, implacably waging war against existing conditions. He sought spiritual companionship, yet found nothing but disruption, animosity, and pettiness—lack of courage and initiative.

His vague, indefinite yearnings gradually ripened into the quiet determination to carry out an independent act—an act to bring relief to his own oppressed soul and possibly disturb the lethargy of the masses.

For various reasons the motives and character of Czolgosz were ignored. Peter, the most jealous disciple of Christ, at the critical moment denied his master, vowing that he knew not this lawbreaker. Such is the historical fate of him that stakes his life for an ideal. The experience with the "human, all-too-human" found a repetition after the shot at Buffalo. But few sought the explanation within the spirit of our times; the rest failed to realize that it was the bursting of a human heart, quivering under the pressure of an unbearable life.

It required neither judgment nor wit to prate about the "normality" or "insanity" of the man. I know of no instance in the revolutionary annals where a man faced a condemning world so absolutely alone and forsaken— a world of cold, cruel judges flippantly passing the sentence of death. But lo! the contrast between the executioners and the simple grandeur of their victim.

One there was that dared to voice human sentiments in an article published in *Free Society,* October 6th, 1901.

As the governmental and press flunkies strenuously endeavored to associate the author with the Buffalo tragedy, such an expression of sympathy, at such a time, was courageous indeed.

The act of September 6th still affects me like the lifting of a veil designed to hide a dangerous truth. For years we are maintaining the illusion that no social question exists in this country; that *our* republic has no place for the struggle of poor and rich. The voices of the deep, crying of human misery and distress, were thought to be silenced by the formula, "We are free and equal in this country; we have no social problems here." The empty phrase of political liberty has been made to serve as a panacea for all social ills. Those that dare to suggest that political freedom is but a farce, so long as social and economic slavery exists, are branded criminals. Mere declarations of independence and political rights dissolve into nothing if the few may monopolize the earth, control the sources of subsistence, and thus force mankind to a life of poverty and servitude. Under such conditions alleged political liberty is but a means to blind the masses to the real necessities of the times and to create artificial campaign issues, the solution of which is in reality of little consequence to the general welfare.

All this was echoed to me by the Buffalo shot. McKinley fell as the first and chief representative of a republic, the main mission of which is to protect by force the wealth stolen from the people.

This mission of government—the violent suppression of every human right—becomes more accentuated with the growing intensity of commercial and industrial exploitation.

In the 80's, the labor movement for an eight-hour workday was forcibly subdued, and five men judicially killed at Chicago. Under the régime of President Cleveland the Federal forces are employed as the executioners of striking workingmen. Capitalists wire for soldiers and their demand is readily complied with at the White House. The last true Democrat, John P. Altgeld, protests as Governor of Illinois against this arbitrary invasion of State rights. For this crime he later pays with his political life. What? Shall the government not serve monopolists à la Pullman? What else is it here for?!

The régime of McKinley proved even more servile. It lost no opportunity in aiding capitalism in mercilessly crushing the aspirations of labor. The use of Federal troops during strikes becomes a daily occurrence. Thus the mask slowly falls from the lying Goddess. Her chief priest, however, proudly carries his starched dignity and pretended piety.

McKinley personified at once social corruption and political servility. Indeed, he was the ideal President of the secret kings of the republic; both in character and appearance a Jesuit, he was eminently fitted to shield the traitors of the country. He always reminded me of the typical porter, whose severe, dignified appearance proclaims his master's gilded respectability, veneering a rotten core.

Such were the environments that prompted Czolgosz's act. Many felt this; few dared to express it. The amazement that such a thing should happen in America really had something artificial about it. To the close observer there exists but an insignificant difference between the social conditions in this country and that of European monarchies, upon whose horizon revolutionary flashes had been playing for years. There, as well as here, the governments are the willing gendarmes and sheriffs of the possessing class; we, however, still cling to the superstition of political liberty.

Pure in aspiration and motive, the personality of Leon Czolgosz towers above our stifling social existence. Purer, indeed, than his accusers and judges wished. They have left nothing undone to make him appear a low, vile creature, since it was necessary to lull the nation into the belief that only the basest of men could be guilty of such a deed.

In vain unscrupulous torturers attempted to defile the sensitive soul—no confession, unworthy of the man, could be forced. His alleged statement, that a lecture of Emma Goldman inspired his act, emanated from a lying press.

The State of New York employed 200 detectives and spent 30,000 dollars to trump up evidence to convict Emma Goldman as the intellectual instigator of McKinley's death. Is it reasonable to suppose, then, that such efforts and means would have been used had Czolgosz been induced to make statements in the least incriminating?

Even the peace of death was denied him. His last moments were poisoned by the Christian kindness of the prison warden. To the last he was tortured by insinuations reflecting on his character; in the hope of obtaining a confession the dying man was annoyed; he was told, among other things, that Emma Goldman had denounced him as tramp and beggar. But even such brutality failed to touch his lofty spirit. "I care not what Emma Goldman or others say about me. I had no accomplices. I did it for the dear people, and I am ready to die."

These were the only words Leon Czolgosz uttered during all those terrible weeks. Not even at his trial, which mocked every conception of justice, could he be induced to speak.

The only decent reporter present at the trial—a woman—relates that she was so overcome by the farcical proceedings that she was unfitted to do newspaper work for months. Czolgosz impressed her, she says, as a visionary, totally oblivious to his surroundings.

His large, dreamy eyes must have beheld in the distance the rising dawn, heralding a new and glorious day.

Five years have since rolled into eternity. His spirit still hovers over me. In tender love I lay these immortelles on his grave.

VOL. II, NO. 8, OCTOBER 1907

McKinley's Assassination from the Anarchist Standpoint

By Voltairine de Cleyre

At the time of her untimely death in 1912 at the age of forty-five, Voltairine de Cleyre was a regular contributor to *Mother Earth,* composing elegant and independent-minded essays, poems, and even fiction, and her work continued to appear in the magazine posthumously. She was one of the most original writers associated with *Mother Earth,* counterpoising her mastery of the flowery, complex sentence with a cool, often wry sensibility. For the sixth anniversary of McKinley's assassination, she contributed a classic anarchist analysis of the causes underlying the president's death and Leon Czolgosz's "martyrdom." It was reprinted as a separate pamphlet later that year by the Mother Earth Publishing Association.

SIX YEARS HAVE PASSED SINCE William McKinley met his doom at Buffalo and the return stroke of justice took the life of his slayer, Leon Czolgosz. The wild rage that stormed through the brains of the people, following that revolver shot, turning them into temporary madmen, incapable of seeing, hearing, or thinking correctly, has spent itself. Figures are beginning to appear in their true relative proportions, and there is some likelihood that sane words will be sanely listened to. Instead of the wild and savage threats, "Brand the Anarchists with hot iron," "Boil in oil," "Hang to the first lamppost," "Scourge and shackle," "Deport to a desert island," which were the stock phrases during the first few weeks following the tragedy, and were but the froth of the upheaved primitive barbarity of civilized men, torn loose and raging like an unreasoning beast, we now hear an occasional serious inquiry: "But what have the Anarchists to say about it? Was Czolgosz really an Anarchist? Did he say he was? And what has Anarchism to do with assassination altogether?"

To those who wish to know what the Anarchists have to say, these words are addressed. We have to say that *not Anarchism, but the state of society which creates men of power and greed and the victims of power and greed,* is responsible for the death of both McKinley and Czolgosz. Anarchism has this much to do with assassination, that as it teaches the possibility of a society in which the needs of life may be fully supplied for all, and in which the opportunities for complete development of mind and body shall be the heritage of all; as it teaches that the present unjust organization of the production and distribution of wealth must finally be completely destroyed, and replaced by a system which will insure to each the liberty to work, without first seeking a master to whom he must surrender a tithe of his product, which will guarantee his liberty of access to the sources and means of production; as it teaches that all this is possible without the exhaustion of body and mind which is hourly wrecking the brain and brawn of the nations in the present struggle of the workers to achieve a competence, it follows that Anarchism does create rebels. Out of the blindly submissive, it makes the discontented; out of the unconsciously dissatisfied, it makes the consciously dissatisfied. Every movement for the social betterment of the peoples, from time immemorial, has done the same. And since among the ranks of dissatisfied people are to be found all manner of temperaments and degrees of mental development—just as are found among the satisfied also—it follows that there are occcasionally those who translate their dissatisfaction into a definite act of reprisal against the society which is crushing them and their fellows. Assassination of persons representing the ruling power is such an act of reprisal. There have been Christian assassins, Republican assassins, Socialist assassins, and Anarchist assassins; in no case was the act of assassination an expression of any of these religious or political creeds, but of temperamental reaction against the injustice created by the prevailing system of the time (excluding, of course, such acts as were merely the result of personal ambition or derangement). Moreover, Anarchism less than any of these can have anything to do in determining a specific action, since, in the nature of its teaching, every Anarchist must act purely on his own initiative and responsibility; there are no secret societies nor executive boards of any description among Anarchists. But that among a mass of people who realize fully what a slaughterhouse capitalism has made of the world, how even little children are daily and hourly crippled, starved, doomed to the slow death of poisoned air, to ruined eyesight, wasted limbs, and polluted blood; how through the sapping of the present generation's strength the unborn are condemned to a rotten birthright, all that riches may be heaped where they are not needed; who realize that all this is as unnecessary and stupid as it is wicked and revolting; that among these there should be some who rise up and strike back, whether wisely or unwisely, effectively or ineffectively, is no matter for wonder; the wonder is there are not more. *The hells of capitalism create the desperate; the desperate act—desperately!*

And insofar as Anarchism seeks to arouse the consciousness of oppression, the desire for a better society, and a sense of the necessity for unceasing warfare against capitalism and the State, the authors of all this unrecognized but Nemesis-bearing crime, insofar it is responsible and does not shirk its responsibility: "For it is impossible but that offences come; but woe unto them through whom they come."

Many offences had come through the acts of William McKinley. Upon his hand was the "damned spot" of official murder, the blood of the Filipinos, whom he, in pursuance of the capitalist policy of Imperialism, had sentenced to death. Upon his head falls the curse of all the workers against whom, time and time again, he threw the strength of his official power. Without doubt he was in private life a good and kindly man; it is even probable he saw no wrong in the terrible deeds he had commanded done. Perhaps he was able to reconcile his Christian belief, "Do good to them that hate you," with the slaughters he ordered; perhaps he murdered the Filipinos "to do them good"; the capitalist mind is capable of such contortions. But whatever his private life, he was the representative of wealth and greed and power; in accepting the position he accepted the rewards and the dangers, just as a miner, who goes down in the mine for $2.50 a day or less, accepts the danger of the firedamp. McKinley's rewards were greater and his risks less; moreover, he didn't need the job to keep bread in his mouth; but he, too, met an explosive force—the force of a desperate man's will. And he died; *not as a martyr, but as a gambler who had won a high stake and was struck down by the man who had lost the game:* for that is what capitalism has made of human well-being—a gambler's stake, no more.

Who was this man? No one knows. A child of the great darkness, a specter out of the abyss! Was he an Anarchist? We do not know. None of the Anarchists knew him, save as a man with whom some few of them had exchanged a few minutes' conversation, in which he said that he had been a Socialist, but was then dissatisfied with the Socialist movement. The police said he was an Anarchist; the police said he attributed his act to the influence of a lecture of Emma Goldman. But the police have lied before, and, like the celebrated Orchard, they need "corroborative evidence." All that we really know of Czolgosz is his revolver shot and his dying words: "I killed the President because he was the enemy of the people, the good, working people." All between is blank. What he really said, if he said anything, remains in the secret papers of the Buffalo Police Department and the Auburn prison. If we are to judge inferentially, considering his absolutely indifferent behavior at his "trial," he never said anything at all. He was utterly at their mercy, and had they been able to twist or torture any word of his into a "conspiracy," they would have done it. Hence it is most probable he said nothing.

Was he a normal or an abnormal being? In full possession of his senses, or of a disturbed or weak mentality? Again we do not know. All manner of fables arose immediately after his act as to his boyhood's career; people knew him in his childhood as evil, stupid, cruel; even some knew him who had heard him talk about assassinating the President years before; other legends contradicted these; all were equally unreliable. His indifference at the "trial" may have been that of a strong man enduring a farce, or of a clouded and nonrealizing mind. His last words were the words of a naive and devoted soul, a soul quite young, quite unselfish, and quite forlorn. If martyrdom is insisted upon, which was the martyr, the man who had had the good of life, who was past middle years, who had received reward and distinction to satiety, who had ordered others killed without once jeopardizing his own life, and to whom death came more easily than to millions who die of long want and slow tortures of disease, or this young strong soul which struck its own blow and paid with its own life, so capable of the utterest devotion, so embittered and ruined in its youth, so hopeless, so wasted, so cast out of the heart of pity, so altogether alone in its last agony? This was the greater tragedy—a tragedy bound to be repeated over and over, until "the good working people" (in truth they are not so good) learn that the earth is theirs and the fullness thereof, and that there is no need for anyone to enslave himself to another. This Anarchism teaches, and this the future will realize, though many martyrdoms lie between.

VOL. III, NO. 2, APRIL 1908

Violence and Anarchism

By Alexander Berkman

Ever since his attempt on the life of Henry Clay Frick, Alexander Berkman has been inextricably associated with the nagging issue of revolutionary violence and its presumed centrality to anarchism. In March 1908, the United States was in its second year of a severe economic depression. During a demonstration by unemployed workers in New York's Union Square, a bomb exploded. A number of anarchists were arrested, including Berkman and a young man named Selig Silverstein who, although critically injured in the blast, was clubbed by the police and died in custody after interrogation. The bomb thrower was never discovered. The police's efforts to implicate Berkman in the incident proving futile, he was then charged with inciting to riot—a charge that was also dismissed for lack of evidence. Recalling the affair a month later in *Mother Earth,* Berkman answered his own rhetorical question: "Is violence specifically Anarchistic?"

I T IS GROWING RATHER MONOTONOUS to hear the cry of "Anarchist conspiracy" raised whenever and wherever there happens an "unlawful" shot or bomb explosion.

Let us consider the matter dispassionately. Is violence specifically Anarchistic? Is the taking of human life such a very unusual occurrence among "civilized" peoples? Is our whole social existence anything but an uninterrupted series of murder, assassination, eradication? All our honored institutions are rooted in the very spirit of murder. Do we build warships for educational purposes? Is the army a Sunday school? Our police, jails, and penitentiaries—what purpose do they serve but to suppress, kill, and maim? Is the gallows the symbol of our brotherhood, the electric chair the proof of our humanitarianism?

"All these things are necessary evils," we are told by the self-satisfied.

True, they are necessary; necessary to preserve society as it is. But has it ever occurred to the "good citizen" whether it is really necessary to preserve things as they are? Is it indeed worthwhile?

Organized society can have but one *raison d'être*, namely, the greatest good of its members. Let us examine, then, whether society, as at present constituted, can be justly said to fulfill its mission.

No life, individual or collective, is possible without the means of subsistence. The social members supplying these means are, consequently, the life-givers of the community. And who are they? The question answers itself automatically, so to speak: the producers of the country's wealth are the conservators of its life. All members and classes of society should equally benefit by the fact of our combined effort as a society. But if, for any reason, distinctions are to be made, the producing class, the real backbone of the social body, should have the preference.

In other words, the workers are the ones who should enjoy the greatest benefits arising from social organization. That is the true mission of human society. Does the latter accomplish it? Does it come anywhere near accomplishment?

By no means. The producers are the very ones on whose shoulders rests the whole burden of our social evils. They are the disinherited, the submerged. Their products are the property of someone else; the land and machinery, without which no production is possible, are not owned by them; as a result, they are forced to sell their labor for whatever pittance the employers condescend to give. Hence poverty, starvation, and widespread misery among the very class which, as the sole producer, has the best claim to enjoy the blessings of organized social life.

To support, defend, and perpetuate these unjust and terrible conditions, it is necessary to have police, prisons, laws, and government. For the disinherited are not content to forever starve in the midst of plenty, and the exploited are beginning to cry out against their cruel bondage.

These cries, these signs of rebellious dissatisfaction must be stifled. That is the mission of law and government: to preserve things as they are; to secure to the rich their stolen wealth; to strangle the voice of popular discontent.

Such is the social life of "civilized" countries. A life of misery and degradation, economic exploitation, governmental suppression, lawful brutality, judicial murder. Sham, injustice, and tyranny are the synonyms of organized society. Shall we preserve it as it is? Is it necessary and desirable? Is it even possible?

"But you can't regenerate society by violence, by a Union Square bomb," the well-meaning people argue.

Indeed, full well we know we cannot. Be fair; give ear. Do not confound the philosophy of a better, freer, and happier life with an *act resulting from the very evils which that philosophy seeks to abolish.*

Anarchism is the science of social order, as opposed to existing disorder; of brotherhood, as against present Ishmaelitism; of individual liberty and well-being, as opposed to legal oppression, robbery, and universal misery.

This condition of social regeneration cannot be achieved by the will or act of any man or party. The enlightenment of the masses as to the evils of government, the awakening of the public conscience to a clear understanding of justice and equity—these are the forces which will abolish all forms of bondage, political, economical, and social, replacing present institutions by free co-operation and the solidarity of communal effort.

"But the bomb?" cry the judges in and out of court. The bomb is the echo of your cannon, trained upon our starving brothers; it is the cry of the wounded striker; 'tis the voice of hungry women and children; the shriek of those maimed and torn in your industrial slaughterhouses; it is the dull thud of the policeman's club upon a defenseless head; 'tis the shadow of the crisis, the rumbling of suppressed earthquake—it is manhood's lightning out of an atmosphere of degradation and misery that king, president, and plutocrat have heaped upon humanity. The bomb is the ghost of your past crimes.

You may foam and legislate, arrest, imprison, and deport. You may still further tighten the thumbscrews of persecution, erect more gallows, and build electric chairs. Pitiful fools! Thus was Christ crucified as a disturber of "Caesar's peace." Did Golgotha suppress his teaching? Have the unspeakable tortures of the Inquisition eradicated free thought? Did Louis XVI save his crown—or his head—by *lettre de cachet?* Has the cause of the Abolitionists been exterminated by the judicial murder of John Brown?

"Our graves will speak louder than the voices you strangle." In spite of all the strenuous governmental, capitalistic, and journalistic efforts to misrepresent and suppress Anarchists and Anarchism—because of those efforts—the people will yet learn the truth.

Though well aware that the Union Square bomb—whoever its thrower—was no result of any conspiracy, the police insisted on my arrest. As usual, they were the first to break their sacred law: my protest notwithstanding, I was photographed and Bertillioned, in contempt of a recent decision of the Supreme Court of the State, declaring such police methods illegal before the conviction of an arrested person. Having absolutely no evidence against me, the police resorted to the ever-ready charge of "inciting to riot." Naturally, when my hearing took place, the case collapsed like an empty flour sack; however, the authorities grasped the opportunity to air their wisdom. The detectives triumphantly announced that they had made the "important discovery" that I am an Anarchist, and the presiding magistrate assured me that Tolstoy could not possibly be an Anarchist, since "all Anarchism is criminal Anarchism." The learned Cadi suggested that I "change the name of the party." "As long as you persist in calling yourself an Anarchist, and evidently take pride in it, it is the duty of the police to keep you under surveillance." I assured the honorable man that the name suited *me* perfectly; if it did not sound pleasant in the long ears of authority, so much the worse for the latter.

The brutal stupidity of the police is equalled only by the lack of decency on the part of some Socialists and other kid-glove heroes. These, our step-brothers, try to curry favor with popular prejudice by classifying—against their better knowledge—Anarchists with the police. The Socialists, once themselves the victims of calumny and persecution, have now in their turn become calumniators and persecutors. They have learned and are practicing capitalistic tactics while yet an insignificant sociopolitical factor. What, then, would be the effect of the "materialistic conception of history" upon the Socialists, if they should ever grasp the reins of government and achieve real power? Will there be found sufficient jailers in the world to supply the needs of triumphant Socialism?

But neither plutocratic nor Socialistic misrepresentation and persecution will halt the march of humanity towards light, liberty, and Anarchy.

VOL. III, NOS. 10–11, DECEMBER 1908–JANUARY 1909

Anarchism and American Traditions

By Voltairine de Cleyre

A native Midwesterner, Voltairine de Cleyre saw the seeds of anarchism in Jeffersonian democracy. It was a short step from "that government is best which governs least" to "no government whatsoever." In "Anarchism and American Traditions," her best-known work, de Cleyre called for a revival of the libertarian spirit of America's Revolutionary Republicans, which by the turn of the twentieth century had been corrupted by commerce and manufacturing. Subsequent to the essay's magazine publication, it was brought out as a separate pamphlet by the Mother Earth Publishing Association.

AMERICAN TRADITIONS, BEGOTTEN of religious rebellion, small self-sustaining communities, isolated conditions, and hard pioneer life, grew during the colonization period of one hundred and seventy years from the settling of Jamestown to the outburst of the Revolution. This was in fact the great constitution-making epoch, the period of charters guaranteeing more or less of liberty, the general tendency of which is well described by Wm. Penn in speaking of the charter for Pennsylvania: "I want to put it out of my power, or that of my successors, to do mischief."

The Revolution is the sudden and unified consciousness of these traditions, their loud assertion, the blow dealt by their indomitable will against the counterforce of tyranny, which has never entirely recovered from the blow, but which from then till now has gone on remolding and regrappling the instruments of governmental power, that the Revolution sought to shape and hold as defenses of liberty.

To the average American of today, the Revolution means the series of battles fought by the patriot army with the armies of England. The millions of schoolchildren who attend our public schools are taught to draw maps of the siege of Boston and the siege of Yorktown, to know the general plan of the several campaigns, to quote the number of prisoners of war surrendered with Burgoyne; they are required to remember the date when Washington crossed the Delaware on the ice; they are told to "Remember Paoli," to repeat "Molly Stark's a widow," to call General Wayne "Mad Anthony Wayne," and to execrate Benedict Arnold; they know that the Declaration of Independence was signed on the Fourth of July, 1776, and the Treaty of Paris in 1783; and then they think they have learned the Revolution—blessed be George Washington! They have no idea why it should have been called a "revolution" instead of the "English war," or any similar title; it's the name of it, that's all. And name-worship, both in child and man, has acquired such mastery of them, that the name "American Revolution" is held sacred, though it means to them nothing more than successful force, while the name "Revolution" applied to a further possibility, is a specter detested and abhorred. In neither case have they any idea of the content of the word, save that of armed force. That has already happened, and long happened, which Jefferson foresaw when he wrote:

"The spirit of the times may alter, will alter. Our rulers will become corrupt, our people careless. A single zealot may become persecutor, and better men be his victims. It can never be too often repeated that the time for fixing every essential right, on a legal basis, is while our rulers are honest, ourselves united. *From the conclusion of this war we shall be going down hill.* It will not then be necessary to resort every moment to the people for support. They will be forgotten, therefore, and their rights disregarded. They will forget themselves in the sole faculty of making money, and will never think of uniting to effect a due respect for their rights. The shackles, therefore, which shall not be knocked off at the conclusion of this war, will be heavier and heavier, till our rights shall revive or expire in a convulsion."

To the men of that time, who voiced the spirit of that time, the battles that they fought were the least of the Revolution; they were the incidents of the hour, the things they met and faced as part of the game they were playing; but the stake they had in view, before, during, and after the war, the real Revolution, was a change in political institutions which should make of government not a thing apart, a superior power to stand over the people with a whip, but a serviceable agent, responsible, economical, and trustworthy (but never so much trusted as not to be continually watched), for the transaction of such business as was the common concern, and to set the limits of the common concern at the line where one man's liberty would encroach upon another's.

They thus took their starting point for deriving a minimum of government upon the same sociological ground that the modern Anarchist derives the no-government theory; viz., that equal liberty is the practical ideal. The difference lies in the belief, on the one hand, that the closest approximation to equal liberty might be best secured by the rule of the majority in those matters involving united action of any kind (which rule of the majority they thought it possible to secure by a few simple arrangements for election), and, on the other hand, the belief that majority rule is both impossible and undesirable; that any government, no matter what its forms, will be manipulated by a very small minority, as the development of the State and United States governments have strikingly proved; that candidates will loudly profess allegiance to platforms before elections, which as officials in power they will openly disregard, to do as they please; and that even if the majority will could be imposed, it would also be subversive of equal liberty, which may be best secured by leaving to the voluntary association of those interested the management of matters of common concern, without coercion of the uninterested or the opposed.

Among the fundamental likenesses between the Revolutionary Republicans and the Anarchists is the recognition that the little must proceed the great; that the local must be the basis of the general; that there can be a free federation only when there are free communities to federate; that the spirit of the latter is carried into the councils of the former, and a local tyranny may thus become an instrument for general enslavement. Convinced of the supreme importance of ridding the municipalities of the institutions of tyranny, the most strenuous advocates of independence, instead of spending their efforts mainly in the general Congress, devoted themselves to their home localities, endeavoring to work out of the minds of their neighbors and fellow-colonists the institutions of entailed property, of a State-Church, of a class-divided people, even the institution of African slavery itself. Though largely unsuccessful, it is to the measure of success they did achieve that we are indebted for such liberties as we do retain, and not to the general government. They tried to inculcate local initiative and independent action. The author of the Declaration of Independence, who in the fall of '76 declined a reelection to Congress in order to return to Virginia and do his work in his own local assembly, in arranging there for public education which he justly considered a matter of "common concern," said his advocacy of public schools was not with any "view to take its ordinary branches out of the hands of private enterprise, which manages *so much better* the concerns to which it is equal"; and in endeavoring to make clear the restrictions of the Constitution upon the functions of the general government, he likewise said: "Let the general government be reduced to foreign concerns only, and let our affairs be disentangled from those of all other nations, except as to commerce, *which the merchants will manage the better the more they are left free to manage for themselves,* and the general government may be reduced to a very simple organization, and a very inexpensive one; a few plain duties to be performed by a few servants." This then was the American tradition, that private enterprise manages better all that to which it is equal. Anarchism declares that private enterprise, whether individual or co-operative, is equal to all the undertakings of society. And it quotes the particular two instances, Education and Commerce, which the governments of the States and of the United States have undertaken to manage and regulate, as the very two which in operation have done more to destroy American freedom and equality, to warp and distort American tradition, to make of government a mighty engine of tyranny, than any other cause, save the unforeseen developments of Manufacture.

It was the intention of the Revolutionists to establish a system of common education, which should make the teaching of history one of its principal branches; not with the intent of burdening the memories of our youth with the dates of battles or the speeches of generals, nor to make of the

Boston Tea Party Indians the one sacrosanct mob in all history, to be revered but never on any account to be imitated, but with the intent that every American should know to what conditions the masses of people had been brought by the operation of certain institutions, by what means they had wrung out their liberties, and how those liberties had again and again been filched from them by the use of governmental force, fraud, and privilege. Not to breed security, laudation, complacent indolence, passive quiescence in the acts of a government protected by the label "homemade," but to beget a wakeful jealousy, a never-ending watchfulness of rulers, a determination to squelch every attempt of those entrusted with power to encroach upon the sphere of individual action—this was the prime motive of the Revolutionists in endeavoring to provide for common education.

"Confidence," said the Revolutionists who adopted the Kentucky Resolutions, "is everywhere the parent of despotism; free government is founded in jealousy, not in confidence; it is jealousy, not confidence, which prescribes limited constitutions to bind down those whom we are obliged to trust with power; that our Constitution has accordingly fixed the limits to which, and no further, our confidence may go. . . . In questions of power, let no more be heard of confidence in man, but bind him down from mischief by the chains of the Constitution."

These resolutions were especially applied to the passage of the Alien laws by the monarchist party during John Adams's administration, and were an indignant call from the State of Kentucky to repudiate the right of the general government to assume undelegated powers, for, said they, to accept these laws would be "to be bound by laws made, not with our consent, but by others against our consent—that is, to surrender the form of government we have chosen, and to live under one deriving its powers from its own will, and not from our authority." Resolutions identical in spirit were also passed by Virginia, the following month; in those days the States still considered themselves supreme, the general government subordinate.

To inculcate this proud spirit of the supremacy of the people over their governors was to be the purpose of public education! Pick up today any common school history, and see how much of this spirit you will find therein. On the contrary, from cover to cover you will find nothing but the cheapest sort of patriotism, the inculcation of the most unquestioning acquiescence in the deeds of government, a lullaby of rest, security, confidence—the doctrine that the Law can do no wrong, a Te Deum of the continuous encroachments of the powers of the general government upon the reserved rights of the States, shameless falsification of all acts of rebellion, to put the government in the right and the rebels in the wrong, pyrotechnic glorifications of union, power, and force, and a complete ignoring of the essential liberties to maintain which was the purpose of the revolutionists. The anti-Anarchist law of post-McKinley passage, a much worse law than the Alien and Sedition Acts which roused the wrath of Kentucky and Virginia to the point of threatened rebellion, is exalted as a wise provision of our All-Seeing Father in Washington. Such is the spirit of government-provided schools. Ask any child what he knows about Shays's rebellion, and he will answer, "Oh, some of the farmers couldn't pay their taxes, and Shays led a rebellion against the courthouse at Worcester, so they could burn up the deeds; and when Washington heard of it he sent over an army quick and taught 'em a good lesson"—"And what was the result of it?" "The result? Why—why—the result was—Oh yes, I remember—the result was they saw the need of a strong federal government to collect the taxes and pay the debts." Ask if he knows what was said on the other side of the story, ask if he knows that the men who had given their goods and their health and their strength for the freeing of the country now found themselves cast into prison for debt, sick, disabled, and poor, facing a new tyranny for the old; that their demand was that the land should become the free communal possession of those who wished to work it, not subject to tribute, and the child will answer "No." Ask him if he ever read Jefferson's letter to Madison about it, in which he says:

"Societies exist under three forms, sufficiently distinguishable. 1. Without government, as among our Indians. 2. Under government wherein the will of every one has a just influence; as is the case in England in a slight degree, and in our States in a great one. 3. Under government of force, as is the case in all other monarchies, and in most of the other republics. To have an idea of the curse of existence in these last, they must be seen. It is a government of wolves over sheep.—It is a problem not clear in my mind that the first condition is not the best. But I believe it to be inconsistent with any great degree of population. The second state has a great deal of good in it. . . . It has its evils, too, the principal of which is the turbulence to which it is subject. . . . But even this evil is productive of good. It prevents the degeneracy of government, and nourishes a general attention to public affairs. I hold that a little rebellion now and then is a good thing."

Or to another correspondent: "God forbid that we should ever be twenty years without such a rebellion! . . . What country can preserve its liberties if its rulers are not warned from time to time that the people preserve the spirit of resistance? Let them take up arms. . . . The tree of liberty must be refreshed from time to time with the blood of patriots and tyrants. It is its natural manure." Ask any schoolchild if he was ever taught that the author of the Declaration of Independence, one of the great founders of the common school, said these things, and he will look at you with open mouth and unbelieving eyes. Ask him if he ever heard that the man who sounded the bugle note in the darkest hour of the Crisis, who roused the courage of the soldiers when Washington saw only mutiny and despair ahead, ask him if he knows that this man also wrote, "Government at best is a necessary evil, at worst an intolerable one," and if he is a little better informed than the average he will answer, "Oh well, *he* was an infidel!" Catechize him about the merits of the Constitution which he has learned to repeat like a poll-parrot, and you will find his chief conception is not of the powers withheld from Congress, but of the powers granted.

Such are the fruits of government schools. We, the Anarchists, point to them and say: If the believers in liberty wish the principles of liberty taught, let them never intrust that instruction to any government; for the nature of government is to become a thing apart, an institution existing for its own sake, preying upon the people, and teaching whatever will tend to keep it secure in its seat. As the fathers said of the governments of Europe, so say we of this government also after a century and a quarter of independence: "The blood of the people has become its inheritance, and those who fatten on it will not relinquish it easily."

Public education, having to do with the intellect and spirit of a people, is probably the most subtle and far-reaching engine for molding the course of a nation; but commerce, dealing as it does with material things and producing immediate effects, was the force that bore down soonest upon the paper barriers of constitutional restriction and shaped the government to its requirements. Here, indeed, we arrive at the point where we, looking over the hundred and twenty-five years of independence, can see that the simple government conceived by the Revolutionary Republicans was a foredoomed failure. It was so because of—1. The essence of government itself; 2. the essence of human nature; 3. the essence of Commerce and Manufacture.

Of the essence of government I have already said, it is a thing apart, developing its own interests at the expense of what opposes it; all attempts to make it anything else fail. In this Anarchists agree with the traditional enemies of the Revolution, the monarchists, federalists, strong government believers, the Roosevelts of today, the Jays, Marshalls, and Hamiltons of then—that Hamilton, who, as Secretary of the Treasury, devised a financial system of which we are the unlucky heritors, and whose objects were twofold: To puzzle the people and make public finance obscure to those that paid for it; to serve as a machine for corrupting the legislatures; "for he avowed the opinion that man could be governed by two motives only, force or interest"; force being then out of the question, he laid hold of interest, the greed of the legislators, to set going an association of persons having an entirely separate welfare from the welfare of their electors, bound together by mutual corruption and mutual desire for plunder. The Anarchist agrees that Hamilton was logical and understood the core of government; the difference is, that while strong governmentalists believe this is necessary and desirable, we choose the opposite conclusion, NO GOVERNMENT WHATEVER.

As to the essence of human nature, what our national experience has made plain is this, that to remain in a continually exalted moral condition is not human nature. That has happened which was prophesied: We have gone downhill from the Revolution until now; we are absorbed in "mere money-getting." The desire for material ease long ago vanquished the spirit of '76. What was that spirit? The spirit that animated the people of Virginia, of the Carolinas, of Massachusetts, of New York, when they refused to import goods from England; when they preferred (and stood by it) to wear coarse homespun cloth, to drink the brew of their own growths, to fit their appetites to the home supply, rather than submit to the taxation of the imperial ministry. Even within the lifetime of the Revolutionists this spirit decayed. The love of material ease has been, in the mass of men and permanently speaking, always greater than the love of liberty. Nine hundred and ninety-nine women out of a thousand are more interested in the cut of a dress than in the independence of their sex; nine hundred and ninety-nine men out of a thousand are more interested in drinking a glass of beer than in questioning the tax that is laid on it; how many children are not willing to trade the liberty to play for the promise of a new cap or a new dress? This it is which begets the complicated mechanism of society; this it is which, by multiplying the concerns of government, multiplies the strength of government and the corresponding weakness of the people; this it is which begets indifference to public concern, thus making the corruption of government easy.

As to the essence of Commerce and Manufacture, it is this: to establish bonds between every corner of the earth's surface and every other corner, to multiply the needs of mankind, and the desire for material possession and enjoyment.

The American tradition was the isolation of the States as far as possible. Said they: We have won our liberties by hard sacrifice and struggle unto death. We wish now to be let alone and to let others alone, that our principles may have time for trial; that we may become accustomed to the exercise of our rights; that we may be kept free from the contaminating influence of European gauds, pageants, distinctions. So richly did they esteem the absence of these that they could in all fervor write: "We shall see multiplied instances of Europeans coming to America, but no man living will ever see an instance of an American removing to settle in Europe, and continuing there." Alas! In less than a hundred years the highest aim of a "Daughter of the Revolution" was, and is, to buy a castle, a title, and a rotten lord, with the money wrung from American servitude! And the commercial interests of America are seeking a world-empire!

In the earlier days of the revolt and subsequent independence, it appeared that the "manifest destiny" of America was to be an agricultural people, exchanging food stuffs and raw materials for manufactured articles. And in those days it was written: "We shall be virtuous as long as agriculture is our principal object, which will be the case as long as there remain vacant lands in any part of America. When we get piled upon one another in large cities, as in Europe, we shall become corrupt as in Europe, and go to eating one another as they do there." Which we are doing, because of the inevitable development of Commerce and Manufacture, and the concomitant development of strong government. And the parallel prophecy is likewise fulfilled: "If ever this vast country is brought under a single government, it will be one of the most extensive corruption, indifferent and incapable of a wholesome care over so wide a spread of surface." There is not upon the face of the earth today a government so utterly and shamelessly corrupt as that of the United States of America. There are others more cruel, more tyrannical, more devastating; there is none so utterly venal.

And yet even in the very days of the prophets, even with their own consent, the first concession to this later tyranny was made. It was made when the Constitution was made; and the Constitution was made chiefly because of the demands of Commerce. Thus it was at the outset a merchant's machine, which the other interests of the country, the land and labor interests, even then foreboded would destroy their liberties. In vain their jealousy of its central power made them enact the first twelve amendments. In vain they endeavored to set bounds over which the federal power dare not trench. In vain they enacted into general law the freedom of speech, of the press, of assemblage and petition. All of these things we see ridden roughshod upon every day and have so seen with more or less intermission since the beginning of the nineteenth century. At this day, every police lieutenant considers himself, and rightly so, as more powerful than the General Law of the Union; and that one who told Robert Hunter that he held in his fist something stronger than the Constitution was perfectly correct. The right of assemblage is an American tradition which has gone out of fashion; the police club is now the mode. And it is so in virtue of the people's indifference to liberty and the steady progress of constitutional interpretation towards the substance of imperial government.

It is an American tradition that a standing army is a standing menace to liberty; in Jefferson's presidency the army was reduced to 3,000 men. It is American tradition that we keep out of the affairs of other nations. It is American practice that we meddle with the affairs of everybody else from the West to the East Indies, from Russia to Japan; and to do it we have a standing army of 83,251 men.

It is American tradition that the financial affairs of a nation should be transacted on the same principles of simple honesty that an individual conducts his own business; viz., that debt is a bad thing and a man's first surplus earnings should be applied to his debts; that offices and officeholders should be few. It is American practice that the general government should always have millions of debt, even if a panic or a war has to be forced to prevent its being paid off; and as to the application of its income, officeholders come first. And within the last administration it is reported that 99,000 offices have been created at an annual expense of $63,000,000. Shades of Jefferson! "How are vacancies to be obtained? Those by deaths are few; by resignation none." Roosevelt cuts the knot by making 99,000 new ones! And few will die—and none resign. They will beget sons and daughters, and Taft will have to create 99,000 more! Verily, a simple and a serviceable thing is our general government.

It is American tradition that the Judiciary shall act as a check upon the impetuosity of Legislatures, should these attempt to pass the bounds of constitutional limitation. It is American practice that the Judiciary justifies every law which trenches on the liberties of the people and nullifies every act of the Legislature by which the people seek to regain some measure of their freedom. Again, in the words of Jefferson: "The Constitution is a mere thing of wax in the hands of the Judiciary, which they may twist and shape in any form they please." Truly, if the men who fought the good fight for the triumph of simple, honest, free life in that day were now to look upon the scene of their labors, they would cry out together with him who said: "I regret that I am now to die in the belief that the useless sacrifice of themselves by the generation of '76 to acquire self-government and happiness to their country, is to be thrown away by the unwise and unworthy passions of their sons, and that my only consolation is to be that I shall not live to see it."

And now, what has Anarchism to say to all this, this bankruptcy of republicanism, this modern empire that has grown up on the ruins of our early freedom? We say this, that the sin our fathers sinned was that they did not trust liberty wholly. They thought it possible to compromise between liberty and government, believing the latter to be "a necessary evil"; and the moment the compromise was made, the whole misbegotten monster of our present tyranny began to grow. Instruments which are set up to safeguard rights become the very whip with which the free are struck.

Anarchism says, Make no laws whatever concerning speech, and speech will be free; so soon as you make a declaration on paper that speech shall be free you will have a hundred lawyers proving that "freedom does not mean abuse, nor liberty license"; and they will define and define freedom out of existence. Let the guarantee of free speech be in every man's determination to use it, and we shall have no need of paper declarations. On the other hand, so long as the people do not care to exercise their freedom, those who wish to tyrannize will do so; for tyrants are active and ardent and will devote themselves in the name of any number of gods, religious and otherwise, to put shackles upon sleeping men.

The problem then becomes, Is it possible to stir men from their indifference? We have said that the spirit of liberty was nurtured by colonial life; that the elements of colonial life were the desire for sectarian independence and the jealous watchfulness incident thereto; the isolation of pioneer communities which threw each individual strongly on his own resources and thus developed all-around men, yet at the same time made very strong such social bonds as did exist; and, lastly, the comparative simplicity of small communities.

All this has mostly disappeared. As to sectarianism, it is only by dint of an occasional idiotic persecution that a sect becomes interesting; in the absence of this, outlandish sects play the fool's role, are anything but heroic, and have little to do with either the name or the substance of liberty. The old colonial religious parties have gradually become the "pillars of society," their animosities have died out, their offensive peculiarities have been effaced, they are as like one another as beans in a pod, they build churches and—sleep in them.

As to our communities, they are hopelessly and helplessly interdependent, as we ourselves are, save that continuously diminishing proportion engaged in all-around farming; and even these are slaves to mortgages. For our cities, probably there is not one that is provisioned to last for a week, and certainly there is none which would not be bankrupt with despair at the proposition that it produce its own food. In response to this condition and its correlative political tyranny, Anarchism affirms the economy of self-sustenance, the disintegration of the great communities, the use of the earth.

I am not ready to say that I see clearly that this *will* take place; but I see clearly that this *must* take place if ever again men are to be free. I am so well satisfied that the mass of mankind prefer material possessions to liberty, that I have no hope that they will ever, by means of intellectual or moral stirrings merely, throw off the yoke of oppression fastened on them by the present economic system, to institute free societies. My only hope is in the blind development of the economic system and political oppression itself. The great characteristic looming factor in this gigantic power is Manufacture. The tendency of each nation is to become more and more a manufacturing one, an exporter of fabrics, not an importer. If this tendency follows its own logic, it must eventually circle round to each community producing for itself. What then will become of the surplus product when the manufacturer shall have no foreign market? Why, then mankind must face the dilemma of sitting down and dying in the midst of it or confiscating the goods.

Indeed, we are partially facing this problem even now; and so far we are sitting down and dying. I opine, however, that men will not do it forever; and when once by an act of general expropriation they have overcome the reverence and fear of property, and their awe of government, they may waken to the consciousness that things are to be used, and therefore men are greater than things. This may rouse the spirit of liberty.

If, on the other hand, the tendency of invention to simplify, enabling the advantages of machinery to be combined with smaller aggregations of workers, shall also follow its own logic, the great manufacturing plants will break up, population will go after the fragments, and there will be seen not indeed the hard, self-sustaining, isolated pioneer communities of early America, but thousands of small communities stretching along the lines of transportation, each producing very largely for its own needs, able to rely upon itself, and therefore able to be independent. For the same rule holds good for societies as for individuals—those may be free who are able to make their own living.

In regard to the breaking up of that vilest creation of tyranny, the standing army and navy, it is clear that so long as men desire to fight, they will have armed force in one form or another. Our fathers thought they had guarded against a standing army by providing for the voluntary militia. In our day we have lived to see this militia declared part of the regular military force of the United States and subject to the same demands as the regulars. Within another generation we shall probably see its members in the regular pay of the general government. Since any embodiment of the fighting spirit, any military organization, inevitably follows the same line of centralization, the logic of Anarchism is that the least objectionable form of armed force is that which springs up voluntarily, like the Minutemen of Massachusetts, and disbands as soon as the occasion which called it into existence is past: that the really desirable thing is that all men—not Americans only—should be at peace; and that to reach this, all peaceful persons should withdraw their support from the army and require that all who make war shall do so at their own cost and risk; that neither pay nor pensions are to be provided for those who choose to make man-killing a trade.

As to the American tradition of nonmeddling, Anarchism asks that it be carried down to the individual himself. It demands no jealous barrier of isolation; it knows that such isolation is undesirable and impossible; but it teaches that by all men's strictly minding their own business, a fluid society, freely adapting itself to mutual needs, wherein all the world shall belong to all men, as much as each has need or desire, will result.

And when Modern Revolution has thus been carried to the heart of the whole world—if it ever shall be, as I hope it will—then may we hope to see a resurrection of that proud spirit of our fathers which put the simple dignity of Man above the gauds of wealth and class and held that to be an American was greater than to be a king.

In that day there shall be neither kings nor Americans—only Men; over the whole earth, MEN.

VOL. IV, NO. 9, NOVEMBER 1909

Francisco Ferrer

By Emma Goldman

The educational reformer and freethinker Francisco Ferrer, who introduced secular schools into Catholic Spain, was executed on October 13, 1909, on the patently false charge of fomenting a popular uprising in Barcelona earlier that summer. His mock trial and the collusion of the military and the Spanish Church that led to his conviction provoked worldwide protest. In the United States his death galvanized a successful libertarian experiment in education—the Modern School movement—that lasted into the 1960s. The November 1909 issue of *Mother Earth* was largely devoted to an appreciation of Ferrer's life and work, and the anniversary of his death was noted yearly thereafter. (See Ferrer, "L'École Rénovée," page 257, and Illustration 6, following page 220.)

NEVER BEFORE IN THE HISTORY OF THE WORLD has one man's death so thoroughly united struggling mankind.

Never before has one man's death called forth such a universal cry of indignation.

Never before has one man's death so completely torn the veil from the sinister face of the hydra-headed monster, the Catholic Church.

Never before in the history of the world has one man's death so shaken the thrones of the golden calf and spread ghastly fear among its worshippers.

One solitary death, yet more powerful than a million cringing lives. More powerful even than that black specter which, for almost two thousand years, has tortured man's soul and poisoned his mind.

Francisco Ferrer stretched in the ditch at Montjuich, his tender, all-too-loving heart silenced by twelve bullets—yet speaking, speaking in a voice so loud, so clear, so deep. . . . Wherein lies the secret of this wonderful phenomenon?

Francisco Ferrer, the Anarchist and teacher? Yes, but there were other Anarchists and teachers: Louise Michel and Elisée Reclus, for instance, beloved by many. Yet why has their death not proved such a tremendous force?

Francisco Ferrer, the founder of the Modern School? But, then, the Modern School did not originate with Francisco Ferrer, though it was he who carried it to Spain. The father of the Modern School is Paul Robin, the latter-day Dr. Pascal—old in years, with the spirit of Spring, tender and loving, he taught modern methods of education long before Ferrer. He organized the first Modern School at Cempuis, near Paris, wherein children found a home, a warm, beautiful atmosphere.

Again, there is Sébastien Faure and his Beehive. He, too, has founded a Modern School, a free, happy, and harmonious place for children. There are scores of modern schools in France, yet no other man's death will act as a fertilizing force as that of Francisco Ferrer.

Was Ferrer's influence so great because of a lifetime of devoted effort? During eight years his heroic spirit strove to spread the light in the dark land of his birth. For eight years he toiled, ceaselessly, to rescue the child from the destructive influence of superstition. One hundred and nine schools with seventy thousand pupils crowned the gigantic efforts of our murdered comrade, while three hundred and eight liberal schools sprang into being, thanks to his beneficial influence. Yet all this and more fails to account for the tremendous volcano that swept the civilized world at Francisco Ferrer's death.

His trial was a farce. The evidence against him perjured. But was there ever a time when the State hesitated to resort to perjury when dealing with opponents? Was there ever a time when it exercised justice toward those who endangered its stronghold? The State is the very embodiment of injustice and perjury. Some make a pretence at fairness: Spain was brazen; that is all.

What, then, is the secret of the phenomenon?

Driven from its omnipotent position of open crime by the world's progress, the Catholic Church had not ceased to be a virulent poison within the social body. Its Borgia methods merely became more hidden, more secret, yet nonetheless malignant and perfidious. Cowed into apparent submission, it had not dared since the days of Huss and Bruno to openly demand a noble victim's blood. But at last, blinded by arrogance and conceit and the insatiable thirst for martyrs' blood, the Catholic Church forgot the progress of the world, forgot the spirit of our age, forgot the growth of free ideas. As of old, it was the Jesuit hand that stretched forth its bloody fingers to snatch its victim. It was the Archbishop of Barcelona who, in a statement signed by the prelates of the Church, first denounced Ferrer and demanded his life. As of old, Inquisition methods were used in the incarceration and mock trial of Ferrer. No time was to be given the progressive world to check the premeditated murder. Hastily and secretly was the martyr assassinated. Full well the Church knew that the dead cannot be saved.

In vain the frantic efforts of Church and State to connect Francisco Ferrer with the uprising at Barcelona. In vain their delirious cries defaming the character of the dead. In vain the scurrilous attacks of their harlots upon the ideas and comrades of Ferrer—attacks which have now reached even the American press.

Before the awakened consciousness of mankind the world over the Catholic Church stands condemned as the instigator and perpetrator of the foul crime committed at Montjuich. It is this awakened human consciousness which has resurrected Francisco Ferrer.

Therein lies the secret of the force of one man's death, of one solitary man in the ditch of Montjuich.

VOL. V, NO. 7, SEPTEMBER 1910

Anarchist Symposium: Kropotkin

In 1910, *Mother Earth* published a short-lived series, an "Anarchist Symposium," comprised of unsigned discussions about such eminent libertarians as Pierre-Joseph Proudhon, Josiah Warren, Leo Tolstoy, Ralph Waldo Emerson, and Peter Kropotkin. The foremost living philosopher of anarchism, and a proponent of the communist anarchism espoused by *Mother Earth*, Kropotkin was then living in exile in England, having long since renounced his Russian patrimony and the title of "prince." He was a frequent contributor to the magazine, and his photograph appeared on the cover of the issue for December 1912, in honor of his seventieth birthday (see Illustration 9 following page 220).

PETER ALEXEYEVITCH KROPOTKIN, A PRINCE who objects to his title, was born in Moscow, in 1842. He was at one time secretary of the Russian Geographical Society, for which he made long and important researches in Asia, and, in addition to his voluminous writings on sociological subjects, he has published much on geographical and other purely scientific questions. Naturally, therefore, he approaches the consideration of the social question exclusively from the modern scientific point of view, and he considers that the sole object of evolution is the increasing happiness of the human race.

For the attainment of universal happiness one fundamental principle must be recognized, via.: "Do to others as you would have it done to you in the like case," which is practically the Golden Rule, and he explains that this expresses the principles of equality, solidarity, and justice. In all which he is entirely at one with Proudhon and Tolstoy.

But, as might be expected from his scientific training, he is differentiated from them by the conviction that nature preaches an even higher doctrine than any of these, and that is ENERGY. "Be strong," he says. "Overflow with the passion of thought and action; so shall your understanding, your love, your energy, pour itself into others." "What has not the engineer's art

DARED, and what do not literature, painting, music, the drama, DARE today?" Where institutions block the way of progress toward greater happiness we "DARE to fight, to make a rich and overflowing life possible to all."

Kropotkin is every bit as much of an evolutionist as is Herbert Spencer, but the two men look at evolution through somewhat different spectacles, Spencer being inclined to emphasize the slow and steady progress of evolution, while Kropotkin's view is well expressed in the following:

"Evolution never advances so slowly and evenly as has been asserted. Evolution and revolution alternate, and the revolutions—that is, the times of accelerated evolution—belong to the unity of nature just as much as do the times in which evolution takes place more slowly." He also points out that order is the free equilibrium of all forces that operate upon the same point—a mathematical way of stating the problem, which is entirely natural to Kropotkin, and he emphasizes the fact that, "if any of these forces are interfered with in their operation by a human will, they operate nonetheless, but their effects accumulate till someday they break the artificial dam and provoke a revolution."

This is, in reality, a most condensed statement of the main individualistic position. The free working of an individual life is unjustly interfered with. In itself it has a force that appears insignificant, and the wrongdoer feels safe in ignoring its protest. But it links itself to other individualities similarly injured; its force, though perhaps hidden, continues and gathers strength by combination, until finally the wrong, in accord with the strict processes of nature, has to be righted.

This insistence on energy, the bold and free assertion of right life and all its powers, coupled with the conviction that revolution is only accelerated evolution, rendered necessary by the accumulation of individual wrongs, carries Kropotkin to conclusions as regards action widely different from the opinions held by Tolstoy, to whom "love" is the supreme law. I think it would be correct to say that Tolstoy is the Puritan of Love, insisting on its direct observance at all times, and condemning anything that at any moment contravenes the law of love, even though it may seem to pave the way to greater and more generally occupied heights of love.

To Kropotkin, on the other hand, the command of nature to exercise energy, daring, the bold initiative that shall overthrow, at the earliest moment possible, whatever stands in the way of the progress toward greater happiness for the individual and the race, is the imperative command, before which all other moral axioms must bend. He exhausts language to convince his readers that "there is need of great events which rudely break the thread of history and hurl mankind out of its ruts into new roads"; that "the Revolution becomes a peremptory necessity," and that "the building which has become uninhabitable hinders the development of what is sprouting in its crevices and around it."

Kropotkin, as absolute a materialist as Bakunin, and as bitterly opposed to the teachings of the Church as Tolstoy, declares that today, under the influence of science, "man has recognized his place in nature; he has recognized that his institutions are his work and can be refashioned by him alone."

Kropotkin is fully as emphatic as are Proudhon and Tolstoy in his condemnation of State-enacted law. He declares that it has no claim to men's respect; that "it is an adroit mixture of such customs as are beneficial to society, and would be observed even without a law, with others which are to the advantage only of a ruling minority, but are harmful to the masses, and can be upheld only by terror."

He emphasizes the point dwelled on with much persistence by Herbert Spencer in his "Plea for Liberty," that "the law puts rigid immobility in the place of progressive development," and insists that, instead of being for the purpose of securing to the individual or society the product of their labor, it exists "to rob the producer of a part of his product, and to protect a few in the enjoyment of what they have stolen from the producer or from the whole of society."

Furthermore, Kropotkin asserts that the law is a comparatively new formation, mankind having lived for ages without any written law, and that it came into being only when society split into two hostile camps, one of which desired to rule the other. He holds that its days already are numbered.

In the next stage of evolution "the laws will be totally abrogated," and unwritten customs will "suffice to maintain a good understanding." With Proudhon he considers that in the society of the future contracts must be lived up to, but he explains that the compelling motives will be the general will, "the necessity, which everyone feels, of finding co-operation, support and sympathy," and the fear of expulsion from the fellowship. He grants, however, that cases may arise where private or public intervention will be necessary to compel right doing.

With Tolstoy, Proudhon and all other Anarchists, Kropotkin has nothing but condemnation for the State. He follows the general line of argument as to the multiplication of laws and officeholders who live at the expense of the toilers, but specially emphasizes the fact that the modern State is bringing every country to bankruptcy and mortgaging the lives of future generations. He further lays great stress on the argument that the State is tantamount to war.

"One State seeks to weaken and ruin another in order to force upon the latter its law, its policy, its commercial treaties, and to enrich itself at its expense. War is today the usual condition of Europe; there is a thirty-years' supply of causes of war on hand. And civil war rages at the same time with foreign war; the State, which was originally to be a protection for all, and especially for the weak, has today become a weapon of the rich against the exploited, of the propertied against the propertyless."

Like the writers already considered he declares in the most pronounced manner that no distinction can be made between the various forms of the State, and that, as the result of the evolution that has been in progress from absolute monarchies to limited monarchies, and from these latter to so-called republics, it is now clear that government by representation is just as bad as any of its predecessors.

"Precisely like any despot, the body of representatives of the people—be it called Parliament, Convention, or anything else; be it appointed by the prefects of a Bonaparte or elected with all conceivable freedom by an insurgent city—will always try to enlarge its competence, to strengthen its power by all sorts of meddling, and to displace the activity of the individual and the group by the law." "The six-hundred-headed beast without a name has outdone Louis IX and Ivan IV."

It may be noted that the tendency of governing bodies to seek continually to increase their power is an argument that Herbert Spencer dwells on repeatedly.

Such rights as are granted by parliamentary representatives, Kropotkin insists, are entirely worthless, vanishing into thin air the moment the privileges of the favored few are seriously attacked, and he naturally instances the alleged freedom of the press in England, the United States, and Switzerland. "That is what political rights are. Freedom of the press and freedom of association, the inviolability of the home and all the rest, are respected only so long as the people make no use of them against the privileged class. But on the day when the people begin to use them for the undermining of privileges, all these rights are thrown overboard."

That the State is doomed is a fixed conviction that Kropotkin spares no pains to drive home. He maintains that it has reached the zenith of its power and become a tyranny that is no longer endurable, and the method by which this has been accomplished is thus described. "Church, law, military power, and wealth acquired by plunder, have for centuries made common cause; have in slow labor piled stone on stone, encroachment on encroachment, and thus created the monstrous institution which has finally fixed itself in every corner of social life—nay, in the brains and hearts of men—and which we call the State." All which, it will be observed, is entirely in the Tolstoy style.

The process of dissolution has begun already, and the hour of the State's death is near at hand. In Kropotkin's judgment the Latin races are those which are in the lead in the attack on an institution that has had its day; "they want the independence of the provinces, communes and groups of laborers; they want not to submit to any dominion, but to league themselves together freely."

"After having tried all kinds of government, humanity is trying now to free itself from the bonds of any government whatever, and to respond to its needs of organization by the free understanding between individuals prosecuting the same common aims."

Reading the last quotation it will be seen that the ideal setup is precisely the same as that held by Proudhon and Tolstoy, and with them Kropotkin enlarges on the enormous field occupied today by private co-operation and on the possibilities that have been opened to it with every improvement in the methods of communication. Not only does this hold good with commercial organizations, but "there is also no lack of free organizations for nobler pursuits; the Lifeboat Association, the Hospitals Association, and hundreds of like organizations. One of the most remarkable societies which has recently arisen is the Red Cross Society. To slaughter men on the battlefields, that remains the duty of the State; but these very States recognize their inability to take care of their own wounded; they abandon the task, to a great extent, to private initiative."

Inasmuch as one constant charge made against Anarchists is that they wish to relegate humanity to conditions of primitive isolation, it is thought necessary to emphasize the point just made.

With Tolstoy, Kropotkin holds that "to rack our brains about the details of the form which public life shall take in the future society would be silly," but he insists that it is necessary to come to an agreement about the main features. One principle is imperative—freedom from authority. People will group themselves freely in communes, but it will and must be freely.

VOL. V, NO. 12, FEBRUARY 1911

Long Live Anarchy!

By Hippolyte Havel

Hippolyte Havel, born in Bohemia, was one of the most cosmopolitan contributors to *Mother Earth* and a member of the magazine's inner circle, along with Max Baginski, Alexander Berkman, Emma Goldman, and Ben L. Reitman. In several issues, from December 1910 to September 1911, he took up the cause of Denjiro Kotoku, a Japanese journalist and translator of Western socialist and anarchist literature, his wife Sugano Kano, and ten other radicals who were executed in Tokyo for plotting to assassinate Emperor Mutsuhito. With no apparent evidence against them, their death was yet another judicial murder after the manner of Francisco Ferrer's.

> The greatest men of a nation are those whom it puts to death.
> *Ernest Renan.*

T HE BLACK DEED IS DONE. THE BEST AND NOBLEST of the people have fallen, murdered in the most fiendish and barbaric manner.

A crime, unparalleled in atrocity, has been committed on January twenty-fourth, nineteen hundred and eleven. A terrible blow has been dealt humanity, and the gauntlet thrown in the face of civilization. Ruthless barbarism cold-bloodedly strangled the heroic pioneers of a new idea and gloated over the agony of its helpless victims.

Yet we mourn not. Rather is it our task to discover to the world the innocence and purity, the honesty and faithfulness, the self-sacrifice and devotion of our murdered comrades. We mourn not: our friends have achieved immortality.

A new epoch has struck for Japan with the date of their martyrdom. When the era of Mikado Mutsuhito shall have passed from man's memory, when *bushido* is but a fable and a myth, the names of the martyred Anarchists will be glorified on the pages of human progress. When the members of the *Daishinin,* who delivered the noblest of mankind into the hangman's hands, shall have been long forgotten, the martyrs of Tokyo will be respected and admired by future generations.

The revolutionary movement in the Orient has received its baptism of blood. The barbaric rulers think to have eradicated the movement for emancipation. What stupidity! They have destroyed the bodies of twelve representatives of the new, world-conquering idea and silenced other representatives in the dungeons; but the spirit lives! That spirit, the eternal cry for liberty—it is not to be silenced, it cannot be killed. It was, it is, and will be. Conquering it marches onward, ever onward, toward liberty and life.

Long live Anarchy! The historic cry has found its echo in the Far East. Often it has resounded, from the lips of the martyrs of Chicago, Paris, Buenos Aires, Vienna, St. Petersburg, Barcelona, and numerous other places. For decades it has been terrifying the tyrants and oppressors of every land. They have tortured, beheaded, electrocuted, quartered, shot, and strangled the pioneers of the new idea. But their voices have not been silenced.

Denjiro Kotoku

Long live Anarchy! On the twenty-fourth of January the cry once more rang from the lips of twelve new martyrs. The solidarity of the international proletariat has been crowned. The West and the East have found each other.

Proudly and joyfully our comrades faced death. *Long live Anarchy!* cried Denjiro Kotoku. *Banzai* (i. e., forever) replied his companions in struggle and death.

They were very dear to us. We mourn not; yet our hearts are saddened at the thought of the charming Sugano. Lovingly we dwell upon her memory. We see the tender lotus ruthlessly destroyed by the hand of the hangman; we behold her, weakened through illness, broken by long imprisonment, yet joyfully and calmly meeting her terrible doom. *I have lived for liberty and will die for liberty, for liberty is my life.* Thus she wrote but recently to her English teacher in San Francisco.

Gentle Sugano! You, the daughter of a Samurai, daughter of a member of your country's Parliament, talented author and writer, you went, like your Russian sisters, into the people, voluntarily exposing yourself to danger, hardships, and hunger. They have sought to besmirch your character and name. The representatives of a Mutsuhito, himself leading a life of polygamy; his son, the heir apparent, offspring of a concubine; the lackeys of Premier Katsura, who chose the daughter of a brothelkeeper for his wife—all these honorable men have sought to besmirch you, lovely lotus flower, because of your friendship for Denjiro Kotoku.

Sugano Kano

What contemptible scoundrels! But someday there will arise a Turgenev in the land of Nippon, and the name of Sugano Kano will be hailed with the Sophia Perovskayas, the Vera Figners, and Maria Spiridonovas.

In Denjiro Kotoku the international movement has lost one of its noblest representatives. He was the pioneer of Socialist and Anarchist thought in the Far East. His numerous translations—Karl Marx's *Capital*, Peter Kropotkin's *Mutual Aid, The Conquest of Bread, Fields, Factories, and Workshops*, and "An Appeal to the Young," as well as of other modern works—have accomplished the *real* opening of Japan to Western civilization.

Denjiro Kotoku was, next to Tolstoy, the severest opponent of war; and—like Hervé—a most courageous, uncompromising propagator of antimilitarist ideas. While the patriotic jingoes celebrated, during the Russo-Japanese war, orgies of wholesale man-killing, Kotoku was engaged in exposing the murderous business by his brilliant articles in the *Yorozu-Choho*. But the voice of the prophet was lost in the wilderness. Like Victor Hugo, Mazzini, Blanqui, Bakunin, Marx, and scores of other pioneers of liberty before him, he was forced to flee his native land, to live in exile at San Francisco, and here, in the land of Patrick Henry, Thomas Paine, and Jefferson, he was to suffer new persecutions at the hands of the government of Washington. O shame, O disgrace!

Denjiro Kotoku, Sugano Kano, Dr. Oishi, and their comrades legally assassinated; these, the noblest and most intelligent of their people: writers, physicians, representatives of pure Buddhist philosophy of human brotherhood, and awakened, intellectual proletarians—these are the men slaughtered in the hope of annihilating every vestige of modern world-thought.

Great, brave men. Lovingly and tenderly we peruse over again an old letter from Dr. Oishi, a reader of MOTHER EARTH. In strong, clear English he sends greetings to his American comrades and requests Anarchist literature for distribution among his countrymen. The much beloved, genial physician of Shingo-Key, bringing cheer and relief to the thousands of sick and afflicted. His only reward, the gallows.

Our eyes have at last been opened to the true character of the government of the Mikado. We know now the infamous conspiracy hatched by the Japanese government. We realize the full significance of the atrocious plot. We can follow to their source the false reports, misrepresentations, and lies put in circulation by Reuter's Agency, the Japanese Ambassadors and Consuls, and especially by the Oriental Information Bureau of New York. The mysterious Oriental veil has been partly lifted. The civilized world is now aware that the trial of our martyred comrades was conducted in secret; that the accused were deprived of impartial hearing or defense; that the claim that they had confessed their guilt was pure fabrication; and that, finally, the official statement regarding the presence at the trial of the members of foreign embassies was also absolutely false.

The trial of Francisco Ferrer was ideal justice in comparison with this judicial wholesale slaughter. Since the days of the Dekabrists in Russia humanity has witnessed no crime so monstrous, so monumental as that committed by the government of Japan.

The rulers of Japan have succeeded in accomplishing one thing. They have drawn upon themselves the hatred of the libertarian elements of every country, who will join hands with the awakening proletariat of Japan in the great work of social emancipation.

The massacre has not only made our comrades martyrs; it has made them immortal. Out of their blood will rise new rebels, avengers who will sweep off the face of the earth the murderers and their institutions.

Long live Anarchy!

VOL. VI, NO. I, MARCH 1911

The Pioneer of Communist Anarchism in America

By Max Baginski

Johann Most died in March 1906, the month that *Mother Earth* came into being. Himself an accomplished orator, Most was an early mentor of Emma Goldman's and introduced her to a thumping style of public speaking in which she quickly excelled. Alexander Berkman, soon after immigrating to America, worked as a typesetter for Most's newspaper, *Freiheit*. Yet following Berkman's arrest and imprisonment for attempting to assassinate Henry Clay Frick, Most belittled the act, and Goldman horsewhipped her former teacher at one of his lectures in full view of the audience. Nevertheless, he was always written of with great admiration in the pages of *Mother Earth*. Max Baginski marked the fifth anniversary of Most's death (calling him John) with a "tender memorial" to one of anarchism's truest torchbearers.

∞

THESE LINES ARE IN TENDER MEMORIAM OF John Most, who died in Cincinnati, five years ago, on the seventeenth of March, 1906.

In the year 1882 Most came to America, as an exile, and continued the publication of the *Freiheit*, whose existence had been made impossible in England. After the execution of Alexander II, on the thirteenth of March, 1881, Most voiced his hope in a leading article in the *Freiheit* that all tyrants may thus be served. That article proved too much for the muchboasted-of British freedom. Prussian and Russian spies and diplomats intrigued an interpellation in the British Parliament, as a result of which Most was indicted for "inciting to kill the reigning sovereigns." The court sentenced our comrade to sixteen months at hard labor, and life in the prison of free England proved a veritable hell.

Most had previously been incarcerated in German and Austrian prisons, and his treatment there was always that of a political prisoner. In free England, however, he found himself treated even more brutally than the ordinary thief or murderer. His complaints against the barbaric methods elicited the sole reply that there were no political prisoners in a free country like England.

When he had paid the penalty for the free expression of his opinions, John Most was invited, immediately upon his discharge from prison, to come to America, there to begin an energetic propaganda along revolutionary Anarchist lines. This comradely invitation was signed, among others, by Justus Schwab, whom most of our old-time comrades no doubt still remember.

Most followed the call. An enthusiastic reception meeting in Cooper Union, in which thousands participated, was his greeting in the new land. A tour of agitation followed, during which Most succeeded in organizing a large number of propaganda groups among the German-speaking workingmen.

Most was the first to initiate, on a comparatively extensive scale, the propaganda of Communist Anarchism in America.

The German element in this country was at that time far more mentally alert and energetic than it is today: the Bismarckian muzzle-law, the expulsion of hundreds of socialistically inclined proletarians, the suppression of

Socialist literature, and the brutal police persecution made the thinking workers rebellious. The lines between governmental and revolutionary Socialism, and between the latter and Anarchism, were not so sharply drawn at the time when Most, the fiery agitator of the social revolution, arrived in America. He was an orator of convincing power, his methods direct, his language concise and popular, and he possessed the genius for glowing word-portrayal which had far more effect upon his auditors than long theoretic argumentation. He lived and felt entirely with the people, the men of toil. The great tragedy of his latter years was that the very people he loved so well turned from him, many of them even joining the general howl of the capitalistic press, which never abated its denunciations of Most as a veritable monster of degradation and bloodthirstiness.

In the meantime there widened the breach between the ballot-box Socialists, on the one hand, and the revolutionary Socialists and Anarchists on the other. Many of those who had so enthusiastically welcomed Most on his arrival in America joined the ballot-box party and now even denounced our comrade because he persisted in warning the people against the game of deception called politics. In this respect he spoke from personal experience: as former member of the Reichstag he felt convinced that parliamentarism could never serve as an aid in the emancipation of the working class.

The American labor movement followed its course. It was able to stand a Powderly, and it has not even now grown strong enough to rid itself of men like Gompers and Mitchell. Naturally there was no room in it for a Most, a Parsons, a Spies, or a Dyer D. Lum. Gompers, a rising star on the labor firmament, may indeed not have been averse to making use of Lum's superior intellect and experience, even to the extent of signing his articles, it is said. But after he had attained bureaucratic power, he found it more politic to withdraw from such compromising associates.

The German movement, in particular, gradually grew weaker. The atmosphere of this country is not very conducive to the mental development of the Germans; as a rule, they lose here all incentive to intellectual pursuit. They either conserve the ideas they have brought over with them, till these become petrified, or they entirely throw idealism overboard and become "successful businessmen," philistines who are far more concerned with their little house and property than with the great events of the world.

Under these circumstances his exile was growing more and more unbearable for Most, his hounding ever more severe and base, the indifference and apathy of the Germans more impenetrable.

His friends had told Most, upon his arrival: "Here, at least, you are secure against imprisonment." Most had waved the remark aside as altogether too optimistic, saying that it was only a question of time when he would come in conflict with the sham liberties of the Republic. He was only too justified in this view. When, in the eighties, the waves of the labor movement rose to exceptional height, and the proletariat began preparations for a general strike to secure the eight-hour day, the plutocrats and financiers grew alarmed. "Order"—that is, profits—seemed in danger. The lackeys of the press were mobilized to denounce to the police and the courts every expression of rebellious independence on the part of the working people.

In April, 1886, there took place in New York a large meeting, addressed, among others, by Most, who called upon the audience to prepare and arm themselves for the coming great struggle. The speech was taken down stenographically and submitted to the grand jury, which found indictments against John Most, Braunschweig, and Schenk. On the second of July, Judge Smyth condemned Most to one year's imprisonment in the penitentiary and five hundred dollars' fine, while the other two comrades were doomed to nine months' prison and two hundred and fifty dollars' fine.

It was the old wretched method. The police of various cities had systematically interfered with the numerous strikes and committed repeated assaults upon the workingmen, establishing "order" in the most brutal manner. The violence of the police naturally resulted in bitterness, riots, and killings. But instead of calling the uniformed ruffians to account, the authorities fell upon the spokesmen of the movement, marking them as their victims. The crimes of the guardians of the law were "legally" laid at the door of the Anarchists: in New York, upon Most; in Chicago, upon Spies and comrades, who—eighteen months later—paid for their love of humanity with their lives.

It became evident that freedom of speech and press was not tolerated in the Republic and that it was as severely persecuted in "free" America as in Germany, Austria, and England.

That was not Most's only conviction. He was repeatedly condemned to serve at Blackwell's Island. The press had so systematically lied about and misrepresented his ideals and personality that the "desirable citizen" came to regard our comrade as a veritable Satan. Especially were the German papers venomous in their denunciations and ceaselessly active in the manhunt against one who had sacrificed everything for his ideals.

When McKinley was shot at Buffalo, the *Freiheit* happened to reprint an article from the then long-deceased radical writer, Karl Heinzen. The article had no bearing whatever upon American conditions, and it was the greatest outrage and travesty upon the most elementary principles of justice that Most was condemned to serve nine months in prison—for reprinting an article written decades before. The New York *Staatszeitung*, "leading organ of the German intelligence," bravely assisted in this shameful proceeding by the most infamous denunciation.

Yet all this persecution and suffering Most could have borne much better than the growing apathy of the very elements to whom he was appealing. He found himself more and more isolated. The struggle for existence—of the *Freiheit,* and his family—grew more difficult. He had dreamed beautiful dreams of the masses who would march side by side with him against the bulwarks of tyranny. And now he discovered himself a revolutionary freelance, standing almost alone. With grim humor he wrote in the *Freiheit:* "Henceforth I shall no more say 'we,' but 'I.'" In spite of it all, however, he fought bravely to the very end. His courage and Rabelaisian humor never forsook him. In the latter years there was even a noticeable improvement in his literary originality. After all, in the words of the Chantecler, "it is beautiful to behold the light when everything around is enveloped in darkness."

VOL. VII, NO. 5, JULY 1912

Voltairine de Cleyre

By Alexander Berkman

Voltairine de Cleyre and Alexander Berkman were kindred spirits in many ways—analytical, ascetic, uncompromising in their beliefs, yet personally warm and generous. They corresponded throughout his long imprisonment in the Western Penitentiary, her letters, he said, with their "great charm and rebellious thought" bringing "color to my existence." His tribute to her was one of several to appear in a memorial issue of *Mother Earth* in July 1912, following her death the previous month (see Illustration 8, following page 220). Berkman also edited her *Selected Works,* published two years later by the Mother Earth Publishing Association (see Leonard D. Abbott, "Voltairine de Cleyre's Posthumous Book," page 214).

VOLTAIRINE DIED SO UNEXPECTEDLY, I can hardly realize even now that she is no more. We were such constant and intimate correspondents for the past six years—almost till her last days—that I still cannot free myself from the peculiar feeling that I may get a letter from her at any moment.

She has been in our midst too recently for us to be able to appreciate fully her exceptional character, brilliant mind, and revolutionary activity. We need better perspective of time to estimate correctly the influence and inspiration she exerted on her comrades and the movement.

But this I know: Voltairine was a martyr, as truly as anyone that was ever crucified by a stupid and petty world.

Some die for their ideal; fewer live for it. And I am quite sure that it is much harder and requires more character and strength to live in accordance with one's purpose and ideas than to die for them. Such are the greatest martyrs, and of them was Voltairine.

Most of us, even revolutionists and Anarchists, often conform, trim a little here, compromise a bit there, and too often we persuade ourselves that the means justify the end. But only those means justify the end which are in their character and tendency in accord with it; and then they are *of* the end, a part of the end itself. If not, then the means gradually master us, and finally master our end.

This we all know; it is history, and it is personal experience. But how few of us dare admit it even in the solitude of our own heart; how few have the courage and honesty to question their activity and life, and ask themselves, *Do* my means justify my end? are they in accord? are they one and the same?

Voltairine had the courage and the honesty. Her whole life was motived by unswerving devotion to the cause she had made her own, by never-conforming and never-compromising loyalty to herself. She was human: she had her faults and failings; black days of doubt and agony of despair. But because of them she towered a giant above her time, for—human as she was—she yet proved victor. She was too strong in her humanity to be the plaything of Circumstance, that "inexorable" master of all ye that are weak in spirit. She would not be dominated by the Dominant Idea of the Age, nor yet by the power of her immediate environment. For the really strong, even if they cannot change their environment, do not suffer the environment to change them.

Thus Voltairine de Cleyre went her way, standing almost alone, often embittered by apathy and corruption and the lack of understanding even among friends, yet growing stronger and firmer in her isolation. For she was one of those rare spirits whose staunch devotion to the ideal permeated her every act and every breath of her life and gave strength and encouragement to all her friends and co-workers in the cause of uncompromising Anarchism.

Her life was a protest against all sham, a challenge to all hypocrisy, and an inspiration for social rebellion.

I am proud to have called you friend and comrade, Voltairine! I do not mourn your death—your poor body is freed from pain, and your spirit is victor! You were one of those who, in your own beautiful words, "choose their own allegiance and serve it. Who will say a word to their souls and keep it—keep it not when it is easy, but when it is hard—keep it when the storm roars and there is a white-streaked sky and blue thunder before, and one's eyes are blinded and one's ears deafened with the war of opposing things; and keep it under the long leaden sky and the gray dreariness that never lifts."

Such as you, Voltairine, that "hold unto the last," Circumstance cannot break. They make and unmake Circumstance, for in them is "the immortal fire of Individual Will, which is the salvation of the Future."

VOL. VII, NO. 9, NOVEMBER 1912

The Causes of the Chicago Martyrdom

By Alexander Berkman

No single event had a greater impact on the incipient anarchist movement in America than the hanging in 1887 of four anarchists wrongly convicted of the bombing near Chicago's Haymarket Square on May 4 of the previous year: Albert Parsons, August Spies, George Engel, and Adolph Fischer. (Three other men, Samuel Fielden, Oscar Neebe, and

Michael Schwab, received prison sentences but were pardoned in 1893. A fourth, Louis Lingg, committed suicide on the eve of the executions.) For Emma Goldman, as for thousands of others, the hangings were a turning point in social awareness. The date, November 11, was permanently marked in the anarchist calendar and occasioned impassioned articles in *Mother Earth* year after year. Alexander Berkman's capsule history in the November 1912 issue placed the Haymarket tragedy within the context of the American labor struggle and the larger war against the "Beast of Law and Order," capital and government. (See Berkman, *"The Bomb,"* page 174.)

A QUARTER OF A CENTURY HAS PASSED since the hanging of our comrades in Chicago, on the 11th of November, 1887. The perspective of time has helped to dissipate the fog of prejudice and passion that at the time beclouded the grave questions at issue: the passage of the years has clarified the situation which resulted in the Haymarket tragedy. An impartial analysis of the events that culminated in the hanging of the Chicago Anarchists compels the unbiased mind to the conclusion that our comrades were the victims of a judicial murder, the direct result of a conspiracy of privilege and authority.

The gallows of 1887 was no accident. Labor events of the preceding decade cast their shadow before. Already in the early seventies—in 1872 and 1873—began the movement for an eight-hour workday. By degrees it assumed such proportion as to force the legislatures of several States to pass laws making eight hours a legal working day for State employees. The agitation kept up, and within a few years the movement became national and powerful enough to induce Congress to pass, in 1878, an eight-hour law for Federal employees.

But the Federal eight-hour law, as well as the similar State statutes, remained a dead letter, in spite of all the resolutions, appeals, and protests of labor. The lords of industry refused to introduce the shorter workday, and their word was the supreme law.

The working masses began to awaken to the realization that parliamentary methods were a farce. The conviction was ripening that no amelioration of labor conditions could be hoped for from political sources. The idea was germinating in the mind of Toil that victory cannot be had for the asking; that it must be fought for—fought in the industrial arena, by the means nearest and most effective in the hands of labor—the method that has since become known as direct action.

It was the dawning of a new consciousness. It found clear expression in the International Congress of Organized Labor, held in Chicago, in 1884, by the Federated Trades Unions of United States and Canada. That congress decided that organized labor must make a determined effort by the direct means of its economic weapons to win the eight-hour day. The 1st of May, 1886, was chosen as the great Labor Day, on which a united attempt was to be made for the recognition of the demands of the workers.

The more radical labor element of the country—the revolutionary Socialists and Anarchists of the time—had already before realized that the road of labor's advancement and ultimate emancipation was not to be sought along political lines, but in direct economic and industrial warfare. Already in 1883, at the Pittsburgh Convention, the revolutionists of the International Working People's Association issued a proclamation, condemning all indirect political activity as ineffectual and misleading, and emphatically advocating revolutionary methods, direct action, and the general strike. The ablest and most energetic spirits of the International Working People's Association were Parsons, Spies, Fielden, and their comrades. They were indefatigable in the labor movement, and their activity in no small degree helped to revolutionize and enlighten the working masses.

The month of May, 1886, was approaching. Capital and labor faced each other in grim determination. Never before had the workers of America given such a demonstration of united, solidaric effort. Capitalism was in a panic.

On the 1st of May a tremendous strike-wave swept the country. In the very forefront of the struggle stood Chicago. Twenty-five thousand workers laid down their tools on the 1st of May, and within two days the number was doubled. By the 4th of May practically all the workers of the great city were on a general strike.

The enemy resorted to every means to stifle the revolt of labor. The capitalist press advised strychnine and lead for the discontented wage slaves, and the armed fist of the law hastened to the service of Mammon. The paid myrmidons of capital vied with each other in shooting down the workers. Bloody encounters between police and strikers were numerous. The most brutal assault took place at the McCormick Works, where conditions were so unbearable that the men were forced to go on strike already in February. At this place the police and Pinkertons deliberately shot a volley into the assembled strikers, killing four workers and wounding a score of others.

It was to protest against these cold-blooded police murders that the Haymarket meeting was called, on the 4th of May, 1886.

It was a perfectly orderly meeting, such as were daily taking place in Chicago in those days. The Mayor of the city, Carter Harrison, was present;

he listened to several speeches and then—according to his own sworn testimony later on in court—he returned to police headquarters to inform the
Chief of Police that the meeting was all right. It was growing late—about
ten in the evening. Heavy clouds appeared on the sky; it looked like rain.
The audience began to disperse, till only about two hundred were left.
Then suddenly a hundred police rushed upon the scene. They halted at the
speakers' wagon, from which Fielden was addressing the remnant of the
audience. The police captain in charge commanded the meeting to disperse. Fielden replied: "This is a peaceful assembly." Without further warning the police threw themselves upon the people, mercilessly clubbing men
and women. At that moment something whizzed through the air, and seven
policemen lay dead on the ground, and about sixty wounded.

The beast of Law and Order thirsted for blood. The fury of the masters
knew no limits. Rebellious labor was to be crushed with an iron hand; the
spirit of discontent was to be stifled, its voice drowned in the blood of the
most devoted and able men of the people. Our Chicago Comrades were the
chosen victims.

It took six long years till there was found a man in an official position—
Governor Altgeld, of the State of Illinois—a man of supreme honesty and
sincere conviction, with moral courage officially to stamp the hanging of
our Chicago comrades as a premeditated judicial murder. By incontrovert-
ible facts and evidence he proved that our martyrs were the victims of a
police conspiracy to convict, prompted and financed by the plutocracy of
Chicago. Governor Altgeld adduced merciless proof upon proof that the
conviction of our comrades was based upon willful and conscious perjury;
that the jury was packed by the official specially chosen by the court for the
purpose; that the judge was bitterly prejudiced, and that he openly intimi-
dated jury and witnesses; and that finally the Anarchists were convicted for
conspiracy to throw a bomb, the actual thrower of which has remained
unknown and therefore in no way shown to have been connected with the
accused. They were convicted and hanged because it was intended they
should die. For they were guilty of enlightening and revolutionizing the
proletariat—a crime tyranny ever punishes with death.

The historic rôle of government is *murder*. The law is the statutory reflection of Mammon. When the interests of capital demand it, when the fabric
of oppression and exploitation is threatened, government steps in to
strengthen the foundation of Things As They Are and to crush everything
that appears to menace their continued existence. 'Tis the triumph of Law
and Order.

If the Chicago tragedy had accomplished nothing more than to clarify the function of capital and the true role of government, the martyrdom of our comrades has not been in vain.

VOL. IX, NO. I, MARCH 1914

The Paris Commune

By Voltairine de Cleyre

If Haymarket was for anarchists a defining event, the same can be said of the Paris Commune of 1871 for militant radicals of every stripe. The Commune was seen as the harbinger of the great proletarian revolution to come. The date of its rise, March 18, was added to the anarchists' calendar, together with May 1, the celebration day of international labor, and November 11, in memory of the Haymarket martyrs. *Mother Earth* published Voltairine de Cleyre's "The Paris Commune" posthumously. The verses at the end were written by an unknown poet and were quoted by de Cleyre in other pieces about the Commune as well as the Haymarket hangings, having been recited by Albert Parsons before the gallows. (See Peter Kropotkin, "The Commune of Paris," page 333.)

THERE ARE TIMES AND OCCASIONS WHICH REDUCE all men to direct, primitive feeling, so strong that to whatever degree of sophistication one may have trained oneself about what one ought to feel or ought not to feel, what is logical or what is not logical, reasonable or unreasonable, one is no longer able, or even disposed, to battle with the imperative mandate of the Man Within. The surge is irresistible: to the faint Reason that would offer argument, there rises up an all-silencing rebuke, a stern scorn, as of one who may in less intense moments hearken placidly and be ruled, but who now is possessed of a single sentiment and has no time for vain palavering.

To me, the commemoration of the 18th of March is one of those times. I cannot remember, at this moment, and I do not wish to remember, that I have a philosophy, a creed of any kind, to set limits upon what I feel, or to measure my passion with a yardstick. And in speaking now, I speak simply as a human being, not as an Anarchist. For the feelings that take possession of me, when I remember what the Commune was, what it struggled to be, what its enemies have made of it, and what they did to the thousands of men, women, and little children who filled the graves, the prisons, and the exile posts of France in the Commune's name, are not at all in accord with a high and calm philosophy which looks upon the struggles of men with still, impartial eyes, and accepts successes and failures alike as part of a drama with an assured dénouement, the final liberation of all. I will not say to myself, "Can I, dare I, feel so, being an Anarchist? What right have I to feel so?" I feel, and the feeling will not be gainsaid.

I feel that there is too much of the blood of the innocent on our enemies' hands for us to contemplate shaking them and talking of a pleasant understanding in the future. Some other time perhaps—afterward—when things shall have been evened. Not now.

Not now, remembering the beleaguered city, Paris the Beautiful, Paris the Devoted, Paris the Eternal Rebel, set round with a foreign army and forsaken by the traitor government of Versailles, which had neither helped her nor allowed her to help herself! And so, encompassed and deserted, and betrayed, she rose up alone under that black pall, flinging it from her, and lifting her proud face, beaded with struggle and white with purpose, and broke the fetters from her hands and feet and flung them in the traitors' teeth. Out of her darkest need, her netherest depth, her bitterest betrayal, she sought and found the strength to rise, alone and free. She sought deliverance where only deliverance can be found, within herself. And though she struggled and was conquered, she set that day a beacon light upon a hill—a light they could not drown with all the blood they spilled.

But oh, what false colors they have given that light—the preachers and the teachers who have miswritten history, and lied, and lied, and lied. What have they not said about the Commune? That it was a carnival of burning, of thuggery, of theft, of murder! That it was the triumph of indecency over moral order and virtue! That it was the idle, the vicious, the jealous, and the envious who made it! That it arose without an accountable reason like a great fungus out of the scum of men.

Oh, how they have lied, these pillars of society, these educators of our children! The sons and daughters of the Commune were of all walks in life, their thousands ranging through all the skilled crafts that have made Paris the art workshop of the world, through the simpler yet more necessary workers, and around the circle of labor, to the scholars, students, journalists, authors, engineers, publicists, and men of military training, but of free spirit.

If the long roll of the 3,600 prisoners taken by the butchers of Versailles were read, there would be found among them so many names decorated with honor by their very enemies that the mere data of their biographies would make a book. There was more learning, more skill, more devotion and purity of sacrifice brought to the service of the Commune, and freely given, than her detractors ever conceived as in existence.

And their purpose was to realize that for which previous revolutions had been fought and had failed—the independence of a people with common interests and common needs against the tyranny of an external force, organized for the purpose of drawing blood and treasure from them in the name of their defense.

In the name of protection and defense, the government of Versailles had taxed them, deserted them, sold them—and having completed the sale and bought off the Prussians, they turned like tigers to tear them.

And on the night before the 23d of May they entered the city, like foreign invaders, and the storm began; lightning of flashing powder, the thunder of cannon, the hail of lead, the patter of blood. The spring sun broke over the cemeteries where the living fought, barricaded by the dead, over the streets where the soldiers rode up and down firing as they pleased, over the houses where women and children waited to be dragged out and murdered. It shone upon the earlier and happier victims who died fighting, upon the cold-blooded massacres of citizens lined up in groups against the walls of their homes, shot and thrown in heaps, upon the butcheries of the wounded in the very hospitals, doctors and nurses shot by the side of those they tended or driven off to the bastions to await still greater suffering.

And at night the fires arose; and they who had devastated Paris threw the blame of her burning on her own children.

And then—the stakes of Satory! The midnight executions when prisoner after prisoner was led out by the lantern light, pinned to a stake, shot, buried in the trench that stretched at his feet! And the torture of mothers to make them reveal the whereabouts of their sons; the hungering and the beating of little children to make them reveal the whereabouts of their parents! The long and terrible marches from prison to prison, in the night, in the mud, in the rain, under the insults of the soldiers, under the blows of their rifle butts, marching, falling, dying in the ditches, under the prison walls. Then the long-drawn tortures of waiting in cold and pale-lit cellars, sleeping on the water-soaked earth—yea, and blood-soaked—kept worse than rats in holes, waiting for—justice! The "justice" of the conqueror.

Then for months and months, the processions to the convict ships, the gruesome journey under the shadow of the cannon over long seas to the marsh-fevered shores of Guiana and the coral-reefed wastes of New Caledonia and the Isle of Pines. And there, the fiendish ingenuity of torture developed by the professional prisonkeeper, year after year poisoning and crushing, till many died, and many went mad, and all were wasted in body and embittered in spirit.

With all these images before my eyes, distinct and lit with a white, awful clearness, as in the paralysis of a lightning flash—I do not want to "love my enemies," nor "let bygones be bygones." I do not want to be philosophical, nor preach their inclusion in the brotherhood of man. I want to *hate* them—utterly. They have the power, they have the weapons, they have the law, they have the prisons; and what they have done before they will do again, whenever and wherever people try to be rid of them. They will do it until the people become the stronger. And then—perhaps—then when they are beaten and thrown down, when they are made to understand how useless they are as they are, will be the time to think about forgiving them and teaching them to do some useful service in the world.

The patience that we need, we who want the free community, is not patience with them, but with the stupidity and stolidity of the people, by whom our enemies enslave us, together with themselves.

I wish that every inconscient child of Labor might feel upon his head the club of power and on his wrist the chain; might see before his eyes, forever, the sacrifice of those who have hurled themselves against the barriers and broken themselves in a self-regardless endeavor to bring freedom into the world—freedom to these others who have never wanted it nor conceived it, these others who are ready slaves to do the will of tyrants upon their fellows who want to be men. If they, these wretched creatures, who live as beasts in sleep, and lend themselves to drag any load at any beggar's price, who accept their existence as an alms allowed them by a Court of Charity—if they were once awakened—Oh, for our conscious and intending enemies there would be no very long story to tell. They might take their Bibles and read, "With what judgment ye judge, ye shall be judged," and remember the stakes of Satory, and say to themselves, "It is better to do like Judas, and buy a rope with the price of our iniquity and go away and hang ourselves!"

Ah, but Paris failed!

Yes, Paris failed; and many another uprising of the spirit of Paris will fail, before the great insurrection comes which will *not* fail.

They will fail because the people do not demand enough, are too patient and law-abiding in their suffering, too naive not to expect good from their enemies, too nurtured in respect of power to offer resistance to the Club. They will fail because they will not attack the essential thing which is their hurt—they will not take back the sources of life from those who have seized them, but play a stupid game of spilling their blood for the winning of a few cents wages, which will be taken away from them again, at the next economic crisis, no matter what form of political power rules them. They will fight for little things and leave the power to precipitate the same struggle over and over in the hands of those with whom they fight. They will go on losing as much flesh and blood in every struggle as would serve to win the whole battle, did they but understand that the thing to fight for was the expropriation of the world's sources of production, and the machinery of it, and their reinvestment in the whole people.

Paris was a blow for the decentralization of political power; it must at any rate have failed (unless the other Communes of France had followed its example), because the centralized State power was too mighty for even its heroism to prevail against. But Paris failed to strike at economic tyranny, and so came short of what it could have achieved, had it possessed itself of what resources it could have had. The lesson is long in the learning, and sometimes it seems that one generation quite forgets what is taught to its predecessor; but the school is a large one, and each section has to do its own learning, probably.

We in America are still in the primer class; we have to learn the very A B C, which is that all trades, all workers, skilled or unskilled, have a common interest, and that all police clubs feel alike. That the rights of assemblage, speech, and petition exist for none except those who assemble in the interests of corporate bodies and political gangs, for those who have nothing to say and nothing to petition for; that as for the rest, they may neither meet, nor talk, nor march, nor petition without feeling the club; so the best thing is to meet and march and demand—not petition—for the club will be no heavier for the one than the other. So far the people have learned not even this, being drunk with their government-school-drilled tradition that everything is done by the people and for the people, by our best of all possible governments, which is of the people. They have to learn what the people of monarchical governments know from the start, that the government is "agin' em," and they must be "agin' it."

It is a far cry from this baby lesson which the workers of America are learning to the conception of the free community whose economic affairs shall be arranged by the groups of actual producers and distributors, eliminating the useless and harmful element now in possession of the world's capital; and whose political rights will never be embodied in useless papers, called Constitutions, which every petty city official may violate at his pleasure—but will exist actively in the free and active personalities of its members, in their desire and determination to assert themselves.

It is a far cry from the strike of the people simply to inflict suffering on themselves, to the strike of the people which will transfer that suffering to their oppressors; from the strike which "quits" to the strike which "takes possession," from that which lays down its tools to that which takes possession of its tools and instead of absenting itself from the shops turns its masters out. But the first page of the lesson has been begun; and there is hope for more speedy learning with the acceleration of solidarity among our enemies.

The Commune went down, as many another Commune will go down. But she went down gloriously, with flashing eyes; low in the blood-spilled dust, by the wall of Père-la-Chaise her face was lifted still; and the haunting ghost of its defiant, dying light yet flickers on the wreath-hung stone. And wherever the people rise in spontaneous rebellion, recognizing their common brotherhood, there the light flashes out again, and the old voice cries:

> They say she is dead, the Commune is dead;
> That if she were living her earthquake tread
> Would scatter the honeyless hornet's hive.
>
> ·　　·　　·　　·　　·
>
> Go revel once more ye cowardly knaves
> With the wantons your lusts have made,
> Be drunken again on the blood of the slave,
> That are slain in your shambles of trade,
> But know ye this, I am not dead.
>
> ·　　·　　·　　·　　·
>
> 　I am not dead, I am not dead,
> 　　I live a life intense, divine;
> 　Yours be the days forever fled,
> 　　But all the morrows shall be mine.

VOL. IX, NO. 3, MAY 1914

Michael Bakunin (1814–1914)

By Max Baginski

Max Baginski marked the birth centennial of Mikhail Bakunin with an appreciation that reflected the awe in which one of anarchism's most heroic founding figures was held. A large man of huge and restless appetites, Michael Bakunin (as Baginski called him) was among that new breed of international, peripatetic revolutionaries that emerged during the European uprisings of 1848. He is perhaps best known for his terrifying words, "The passion for destruction is also a creative passion," which ever since has alarmed both antianarchist revolutionaries and antirevolutionists alike. The force of Bakunin's personality was manifest in the fatal factionalism that split the International Workingmen's Association of 1864–76 (the "First International") between his followers and those of his greatest rival, Karl Marx, who engineered his expulsion from the organization in 1872. Bakunin died in 1876, the same year the First International dissolved.

I N THE SPRING OF 1861 THERE ARRIVED IN San Francisco a man who had a long and eventful journey behind him. He came all the way from Siberia, where he had passed four years in exile. Previous to that he was imprisoned in the dungeons of Saxony, Austria, and Russia. In Saxony he had been sentenced to death because of his participation in the Dresden uprising. Extradited to Austria, he was again condemned to die. Then followed his extradition to Russia, where he was kept six years in the Petro-Pavlov Fortress. Transferred to the dreaded Schlüsselburg casemates, he was subsequently doomed to lifelong exile in Siberia.

Twelve years of this persecution and torture passed before he succeeded in finding his way to liberty. Under many difficulties he escaped from Siberia, crossed Japan, and thence reached the United States. Soon he was in London, where he immediately renewed his revolutionary connections and threw himself into his former work with an energy and enthusiasm as if all the persecution he had suffered merely served to rejuvenate him.

The name of this refugee was Michael Bakunin. Born May 20th (May 8th, according to the Russian calendar), 1814, he enjoyed all the advantages of a child of a wealthy family that belonged to the oldest Russian nobility. Young Bakunin might have easily attained to something "great" in the official circles of Russia, after he graduated from the Imperial Artillery School and became an army officer. But his rebellious temperament, his passionate love of liberty, and his rich mental endowments all combined to alienate him from the world of bureaucracy, and made him one of the great, significant personalities whose name will for all time be associated with the noblest struggles of humanity to break its fetters.

In the personality of Bakunin was incarnate the spirit of the Social Revolution. He was the very reverse of the *genus* politician who cunningly builds up his party and becomes absorbed therein. He gave himself fully, abandoned himself completely to his ideal, while the politician carefully calculates the steps he must climb to reach his goal. 'Tis the eternal contrast between the idealist and the politician: the one espouses liberty as wide as the world, the other awaits a favorable opportunity for advancement; the one devotes himself entirely to revolution, the other adapts himself to circumstances. It is because of this contrast that the politician wins momentary triumph, the real value of which soon shrinks, while the revolutionist achieves little success during his lifetime and personally often suffers a tragic fate—but the fire of his being, the directness and oneness of his purpose continue to inspire the hearts and minds of mankind long after his death.

No doubt Karl Marx, Bakunin's antagonist in the International Workingmen's Association—organized fifty years ago—is still held in high esteem. But one thinks of him as a scholastic, a theoretician, the founder of a system that began with the claim of infallibility, but which is now doomed to disintegration, its very foundations crumbling to dust. No such musty chill breathes from Bakunin. His lifework is not an appeal to mere intellectuality; he speaks to the whole man, the most precious part of whom is still his strong will, his instincts and passions.

Young Bakunin worked his way through the abstruse books of the German philosophers and later became active in the conspiratory and revolutionary uprisings of almost every country in Europe. In all these struggles his efforts were directed towards the demolition of every form of tyranny: God, State, capitalism, every metaphysical as well as physical despotism was to be destroyed before justice and liberty could triumph. His manifold activities brought him in personal contact with most of the thinkers and propagandists of the social revolutionary movement of his time. He carried on long discussions of social problems with Proudhon; he was in close touch with Nechayev, the most zealous and reckless of Russian revolutionists, as well as with Alexander Herzen. Common ideas made Richard Wagner kin to him in the days of the Dresden uprising, and he was an intimate friend of the poet-revolutionist Georg Herwegh. There was hardly any individual type of revolutionist that Bakunin failed to meet in his stormy career. From the wealth of his experience—with individuals, events, theories, principles—there crystallized in his later years the conviction that the proletariat can never hope for liberation except through its own efforts. In a letter to the members of the Jura Federation, with whom he had worked and struggled and who stood by him in spite of all the slanders of the Marx clique, he left a sort of testament that is of especial significance at the present time, when the workers throughout the world are beginning to see the emptiness of political phrases. In this letter—the last greeting to his former comrades—he says:

"By birth and personal position I am a bourgeois, and as such I could carry on only theoretical propaganda amongst you. But I have come to the conclusion that the time for theoretical work, written or spoken, is past. . . . This is not a time for ideas; it is the time for action, for deeds. And first of all it is necessary to organize the power of the proletariat. But this organization must be the work of the proletariat itself. If I were young I would go into the midst of the workers and by taking part in the daily life and struggles of my brothers, I would aid in this most important work of organization. But neither my age nor my health permit it now. Organize, constantly organize the international militant solidarity of the workers, in every trade and country, and remember that however weak you are as isolated individuals or districts, you will constitute a tremendous, invincible power by means of universal coöperation."

This is the same militant spirit that breathes now in the best expressions of the Syndicalist and I. W. W. movements. Indeed, the 100th anniversary of Michael Bakunin comes at a time of a strong worldwide revival of the ideas for which Bakunin labored throughout his life with such wonderful devotion, perseverance, and courage.

VOL. IX, NO. 4, JUNE 1914

Mutual Aid:
An Important Factor in Evolution

By Peter Kropotkin

Peter Kropotkin's best-known book, *Mutual Aid,* provided a scientific framework for the central concept of communist anarchism: voluntary cooperation as the natural basis for society. It was also a counter to the arguments of the Social Darwinists, who held that "survival of the fittest" explained, if not justified, the innate competitive spirit of capitalism. On the eve of the Great War, Kropotkin expanded on his position, addressing the "principles of independence and free federation" in contrast to centralized government and the nation-state.

AT FIRST RECEIVED WITH DISTRUST, the idea that mutual aid and mutual support represent an important factor in the progressive evolution of animal species seems to be accepted now by many biologists. In most of the chief works of Evolution, appeared lately in Germany, it is already recognized that two different aspects of the struggle for life must be distinguished: the struggle of the whole, of large divisions, of a species against adverse natural conditions and rival species, and the struggle between individuals within the species; in other words: *exterior* warfare and *inner* war. At the same time it begins also to be recognized that the struggle for life *within* the species has been exaggerated and that *mutual aid is,* to say the least, *as much a fundamental principle in Nature as mutual struggle; while for progressive evolution* it is without doubt the most important of the two.

The value of this recognition cannot be overlooked. Darwin already foresaw it. Once it is recognized that the social instinct is a permanent and powerful instinct in every animal species, and still more so in man, we are enabled to establish the foundations of Ethics (the Morality of Society) upon the sound basis of the observation of Nature and need not look for it in supernatural revelation. The idea which Bacon, Grotius, Goethe, and Darwin himself (in his second work, *The Descent of Man*) were advocating is thus finding a full confirmation, once we direct our attention to the extent to which mutual aid is carried on in Nature. We see at once what a powerful weapon it represents even for the feeblest species in their struggle against adverse natural conditions, the longevity it secures to the individuals, the accumulation of experience, and the development of higher instincts and intelligence that it renders possible within the species.

To show this importance of the social instinct as a basis of Ethics is the work which I am now engaged in.

Another important consideration to which the study of mutual aid in Nature brings us is that it enables us better to realize how much the evolution of every animal species, and still more so of human societies and separate individuals, depends upon *the conditions of life under which they are developing.* This idea, so energetically advocated by the French Encyclopaedists at the end of the eighteenth century, and by their Socialist and Anarchist followers in the succeeding century, beginning with Godwin, Fourier, and Robert Owen, is bitterly combated by the defenders of Capitalism and the State, as well as by the religious preachers; and we all know what advantage they took of the struggle-for-life idea for the defence of their position—much to the despair of Darwin himself. Now that we see that the idea of an inner struggle within the species had been grossly exaggerated by Darwin's followers, we understand that if in his works, subsequent to his *Origin of Species* (*The Descent of Man* and especially *Variation in Animals and Plants*), he gave more and more importance to the action of exterior conditions in determining the lines of evolution of all living beings—he did not make "a concession" to his opponents, as we are told by some of his English followers. He merely summed up the result of the immense researches he had made into the causes of variation after he had published in 1859 his first epoch-making work, *The Origin of Species.*

A careful, dispassionate study of the effects of environment upon the development of both societies and individuals can thus be made now, and it is sure to open new, important vistas upon Evolution as a whole, while at the same time it frees the social reformer from the doubts he might have had concerning his efforts of changing first the present conditions of life of mankind and saying that better conditions of social life, based on mutual support and equality, would already raise man's moral conceptions to a level they never could attain under the present system of slavery and exploitation of man by man.

A third point upon which the researches made can throw a new light is *the origin of the State.* Some ideas upon this subject, derived from the studies of the development of Society, and contained in *Mutual Aid,* I have embodied in a pamphlet, "The State and Its Historical Role." But much more could be said upon this important subject; and, as every careful reader will see himself, the chapters I give in the book to "Mutual Aid in the Mediaeval City" and, the preceding chapter, to the Village Community, open new lines of research which would be rich in important *practical* results. Unfortunately, the worship of the centralized Roman State and Roman Law, which reigns supreme in our universities, stands in the way of such researches. The more so, as such studies, if they were made, would give support to the ideas growing now in the Latin and the Anglo-Saxon communities as regards the necessity of independence, or "home rule," not only for separate nationalities but also for every geographically separate territory, every commune and parish. Such an independence—it begins now to be understood—would be the only proper way for establishing a real union between the different parts of a territory, in lieu of the artificial cohesion enforced now by a common submission to some outside authority. It has been said in some reviews of this book that I have to some extent exaggerated the good features of the mediaeval free republics. But if this book were not written for the general reader, and if I had incorporated into it the immense mass of material I have collected in the reliable contemporary sources and serious modern works on the subject, one would have seen that, far from having exaggerated, I was compelled to limit my illustrations to quite a small number of those I might have given. Those illustrations which I have in my manuscript notes alone would do to make a second volume.

Now that we see such a great movement among the workingmen of Europe and America towards themselves working out the forms which production and exchange ought to take in a society freed from the yoke of Capital and State, I earnestly advise those workers who are already thinking in that direction to meditate about what we know of the first two centuries of independent life in the mediaeval cities, after they had thrown off the yoke of feudal barons, bishops, and kings, and started a new development on the lines of freedom and federation. Of course, we must not try to imitate the past—history does not repeat itself, and I have indicated in *Mutual Aid* the mistakes the mediaeval cities committed when they worked out their freedom charts. What we have to do is to see whether the *principles of independence and free federation* were not infinitely better, leading to prosperity and a higher intellectual development, than the submission to outside authorities and the enslavement to Church and State, which characterized the epoch that followed the fall of the free cities and inaugurated the growth of military States.

At the present time the idea of centralization and centralized States is so much in vogue, even among Socialists, that we often hear people saying that the smaller nationalities have no reason to exist; the sooner they will be swallowed by the more numerous ones, the sooner they forget their mother tongue, the better.

All my life, experience has taught me quite the reverse. All that I have learned in my life has persuaded me, on the contrary, that the surest way to bring about a harmony of aspirations among the different nations is for every fraction of mankind to further develop and to enrich the language that is spoken by the masses of that fraction of humanity. This will also be the surest way for all those fractions to agree among themselves as to the one or two languages that will be accepted later on as the chief means of international intercourse. The more so as learning a language would be a knowledge quite easy to acquire under the perfected methods of teaching languages which are already worked out now.

Besides, this is also the surest way to stimulate every nationality to develop the best that it has worked out in the course of centuries in its own surroundings: the surest way to enrich our common inheritance with those national features which give a special value to philosophical conceptions, to poetry, and to art.

VOL. IX, NO. 5, JULY 1914

Dynamite!

By Charles Robert Plunkett

On the morning of July 4, 1914, an explosion in a tenement building on upper Lexington Avenue, in Harlem, killed three young men, all anarchists, and a woman friend. The men—Arthur Caron, Carl Hanson, and Charles Berg—had been active in recent demonstrations, organized by

Frank Tannenbaum and Alexander Berkman, to demand food and shelter for the homeless unemployed during the depression winter of 1913–14. (See Berkman, "Tannenbaum before Pilate," page 277, and "The Movement of the Unemployed," page 338.) More significant still, they had protested the massacre of men, women, and children on April 20 in Ludlow, Colorado, at a tent colony of striking workers and their families near the Colorado Fuel and Iron Company, controlled by John D. Rockefeller, Jr. (see "Remember Ludlow!" by Julia May Courtney, page 344). It was generally supposed that the Lexington Avenue bomb had been intended for the Rockefeller family estate, Pocantico Hills, near Tarrytown, New York, though no connection was ever proved. The July 1914 issue of *Mother Earth,* under Berkman's editorship, was an emotional outpouring in honor of the "martyrs" of the explosion, taken to a pitch by Charles Robert Plunkett's "Dynamite!" In the last paragraph, Plunkett misquoted Louis Lingg, one of the men falsely convicted in the Haymarket bombing of 1886, who committed suicide in his jail cell on the eve of the executions. Lingg's actual words were: "If you cannonade us, we shall dynamite you."

Emma Goldman was on a lecture tour at the time of the issue's publication and was, as she wrote in her memoirs, "dismayed at its content . . . the harangues were of a most violent character. I had tried always to keep our magazine free from such language, and now the whole number was filled with prattle about force and dynamite. I was so furious that I wanted the entire issue thrown into the fire. But it was too late; the magazine had gone out to the subscribers." Plunkett's association with anarchism was short-lived, and he later became a professor of biology at New York University.

IT HAD TO COME. IT WAS THE LOGICAL culmination of events. The past five months have witnessed a period of Anarchist activity in New York City unequaled in this country since the stirring days of 1886 in Chicago. Also, and consequently, they have witnessed unexampled police brutality, court persecution, newspaper slander, and popular prejudice. The end was inevitable.

It began in the stormy days of February with the Revolt of the Unemployed—well-fed, pharisaical clergymen and their smug, self-righteous congregations rudely awakened from their fatuous dreams of seventeenth-century theology by hordes of hungry men demanding food and shelter—mass meetings and demonstrations, the greatest ever held in New York, at which thousands of workers listened to and applauded the speeches of avowed Anarchists—the Black Flag of Hunger borne by ragged, starving men through the residential street of the world's industrial potentates—the city stirred, the country aroused, the pillars of capitalist society shaken. Hunger had become articulate, Misery had found its voice! The authorities, deaf to the groans of Starvation, quickly gave ear to the first murmurs of Revolt. One hundred and ninety-two men arrested at once for seeking food; Frank Tannenbaum sentenced to practically two and a half years in jail for declaring that a hungry man has the right to eat; meetings forcibly broken up by the police, workingmen clubbed, arrested, and jailed for expressing their opinions—and they ask if we believe in violence!

Then came the massacre of Ludlow—two hundred men, women, and children of the working class shot down or burned alive by the hired butchers of Standard Oil. Again it was the Anarchists who took up the fight of the workers and brought home the responsibility where it belonged—to the oily murderer who teaches a Bible class on Sunday and roasts alive defenseless women on Monday. "My conscience acquits me," said young Rockefeller. We replaced his conscience; we became his Nemesis. His well-oiled conscience acquitted him; but we, the militant workers, have convicted him and passed judgment from his own Bible—"A life for a life."

Driven from his office at 26 Broadway, from his city home and his pet Sunday School—the world's most potent monarch was forced to take refuge behind barred gates and armed guards at his Tarrytown estate. Having driven the rat into his hole, we followed him there. We went to Tarrytown. More clubs, more arrests, more jail, more persecution. A dozen men and women thrown into a filthy, stinking jail for speaking on the street, more arrested and clubbed the next day, jail sentences of thirty to ninety days punished the temerity of the rebels who dared invade Rockefeller's hometown. Finally, finding his town police, his private guards and special deputies unable to cope with the situation, a hired "mob" was organized, which, inflamed with patriotism, rural bigotry, and Rockefeller's whiskey, and gratuitously aided by the New York City authorities, attacked, stoned, and—had not their "Dutch courage" failed them—would have lynched the Anarchist speakers.

After this, the mask was off. Not content with legal violence, the ruling class itself had first appealed to extralegal violence. None could suppose that the Anarchists would not accept the challenge.

This was the situation on the morning of July 4th. Then came the explosion, startling the country and striking terror into the hearts of the reaction. A large tenement house on Lexington Avenue was destroyed and three well-known Anarchists—Arthur Caron, Charles Berg and Carl Hanson—were killed. The ruin was evidently caused by a large quantity of dynamite exploding in the flat occupied by our comrades. These are the facts. More than this no one knows, and probably never will know.

Whatever may be the truth of the matter, the police and the capitalist press immediately assumed that the dynamite was being made into a bomb for use against Rockefeller or in Tarrytown. This was the story flashed over the country, and the moral effect of the explosion was as great as if our comrades had succeeded in their purpose, whatever it may have been.

As usual, many of the lip-revolutionists scurried to cover and hastened to "repudiate" violence, Anarchy, the dead men, and everything connected with them. The Anarchists, however, have stood their ground. Although we know nothing of the facts, we do not hesitate to admit the possibility, nor fear to face the accusation that our comrades met their death in an attempt to retaliate upon the violence of the ruling classes in the only possible way—with violence.

If they did, we own them proudly, and we honor them for their intelligence, their initiative, and their courage. They did the only logical thing, the only courageous thing, the only revolutionary thing under the circumstances. When Free Speech is suppressed, when men are jailed for asking for food, clubbed for assembling to discuss their grievances, and stoned for expressing their opinions, there is but one recourse—violence. The ruling class has guns, bullets, bayonets, police, jails, militia, armies and navies. To oppose all this the worker has only—dynamite.

All honor to the men who acted, while others talked. All honor to the men who were preparing to strike a blow of terror into the hearts of the enemy. They are dead—the last in the long list of martyrs to the cause of human liberty—but there are hundreds and thousands still alive who, inspired by their act, will follow their example—with better success.

Off with the mask! This is war. Violence can be met only with violence. "If they attack us with cannon, we will attack them with dynamite"—and, whenever possible, let us attack first. To oppression, to exploitation, to persecution, to police, jails, militia, armies and navies, there is but one answer—DYNAMITE!

VOL. IX, NO. 5, JULY 1914

Anarchism: Communist or Individualist?—Both

By Max Nettlau

In its pages, *Mother Earth* tried to reconcile the often antagonistic varieties of anarchism. Thus Max Nettlau, the movement's premier historian,
pointed to a necessary middle ground between the two extremes of individualist and communist anarchism. Ironically, his reasoned argument
appeared in the same issue that expressed the most radical views on the
need for revolutionary violence, following the Lexington Avenue explosion.

ANARCHISM IS NO LONGER YOUNG, AND IT MAY be time to ask
ourselves why, with all the energy devoted to its propaganda, it does
not spread more rapidly. For even where local activity is strongest, the results are limited, whilst immense spheres are as yet hardly touched by any
propaganda at all. In discussing this question, I will not deal with the
problem of Syndicalism, which, by absorbing so much of Anarchist activity and sympathies, cannot by that very fact be considered to advance the
cause of Anarchism proper, whatever its other merits may be. I will also try
not to repeat what I put forward in other articles in years gone by as possible means of increasing the activity of Anarchists. As my advice was not
heeded, it cannot, in any case, be considered to have hampered the progress of our ideas.

I will consider the theories of Anarchism only; and here I have been
struck for a long time by the contrast between the largeness of the aims of
Anarchism—the greatest possible realization of freedom and well-being for

all—and the narrowness, so to speak, of the economic program of Anarchism, be it Individualist or Communist. I am inclined to think that the feeling of the inadequacy of this economic basis—exclusive Communism or exclusive Individualism, according to the school—hinders people from acquiring practical confidence in Anarchism, the general aims of which appeal as a beautiful ideal to many. I feel myself that neither Communism nor Individualism, if it became the sole economic form, would realize freedom, which always demands a choice of ways, a plurality of possibilities. I know that Communists, when asked pointedly, will say that they should have no objection to Individualists who wished to live in their own way without creating new monopolies or authority, and *vice versa*. But this is seldom said in a really open and friendly way; both sections are far too much convinced that freedom is only possible if *their* particular scheme is carried out. I quite admit that there are Communists and Individualists to whom their respective doctrines, and these alone, give complete satisfaction and leave no problem unsolved (in their opinion); these would not be interfered with, in any case, in their lifelong constancy to *one* economic ideal. But they must not imagine that all people are constituted after their model and likely to come round to their views or remain "unreclaimed" adversaries on whom no sympathy is to be wasted. Let them but look on real life, which is bearable at all only by being varied and differentiated, in spite of all official uniformity. We all see the survivals of earlier Communism, the manifold workings of present-day solidarity, from which new forms of future Communism may develop—all this in the teeth of the cutthroat capitalist Individualism which predominates. But this miserable bourgeois Individualism, if it created a desire for solidarity, leading to Communism, certainly also created a desire for a genuine, free, unselfish Individualism, where freedom of action would no longer be misused to crush the weaker and to form monopolies, as today.

Neither Communism nor Individualism will ever disappear; and if by some mass action the foundations of some rough form of Communism were laid, Individualism would grow stronger than ever in opposition to this. Whenever a uniform system prevails, Anarchists, if they have their ideas at heart, will go ahead of it and never permit themselves to become fossilized upholders of a given system, be it that of the purest Communism.

Will they, then, be always dissatisfied, always struggling, never enjoying rest? They might feel at ease in a state of society where all economic possibilities had full scope, and then their energy might be applied to peaceful emulation and no longer to continuous struggle and demolition. This desirable state of things could be prepared from now, if it were once for all frankly understood among Anarchists that both Communism and Individualism are equally important, equally permanent; and that the exclusive predominance of either of them would be the greatest misfortune that could befall mankind. From isolation we take refuge in solidarity, from too much society we seek relief in isolation: both solidarity and isolation are, each at the right moment, freedom and help to us. All human life vibrates between these two poles in endless varieties of oscillations.

Let me imagine myself for a moment living in a free society. I should certainly have different occupations, manual and mental, requiring strength or skill. It would be very monotonous if the three or four groups with whom I would work (for I hope there will be no Syndicates then!) would be organized on exactly the same lines; I rather think that different degrees or forms of Communism will prevail in them. But might I not become tired of this, and wish for a spell of relative isolation, of Individualism? So I might turn to one of the many possible forms of "equal exchange" Individualism. Perhaps people will do one thing when they are young and another thing when they grow older. Those who are but indifferent workers may continue with their groups; those who are efficient will lose patience at always working with beginners and will go ahead by themselves, unless a very altruist disposition makes it a pleasure to them to act as teachers or advisers to younger people. I also think that at the beginning I should adopt Communism with friends and Individualism with strangers and shape my future life according to experience. Thus, a free and easy change from one variety of Communism to another, thence to any variety of Individualism, and so on, would be the most obvious and elementary thing in a really free society; and if any group of people tried to check this, to make one system predominant, they would be as bitterly fought as revolutionists fight the present system.

Why, then, was Anarchism cut up into the two hostile sections of Communists and Individualists? I believe the ordinary factor of human shortcomings, from which nobody is exempt, accounts for this. It is quite natural that Communism should appeal more to some, Individualism to others. So each section would work out their economic hypothesis with full ardor and conviction and by and by, strengthened in their belief by opposition, consider it the *only* solution and remain faithful to it in the face of all. Hence the Individualist theories for about a century, the Collectivist and Communist theories for about fifty years, acquired a degree of settledness, certitude, apparent permanency, which they never ought to have assumed, for stagnation—this is the word—is the death of progress. Hardly any effort was made in favor of dropping the differences of schools; thus both had full freedom to grow, to become generalized, if they could. With what result?

Neither of them could vanquish the other. Wherever Communists are, Individualists will originate from their very midst; whilst no Individualist wave can overthrow the Communist strongholds. Whilst here aversion or enmity exists between people who are so near each other, we see Communist Anarchism almost effacing itself before Syndicalism, no longer scorning compromise by accepting more or less the Syndicalist solution as an inevitable stepping-stone. On the other hand, we see Individualists almost relapse into bourgeois fallacies—all this at a time when the misdeeds of authority, the growth of State encroachments, present a better occasion and a wider field than ever for real and outspoken Anarchist propaganda.

It has come to this, that at the French Communist Anarchist Congress held in Paris last year Individualism was regularly stigmatized and placed outside the pale of Anarchism by a formal resolution. If ever an international Anarchist Congress was held on these lines, endorsing a similar attitude, I should say good-bye to all hopes placed in this kind of sectarian Anarchism.

By this I intend neither to defend nor to combat Communism or Individualism. Personally, I see much good in Communism; but the idea of seeing it generalized makes me protest. I should not like to pledge my own future beforehand, much less that of anybody else. The question remains entirely open for me; experience will show which of the extreme and of the many intermediate possibilities will be the best on each occasion, at each time. Anarchism is too dear to me that I should care to see it tied to an economic hypothesis, however plausible it may look today. Unique solutions will never do, and whilst everybody is free to believe in and to propagate his own cherished ideas, he ought not to feel it right to spread them except in the form of the merest hypothesis, and everyone knows that the literature of Communist and Individualist Anarchism is far from keeping within these limits; we have all sinned in this respect.

In the above I have used the terms "Communist" and "Individualist" in a general way, wishing to show the useless and disastrous character of sectional exclusiveness among Anarchists. If any Individualists have said or done absurd things (are Communists impeccable?), to show these up would not mean to refute me. All I want is to see all those who revolt against authority work on lines of general solidarity instead of being divided into little chapels because each one is convinced he possesses a correct *economic* solution of the social problem. To fight authority in the capitalist system and in the coming system of State Socialism, or Syndicalism, or of both, or all the three combined, an immense wave of real Anarchist feeling is wanted before ever the question of economic remedies comes in. Only recognize this, and a large sphere of solidarity will be created, which will make Communist Anarchism stand stronger and shine brighter before the world than it does now.

P. S.—Since writing the above I have found an early French Anarchist pamphlet, from which I translate the following:

"Thus, those who feel so inclined will unite for common life, duties, and work, whilst those to whom the slightest act of submission would give umbrage will remain individually independent. The real principle [of Anarchism] is this far from demanding integral Communism. But it is evident that for the benefit of certain kinds of work many producers will unite, enjoying the advantages of co-operation. But I say once more, Communism will never be a fundamental [meaning unique and obligatory] principle, on account of the diversity of our intellectual faculties, of our needs, and of our will."

This quotation (the words in brackets are mine) is taken from p. 72 of what may be one of the scarcest Anarchist publications, on which my eye lit on a bookstall ten days after writing the above article: *Philosophie de l'Insoumission ou Pardon à Cain,* par Félix P. (New York, 1854, iv. 74 pp., 12mo)—that is, "Philosophy of Non-Submission," the author's term for Anarchy. I do not know who Félix P. was; apparently one of the few French Socialists, like Déjacque, Bellegarrigue, Cœurderoy, and Claude Pelletier, whom the lessons of 1848 and other experiences caused to make a bold step forward and arrive at Anarchism by various ways and independent of Proudhon. In the passage quoted he put things into a nutshell, leaving an even balance between the claims of Communism and Individualism. This is exactly what I feel in 1914, sixty years after. The personal predilections of everybody would remain unchanged and unhurt, but exclusivism would be banished, the two vital principles of life allied instead of looking askance at each other.

Authority and ordinary selfishness are far too powerful and common enemies to all of us that we can afford to waste energy on internal struggles which, by establishing dogmatism, would sap the very roots of Anarchism.

VOL. IX, NO. 10, DECEMBER 1914

Emma Goldman in Chicago

By Margaret Anderson

Although anarchists had their own pantheon of heroes and martyrs, for most Americans the predominant figure in the movement was Emma Goldman; whether as a demonic presence to her detractors or as an inspiration to her supporters, her public persona was outsized. Margaret Anderson founded the avant-garde *Little Review* in Chicago in March 1914. Her articles on philosophical anarchism attracted Goldman; the two began corresponding and afterward became friends. In the December 1914 issue of *Mother Earth,* Anderson reported her impressions of Goldman's recent series of lectures during a three-week stay in Chicago, concluding: "She is always a giant. . . . Perhaps because, like science, she defies finalities."

Emma goldman has just finished her three weeks of lecturing in Chicago, and those of us who went every night to hear her have a feeling that something tremendous has dropped out of life with her going. The exasperating thing about Emma Goldman is that she makes herself so indispensable to her audiences that it is always tragic when she leaves; the amazing thing about her is that her inspiration seems never to falter. Life takes on an intenser quality when she is present: there is something cosmic in the air, a feeling of worlds in the making which Hardy once put into a single line: "while universe after universe drifts by."

Most of these new lectures were devoted to the modern drama and were given in the Assembly Hall of the Fine Arts Building. This is the first time in her life that Miss Goldman has talked in just that kind of hall and before just that kind of people. The thing was in the nature of an experiment and was made possible by the efforts of a few people who became interested in her work last year. Their plan to enlighten a certain type of benighted human being—the type that will go to anything which happens to be featured in the Fine Arts Building but that shudders at the mere thought of Emma Goldman in Labor Hall—had its interesting and its amusing sides. But more of that later. The other lectures—the propaganda ones—were given on Monday and Wednesday nights at East End Hall and in Jewish on Friday nights and Sunday afternoons at Hodcarrier's and Workman's Hall. There were also three Sunday night War lectures in the Fine Arts; and these of course were the most important in point of attendance and general value.

But the outstanding event of the whole three weeks was Miss Goldman's appearance at the Chicago Press Club, where she was invited to talk during luncheon. It was one of the most stirring things I have ever sat through. Picture a large club dining room filled with about five hundred hard-faced men ("Oh! those faces!" Miss Goldman said afterward; "how they seared me!"); imagine their cynical indifference as she began to speak amid all the clattering of dishes and the rushing of waitresses; and then imagine the stillness that gradually descended upon them as she poured out her magnificent denouncement.

Her subject was "The Relationship of Anarchism to Literature," and she talked to those men about making their lives and their work free and true and beautiful in a way that would pull the heart out of anything but a veteran newspaper man. "You are mental prostitutes!" she hurled at them. "You sell yourselves and your work to your editors or your publishers. There is no such thing as a free man among you. You say what you're told to say—whether it's the truth or not; you must not have an opinion of your own; you dare not have any ideas; you'd die of indigestion if you had. It is men like you who are responsible for public crimes such as the hanging of my five Anarchist comrades in this city twenty-seven years ago." She berated them for an hour; she told them what her Anarchism means—how it can contribute to the living of a rich life; "You call it a dream, gentlemen; well, I plead guilty. But when we can't dream any longer we die. That's what is the matter with you. You've lost your dreams!" She sat down under an applause that burst out like bullets. Even some of the sodden ones looked almost awakened for a moment. One man rushed up to her saying: "I'm a Socialist by birth, education, and choice, but I want to say that you're splendid. We needed just this kind of talk, and I for one thank you." The majority of men there, like the one who sat next to me, said the typical thing: "Of course it's all true, but I can't agree with her." But the most humorous aspect of the affair was the report of it in the Press Club *Scoop* a few days later. A column was devoted to the man who introduced Miss

Goldman, giving his speech in detail; and then there was a last short paragraph: "Miss Goldman spoke for the better part of an hour." Not a word of what she had said, though a reporter at the speaker's table had taken it all down industriously. Of course Miss Goldman had no faith that she roused anyone there—but she did talk inspiredly! It all came out with such a rush of pleading—just as though she really could put youth and hope and dreams back into the lives of those listeners. And how glorious she was standing there at the table like some Victory that Meunier might have modeled, soaring straight through lies and compromises and cowardices, bearing her banner so bravely toward the mountain tops.

This is the function of Emma Goldman. She stirs and inspires and endows with new life; and all these elements were strongly in evidence at her propaganda lectures, with the exception perhaps of the one on "Woman and War," which was not so good a lecture as Miss Goldman might have been expected to give on that subject. One agreed with everything she said; but then Olive Schreiner had said it before, and Emma Goldman should have had some distinct contribution to make on such a theme. There are few subjects which so lend themselves her special gift—by which I mean, predominately, the gift of life. Emma Goldman's genius is not so much that she is a great thinker as that she is a great woman; she preaches, but she is a better artist than she is a preacher. "Woman and War" gave her a chance to say things that few other women can say with the conviction which comes from having tested a philosophy in terms of life. Therefore that lecture was something of a disappointment. But she more than compensated for it in her "Misconceptions of Free Love," which was a beautiful thing. The hall was filled that night with many of the people who had been going to the drama lectures, beside the usual East End Hall attendance and the crowd of I. W. W. boys in the gallery, whose chief purpose in going to any meeting seems to be to make a loud noise. The first were in a state of excited curiosity, giggling in apprehension of how shocked they might be—and really hoped they would be; the second were earnest and quiet; the third sang songs and acted as if it were a gala occasion of some sort. Miss Goldman walked on to the platform and began to speak with a seriousness which silenced the tittering ones, though it didn't seem to convince them that something fine and big was being said. They went away without any deeper impressions, I suppose, than that they had been daring enough to go to a "terrible" lecture and had found nothing terrible about it.

Some of the drama lectures had one serious shortcoming: they were not interesting. Miss Goldman divided her drama talks into nine groups—Scandinavian, German, French, Spanish, Italian, English, American, Jewish, and Russian—and talked each evening about three or four plays which sometimes were not related except insofar as they all emphasized the social significance of modern playwriting. As a result of such an arrangement, all she could do in an hour's time was to tell the story of each play and point out its social value. And she did it well; instead of being indiscriminate and uncritical, as some of her critics have it, she proved how creatively critical she is: she understands what the authors were trying to do, and she doesn't distort and misinterpret in an effort to say something clever on her own account. Heaven knows that is the sort of criticism we are looking for in a day when the other kind is so predominate. But it is not enough from Emma Goldman. Unless she can link up a drama talk with her special function—with her own reactions—the essence of her personality is lacking and the thing misses fire. I mean in this way: suppose she were to take one play at a time—*Fanny's First Play,* for instance—and incorporate it in a lecture which had for its title something like "The Spiritual Awakening of the Younger Generation." That would give her a chance to be herself most of the evening, instead of being the dramatist's mouthpiece; and it is only by talking of her own ideas, not merely by explaining the ideas of other people, that Emma Goldman will build up a real following for her drama talks. One of the results of her present method was that many people in the audience exclaimed "Oh, why isn't she more radical?"—though as she herself said quite rightly, she couldn't be radical simply for the sake of being radical. What those people meant to say was: "Why isn't she more interesting?" And it was a legitimate question because, with the exception of two or three lectures, she didn't get away from the obvious sufficiently to make the series distinctive.

Another stirring occasion was that of the eleventh of November when the hanging of the Chicago Anarchists was commemorated. Several people spoke in various languages in East End Hall, and the meeting closed with Emma Goldman on the platform, like the "Fire Brand" she was called years ago, telling how that horrible murder made her an Anarchist and compelled her to go from one end of the country to the other urging human beings to become something finer than they are.

As for the lectures on the War—they were excellent and were so well attended that people were forced to stand around the room or, as on the last night, be turned away. The first on "The Psychology of War"; the second—perhaps the least inspired of the three—on "Religion and War"; the third, "The Czar and My Beloved Jews." Miss Goldman was in her element on these occasions and answered questions with an extraordinary sweep and insight. The second lecture reflected something of her tendency to make her point at any price—to push an attitude into the place of an argument. But even with that it stood out somehow as fundamentally sound. All of which brings me to the very amusing attitude of the pedagogues toward

Miss Goldman. They say, "Let her give us more hard thinking and we'll be more sympathetic." But I have rarely seen one who has taken the trouble to talk to her after a lecture—to argue out a point of disagreement—who hasn't left her with a feeling of capitulation. She somehow always says the big thing. And with all her lack of "science" as they claim, her attitude has little in it that is incompatible with a very masterly essay which John Burroughs contributed recently to *The Yale Review.* He called it "Life as the Scientist Sees It," and it made the specialists look like pygmies. That is what Emma Goldman does. She is always a giant—for some reason that no one has yet expressed very well. Perhaps because, like science, she denies finalities.

VOL. X, NO. 12, FEBRUARY 1916

The Philosophy of Atheism

By Emma Goldman

Most varieties of anarchism rejected religion on three grounds: for its essential superstition, for its historical interdependence with and support of the state, and for its opposition to the libertarian principles of free existence and free choice in all things. There was no quarter given. As Mikhail Bakunin wrote in *God and the State,* turning a well-known saying of Voltaire's on its head, "If God really existed it would be necessary to abolish him." For her essay "The Philosophy of Atheism," Emma Goldman drew largely from Bakunin's book, which was published by the Mother Earth Publishing Association in 1916, in a translation by Benjamin Tucker, the former editor of the individualist anarchist journal *Liberty* (1881–1908).

∽

To GIVE AN ADEQUATE EXPOSITION OF THE philosophy of Atheism, it would be necessary to go into the historical changes of the belief in a Deity, from its earliest beginning to the present day. But that is not within the scope of the present paper. However, it is not out of place to mention, in passing, that the concept God, Supernatural Power, Spirit, Deity, or in whatever other term the essence of Theism may have found expression, has become more indefinite and obscure in the course of time and progress. In other words, the God idea is growing more impersonal and nebulous in proportion as the human mind is learning to understand natural phenomena and in the degree that science progressively correlates human and social events.

God, today, no longer represents the same forces as in the beginning of His existence; neither does He direct human destiny with the same iron hand as of yore. Rather does the God idea express a sort of spiritualistic stimulus to satisfy the fads and fancies of every shade of human weakness. In the course of human development the God idea has been forced to adapt itself to every phase of human affairs, which is perfectly consistent with the origin of the idea itself.

The conception of gods originated in fear and curiosity. Primitive man, unable to understand the phenomena of nature and harassed by them, saw in every terrifying manifestation some sinister force expressly directed against him; and as ignorance and fear are the parents of all superstition, the troubled fancy of primitive man wove the God idea.

Very aptly, the world-renowned atheist and anarchist, Michael Bakunin, says in his great work *God and the State:* "All religions, with their gods, their demigods, and their prophets, their messiahs and their saints, were created by the prejudiced fancy of men who had not attained the full development and full possession of their faculties. Consequently, the religious heaven is nothing but the mirage in which man, exalted by ignorance and faith, discovered his own image, but enlarged and reversed—that is divinized. The history of religions, of the birth, grandeur, and the decline of the gods who had succeeded one another in human belief, is nothing, therefore, but the development of the collective intelligence and conscience of mankind. As fast as they discovered, in the course of their historically progressive advance, either in themselves or in external nature, a quality, or even any great defect whatever, they attributed them to their gods, after having exaggerated and enlarged them beyond measure, after the manner of children, by an act of their religious fancy. . . . With all due respect, then, to the metaphysicians and religious idealists, philosophers, politicians, or poets: the idea of God implies the abdication of human reason and justice; it is the most decisive negation of human liberty and necessarily ends in the enslavement of mankind, both in theory and practice."

Thus the God idea revived, readjusted, and enlarged or narrowed, according to the necessity of the time, has dominated humanity and will continue to do so until man will raise his head to the sunlit day, unafraid and with an awakened will to himself. In proportion as man learns to realize himself and mold his own destiny theism becomes superfluous. How far man will be able to find his relation to his fellows will depend entirely upon how much he can outgrow his dependence upon God.

Already there are indications that Theism, which is the theory of speculation, is being replaced by Atheism, the science of demonstration; the one hangs in the metaphysical clouds of the Beyond, while the other has its roots firmly in the soil. It is the earth, not heaven, which man must rescue if he is truly to be saved.

The decline of Theism is a most interesting spectacle, especially as manifested in the anxiety of the Theists, whatever their particular brand. They realize, much to their distress, that the masses are growing daily more Atheistic, more antireligious; that they are quite willing to leave the Great Beyond and its heavenly domain to the angels and sparrows; because more and more the masses are becoming engrossed in the problems of their immediate existence.

How to bring the masses back to the God idea, the spirit, the First Cause, etc.—that is the most pressing question to all Theists. Metaphysical as all these questions seem to be, they yet have a very marked physical background. Inasmuch as religion, "Divine Truth," rewards and punishments are the trademarks of the largest, the most corrupt and pernicious, the most powerful and lucrative industry in the world, not excepting the industry of manufacturing guns and munitions. It is the industry of befogging the human mind and stifling the human heart. Necessity knows no law; hence the majority of Theists are compelled to take up every subject, even if it has no bearing upon a deity or revelation or the Great Beyond. Perhaps they sense the fact that humanity is growing weary of the hundred and one brands of God.

How to raise this dead level of Theistic belief is really a matter of life and death for all denominations. Therefore their tolerance; but it is a tolerance not of understanding, but of weakness. Perhaps that explains the efforts fostered in all religious publications to combine variegated religious philosophies and conflicting Theistic theories into one denominational trust. More and more, the various concepts "of the only true God, the only pure spirit, the only true religion" are tolerantly glossed over in the frantic effort to establish a common ground to rescue the modern mass from the "pernicious" influence of Atheistic ideas.

It is characteristic of Theistic "tolerance" that no one really cares what the people believe in, just so they believe or pretend to believe. To accomplish this end, the crudest and vulgarest methods are being used. Religious endeavor meetings and revivals with Billy Sunday as their champion— methods which must outrage every refined sense, and which in their effect upon the ignorant and curious often tend to create a mild state of insanity not infrequently coupled with erotomania. All these frantic efforts find approval and support from the earthly powers; from the Russian despot to the American President; from Rockefeller and Wanamaker down to the pettiest business man. They know that capital invested in Billy Sunday, the Y. M. C. A., Christian Science, and various other religious institutions will return enormous profits from the subdued, tamed, and dull masses.

Consciously or unconsciously, most Theists see in gods and devils, heaven and hell, reward and punishment, a whip to lash the people into obedience, meekness, and contentment. The truth is that Theism would have lost its footing long before this but for the combined support of Mammon and power. How thoroughly bankrupt it really is, is being demonstrated in the trenches and battlefields of Europe today.

Have not all Theists painted their Deity as the god of love and goodness? Yet after thousands of years of such preachments the gods remain deaf to the agony of the human race. Confucius cares not for the poverty, squalor, and misery of the people of China. Buddha remains undisturbed in his philosophical indifference to the famine and starvation of the outraged Hindoos; Jahve continues deaf to the bitter cry of Israel; while Jesus refuses to rise from the dead against his Christians who are butchering each other.

The burden of all song and praise, "unto the Highest," has been that God stands for justice and mercy. Yet injustice among men is ever on the increase; the outrages committed against the masses in this country alone would seem enough to overflow the very heavens. But where are the gods to make an end to all these horrors, these wrongs, this inhumanity to man? No, not the gods, but MAN must rise in his mighty wrath. He, deceived by all the deities, betrayed by their emissaries, he, himself, must undertake to usher in justice upon the earth.

The philosophy of Atheism expresses the expansion and growth of the human mind. The philosophy of Theism, if we can call it philosophy, is static and fixed. Even the mere attempt to pierce these mysteries represents, from the Theistic point of view, nonbelief in the all-embracing omnipotence and even a denial of the wisdom of the divine powers outside of man. Fortunately, however, the human mind never was, and never can be, bound by fixities. Hence it is forging ahead in its restless march towards knowledge and life. The human mind is realizing "that the universe is not the result of a creative fiat by some divine intelligence, out of nothing, producing a masterpiece chaotic in perfect operation," but that it is the product of chaotic forces operating through aeons of time, of clashes and cataclysms, of repulsion and attraction crystalizing through the principle of selection into what the Theists call, "the universe guided into order and beauty." As Joseph McCabe well points out in his *Existence of God:* "a law of nature is not a formula drawn up by a legislator, but a mere summary of the observed facts—a 'bundle of facts.' Things do not act in a particular way because there is a law, but we state the 'law' because they act in that way."

The philosophy of Atheism represents a concept of life without any metaphysical Beyond or Divine Regulator. It is the concept of an actual, real world with its liberating, expanding, and beautifying possibilities, as against an unreal world, which, with its spirits, oracles, and mean contentment, has kept humanity in helpless degradation.

It may seem a wild paradox, and yet it is pathetically true, that this real, visible world and our life should have been so long under the influence of metaphysical speculation, rather than of physical demonstrable forces. Under the lash of the Theistic idea, this earth has served no other purpose than as a temporary station to test man's capacity for immolation to the will of God. But the moment man attempted to ascertain the nature of that will, he was told that it was utterly futile for "finite human intelligence" to get beyond the all-powerful infinite will. Under the terrific weight of this omnipotence, man has been bowed into the dust—a willless creature, broken and sweating in the dark. The triumph of the philosophy of Atheism is to free man from the nightmare of gods; it means the dissolution of the phantoms of the beyond. Again and again the light of reason has dispelled the Theistic nightmare, but poverty, misery, and fear have recreated the phantoms—though whether old or new, whatever their external form, they differed little in their essence. Atheism, on the other hand, in its philosophic aspect refuses allegiance not merely to a definite concept of God, but it refuses all servitude to the God idea and opposes the Theistic principle as such. Gods in their individual function are not half as pernicious as the principle of Theism which represents the belief in a supernatural, or even omnipotent, power to rule the earth and man upon it. It is the absolutism of Theism, its pernicious influence upon humanity, its paralyzing effect upon thought and action, which Atheism is fighting with all its power.

The philosophy of Atheism has its root in the earth, in this life; its aim is the emancipation of the human race from all Godheads, be they Judaic, Christian, Mohammedan, Buddhistic, Brahministic, or what not. Mankind has been punished long and heavily for having created its gods; nothing but pain and persecution have been man's lot since gods began. There is but one way out of this blunder: Man must break his fetters which have chained him to the gates of heaven and hell, so that he can begin to fashion out of his reawakened and illumined consciousness a new world upon earth.

Only after the triumph of the Atheistic philosophy in the minds and hearts of man will freedom and beauty be realized. Beauty as a gift from heaven has proved useless. It will, however, become the essence and impetus of life when man learns to see in the earth the only heaven fit for man. Atheism is already helping to free man from his dependence upon punishment and reward as the heavenly bargain counter for the poor in spirit.

Do not all Theists insist that there can be no morality, no justice, honesty, or fidelity without the belief in a Divine Power? Based upon fear and hope, such morality has always been a vile product, imbued partly with self-righteousness, partly with hypocrisy. As to truth, justice, and fidelity, who have been their brave exponents and daring proclaimers? Nearly always the godless ones: the Atheists; they lived, fought, and died for them. They knew that justice, truth, and fidelity are not conditioned in heaven, but that they are related to and interwoven with the tremendous changes going on in the social and material life of the human race; not fixed and eternal, but fluctuating, even as life itself. To what heights the philosophy of Atheism may yet attain no one can prophesy. But this much can already be predicted: only by its regenerating fire will human relations be purged from the horrors of the past.

Thoughtful people are beginning to realize that moral precepts, imposed upon humanity through religious terror, have become stereotyped and have therefore lost all vitality. A glance at life today, at its disintegrating character, its conflicting interests with their hatreds, crimes, and greed, suffices to prove the sterility of Theistic morality.

Man must get back to himself before he can learn his relation to his fellows. Prometheus chained to the Rock of Ages is doomed to remain the prey of the vultures of darkness. Unbind Prometheus, and you dispel the night and its horrors.

Atheism in its negation of gods is at the same time the strongest affirmation of man, and through man, the eternal yea to life, purpose, and beauty.

PART TWO

THE WOMAN
QUESTION

In the first two decades of the twentieth century, the focus of the feminist movement in the United States, as in England, was largely on the right to vote. For anarchists, suffrage was a hollow political gesture that could in no way improve the condition of women or of society itself. The true answer to "the woman question," as it was often called, was individualist in its most profound sense: complete freedom to live as one chose, without the constraints of law or hypocritical custom in one's personal and public affairs. The debate in the pages of *Mother Earth* on conventional morality, marriage and the family, birth control (and the related issues of abortion and eugenics), and prostitution, not to mention the vote, anticipated in its breadth and outspokenness the feminist revival that began in the 1960s and alarmed suffragists and opponents of anarchism quite as much as did the fear of revolutionary violence. Once at the Manhattan Liberal Club, a woman fainted during a lecture by Emma Goldman on woman's "emancipation." Unfazed, the speaker afterward remarked: "She is an example of woman's emancipation. If she had her clothes looser she would not have fainted."

VOL. I, NO. 6, AUGUST 1906

Modesty

By Margaret Grant

A number of satirical essays on conventional morality, clearly intended *pour épater les bourgeois,* appeared in *Mother Earth* under the name of Margaret Grant. The real author of these pieces, however, was John R. Coryell, a regular contributor to the magazine. His *Sex Union and Parenthood, and What Is Seduction?* was brought out by the Mother Earth Publishing Association. He and his wife, Abby, were the first teachers at the anarchist Modern School in New York, founded in 1911 by the Ferrer Association. A prolific writer in many genres, with a variety of pseudonyms, Coryell originated the "Nick Carter" detective series and the "Bertha M. Clay" true romance stories.

IT IS SO WELL UNDERSTOOD THAT MODESTY becomes a woman that it behooves us as women to know just what modesty really is. If we open the dictionary, we find according to Webster that modesty is "natural delicacy or shame regarding personal charms and the sexual relation; purity of thought and manners." Of course every woman will understand that this definition refers especially to her; the rule for men will vary considerably from this, as is no more than right, considering the subordinate position we hold in relation to them.

Certainly it was with a sigh of relief that I read that modesty was a "natural" delicacy or shame, for as a woman I wished a sure guide for my inquiring mind. If modesty were an affair of nature and not of art, then my way would be smoothed before me; and if I might not trust my own instincts, which perhaps were perverted, I might study a child, in whom there was no art, and so come to the truth.

I may as well admit, at the outset, that I had no clear ideas of modesty. There was this in my favor, however, that I earnestly longed to know what modesty was, in order that I might successfully practice it.

Well, I set about the study of a child's conduct. You can imagine the result. I was shocked, appalled; the little wretch had no notions whatever of—I was going to say modesty; but, perhaps, it will be better to say—the rules of the game. That is a phrase men use, and it ought to please them. It was of no use to study more than one child, in the hope of finding a difference, for the abandoned creatures, without regard to sex or color, or previous condition of servitude, all behaved themselves in the same way, that is to say, most immodestly. They did what they were functionally moved to do, or exposed their nakedness, without any evidence of that sense of shame which is necessary to modesty.

But if nature were at fault in children, I argued, no doubt it would assert itself in savages; so I turned to them. Alas! what a strange and disconcerting state of affairs I found. It seemed as if each race, if not each tribe, had its own different notions of what was modest. I found that there were women in Africa who would brave death itself rather than be seen without a shred of cloth or skin hanging down behind from the waist; others who would have felt it equally infamous to appear in public without a narrow strip of some material hanging from the neck between the breasts; others who satisfied their sense of modesty completely by a dozen strips of hide hung from the waist in front, but without hiding any part of the body; others, again, who jeered at any shred of clothing, saying that the person using it must have some deformity to conceal.

In South Africa were women who held it immodest to appear in public unless their naked bodies were painted; others who were equally ashamed without a belt two inches broad about the waist. In the South Sea Islands if a woman were tattooed she was sufficiently clad, and her modesty was satisfied.

So it was with all the savage people living in warm climates; they went naked and were unashamed. Was not that astonishing? I made up my mind at last that Webster was wrong in saying that modesty was a natural delicacy or shame. Still, I was not to be balked; I must know what modesty truly was; so I turned to the people of another civilization than ours, thinking there might be some help there for me. Turkish and kindred Oriental women had a modesty that would not permit them to show their faces in public; but the creatures wore trousers, betraying the fact that they had legs—or should I say limbs? Can a woman be modest who does not hide her le—limbs, I mean? Chinese women were too modest to expose any part of the body but the face, and that well covered with paint. Even their hands kept under cover for the most part of the time; and as for showing their wrists!—not they. All of which was encouraging, but in the midst of my delight over the exquisite modesty, I was told that their private morals were terrible, and that the hussies wore trousers. There remained the Japanese women. Well, the least said of them the better, in this connection. Actually they wore clothing when it was convenient, and went without when that suited them better!

But the worst feature of all this was that travelers insisted that in those countries where women went naked they were more moral and chaste than in those countries where they clothed themselves. Japanese women, for example, are declared to be models of shyness, gentleness, and modesty. And they wear clothing or go without, as it suits their convenience—not as suits modesty, mind you, but convenience! Is the thing credible? H. Crawford Angus, the African traveler, goes so far as to say this: "It has been my experience that the more naked the people and the more, to us, obscene and shameless in their manner and customs, the more moral and strict they are in matters of sexual intercourse." But who wants to pay such a price for mere morality?

Then he goes on to describe what may be called the initiation into womanhood of girls who arrive at puberty, and says these shocking things: "The whole matter is looked upon as a matter of course, and not a thing to be ashamed of and to hide; and being thus openly treated of, and no secrecy made about it, you find in this tribe that the women are very virtuous. They know from the first all that is to be known, and cannot see any reason for secrecy concerning natural laws or the powers and senses that have been given them from birth."

Wallace, the famous traveler and scientist, has the presumption to say of the women of the wild tribes of the Amazon: "There is far more immodesty in the transparent and flesh-colored garments of our stage dancers than in the perfect nudity of these daughters of the forest." Now, of course, stage dancers may be, and very likely, are immodest, but what do you think of a man saying anything in favor of nudity? A respectable gentleman and a scientist, too! For shame!

Do you wonder that I abandoned all ideas of learning anything about modesty, from either children, savages, or peoples of other civilizations? Of course, I no longer had Webster for a guide, since it was certain that there was no such thing as a "natural" delicacy or shame. Consequently, I made up my mind that modesty was a thing of our civilization, and quite artificial it might be, but no less necessary for that reason; so I set about discovering what conduct was modest and what was not.

This was not as easy as you might suppose, but I finally made up a list which received general endorsement, and then set about verifying it by the conduct of those who should know what to do and what not to do. This is the list, which I made as short as possible: A woman may not expose her le—limbs to view; nor her breasts; nor any part of her body nude excepting her hands and face. She must not betray by word or sign or act that she has any bodily functions to perform, save only eating and drinking. She must not be aware that differences of sex consist of anything more than a difference in style of clothing. She must shudder at the thought of anything distinctly sexual. Actual maternity may be referred to, but possible maternity, being noticed even indirectly, is cause for a change of color, or fainting, if possible. It is better that a girl's health should be ruined than that her mother should be so indelicate as to speak to her of the especial functions of her sex. A young woman should pretend that she has no thought whatever about being a wife or mother, but secretly must devote her whole mind to winning a husband. She should strive with all her might to destroy every symptom of animal passion within herself, and should know nothing of wifely relations except as she can learn of them in secret and stealthy talks with ignorant servants or other girls.

I admit, at once, that the list is not complete, and that some of the rules of modesty laid down are somewhat subject to change under conditions not altogether to be defined. For example, a woman may expose her breasts very freely in the evening, although it would be bad form to do so in the daytime; and a woman who would permit herself to be seen nursing her baby could not hope to retain the respect of anyone. Then she may not only betray the fact of being a biped, but may even show her legs with perfect frankness at the seashore, while to do so in mountain climbing or in search of health through any exercise would be shameful. Also, while on the streets, she may draw her skirts so tightly about her lower limbs as to leave the imagination no opportunity for exercise. Also, while she may not display her breasts nude on the streets, she may wear a girdle, which while it injures her internal organs, leaves the breasts to move about in a manner which she has learned is very provocative to men.

I find that some of the rules of modesty lead to ill health and physical weakness, so that few women are well because of them; but if to be modest is necessary, who can complain of the results?

Of course we all know that health demands proper attention to the excretory processes of the body, but what right-minded female would not rather suffer any anguish of mind and body than even hint to a male any such need on her part? Modesty must be maintained though the most serious of internal injuries and permanent illness result.

Hundreds and thousands of girls injure themselves for life by ignorant conduct at the age of puberty; but what modest mother would save her child one pang by soiling her lips with words that would dispel the child's ignorance? And, of course, a young woman would be saved inexpressible suffering if her male companions only knew that once a month she was subject to a functional change; but what girl would consent to share such indecent knowledge with a boy?

I will not say that I know, now, what makes an act modest or the reverse; but I do know and believe that we women will never have good health until we throw modesty to the winds and conduct ourselves like some of those shameless creatures who really seem to glory in their sex. Shall we do so? Indeed, we shall not. Do I not know your answer? Let us go on in the good old modest way; sick and ailing all our lives, but not sacrificing one shred of the precious conventions that we have collected about us at such a terrible cost.

Let us live maimed, deformed, decrepit, ignorant, half-sexed caricatures of women—but let us be modest!

VOL. II, NO. II, JANUARY 1908

They Who Marry Do Ill

By Voltairine de Cleyre

The anarchist position toward marriage was unambiguous: free love meant the natural right of both men and women to choose how to live their intimate lives, whereas marriage—essentially a property arrangement—was a wrongful intrusion by church and state into one's most private affairs. Voltairine de Cleyre took the individualist argument to an extreme. She rejected even a companioniate arrangement as marriage by another name, and thus a relationship that compromised self-fulfillment—whether romantic, sexual, intellectual, or creative—and produced a poor setting for the nurturing of children. Her reasoning was elegant as always, if austere. All the same, most active anarchists continued to form companionships, lifelong and otherwise, or to marry regardless of their opposition to the state.

A lecture presenting the negative side of the question, whose positive was argued under the heading "They Who Marry Do Well," by Dr. Henrietta P. Westbrook; both lectures delivered before the Radical Liberal League, Philadelphia, April 28, 1907.

L ET ME MAKE MYSELF UNDERSTOOD ON two points, now, so that when discussion arises later, words may not be wasted in considering things not in question:

First—How shall we measure doing well or doing ill;

Second—What I mean by marriage.

So much as I have been able to put together the pieces of the universe in my small head, there is no absolute right or wrong; there is only a relativity, depending upon the continuously though very slowly altering condition of a social race in respect to the rest of the world. Right and wrong are social conceptions: mind, I do not say *human* conceptions. The names "right" and "wrong," truly, are of human invention only; but the conception "right" and "wrong," dimly or clearly, has been wrought out with more or less effectiveness by all intelligent social beings. And the definition of Right, as sealed and approved by the successful conduct of social beings, is: That mode of behavior which best serves the growing need of that society.

As to what that need is, certainly it has been in the past and for the most part is now indicated by the unconscious response of the structure (social or individual) to the pressure of its environment. Up till a few years since I believed with Huxley, Von Hartmann, and my teacher, Lum, that it was wholly so determined; that consciousness might discern, and obey or oppose, but had no voice in deciding the course of social development: if it decided to oppose, it did so to its own ruin, not to the modification of the unconsciously determined ideal.

Of late years I have been approaching the conclusion that consciousness has a continuously increasing part in the decision of social problems; that while it is still a minor voice, and must be for a long time to come, it is, nevertheless, the dawning power which threatens to overhurl old processes and old laws and supplant them by other powers and other ideals. I know no more fascinating speculation than this, of the rôle of consciousness in present and future evolution. However, it is not our present speculation. I speak of it only because in determining what constitutes well-being at present, I shall maintain that the old ideal has been considerably modified by conscious reaction against the superfluities produced by unconscious striving towards a certain end.

The question now becomes: What is the growing ideal of human society, unconsciously indicated and consciously discerned and illuminated?

By all the readings of progress, this indication appears to be the *free individual;* a society whose economic, political, social, and sexual organization shall secure and constantly increase the scope of being to its several units; whose solidarity and continuity depend upon the free attraction of its component parts, and in no wise upon compulsory forms.

Unless we are agreed that this is the discernible goal of our present social striving, there is no hope that we shall agree in the rest of the argument. For it would be vastly easy to prove that if the maintenance of the old divisions of society into classes, each with specialized services to perform—the priesthood, the military, the wage earner, the capitalist, the domestic servant, the breeder, etc.—is in accord with the growing force of society, then marriage is the thing, and they who marry do well.

But this is the point at which I stand, and from which I shall measure well- and ill-doing; viz.: that the aim of social striving now is the free individual, implying all the conditions necessary to that freedom.

Now the second thing: What shall we understand as marriage?

Some fifteen or eighteen years ago, when I had not been out of a convent long enough to forget its teachings, nor lived and experienced enough to work out my own definitions, I considered that marriage was "a sacrament of the Church," or it was "a civil ceremony performed by the State," by which a man and a woman were united for life, or until the divorce court separated them. With all the energy of a neophyte freethinker, I attacked religious marriage as a piece of unwarranted interference on the part of the priest with the affairs of individuals, condemned the "until-death-do-us-part" promise as one of the immoralities which made a person a slave through all his future to his present feelings, and urged the miserable vulgarity of both the religious and civil ceremony, by which the intimate personal relations of two individuals are made topic of comment and jest by the public.

By all this I still hold. Nothing is more disgustingly vulgar to me than the so-called sacrament of marriage; outraging all delicacy with the trumpeting of private matters in the general ear. Need I recall, as an example, the unprinted and unprintable floating literature concerning the marriage of Alice Roosevelt, when the so-called "American princess" was targeted by every lewd jester in the country, because, forsooth, the whole world had to be informed of her forthcoming union with Mr. Longworth! But it is neither a religious nor a civil ceremony that I refer to now, when I say that "Those who marry do ill." The ceremony is only a form, a ghost, a meatless shell. By marriage I mean the real thing, the permanent relation of a man and a woman, sexual and economical, whereby the present home and family life is maintained. It is of no importance to me whether this is a polygamous, polyandric, or monogamous marriage, nor whether it was blessed by a priest, permitted by a magistrate, contracted publicly or privately, or not contracted at all. It is the permanent dependent relationship which, I affirm, is detrimental to the growth of individual character, and to which I am unequivocally opposed. Now my opponents know where to find me.

In the old days to which I have alluded, I contended, warmly and sincerely, for the exclusive union of one man and one woman as long as they were held together by love, and for the dissolution of the arrangement upon desire of either. We talked in those days most enthusiastically about the bond of love, and it only. Nowadays I would say that I prefer to see a marriage based purely on business considerations than a marriage based on love. That is not because I am in the least concerned for the success of the marriage, but because I am concerned with the success of love. And I believe that the easiest, surest, and most applicable method of killing love is marriage—marriage as I have defined it. I believe that the only way to preserve love in anything like the ecstatic condition which renders it worthy of a distinctive name—otherwise it is either lust or simply friendship—is to maintain the distances. Never allow love to be vulgarized by the common indecencies of continuous close communion. Better be in familiar contempt of your enemy than of the one you love.

I presume that some who are unacquainted with my opposition to legal and social forms, are ready to exclaim: "Do you want to do away with the relation of the sexes altogether, and cover the earth with monks and nuns?" By no means. While I am not over and above anxious about the repopulation of the earth, and should not shed any tears if I knew that the last man had already been born, I am not advocating sexual total abstinence. If the advocates of marriage had merely to prove a case against complete sexual continence, their task would be easy. The statistics of insanity, and in general of all manner of aberrations, would alone constitute a big item in the charge. No: I do not believe that the highest human being is the unsexed one, or the one who extirpates his passions by violence, whether religious or scientific violence. I would have people regard all their normal instincts in a normal way, neither gluttonizing nor starving them, neither exalting them beyond their true service nor denouncing them as servitors of evil, both of which mankind are wont to do in considering the sexual passion. In short, I would have men and women so arrange their lives that they shall always, at all times, be free beings in this regard as in all others. The limit of abstinence or indulgence can be fixed by the individual alone, what is normal for one being excess for another, and what is excess at one period of life being normal at another. And as to the effects of such normal gratification of normal appetite upon population, I would have them consciously controlled, as they can be, are to some extent now, and will be more and more through the progress of knowledge. The birthrate of France and of native Americans gives evidence of such conscious control.

"But," say the advocates of marriage, "what is there in marriage to interfere with the free development of the individual? What does the free development of the individual mean, if not the expression of manhood and womanhood? And what is more essential to either than parentage and the rearing of young? And is not the fact that the latter requires a period of from fifteen to twenty years the essential need which determines the permanent home?" It is the scientific advocate of marriage that talks this way. The religious man bases his talk on the will of God or some other such metaphysical matter. I do not concern myself with him; I concern myself only with those who contend that as Man is the latest link in evolution, the same racial necessities which determine the social and sexual relations of allied races will be found shaping and determining these relations in Man; and that, as we find among the higher animals that the period of rearing the young to the point of caring for themselves usually determines the period of conjugality, it must be concluded that the greater attainments of Man, which have so greatly lengthened the educational period of youth, must likewise have fixed the permanent family relation as the ideal condition for humanity. This is but the conscious extension of what unconscious, or perhaps semiconscious, adaptation had already determined in the higher animals and in savage races to an extent. If people are reasonable, sensible, self-controlled (as to other people they will keep themselves in trouble anyway, no matter how things are arranged), does not the marriage state secure this great fundamental purpose of the primal social function, which is at the same time an imperative demand of individual development, better than any other arrangement? With all its failures, is it not the best that has been tried or with our present light has been conceived?

In endeavoring to prove the opposite of this contention, I shall not go to the failures to prove my point. It is not my purpose to show that a vast number of marriages do not succeed; the divorce court records do that. But as one swallow doesn't make a summer, nor a flock of swallows either, so divorces do not prove that marriage in itself is a bad thing, only that a goodly number of individuals make mistakes. This is, indeed, an unanswerable argument against the indissolubility of marriage, but none against marriage itself. I will go to the successful marriages—the marriages in which whatever the friction, man and wife have spent a great deal of agreeable time together; in which the family has been provided for by honest work decently paid (as the wage system goes) of the father and preserved within the home by the saving labor and attention of the mother; the children given a reasonable education and started in life on their own account, and the old folks left to finish up life together, each resting secure in the knowledge that he has a tried friend until death severs the bond. This, I conceive, is the best form that marriage can present, and I opine it is oftener dreamed of than realized. But sometimes it is realized. Yet from the viewpoint that the object of life should be the development of individuality, such have lived less successfully than many who may not have lived so happily.

And to the first great point—the point that physical parentage is one of the fundamental necessities of self-expression: here, I think, is where the factor of consciousness is in process of overturning the methods of life. Life, working unconsciously, blindly sought to preserve itself by generation, by manifold generation. The mind is simply staggered at the productivity of a single stalk of wheat, or of a fish, or of a queen bee, or of a man. One is smitten by the appalling waste of generative effort; numbed with helpless pity for the little things, the infinitude of little lives, that must come forth and suffer and die of starvation, of exposure, as a prey to other creatures, and all to no end but that out of the multitude a few may survive and continue the type! Man, at war with Nature and not yet master of the situation, obeyed the same instinct and by prolific parentage maintained his war. To the Hebrew patriarch as to the American pioneer, a large family meant strength, the wealth of brawn and sinew to continue the conquest of forest and field. It was the only resource against annihilation. Therefore, the instinct towards physical creation was one of the most imperative determinants of action.

Now the law of all instinct is that it survives long after the necessity which created it has ceased to exist and acts mischievously. The usual method of reckoning with such a survival is that since such and such a thing exists, it is an essential part of the structure, not obliged to account for itself and bound to be gratified. I am perfectly certain, however, that the more conscious consciousness becomes, or in other words, the more we become aware of the conditions of life and our relations therein, their new demands and the best way of fulfilling them, the more speedily will instincts no longer demanded be dissolved from the structure.

How stands the war upon Nature now? Why, so—that short of a planetary catastrophe, we are certain of the conquest. And what is perfecting the conquest? Consciousness! The alert brain! The dominant will! Invention, discovery, mastery of hidden forces. We are no longer compelled to use the blind method of limitless propagation to equip the race with hunters and trappers and fishers and sheep-keepers and soil-tillers and breeders. Therefore, the original necessity which gave rise to the instinct of prolific parentage is gone; the instinct itself is bound to die, and is dying, but will die the faster as men grasp more and more the whole situation. In proportion as the parenthood of the brain becomes more and more prolific, as ideas spread, multiply, and conquer, the necessity for great physical production declines. This is my first contention. Hence the development of individuality does no longer *necessarily* imply numerous children, nor indeed, *necessarily* any children at all. That is not to say that no one will want children, nor to prophesy race suicide. It is simply to say that there will be fewer born, with better chances of surviving, developing, and achieving. Indeed, with all its clash of tendencies, the consciousness of our present society is having this driven home to it.

Supposing that the majority will still desire, or let me go further and say *do* still desire, this limited parentage, the question now becomes: Is this the overshadowing need in the development of the individual, or are there other needs equally imperative? If there are other needs equally imperative, must not these be taken equally into account in deciding the best manner of conducting one's life? If there are not other needs equally imperative, is it not still an open question whether the married state is the best means of securing it? In answering these questions, I think it will again be safe to separate into a majority and a minority. There will be a minority to whom the rearing of children will be the great dominant necessity of their being and a majority to whom this will be one of their necessities. Now what are the other necessities? The other physical and mental appetites! The desire for food and raiment and housing after the individual's own taste; the desire for sexual association, not for reproduction; the artistic desires; the desire to know, with its thousand ramifications, which may carry the soul from the depths of the concrete to the heights of the abstract; the desire to do, that is, to imprint one's will upon the social structure, whether as a mechanical contriver, a force harnesser, a social rebuilder, a combiner, a dream translator—whatever may be the particular mode of the personal organization.

The necessity for food, shelter, and raiment it should at all times lie within the individual's power to furnish for himself. But the method of home-keeping is such that after the relation has been maintained for a few years, the interdependence of one on the other has become so great that each is somewhat helpless when circumstance destroys the combination, the man less so, and the woman wretchedly so. She has done one thing in a secluded sphere, and while she may have learned to do that thing well (which is not certain, the method of training is not at all satisfactory), it is not a thing which has equipped her with the confidence necessary to go about making an independent living. She is timid above all, incompetent to deal with the conditions of struggle. The world of production has swept past her; she knows nothing of it. On the other hand, what sort of an occupation is it for her to take domestic service under some other woman's rule? The conditions and pay of domestic service are such that every independent spirit would prefer to slave in a factory, where at least the slavery ends with the working hours. As for men, only a few days since a staunch free unionist told me, apparently without shame, that were it not for his wife he would be a tramp and a drunkard, simply because he is unable to keep a home; and in his eyes the chief merit of the arrangement is that his stomach is properly cared for. This is a degree of a helplessness which I should have thought he would have shrunk from admitting, but is nevertheless probably true. Now this is one of the greatest objections to the married condition, as it is to any other condition which produces like results. In choosing one's economic position in society, one should always bear in mind that it should be such as should leave the individual uncrippled—an all-around person, with both productive and preservative capacities, a being pivoted within.

Concerning the sexual appetite, irrespective of reproduction, the advocates of marriage claim, and with some reason, that it tends to preserve normal appetite and satisfaction and is both a physical and moral safeguard against excesses, with their attendant results, disease. That it does not do so entirely we have ample and painful proof continuously before our eyes. As to what it may accomplish, it is almost impossible to find out the truth; for religious asceticism has so built the feeling of shame into the human mind on the subject of sex that the first instinct, when it is brought under discussion, seems to be to lie about it. This is especially the case with women. The majority of women usually wish to create the impression that they are devoid of sexual desires and think they have paid the highest compliment to themselves when they say, "Personally, I am very cold; I have never experienced such attraction." Sometimes this is true; but oftener it is a lie—a lie born of centuries of the pernicious teaching of the Church. A roundly developed person will understand that she pays no honor to herself by denying herself fullness of being, whether to herself or of herself; though, without doubt, where such a deficiency really exists, it may give room for an extra growth of some other qualities, perhaps of higher value. In general, however, notwithstanding women's lies, there is no such deficiency. In general, young, healthy beings of both sexes desire such relations. What then? Is marriage the best answer to the need? Suppose they marry, say at twenty years, or thereabout, which will be admitted as the time when sexual appetite is usually most active: the consequence is (I am just now leaving children out of account) that the two are thrown too much and too constantly in contact and speedily exhaust the delight of each other's presence. Then irritations begin. The familiarities of life in common breed contempt. What was once a rare joy becomes a matter of course and loses all its delicacy. Very often it becomes a physical torture to one (usually the woman), while it still retains some pleasure to the other, for the reason that bodies, like souls, do most seldom, almost never, parallel each other's development. And this lack of parallelism is the greatest argument to be produced against marriage. No matter how perfectly adapted to each other two people may be at any given time, it is not the slightest evidence that they will continue to be so. And no period of life is more deceptive as to what future development may be than the age I have just been speaking of; the age when physical desires and attractions being strongest, they obscure or hold in abeyance the other elements of being.

The terrible tragedies of sexual antipathy, mostly for shame's sake, will never be revealed. But they have filled the earth with murder. And even in those homes where harmony has been maintained, and all is apparently peaceful, it is mainly so through the resignation and self-suppression of either the man or the woman. One has consented to be largely effaced for the preservation of the family and social respect.

But awful as these things are, these physical degradations, they are not so terrible as the ruined souls. When the period of physical predominence is past, and soul-tendencies begin more and more strongly to assert themselves, how dreadful is the recognition that one is bound by the duties of common parentage and the necessities of home-keeping to remain in the constant company of one from whom one finds oneself going farther away in thought every day. "Not a day," exclaim the advocates of "free unions." I find such exclamation worse folly than the talk of "holy matrimony" believers. The bonds are there, the bonds of life in common, the love of the home built by joint labor, the habit of association and dependence; they are very real chains, binding both, and not to be thrown off lightly. Not in a day nor a month, but only after long hesitation, struggle, and grievous, grievous pain, can the wrench of separation come. Oftener it does not come at all.

A chapter from the lives of two men recently deceased will illustrate my meaning. Ernest Crosby, wedded, and I presume happily, to a lady of conservative thought and feeling, himself then conservative, came into his soul's own at the age of thirty-eight, while occupying the position of Judge of the International Court at Cairo. From then on, the whole radical world knows Ernest Crosby's work. Yet what a position was his, compelled by honor to continue the functions of a social life which he disliked! To quote the words of his friend, Leonard Abbott, "a prisoner in his palatial home, waited on by servants and lackeys. Yet to the end he remained enslaved by his possessions." Had Crosby not been bound, had not union and family relations with one who holds very different views of life in faith and honor held him, should we not have had a different life-sum? Like his great teacher, Tolstoy, likewise made absurd, his life contradicted by his works, because of his union with a woman who has not developed along parallel lines.

The second case, Hugh O. Pentecost. From the year 1887 on, whatever were his special tendencies, Pentecost was in the main a sympathizer with the struggle of labor, an opposer of oppression, persecution, and prosecution in all forms. Yet through the influence of his family relations, because he felt in honor bound to provide greater material comfort and a better standing in society than the position of a radical speaker could give, he consented at one time to be the puppet of those he had most strenuously condemned, to become a district attorney, a prosecutor. And worse than that, to paint himself as a misled baby for having done the best act of his life, to protest against the execution of the Chicago Anarchists. That this influence was brought to bear upon him I know from his own lips; a repetition, in a small way, of the treason of Benedict Arnold, who for his Tory wife's sake laid everlasting infamy upon himself. I do not say there was no self-excusing in this, no Eve-did-tempt-me taint, but surely it had its influence. I speak of these two men because these instances are well known; but everyone knows of such instances among more obscure persons and often where the woman is the one whose higher nature is degraded by the bond between herself and her husband.

And this is one side of the story. What of the other side? What of the conservative one who finds himself bound to one who outrages every principle of his or hers? People will not, and cannot, think and feel the same at the same moments throughout any considerable period of life; and therefore, their moments of union should be rare and of no binding nature.

I return to the subject of children. Since this also is a normal desire, can it not be gratified without the sacrifice of individual freedom required by marriage? I see no reason why it cannot. I believe that children may be as well brought up in an individual home, or in a communal home, as in a dual home; and that impressions of life will be far pleasanter if received in an atmosphere of freedom and independent strength than in an atmosphere of secret repression and discontent. I have no very satisfactory solutions to offer to the various questions presented by the child-problem; but neither have the advocates of marriage. Certain to me it is that no one of the demands of life should ever be answered in a manner to preclude future free development. I have seen no great success from the old method of raising children under the indissoluble marriage yoke of the parents. (Our conservative parents no doubt consider their radical children great failures, though it probably does not occur to them that their system is in any way at fault.) Neither have I observed a gain in the child of the free union. Neither have I observed that the individually raised child is any more likely to be a success or a failure. Up to the present, no one has given a scientific answer to the child-problem. Those papers which make a specialty of it, such as *Lucifer,* are full of guesses and theories and suggested experiments; but no infallible principles for the guidance of intentional or actual parents have as yet been worked out. Therefore, I see no reason why the rest of life should be sacrificed to an uncertainty.

That love and respect may last, I would have unions rare and impermanent. That life may grow, I would have men and women remain separate personalities. Have no common possessions with your lover more than you might freely have with one not your lover. Because I believe that marriage stales love, brings respect into contempt, outrages all the privacies, and limits the growth of both parties, I believe that "They who marry do ill."

VOL. IV, NO. 11, JANUARY 1910

The White Slave Traffic

By Emma Goldman

Anarchism approached prostitution not as a moral question but as a social wrong rooted (as was conventional marriage) in economic exploitation and the lack of education for women, conditions aided and abetted by the hypocrisy of organized religion and the state. Emma Goldman, who as a trained nurse spent many years among the needy prostitutes in

New York's brothels, wrote her classic libertarian analysis of "The White
Slave Traffic" for the January 1910 issue of *Mother Earth*. She afterward
revised it and, under the title "The Traffic in Women," included it in her
Anarchism and Other Essays, published in 1910 by the Mother Earth
Publishing Association.

OUR REFORMERS HAVE SUDDENLY MADE a great discovery: the
white slave traffic. The papers are full of these "unheard-of conditions"
in our midst, and the lawmakers are already planning a new set of laws to
check the horror.

How is it that an institution, known almost to every child, should have
been discovered so suddenly? How is it that this evil, known to all sociologists, should now be made such an important issue?

It is significant that whenever the public mind is to be diverted from a
great social wrong, a crusade is inaugurated against indecency, gambling,
saloons, etc. And what is the result of such crusades? Gambling is increasing, saloons are doing a lively business through back entrances, prostitution
is at its height, and the system of pimps and cadets is but aggravated.

To assume that the recent investigation of the white slave traffic by
George Kibbe Turner and others (and by the way, a very superficial investigation) has discovered anything new is, to say the least, very foolish.
Prostitution was and is a widespread evil, yet mankind goes on its business,
perfectly indifferent to the sufferings and distress of the victims of prostitution. As indifferent, indeed, as mankind has so far remained to our industrial system, or to economic prostitution.

Only when human sorrows are turned into a toy with glaring colors will
baby people become interested—for a while at least. The people are a very
fickle baby that must have new toys every day. The "righteous" cry against
the white slave traffic is such a toy. It serves to amuse the people for a little
while, and it will help to create a few more fat political jobs—parasites who
stalk about the world as inspectors, investigators, detectives, etc.

What really is the cause of the trade in women? Not merely white
women, but yellow and black women as well. Exploitation, of course: the
merciless Moloch of capitalism that fattens on underpaid labor, thus driving thousands of women and girls into prostitution. With Mrs. Warren
these girls feel, "Why waste your life working for a few shillings a week in a
scullery, eighteen hours a day?"

Naturally, our reformers say nothing about this cause. George Kibbe

Turner and all other scribblers know the cause well enough, but it doesn't pay to say anything about it. It is so much more profitable to play the Pharisee, to pretend an outraged morality, than to go to the bottom of things. Yet no less an authority than Dr. Sanger, the author of *The History of Prostitution*,* although not a radical, has this to say:

"A prolific cause of female depravity can be found in the several tables, showing the description of the employment pursued and the wages received by the women previous to their fall, and it will be a question for the political economist to decide how far mere business consideration should be an apology on the part of employers for a reduction in their rates of remuneration, and whether the savings of a small percentage on wages is not more than counterbalanced by the enormous amount of taxation enforced on the public at large to defray the expenses incurred on account of a system of vice, *which is the direct result in many cases of insufficient compensation of honest labor.*"

The economic reason given for prostitution in the above quotation can be found in all works of any consequence dealing with the question. Nor is it necessary to seek information in books; one has but to observe everyday life to realize that there are thousands of girls working for two or three dollars a week, withering away in factories and shops, while life passes by in all its joy and glory, leaving them behind. What else are they to do? However, our present-day reformers would do well to look into Dr. Sanger's book. There they will find that out of 2,000 cases under his observation, but few came from the middle classes, from well-ordered conditions, or pleasant homes. By far the largest majority were working girls and working women. Some driven into prostitution through sheer want, others because of a cruel, wretched life at home, others again because of thwarted and crippled physical natures (which I will speak of again later on). Also it will do the maintainers of purity and morality good to learn that out of 2,000 cases 490 were married women, women who lived with their husbands. Evidently there was not much of a guarantee for their safety and purity in the sanctity of marriage.

The very last to cry out against prostitution is our "respectable" class, since it was that class that ushered in prostitution, from Moses to Trinity Church. Dr. H. Bloss, Dr. Alfred Blaschko, Dr. W. W. Sanger, and other eminent writers on this subject convincingly prove that prostitution originated with the so-called upper classes. I quote Dr. Sanger:

"Our most ancient and historical records are believed to be the books of

---

*It is a significant fact that Dr. Sanger's book has been excluded from the U. S. mails. Evidently the authorities are not anxious that the public be informed as to the true cause of prostitution.

Moses; according to them it must be admitted that prostitutes were common among the Jews, many centuries before Christ. Moses appears to have
connived at the intercourse of Jewish young men with foreign prostitutes.
He took an Ethiopian woman himself. Assyrian women, Moabites,
Midianites, and other neighbors of the Jews established themselves as prostitutes in the land of Israel. Jephtha, the son of a prostitute, became none
the less Chief of Israel." Moses evidently believed that therein lay the greatest safeguard for the daughters of his own people. We shall see presently
that the Christians were not so considerate of their own daughters, since
they did not employ foreigners for that purpose.

The history of the Christian Church will also serve as a history of prostitution, since the two always went hand in hand and furnished thereby
great revenues for the Church.

Dr. Sanger cites the case of Pope Clement II, who issued a bull that all
prostitutes were to pay a certain amount of their earnings, or that those
living on prostitution were compelled to give half their income to the
Church. Pope Sixtus IV received 20,000 ducats from a single brothel,
which, incidentally, he himself had built. Nor is it unknown that a great
many cloisters and nunneries were in reality nothing else than brothels.

In modern times the Church is a little more careful in that direction. At
least, it does not openly demand tribute from prostitutes. It finds it much
more profitable to go in for real estate, like Trinity Church, for instance, to
rent out death traps at an exorbitant price to those who live off and on
prostitution.

Much as I should like to, my space will not admit speaking of prostitution in Egypt, Greece, Rome, and during the Middle Ages. The conditions
in the latter period are particularly interesting, inasmuch as prostitution
was organized into guilds, presided over by a Brothel Queen. These guilds
employed strikes as a medium of improving their condition and keeping a
standard price. Certainly that is more practical a method than the one used
by the modern wage slave in society.

Never, however, did prostitution reach its present depraved and criminal
position, because at no time in past ages was prostitution persecuted and
hounded as it is today, especially in Anglo-Saxon countries, where
Pharisaism is at its height, where each one is busy hiding the skeletons in
his own home by pointing to the sore of the other fellow.

But I must not lose sight of the present issue, the white slave traffic. I
have already spoken of the economic cause, but I think a cause much deeper
and by far of greater importance is the complete ignorance on sex matters.
It is a conceded fact that woman has been reared as a sex commodity, and
yet she is kept in absolute ignorance of the meaning and importance of sex.
Everything dealing with that subject is suppressed, and people who attempt

to bring light into this terrible darkness are persecuted and thrown into prison. Yet it is nevertheless true that so long as a girl is not to know how to take care of herself, not to know the function of the most important part of her life, we need not be surprised if she becomes an easy prey to prostitution or any other form of a relationship which degrades her to the position of an object for mere sex gratification.

It is due to this ignorance that the entire life and nature of the girl is thwarted and crippled. We have long ago taken it as a self-evident fact that the boy may follow the call of the wild, that is to say that the boy may, as soon as his sex nature asserts itself, satisfy that nature, but our moralists are scandalized at the very thought that the nature of a girl should assert itself. To the moralist prostitution does not consist so much in the fact that the woman sells her body, but rather that she sells it to many.

Having been looked upon as a mere sex commodity, the woman's honor, decency, morality, and usefulness have become a part of her sex life. Thus society considers the sex experiences of a man as attributes of his general development, while similar experiences in the life of a woman are looked upon as a terrible calamity, a loss of honor and of all that is good and noble in a human being. This double standard of morality has played no little part in the creation and perpetuation of prostitution. It involves the keeping of the young in absolute ignorance on sex matters, which alleged "innocence," together with an overwrought and stifled sex nature, helps to bring about a state of affairs that our Puritans are so anxious to avoid or prevent. This state of affairs finds a masterly portrayal in Zola's *Fecundity*.

Girls, mere children, work in crowded, overheated rooms ten to twelve hours daily at a machine, which tends to keep them in a constant overexcited sex state. Many of these girls haven't any home or comforts of any kind; therefore the street or some place of cheap amusement is the only means of forgetting their daily routine. This naturally brings them into close proximity with the other sex. It is hard to say which of the two factors brings the girl's oversexed condition to a climax, but it certainly is the most natural thing that a climax should follow. That is the first step toward prostitution. Nor is the girl to be held responsible for it. On the contrary, it is altogether the fault of society, the fault of our lack of understanding, of lack of appreciation of life in the making; especially is it the criminal fault of our moralists, who condemn a girl for all eternity because she has gone from "the path of virtue"; that is, because her first sex experience has taken place without the sanction of the Church or State.

The girl finds herself a complete outcast, with the doors of home and society closed in her face. Her entire training and tradition are such that the girl herself feels depraved and fallen, and therefore has no ground to stand upon, or any hold that will lift her up, instead of throwing her

down. Thus society creates the victims that it afterwards vainly attempts
to get rid of.

Much stress is laid on white slaves being imported into America. How
would America ever retain her virtue if she didn't have Europe to help her
out? I will not deny that this may be the case in some instances, any more
than I will deny that there are emissaries of Germany and other countries
luring economic slaves into America, but I absolutely deny that prostitution is recruited, to any appreciable extent, from Europe. It may be true
that the majority of prostitutes of New York City are foreigners, but that is
only because the majority of the population is foreign. The moment we go
to any other American city, to Chicago or the Middle West, we shall find
that the number of foreign prostitutes is by far a minority.

Equally exaggerated is the belief that the majority of street girls in this
city were engaged in this business before they came to America. Most of the
girls speak excellent English, they are Americanized in habits and appearance—a thing absolutely impossible unless they have lived in this country
many years. That is, they were driven into prostitution by American conditions, by the thoroughly American custom for excessive display of finery
and clothes, which, of course, necessitates money, money that can not be
earned in shops or factories. The equanimity of the moralists is not disturbed by the respectable woman gratifying her clothesophobia [*sic*] by
marrying for money; why are they so outraged if the poor girl sells herself
for the same reason? The only difference lies in the amount received, and of
course in the seal society either gives or withholds.

I am sure that no one will accuse me of nationalist tendencies. I am glad
to say that I have developed out of that, as out of many other prejudices. If,
therefore, I resent the statement that Jewish prostitutes are imported, it is
not because of any Judaistic sympathies, but because of the fact inherent in
the lives of these people. No one but the most superficial will claim that the
Jewish girls migrate to strange lands, unless they have some tie or relation
that brings them there. The Jewish girl is not adventurous. Until recent
years, she had never left home, not even so far as the next village or town,
unless it were to visit some relative. Is it then credible that Jewish girls
would leave their parents or families, travel thousands of miles to strange
lands, through the influence and promises of strange forces? Go to any of
the large incoming steamers and see for yourself if these girls do not come
either with their parents, brothers, aunts, or other kinsfolk. There may be
exceptions, of course, but to state that a large number of Jewish girls are
imported for prostitution, or any other purpose, is simply not to know the
Jewish psychology.

On the other hand, it speaks of very little business ability on the part of importers of the white slaves, if they assume that the girls from the peasant regions of Poland, Bohemia, or Hungary in their native peasant crude state and attire would make a profitable business investment. These poor ignorant girls, in their undeveloped state, with their shawls about their heads, look much too unattractive to even the most stupid man. It therefore follows that before they can be made fit for business, they, too, must be Americanized, which would require not merely a week or a month, but considerable time. They must at least learn the rudiments of English, but more than anything else they must learn American shrewdness in order to protect themselves against the many uniformed cadets who prey on them and fleece them at every step.

To ascribe the increase of prostitution to alleged importation, to the growth of the cadet system, or similar causes is highly superficial. I have already referred to the former. As to the cadet system, abhorrent as it is, we must not ignore the fact that it is essentially a phase of modern prostitution—a phase accentuated by suppression and graft, resulting from sporadic crusades against the social evil.

The origin of the cadets, as an institution, can be traced to the Lexow investigation in New York City, in 1894. Thanks to that moral spasm, keepers of brothels, as well as unfortunate victims of the street, were turned over to the tender mercies of the police. The inevitable consequence of exorbitant bribes and the penitentiary followed.

While comparatively protected in the brothels, where they represented a certain value, the unfortunate girls now found themselves on the street, absolutely at the mercy of the graft-greedy police. Desperate, needing protection and longing for affection, these girls naturally proved an easy prey to cadets, themselves the result of the spirit of our commercial age. Thus the cadet system was the direct outgrowth of police persecution, graft, and attempted suppression of prostitution. It was sheer folly to confute this modern phase of the social evil with the causes of the latter.

The serious student of this problem realizes that legislative enactments, stringent laws, and similar methods cannot possibly eradicate nor even ameliorate this evil. Those best familiar with the subject agree on this vital point. Dr. Alfred Blaschko, an eminent authority, convincingly proves in his *Prostitution im 19. Jahrhundert* that governmental suppression and moral crusades accomplish nothing save driving the evil into secret channels, multiplying its dangers to the community. In this claim he is supported by such thorough students as Havelock Ellis, Dr. H. Bloss, and others.

Mere suppression and barbaric enactment can serve but to embitter and further degrade the unfortunate victims of ignorance and stupidity. The

latter has reached its highest expression in the proposed law to make humane treatment of prostitutes a crime, punishing anyone sheltering a prostitute with five years' imprisonment and $10,000 fine. Such an attitude
merely exposes the terrible lack of understanding of the true causes of prostitution, as a social factor, as well as manifesting the Puritanic spirit of the
Scarlet Letter days.

An educated public opinion, freed from the legal and moral hounding
of the prostitute, can alone help to ameliorate present conditions. Willful
shutting of eyes and ignoring of the evil, as an actual social factor of modern life, can but aggravate matters. We must rise above our foolish notions
of "better than thou" and learn to recognize in the prostitute a product of
social conditions. Such a realization will sweep away the attitude of hypocrisy and insure a greater understanding and more humane treatment. As to
a thorough eradication of prostitution, nothing can accomplish that save a
complete transvaluation of all accepted values—especially the moral
ones—coupled with the abolition of industrial slavery.

VOL. VII, NO. IO, DECEMBER 1912

The Sterilization of the Unfit

By Peter Kropotkin

Set ideas of race and racial degeneration, so-called, were strong at the
turn of the twentieth century; with the British empire at its height of
power and American imperialism on the rise, the superiority of the
"Anglo-Saxon race" was touted by many religious and political leaders,
Theodore Roosevelt prominent among them. In this atmosphere, for
some of the middle class the cause of birth limitation graded naturally
into eugenics and forced sterilization as a social good, for the promotion

of racial purity and the elimination of poverty. Peter Kropotkin, a trained scientist with a deep understanding of evolutionary theory, addressed the issue from an anarchist perspective at a Eugenics Congress in 1912, and gently lectured his colleagues about who precisely might best be designated as the "unfit" members of the human race.

Lecture delivered by Peter Kropotkin before the Eugenics Congress held in London in August last.

PERMIT ME TO MAKE A FEW REMARKS: one concerning the papers read by Professor Loria and Professor Kellogg, and another of a more general character concerning the purposes and the limitations of Eugenics.

First of all I must express my gratitude to Professor Loria and to Professor Kellogg for having widened the discussion about the great question which we all have at heart—the prevention of the deterioration and the improvement of the human race by maintaining in purity the common stock of inheritance of mankind.

Granting the possibility of artificial selection in the human race, Professor Loria asks: "Upon which criterion are we going to make the selection?" Here we touch upon the most substantial point of Eugenics and of this Congress. I came this morning with the intention of expressing my deep regret to see the narrow point of view from which Eugenics has been treated up till now, excluding from our discussions all this vast domain where Eugenics comes in contact with social hygiene. This exclusion has already produced an unfavorable impression upon a number of thinking men in this country, and I fear that this impression may be reflected upon science altogether. Happily enough the two papers I just mentioned came to widen the field of our discussions.

Before science is enabled to give us any advice as to the measures to be taken for the improvement of the human race, it has to cover first with its researches a very wide field. Instead of that we have been asked to discuss not the foundations of a science which has still to be worked out, but a number of practical measures, some of which are of a legislative character. Conclusions were already drawn from a science before its very elements had been established.

Thus we have been asked to sanction, after a very rapid examination, marriage certificates, Malthusianism, the notification of certain contagious diseases, and especially the sterilization of the individuals who may be considered as undesirables.

I do not lose sight of the words of our president, who indicated the necessity of concentrating our attention upon the heredity aspects of this portion of social hygiene; but I maintain that by systematically avoiding considerations about the influence of surroundings upon the soundness of what is transmitted by heredity, the Congress conveys an entirely false idea of both Genetics and Eugenics. To use the word à la mode, it risks the "sterilization" of its own discussions. In fact, such a separation between surroundings and inheritance is impossible, as we just saw from Professor Kellogg's paper, which has shown us how futile it is to proceed with Eugenic measures when such immensely powerful agencies, like war and poverty, are at work to counteract them.

Another point of importance is this. Science, that is, the sum total of scientific opinion, does not consider that all we have to do is to pay a compliment to that part of human nature which induces man to take the part of the weak ones and then to act in the opposite direction. Charles Darwin knew that the birds which used to bring fish from a great distance to feed one of their blind fellows were also a part of Nature, and, as he told us in *The Descent of Man,* such facts of mutual support were the chief element for the preservation of the race; because such facts of benevolence nurture the sociable instinct, and without that instinct not one single race could survive in the struggle for life against the hostile forces of Nature.

My time is short, so I take only one question out of those which we have discussed: Have we had any serious discussion of the Report of the American Breeders' Association, which advocated sterilization? Have we had any serious analysis of the vague statements of that Report about the physiological and mental effects of the sterilization of the feebleminded and prisoners? Were any objections raised when this sterilization was represented as a powerful deterring means against certain sexual crimes?

In my opinion, Professor McDonnell was quite right when he made the remark that it was untimely to talk of such measures at the time when the criminologists themselves are coming to the conclusion that the criminal is "a manufactured product," a product of society itself. He stood on the firm ground of modern science. I have given in my book on prisons [*In Russian and French Prisons*] some striking facts, taken from my own close observation of prison life from the inside, and I might produce still more striking facts to show how sexual aberrations, described by Krafft-Ebing, are often the results of prison nurture, and how the germs of that sort of criminality, if they were present in the prisoner, were always aggravated by imprisonment.

But to create or aggravate this sort of perversion in our prisons, and then to punish it by the measures advocated at this Congress, is surely one of the greatest crimes. It kills all faith in justice, it destroys all sense of mutual obligation between society and the individual. It attacks the race solidarity—the best arm of the human race in its struggle for life.

Before granting to society the right of sterilization of persons affected by disease, the feebleminded, the unsuccessful in life, the epileptics (by the way, the Russian writer you so much admire at this moment, Dostoyevsky, was an epileptic), is it not our holy duty carefully to study the social roots and causes of these diseases?

When children sleep to the age of twelve and fifteen in the same room as their parents, they will show the effects of early sexual awakenings with all its consequences. You cannot combat such widely spread effects by sterilization. Just now 100,000 children have been in need of food in consequence of a social conflict. Is it not the duty of Eugenics to study the effects of a prolonged privation of food upon the generation that was submitted to such a calamity?

Destroy the slums, build healthy dwellings, abolish that promiscuity between children and full-grown people, and be not afraid, as you often are now, of "making Socialism"; remember that to pave the streets, to bring a supply of water to a city, is already what they call to "make Socialism"; and you will have improved the germ plasm of the next generation much more than you might have done by any amount of sterilization.

And then, once these questions have been raised, don't you think that the question as to who are the unfit must necessarily come to the front? Who, indeed? The workers or the idlers? The women of the people, who suckle their children themselves, or the ladies who are unfit for maternity because they cannot perform all the duties of a mother? Those who produce degenerates in the slums, or those who produce degenerates in palaces?

VOL. IX, NO. 12, DECEMBER 1915

Feminism in America

By R. A. P.

Robert Allerton Parker, who coined the phrase "birth control," taught English to adult foreigners at the anarchist Ferrer Center in New York, which also housed the Modern School for children. Writing under his initials, he took on "respectable" middle-class feminism and the social havoc it caused. He was the author, years later, of *A Yankee Saint: John Noyes and the Oneida Colony* (1935).

T HE IDEA OF FEMINISM IS ONE WHICH HAS OF LATE been so persistently dinned into the ears of the American that the unwary may be led to believe that it embodies a program of freedom for women. As a matter of fact, our American feminists are the exponents of a new slavery. Though the very basis of this idea is, obviously, founded upon the bisexual character of the human race, these ardent ladies are the bitterest and most uprighteous opponents of those very functions that seem most adequately to indicate such bisexuality. These functions are, we may conclude from the opinions of the eminent Mrs. Charlotte Perkins Gilman—widely heralded as "our leading American feminist"—a wicked and immoral afterthought, pushed into the foreground of consciousness by the lechery of men. For in all her highly moral and edifying tales of "white slavery," cruel seduction, and sinister grape-juice rapine, you cannot escape the continuous harping upon the universal, omnipresent sexual victimization of virtuous females by some low, vulgar male—who is usually, however, brought to "justice" by some highly efficient feminist—in one case the detective mama of the mammalian male himself! All sexual activity must be sanctified by law and sterilized by respectability. In the name of "humanism" the

American feminist would prevent and in every way increase the inhibitions to sexual expression.

Such prudery and hypocrisy could bloom and flourish only in the soil of American "culture." They present a curious contrast to the attitude of the earlier feminists of Europe, with whom we may or may not agree, but who had, at least, the honesty and frankness to realize and to point out that the freedom of women must mean initially the freedom of their bodies. So strong this conviction has been that in the Woman's Congress of 1905, as in practically all of their writings, these women claimed the right of abortion and advocated the abolition of all punishment for abortion except when performed against the will of the pregnant woman herself. Such activity was of importance and value because it tended to emphasize the fact that the true enemies of woman are not men individually, but the corrupt and enslaving forces of the State—representing the industrial masters, the Church, Morality, Custom.

But note the evasion of this problem of the freedom of the body in the works of our leading American feminists—in the pages of Mrs. Gilman's *Forerunner* or in the glib and diffuse ramblings of one Beatrice Hale's *What Women Want*—an interpretation of feminism recently published. These ladies—and if they are not representative, they should be immediately corrected—align themselves squarely with the good old forces of Respectability. They grow eloquent over "work" and "economic independence"—revealing a pathetic detachment from the woman who does work, who might tell them something of the "glory of Labor." They would open all careers to women; but it is painfully evident that they desire only well-paid servile posts of the middle class, that they wish to become only the clean-handed slaves of the State, the Charities, the Churches, and the "captains" of industry. But these champions of chastity and feminism might profitably ask the victims of organized morality whether the cruelty they may have suffered from men has ever equalled that of these female charity and correction experts, these eminent feminists who conduct reformatories and supervise jails and prisons. In a word, whatever so-called feministic progress has already been made has only strengthened and broadened the systematic interference of the Government and the Church with the lives of their victims. This is strikingly the case in the "political freedom" in those States where women have been given the ballot—a "freedom" that has in not a few cases concentrated its activity into the hounding and persecution of other women—prostitutes—note the Redlight Abatement Act in California.

This alliance of the feminists with all the forces that have been the most determined enemies of the working people, of the poor and disinherited, is unconsciously but clearly brought out in Mrs. Hale's book. This book makes it strikingly and curiously evident that American feminism is a by-product of the middle-class habit of thought, instead of being, as it claims, a vital and creative force. Its shallowness and sterility—its failure to strike the fundamental note of human freedom and development—render American feminism of no interest except as an amusing and typical instance of feminine intellectual homosexuality.

Three Letters and a Vindication

By Margaret Sanger

Margaret Sanger, who became the foremost proponent of birth control in the United States, launched her movement under the guidance of Emma Goldman and with the support of *Mother Earth*. Both women were strong-willed, and their inevitable clash led within a few years to Sanger's dissociating her movement from its anarchist beginnings.

A formidable obstacle to the dissemination of birth-control information was the so-called Comstock Law of 1872, which forbade the sending of obscene materials (including literature on family limitation) through the U.S. mail. Anthony Comstock, the ferocious moral crusader by whose name the law was known, was made a special agent of the Post Office Department in 1873 and was personally responsible for some 3,600 arrests until his death in 1915. His influence was such that the New York City Police Department granted his Society for the Suppression of Vice wide prosecutorial powers. Because of him, Sanger's short-lived magazine, *The Woman Rebel,* was impounded and Sanger arrested. She fled to Europe while awaiting trial, and when she returned the charges against her were dismissed. (She later served a monthlong term in the Queens County Penitentiary in February 1917.) In January 1915, while she was still abroad, an undercover Comstock agent visited her husband,

William, and asked to buy a copy of his wife's pamphlet, *Family Limitation*.
William obliged and was arrested not long afterward by Comstock himself and sent to prison for thirty days. *Mother Earth* reported regularly on
the Sangers' persecution, while Goldman on her lecture tours repeatedly
spoke on birth control and distributed copies of *Family Limitation*.
Margaret Sanger's testy responses to the backing she received from the
Mother Earth group—and Goldman's appended comments—foreshad-
owed her break with anarchism.

VOL. X, NO. 2, APRIL 1915

A Letter from Margaret Sanger [I]

THE EDITOR OF MOTHER EARTH, New York City:

Dear Comrade—In the November number of your publication, I have
read with pleasure an article by Harry Breckenridge on my case. Through
your columns I wish to thank Comrade Breckenridge for his article and
also the other comrades of the Ferrer School who, I understand, have also
attempted to get up some agitation on the case.

It may not be known to the readers of MOTHER EARTH that there are
three federal indictments against me, based on the March, May, and July
issues of *The Woman Rebel*. It may be supposed that though I might get
away with these three indictments based solely on an opinion of obscenity,
there remains the August, September, and October issues, which were suppressed and contain material for further forthcoming indictments. So that
if I were to fool about defending myself in the courts, I would be forced to
spend half the winter dallying about at the beck and call of a few officials.

When the case first came up in August before Judge Hazel, I was not
placed under bail, but allowed to go on my own recognizance. When the
case was called in October before Judge Foster, I had no objection to the
case going on the day it was fixed on the calendar, and said that I was ready
to proceed. When, however, day after day dragged on, and I was supposed
to sit at the end of a telephone awaiting the call of the District Attorney, I
objected.

I asked for a postponement in order to do many things I had to do. The Judge refused a postponement. Thrice he refused it, and the only natural thing for me to do was to take it myself, which I did.

There is other work more important to me than fussing over an opinion of obscenity, which is all the case against me was based on. There was no information concerning the prevention of conception given in the columns of my papers; consequently the only things the case was based on were the questions or articles in those three issues which advocated the prevention of conception—articles considered "obscene" "filthy" and "vile."

So far as the freedom of the press is concerned, it is a most important issue, and one which concerns everybody in the United States. Especially does it concern us in the revolutionary movement, for it is here that we need the freedom of expressing our ideas and our thoughts, because they are in direct opposition to the prevailing and stagnant ideas of the day.

But I began a fight for the right of giving out information on the prevention of conception. That is my present and immediate work; and I am not to have that work sidetracked by an opinion on "obscenity"—even though it involves Free Speech, I shall do this first. When I have said all that I have to say and all others have said on this subject, I shall turn to take up the fight of the suppression and confiscation of the five issues of *The Woman Rebel,* and fight for its continuation.

We who have lost faith in the justice of the Courts of law are bound to work out a different method to achieve our purposes than those who still fall into the trap of its ponderous machinery. So that if the way I work may not be along the lines that other comrades have followed, I can only ask your patience and faith in my sincerity in doing what I consider the best and quickest way to accomplish my object. There are always various opinions on these questions and all that we can ask is that each comrade do that which out of his or her years of experience and reflection seems the cleanest and most direct from the revolutionary standpoint.

Again, some of the comrades have sighed and criticized me for mixing the issues, as they say—declaring that had I not published the article on the defense of assassination by Herbert H. Thorpe, that all the rest would have been easy. I take this opportunity to state that I have no apology to make for publishing that article. There would have been no objection to an article against assassination, and if free speech and free press mean anything in the United States, certainly that article, reasoning and scientific, has a right to be published and read and discussed. That one may or may not agree with the material in the article is not the point. The point is that Mr. Thorpe had an opinion on a question which at that time was the cause of throwing all of Europe into a state of war. And he has the right to express his opinion.

The work I am at present engaged in will take at least several weeks longer, I shall then continue the trial.

There is one fact which naturally assuages my conscience, and that is that the federal authorities will always be there to receive me at any time I decide to turn up. I think I can safely say that they will still be "on the job" to gather me into their "fold."

I will frankly say that I was keenly disappointed at the silence of MOTHER EARTH in regard to this outrageous tyrannical attitude of the Post Office authorities toward *The Woman Rebel*. I expect very little publicity on this "delicate subject" from the capitalist press, but naturally I look for an attitude of solidarity and comradeship from the radical press.

But as the indictments were returned in August and there were three suppressions since March—and not a word in any paper until November, it makes one feel quite alone in a fight that so concerns the workers and all of us. However I wish to express my thanks to those comrades who have written me encouraging and sympathizing letters, and to those who are furthering and spreading the propaganda. Gather together all those interested in its spreading influence and together we will fight for the open and free discussion of this subject which so vitally concerns every working man and woman.

Fraternally,
MARGARET H. SANGER

The financial burden of *The Woman Rebel* and all this propaganda has been carried on almost alone. I cannot continue it much longer unless some financial help comes along. If the propaganda has been worth a little to you, let me know.

M. H. S.

Margaret Sanger promised to keep MOTHER EARTH posted on the status of her case, which she failed to do until August—too late for our issue. The September and October numbers of MOTHER EARTH were devoted entirely to the unemployed and antimilitarist agitations. However, during all of that time, we pushed *The Woman Rebel* and discussed its editor's case before thousands of people throughout the country. Under the circumstances it seems very unfair on the part of our comrade to accuse MOTHER EARTH of indifference. But then it is human to feel neglected when one faces one's first great battle with the powers that be, in behalf of an unpopular cause.

We understand our comrade and assure her that MOTHER EARTH and those connected with her never have and never will hesitate to stand by our brave friend, Margaret H. Sanger.　　　　　EMMA GOLDMAN

VOL. X, NO. II, JANUARY 1916

Not Guilty!

THERE SEEMS TO BE CONSIDERABLE misapprehension among those who are interested in my coming trial. Many are under the impression that the indictments pending are for circulation of the forbidden information. This, of course, is not true. I have been indicted under Section 211 of the federal criminal code for alleged obscenity. They were issued against me as editor and publisher of *The Woman Rebel.* My "crime" is not in giving the information, but solely for advocating birth control. There are three indictments, based on twelve articles, eleven of which are for *printing the words*— "prevention of conception." To the elect of federal officialdom these words themselves are considered lewd, lascivious, and obscene. In none of these articles is any information given—simply discussions of the subject, addressed to the working women of this country.

Many "radical" advisers have assured me that the wisest course to follow in fighting the case would be to plead "guilty" to this "obscenity" charge and to throw myself upon the mercy of the court, which would mean, according to those familiar with the administration of "justice," a light sentence or a light fine.

It is unfortunate that so many radicals and so-called revolutionists have failed to understand that my object in this work has been to remove, or to try to remove, the term "prevention of conception" from this section of the penal code, where it has been labeled by our wise legislators as filthy, vile, and obscene, and to obtain deserved currency for this valuable idea and practice.

The problem of staying out of jail or being sent to jail is merely incidental in this fight. It is discouraging to find that advanced revolutionists of this country are frantically trying to save agitators from jail sentences, thereby losing sight of the real and crucial issues of the fight. If we could depend upon a strong and consistently revolutionary support in such battles, instead of weakened efforts to effect a compromise with the courts, there would be much greater stimulation for individuals to enter revolutionary activity.

To evade the issue in this case, as I have been advised, would mean to leave matters as they have been since 1872. But it is time for the people of this country to find out if the United States mails are to be available for their use, as they in their adult intelligence may desire, or is it possible for the United States post office to constitute itself an institution for the promulgation of stupidity and ignorant tyranny.

The first step in the birth control movement or any other propaganda requiring a free press is to open the mails to the people of this country, regardless of class. Nothing can be accomplished without the free and open discussion of any subject.

These indictments have had the effect of opening the discussion of birth control in magazines and papers of the most conservative nature, whose editors would have been horrified at the subject previous to my arrest.

When my case is called in the federal courts* I shall enter a plea of "not guilty," in order to separate the idea of prevention of conception and birth control from the sphere of pornography, from the gutter of slime and filth where the lily-livered legislators have placed it, under the direction of the late unlamented Anthony Comstock, and in which the forces of reaction are still attempting to hold it.

*Trial postponed for two weeks.

From the article by Margaret Sanger, our readers will know she is among us and is determined to make her fight in her usual brave way. But what our readers do not know is that Margaret Sanger has gone through untold hardships the last year, and that very recently she received a staggering blow through the death of her much loved daughter, Peggy.

To face trial under such conditions requires more than ordinary strength, and Margaret Sanger just now is anything but physically strong. The one thing to sustain her in this crucial moment is the moral and material support of all rebels. I therefore appeal to everyone who reads MOTHER EARTH to write to Margaret Sanger, care of E. Byrne, 26 Post Ave., New York City. Send as large a contribution as you can spare and more, for the fight will be hard and bitter. Monies already collected: E. G. Birth Control Meeting, Chicago, $40; St. Louis, $20; Indianapolis, $10; Akron, $6.50; Youngstown, $13.60; Cleveland, $21; Contribution D. Kiefer, $10; per Kiefer, $5; Van Valkenburgh, $2.   EMMA GOLDMAN

VOL. X. NO. 12, FEBRUARY 1916

To My Friends

A T THE REQUEST OF THE UNITED STATES attorney, my trial for advocating Birth Control and protesting against the existing federal statutes which would make such advocacy criminal has been postponed until February 14th, in the Federal District Court in New York City.

Such invaluable aid has been rendered me in answer to my first letter that I am now making this further appeal to you to keep a live interest in this vital question.

I am being prosecuted not because the federal authorities consider Birth Control antisocial and anti-American, but *because they consider the advocacy of Control* LEWD, LASCIVIOUS, AND PORNOGRAPHIC!

You may disagree with me concerning the value of this propaganda for voluntary or prudential parenthood. But do you not believe with me that such an idea of doctrine can in no sense be considered pornographic? Is it not the very opposite?

If it is right and moral to advise: "Be fruitful and multiply!" is it any more lewd or lascivious to teach men and women that the strength of civilization lies in *well-born* children alone?

Does not Birth Control call for the most serious and open discussion, instead of immediate suppression by the Courts?

P L E A S E answer these questions.

Let Judge Clayton of the Federal District Court know YOUR opinion.

Let President Wilson know. Let the newspapers know. Let me know.

I take this opportunity to thank you for the encouragement and help you have extended.

Sincerely,

(Signed)   MARGARET SANGER

Twenty-six Post Avenue, New York City.
January 26, 1916.

VOL. XI, NO. 2, APRIL 1916

A Letter from Margaret Sanger [II]

THERE SEEMS TO BE GENERAL DISSATISFACTION among the readers of MOTHER EARTH over the result of my trial.

Many of them have written me that the law remains unchanged. That any man or woman may still be rushed into prison, whose case may not be "dismissed."

True—all too true.

The Socialists have been telling us this for years. They have been telling us that "direct action" does not accomplish anything until the laws are changed.

You have taken an interest in my trial. You have written letters to Judge Dayton, U. S. Dist. Attorney and other officials requesting the dismissal of my case—You have pleaded the Cause of Birth Control thru thousands of letters to these officials—you have been heard—the authorities dismissed the case, as you requested—and now you are disappointed and "mad" at ME because they did it.

I made no requests of the authorities: on the contrary I informed them, before the case was dismissed, that I should continue my work until working women in America should have the same freedom to get Birth Control knowledge as the women of wealth.

I have tried to tell you that going into jail or staying out of it was of slight importance to me. My work—my Cause, is the cry of anguish which comes to me from the women of the Cotton Belt—the cry of working women tortured with the dread of childbearing and begging for relief from it. I am free and have relieved nearly three hundred of these women in the past four weeks: to continue to do this work—via direct action—is my Cause.

William Sanger went to jail—the law remained the same—I did not go to jail—you say the law remains the same. Then the Socialists must be right. Will Emma Goldman's *trial* change the law, or will it serve as William Sanger's and my case has served—as precedents only? Opinions expressed by several prominent members of the legal profession have been to the effect that the "dismissal" of my case by the Government is of *far greater value* as a precedent than an acquittal by a jury.

Comrades—let's on with our work and stop quibbling.

M. H. S.

VOL. XI, NO. 2, APRIL 1916

The Social Aspects of Birth Control

By Emma Goldman

For Emma Goldman, the fight for birth control was part of the larger social revolution, whereas to Margaret Sanger and her followers it increasingly came to be seen as the panacea for the world's ills. They turned away, as Sanger later wrote, from the "wives of wage slaves" and toward "women of wealth and intelligence" for support—a statement and sentiments unthinkable for an anarchist. Goldman forcefully stated her position in "The Social Aspects of Birth Control," which appeared in the special "Birth Control Number" of *Mother Earth* in April 1916, the same month in which she was tried and convicted in New York for distributing birth control literature at a lecture in February. The quoted remarks by Circuit Judge William Gatens, of Portland, Oregon, were made the previous August, when he overturned the conviction of Goldman and Ben L. Reitman for—once again—the same offense.

IT HAS BEEN SUGGESTED THAT TO CREATE one genius nature uses all of her resources and takes a hundred years for her difficult task. If that be true, it takes nature even longer to create a great idea. After all, in creating a genius nature concentrates on one personality, whereas an idea must eventually become the heritage of the race and must needs be more difficult to mold.

It is just one hundred and fifty years ago when a great man conceived a great idea, Robert Thomas Malthus, the father of Birth Control. That it should have taken so long a time for the human race to realize the greatness of that idea is only one more proof of the sluggishness of the human mind.

It is not possible to go into a detailed discussion of the merits of Malthus' contention, to wit, that the earth is not fertile or rich enough to supply the needs of an excessive race. Certainly if we will look across to the trenches and battlefields of Europe we will find that in a measure his premise was correct. But I feel confident that if Malthus would live today he would agree with all social students and revolutionists that if the masses of people continue to be poor and the rich grow ever richer, it is not because the earth is lacking in fertility and richness to supply the need even of an excessive race, but because the earth is monopolized in the hands of the few to the exclusion of the many.

Capitalism, which was in its baby's shoes during Malthus' time, has since grown into a huge insatiable monster. It roars through its whistle and machine, "Send your children on to me, I will twist their bones; I will sap their blood, I will rob them of their bloom," for capitalism has an insatiable appetite.

And through its destructive machinery, militarism, capitalism proclaims, "Send your sons on to me, I will drill and discipline them until all humanity has been ground out of them; until they become automatons ready to shoot and kill at the behest of their masters." Capitalism cannot do without militarism, and since the masses of people furnish the material to be destroyed in the trenches and on the battlefield, capitalism must have a large race.

In so-called good times, capitalism swallows masses of people to throw them out again in times of "industrial depression." This superfluous human mass, which is swelling the ranks of the unemployed and which represents the greatest menace in modern times, is called by our bourgeois political economists the labor margin. They will have it that under no circumstances must the labor margin diminish, else the sacred institution known as capitalistic civilization will be undermined. And so the political economists, together with all sponsors of the capitalistic regime, are in favor of a large and excessive race and are therefore opposed to Birth Control.

Nevertheless Malthus' theory contains much more truth than fiction. In its modern aspect it rests no longer upon speculation, but on other factors which are related to and interwoven with the tremendous social changes going on everywhere.

First, there is the scientific aspect, the contention on the part of the most eminent men of science who tell us that an overworked and underfed vitality cannot reproduce healthy progeny. Beside the contention of scientists, we are confronted with the terrible fact which is now even recognized by benighted people, namely, that an indiscriminate and incessant breeding on the part of the overworked and underfed masses has resulted in an increase of defective, crippled, and unfortunate children. So alarming is this fact, that it has awakened social reformers to the necessity of a mental clearinghouse where the cause and effect of the increase of crippled, deaf, dumb, and blind children may be ascertained. Knowing as we do that reformers accept the truth when it has become apparent to the dullest in society, there need be no discussion any longer in regard to the results of indiscriminate breeding.

Secondly, there is the mental awakening of woman, that plays no small part in behalf of Birth Control. For ages she has carried her burdens. Has done her duty a thousandfold more than the soldier on the battlefield. After all, the soldier's business is to take life. For that he is paid by the State, eulogized by political charlatans, and upheld by public hysteria. But woman's function is to give life, yet neither the State nor politicians nor public opinion have ever made the slightest provision in return for the life woman has given.

For ages she has been on her knees before the altar of duty as imposed by God, by Capitalism, by the State, and by Morality. Today she has awakened from her age-long sleep. She has shaken herself free from the nightmare of the past; she has turned her face towards the light and is proclaiming in a clarion voice that she will no longer be a party to the crime of bringing hapless children into the world only to be ground into dust by the wheel of capitalism and to be torn into shreds in trenches and battlefields. And who is to say her nay? After all it is woman who is risking her health and sacrificing her youth in the reproduction of the race. Surely she ought to be in a position to decide how many children she should bring into the world, whether they should be brought into the world by the man she loves and because she wants the child, or should be born in hatred and loathing.

Furthermore, it is conceded by earnest physicians that constant reproduction on the part of women has resulted in what the laity terms, "female troubles": a lucrative condition for unscrupulous medical men. But what possible reason has woman to exhaust her system in everlasting child bearing?

It is precisely for this reason that woman should have the knowledge that would enable her to recuperate during a period of from three to five years between each pregnancy, which alone would give her physical and mental well-being and the opportunity to take better care of the children already in existence.

But it is not woman alone who is beginning to realize the importance of Birth Control. Men, too, especially workingmen, have learned to see in large families a millstone around their necks, deliberately imposed upon them by the reactionary forces in society because a large family paralyzes the brain and benumbs the muscles of the masses of workingmen. Nothing so binds the workers to the block as a brood of children, and that is exactly what the opponents of Birth Control want. Wretched as the earnings of a man with a large family are, he cannot risk even that little, so he continues in the rut, compromises and cringes before his master, just to earn barely enough to feed the many little mouths. He dare not join a revolutionary organization; he dare not go on strike; he dare not express an opinion. Masses of workers have awakened to the necessity of Birth Control as a means of freeing themselves from the terrible yoke and still more as a means of being able to do something for those already in existence by preventing more children from coming into the world.

Last, but not least, a change in the relation of the sexes, though not embracing very large numbers of people, is still making itself felt among a very considerable minority. In the past and to a large extent with the average man today woman continues to be a mere object, a means to an end; largely a physical means and end. But there are men who want more than that from woman; who have come to realize that if every male were emancipated from the superstitions of the past nothing would yet be changed in the social structure so long as woman had not taken her place with him in the great social struggle. Slowly but surely these men have learned that if a woman wastes her substance in eternal pregnancies, confinements, and diaper washing, she has little time left for anything else. Least of all has she time for the questions which absorb and stir the father of her children. Out of physical exhaustion and nervous stress she becomes the obstacle in the man's way and often his bitterest enemy. It is then for his own protection and also for his need of the companion and friend in the woman he loves that a great many men want her to be relieved from the terrible imposition of constant reproduction of life, that therefore they are in favor of Birth Control.

From whatever angle, then, the question of Birth Control may be considered, it is the most dominant issue of modern times and as such it cannot be driven back by persecution, imprisonment, or a conspiracy of silence.

Those who oppose the Birth Control Movement claim to do so in behalf of motherhood. All the political charlatans prate about this wonderful motherhood, yet on closer examination we find that this motherhood has gone on for centuries past blindly and stupidly dedicating its offspring to Moloch. Besides, so long as mothers are compelled to work many hard hours in order to help support the creatures which they unwillingly brought into the world, the talk of motherhood is nothing else but cant. Ten percent of married women in the city of New York have to help make a living. Most of them earn the very lucrative salary of $280 a year. How dare anyone speak of the beauties of motherhood in the face of such a crime?

But even the better-paid mothers, what of them? Not so long ago our old and hoary Board of Education declared that mother teachers may not continue to teach. Though these antiquated gentlemen were compelled by public opinion to reconsider their decision, it is absolutely certain that if the average teacher were to become a mother every year, she would soon lose her position. This is the lot of the married mother; what about the unmarried mother? Or is anyone in doubt that there are thousands of unmarried mothers? They crowd our shops and factories and industries everywhere, not by choice but by economic necessity. In their drab and monotonous existence the only color left is probably a sexual attraction which without methods of prevention invariably leads to abortions. Thousands of women are sacrificed as a result of abortions, because they are undertaken by quack doctors, ignorant midwives in secrecy and in haste. Yet the poets and the politicians sing of motherhood. A greater crime was never perpetrated upon woman.

Our moralists know about it, yet they persist in behalf of an indiscriminate breeding of children. They tell us that to limit offspring is entirely a modern tendency, because the modern woman is loose in her morals and wishes to shirk responsibility. In reply to this, it is necessary to point out that the tendency to limit offspring is as old as the race. We have as the authority for this contention an eminent German physician, Dr. Theilhaber, who has compiled historic data to prove that the tendency was prevalent among the Hebrews, the Egyptians, the Persians, and many tribes of American Indians. The fear of the child was so great that the women used the most hideous methods rather than to bring an unwanted child into the world. Dr. Theilhaber enumerates fifty-seven methods. This data is of great importance inasmuch as it dispels the superstition that woman wants to become a mother of a large family.

No, it is not because woman is lacking in responsibility, but because she has too much of the latter that she demands to know how to prevent conception. Never in the history of the world has woman been so race conscious as she is today. Never before has she been able to see in the child, not only in her child, but every child, the unit of society, the channel through which man and woman must pass; the strongest factor in the building of a new world. It is for this reason that Birth Control rests upon such solid ground.

We are told that so long as the law on the statute books makes the discussion of preventives a crime, these preventives must not be discussed. In reply I wish to say that it is not the Birth Control Movement, but the law, which will have to go. After all, that is what laws are for, to be made and unmade. How dare they demand that life shall submit to them? Just because some ignorant bigot in his own limitation of mind and heart succeeded in passing a law at the time when men and women were in the thralls of religious and moral superstition, must we be bound by it for the rest of our lives? I readily understand why judges and jailers shall be bound by it. It means their livelihood; their function in society. But even judges sometimes progress. I call your attention to the decision given in behalf of the issue of Birth Control by Judge Gatens of Portland, Oregon. "It seems to me that the trouble with our people today is, that there is too much prudery. Ignorance and prudery have always been the millstones around the neck of progress. We all know that things are wrong in society; that we are suffering from many evils but we have not the nerve to get up and admit it, and when some person brings to our attention something we already know, we feign modesty and feel outraged." That certainly is the trouble with most of our lawmakers and with all those who are opposed to Birth Control.

I am to be tried at Special Sessions April 5th. I do not know what the outcome will be, and furthermore, I do not care. This dread of going to prison for one's ideas so prevalent among American radicals is what makes the movement so pale and weak. I have no such dread. My revolutionary tradition is that those who are not willing to go to prison for their ideas have never been considered of much value to their ideas. Besides, there are worse places than prison. But whether I have to pay for my Birth Control activities or come out free, one thing is certain, the Birth Control movement cannot be stopped nor will I be stopped from carrying on Birth Control agitation. If I refrain from discussing methods, it is not because I am afraid of a second arrest, but because for the first time in the history of America, the issue of Birth Control through oral information is clear-cut, and as I want it fought out on its merits, I do not wish to give the authorities an opportunity to obscure it by something else. However, I do want to point out the utter stupidity of the law. I have at hand the testimony given by the detectives, which, according to their statement, is an exact transcription of what I spelled for them from the platform. Yet so ignorant are these men that they have not a single contracept spelled correctly now. It is perfectly within the law for the detectives to give testimony, but it is not within the law for me to read the testimony which resulted in my indictment. Can you blame me if I am an anarchist and have no use for laws? Also, I wish to point out the utter stupidity of the American court. Supposedly justice is to be meted out there. Supposedly there are to be no star-chamber proceedings under democracy, yet the other day when the detectives gave their testimony, it had to be done in a whisper, close to the judge as at the confessional in a Catholic Church, and under no circumstances were the ladies present permitted to hear anything that was going on. The farce of it all! And yet we are expected to respect it, to obey it, to submit to it.

I do not know how many of you are willing to do it, but I am not. I stand as one of the sponsors of a world-wide movement, a movement which aims to set woman free from the terrible yoke and bondage of enforced pregnancy; a movement which demands the right for every child to be well born; a movement which shall help free labor from its eternal dependence; a movement which shall usher into the world a new kind of motherhood. I consider this movement important and vital enough to defy all the laws upon the statute books. I believe it will clear the way not merely for the free discussion of contracepts but for the freedom of expression in Life, Art, and Labor, for the right of medical science to experiment with contracepts as it has in the treatment of tuberculosis or any other disease.

I may be arrested, I may be tried and thrown into jail, but I never will be silent; I never will acquiesce or submit to authority, nor will I make peace with a system which degrades woman to a mere incubator and which fattens on her innocent victims. I now and here declare war upon this system and shall not rest until the path has been cleared for a free motherhood and a healthy, joyous, and happy childhood.

VOL. IX, NO. 3, MAY 1916

Reflections on Emma Goldman's Trial

By Leonard D. Abbott

Emma Goldman's trial on April 20, 1916, received full coverage in the newspapers as well as in *Mother Earth,* which included in its May issue Leonard D. Abbott's summary of the proceedings, reprinted here; the complete court transcript; a report by Robert Morris of the dinner held in her honor the evening before at the Hotel Brevoort, which was attended by two hundred people; a piece by Ben L. Reitman (signed the "Manager") on his visits to "Our Lady of Sorrows" at the Queens County Workhouse; and an announcement of a grand welcome for her on May 5, at Carnegie Hall, upon her release from jail. Abbott, a regular contributor to *Mother Earth,* was one of the earliest and most active proponents of the Modern School movement and a founding member of the Ferrer Association.

I T IS TWENTY-THREE YEARS SINCE Emma Goldman suffered a prison sentence as the result of an impassioned speech she made at a demonstration of striking cloakmakers and of the unemployed in Union Square, New York. Her "crime" at that time was that she quoted the famous maxim of Cardinal Manning, "Necessity knows no law, and the starving man has a natural right to a share of his neighbor's bread," and added: "Ask for work. If they do not give you work, ask for bread. If they do not give you work or bread, then take bread."

On April 20th, 1916, Emma Goldman was again sentenced to prison. This time her offense was that she exposed the evils of indiscriminate and incessant breeding and that she told the poor, in language they could understand, how they might limit their families.

Both of her imprisonments have been honorable, and both have been but incidents in the heroic crusade against poverty and superstition to which she has devoted her life.

The appearance of the courtroom on the day of the trial was in itself heartening. Five hundred were in attendance. Two hundred gained admittance.

The routine of the court was totally upset by the influx of liberals. It was as if a gust of fresh air had blown into a musty room. Officialdom, as represented by the uniformed attendants, was restive and apprehensive. An effort was made to exclude some of the young women who had gained admittance. A man carrying a bunch of American Beauty roses for Emma Goldman was excluded. There was no room for roses in a courtroom. When the judges entered, they knew that it was no ordinary case they were to try. Presiding Judge O'Keefe from the start made efforts to be fair in his rulings; he seemed to be more liberal than the colleagues who flanked him and whose wooden faces were positively depressing. Chief Justice Isaac Franklin Russell came in as a spectator, and watched the proceedings with genuine interest. It would have been interesting to know the *real* thoughts and feelings of the judges. They did not seem particularly proud of the job that they had to do.

The lecture for which Emma Goldman had been arrested had been delivered at the New Star Casino in New York on February 8th. She had given the same lecture in English and in Jewish half a hundred times in cities throughout the country. Two detectives were put on the stand to testify as to what they had heard. They were so ignorant that they had not known how to spell correctly the words of the indictment they had framed in connection with Emma Goldman's arrest, and their testimony was inaccurate. They declared that Emma Goldman had spoken at the New Star Casino in German, whereas she had actually spoken in Yiddish. She could have made more than she did of this error, but she refused to take advantage of technicalities and preferred to keep to the main issue.

There was just one point at which Emma Goldman thought it worth while to take a little excursion into the domain of legal technicality. She maintained that the law under which she had been arrested was aimed at those who made financial profit out of advertising and selling contraceptives, not at humanitarians and social reformers. "The information connected with this movement," she said, "is not for personal gain or profit, but for the education of the working and professional classes who, harassed by economic conditions, by the high cost of living, by the terrible congestion of our large cities, cannot decently provide for a large brood of children, as a result of which their children are born weak, are ill cared for and ill nourished."

A dramatic moment came when Emma Goldman spoke of John Galsworthy's drama *Justice*, now running in New York, and pointed out that behind every so-called "crime" is "palpitating life." She wished to explain to the judges the nature of the "palpitating life" that had impelled her in her own conflict with the law. But Life is the one thing that Law is often most afraid of, and her speech at this point was rudely cut short.

Another dramatic moment came when she said that if it constituted a crime to contend for happier childhood and healthier motherhood, she was glad and proud to be a criminal. The crowd in the courtroom burst into applause. Excited attendants strove to quell the clamor. This spontaneous demonstration recalled the cheers and hand-clapping that had heartened William Sanger on his way to jail last September.

"I have committed no offense," continued Emma Goldman. "I have simply given to the poorer women in my audiences information that any wealthy woman can obtain secretly from her physician, who does not fear prosecution. I have offered them advice as to how to escape the burden of large families without resorting to illegal operations."

The judges seemed to be in a quandary. Their three heads came together for a long conference. Finally, Judge O'Keefe cleared his throat and announced: "We find you guilty as charged." He added: "The judgment of this court is that you pay $100 fine or serve fifteen days in the workhouse." Emma Goldman promptly replied: "I will take the workhouse." The words were hardly out of her mouth before she was seized by an attendant and hurried toward the pen. Many of her friends waved their hands as she was being rushed along, and some stuck their fingers through the wire grating of the pen runway. She tried to reach them in farewell as she passed. Her face was alight with enthusiasm.

Immediately following the sentence, the District Attorney's office handed to the press the following statement: "This office has no fault to find with the expression of any honest opinion given in a decent manner. The gravamen of the charge in this case is not the discussion of birth control, *per se,* but the indecency of the manner in which the subject was presented to a promiscuous audience, in which children of tender years were permitted to be present."

All this is but an effort to distract attention from the real issue. Emma Goldman's lecture was no more "indecent" than nature itself is "indecent." She discussed sexual facts frankly and clearly, as her subject required, and in doing so she helped to break down sex superstition and to enlarge human knowledge.

In serving her fifteen days imprisonment in Queen's County Jail on a charge of having educated the masses in a knowledge of the importance of birth control, Emma Goldman has had a quiet mind and a serene faith. She knows that the future will vindicate her—that she is already vindicated in the minds of intelligent and liberty-loving people. She takes her place with the intellectual pioneers who in all ages have been willing to sacrifice themselves in order that truth might be advanced. She takes her place with the path-blazers of the birth control movement in England and America—with Charles Bradlaugh and Annie Besant, with William Sanger and Margaret Sanger, men and women who have never been unwilling to go to prison or to endure any other suffering that the cause demanded.

VOL. XII, NO. 3, MAY 1917

The Woman Suffrage Chameleon

By Emma Goldman

Anarchism rejected the suffragist claims that granting women the right to vote would not only serve to liberate them economically and socially, but also humanize politics under the benevolent influence of their presumed moral superiority. The complicity of the hitherto pacifist suffragists with the government as the United States entered the Great War was, for Emma Goldman, a repugnant, hypocritical turnaround that proved the anarchist argument irrefutable.

FOR WELL-NIGH HALF A CENTURY the leaders of woman suffrage have been claiming that miraculous results would follow the enfranchisement of woman. All the social and economic evils of past centuries would be abolished once woman will get the vote. All the wrongs and injustices, all the crimes and horrors of the ages would be eliminated from life by the magic decree of a scrap of paper.

When the attention of the leaders of the movement was called to the fact that such extravagant claims convince no one, they would say, "Wait until we have the opportunity; wait till we are face to face with a great test, and then you will see how superior woman is in her attitude toward social progress."

The intelligent opponents of woman suffrage, who were such on the ground that the representative system has served only to rob man of his independence, and that it will do the same to woman, knew that nowhere has woman suffrage exerted the slightest influence upon the social and economic life of the people. Still they were willing to give the suffrage exponents the benefit of doubt. They were ready to believe that the suffragists were sincere in their claim that woman will never be guilty of the stupidities and cruelties of man. Especially did they look to the militant suffragettes of England for a superior kind of womanhood. Did not Mrs. Emmeline Pankhurst make the bold statement from an American platform that woman is more humane than man, and that she never would be guilty of his crimes: for one thing, woman does not believe in war and will never support wars.

But politicians remain politicians. No sooner did England join the war, for humanitarian reasons, of course, than the suffrage ladies immediately forgot all their boasts about woman's superiority and goodness and immolated their party on the altar of the very government which tore their clothing, pulled their hair, and fed them forcibly for their militant activities. Mrs. Pankhurst and her hosts became more passionate in their war mania, in their thirst for the enemy's blood than the most hardened militarists. They consecrated their all, even their sex attraction, as a means of luring unwilling men into the military net, into the trenches and death. For all this they are now to be rewarded with the ballot. Even Asquith, the erstwhile foe of the Pankhurst outfit, is now convinced that woman ought to have the vote, since she has proven so ferocious in her hate and is so persistently bent on conquest. All hail to the English women who bought their vote with the blood of the millions of men already sacrificed to the monster War. The price is indeed great, but so will be the political jobs in store for the lady politicians.

The American suffrage party, bereft of an original idea since the days of Elizabeth Cady Stanton, Lucy Stone, and Susan Anthony, must needs ape with parrot-like stupidity the example set by their English sisters. In the heroic days of militancy, Mrs. Pankhurst and her followers were roundly repudiated by the American suffrage party. The respectable, lady-like Mrs. Catt would have nothing to do with such ruffians as the militants. But when the suffragettes of England, with an eye for the fleshpots of Parliament, turned somersault, the American suffrage party followed suit. Indeed, Mrs. Catt did not even wait until war was actually declared by this country. She went Mrs. Pankhurst one better. She pledged her party to militarism, to the support of every autocratic measure of the government long before there was any necessity for it all. Why not? Why waste another fifty years lobbying for the vote if one can get it by the mere betrayal of an ideal? What are ideals among politicians, anyway!

The arguments of the antis that woman does not need the vote because she has a stronger weapon—her sex—was met with the declaration that the vote will free woman from the degrading need of sex appeal. How does this proud boast compare with the campaign started by the suffrage party to lure the manhood of America into the European sea-blood? Not only is every youth and man to be brazenly solicited and cajoled into enlisting by the fair members of the suffrage party, but wives and sweethearts are to be induced to play upon the emotions and feelings of the men, to bring their sacrifice to the Moloch of Patriotism and War.

How is this to be accomplished? Surely not by argument. If during the last fifty years the women politicians failed to convince most men that woman is entitled to political equality, they surely will not convince them suddenly that they ought to go to certain death while the women remain safely tucked away at home sewing bandages. No, not argument, reason, or humanitarianism has the suffrage party pledged to the government; it is the sex attraction, the vulgar persuasive and ensnaring appeal of the female let loose for the glory of the country. What man can resist that? The greatest have been robbed of their sanity and judgment when benumbed by the sex appeal. How is the youth of America to withstand it?

The cat is out of the bag. The suffrage ladies have at last proven that their prerogative is neither intelligence nor sincerity and that their boast of equality is all rot; that in the struggle for the vote, even, the sex appeal was their only resort and cheap political reward their only aim. They are now using both to feed the cruel monster war, although they must know that awful as the price is which man pays, it is as naught compared with the cruelties, brutalities, and outrage woman is subjected to by war.

The crime which the leaders of the American woman suffrage party have committed against their constituency is in direct relation of the procurer to his victim. Most of them are too old to effect any result upon enlistment through their own sex appeal or to render any personal service to their country. But in pledging the support of the party they are victimizing the younger members. This may sound harsh, but it is true nevertheless. Else how are we to explain the pledge, to make a house-to-house canvass, to work upon the patriotic hysteria of women, who in turn are to use their sex appeal upon the men to enlist. In other words, the very attribute woman was forced to use for her economic and social status in society, and which the suffrage ladies have always repudiated, is now to be exploited in the service of the Lord of War.

In justice to the Woman's Political Congressional Union and a few individual members of the suffrage party be it said that they have refused to be cajoled by the suffrage leaders. Unfortunately, the Woman's Political Congressional Union is really between and betwixt in its position. It is neither for war nor for peace. That was all well and good so long as the monster walked over Europe only. Now that it is spreading itself at home, the Congressional Union will find that silence is a sign of consent. Their refusal to come out determinedly against war practically makes them a party to it.

In all this muddle among the suffrage factions, it is refreshing indeed to find one woman decided and firm. Jeannette Rankin's refusal to support the war will do more to bring woman nearer to emancipation than all political measures put together. For the present she is no doubt considered anathema, a traitor to her country. But that ought not to dismay Miss Rankin. All worthwhile men and women have been decried as such. Yet they and not the loudmouthed, weak-kneed patriots are of value to posterity.

PART THREE

LITERATURE

EDITOR'S NOTE

According to the legend on its masthead, *Mother Earth* was published as a "Monthly Magazine Devoted to Social Science and Literature." In the decade preceding World War I, the heady spirit of modernism began to sweep over the arts, and the editors and publisher of *Mother Earth* were far from insensible to it. Emma Goldman, after all, was good friends with Margaret Anderson, the editor of the avant-garde *Little Review*. Even more significant was the involvement of the men and women associated with the magazine with the Ferrer Center, the Provincetown Players, Alfred Stieglitz's "291" gallery, Mabel Dodge's weekly evening salons, and other such centers of intellectual and creative ferment. Yet stylistically, very little of the modernist influence showed itself in the literary contributions to *Mother Earth,* even those by writers who were to become known for their experimentalism. Though the work was lively and competent, the fiction was largely realist, the poetry mostly composed in traditional forms, and the general essays written in the Emersonian mold. This was in part due to the personal preferences in esthetic matters of members of the *Mother Earth* circle, which tended to be impatient with art for art's sake; but also to their intense preoccupation with the political and social causes of the day, which frequently led to picket lines, mass rallies, and the local jails. By force of circumstance, then, and not out of disrespect, "Literature" as such was generally in the service of "Social Science": the contributions that follow—poetry, fiction, book reviews, and essays—were never routinely relegated to the back pages of the magazine or printed as mere fillers.

VOL. I, NO. I, MARCH 1906

The Song of the Storm-Finch

By Maxim Gorky

In a poem well-known in Russia, Maxim Gorky made the storm petrel—here translated as "storm-finch"—the symbolic herald of the revolution that was soon to erupt in the land. "The Song of the Storm-Finch" was, fittingly, the lead contribution to the first issue of *Mother Earth,* immediately following the inaugural editorial by Emma Goldman and Max Baginski. The translator, Alice Stone Blackwell, was the editor of the suffragist *Woman's Journal,* founded by her parents, Henry Blackwell and Lucy Stone.

THE STRONG WIND is gathering the storm-clouds together*
Above the gray plain of the ocean so wide.
The storm-finch, the bird that resembles dark lightning,
Between clouds and ocean is soaring in pride.

Now skimming the waves with his wings, and now shooting
Up, arrow-like, into the dark clouds on high,
The storm-finch is clamoring loudly and shrilly;
The clouds can hear joy in the bird's fearless cry.

*From *Songs of Russia,* rendered into English by Alice Stone Blackwell.

In that cry is the yearning, the thirst for the tempest,
And anger's hot might in its wild notes is heard;
The keen fire of passion, the faith in sure triumph—
All these the clouds hear in the voice of the bird. . . .

The storm-wind is howling, the thunder is roaring;
With flame blue and lambent the cloud-masses glow
O'er the fathomless ocean; it catches the lightnings,
And quenches them deep in its whirlpool below.

Like serpents of fire in the dark ocean writhing,
The lightnings reflected there quiver and shake
As into the blackness they vanish forever.
The tempest! Now quickly the tempest will break!

The storm-finch soars fearless and proud 'mid the lightnings,
Above the wild waves that the roaring winds fret;
And what is the prophet of victory saying?
"Oh, let the storm burst! Fiercer yet—fiercer yet!"

VOL. I, NO. 3, 1906

Comrade

By Maxim Gorky

Maxim Gorky and his common-law wife visited the United States in 1906–7 to raise funds for the revolutionary movement in Russia, which may account for his work appearing twice that year in *Mother Earth,* in addition to an interview (Vol. I, no. 11, February 1907). Although a hero to American radicals, he was not without his critics. Voltairine de Cleyre, for one, admonished him in the magazine ("An Open Letter," Vol. I, no. 7, September 1906) for staying in Philadelphia at the Bellevue-Stratford Hotel, "surrounded by the vulgar gaud of modern riches, paid for—by whom? By those who are down in the lower depths where you once were!" He was, however, subsequently thrown out of the hotel when it was discovered that he and his companion were not in fact legally married.

A LL IN THAT CITY WAS STRANGE, incomprehensible. Churches in great number pointed their many-tinted steeples toward the sky, in gleaming colors; but the walls and the chimneys of the factories rose still higher, and the temples were crushed between the massive façades of commercial houses, like marvelous flowers sprung up among the ruins, out of the dust. And when the bells called the faithful to prayer, their brazen sounds, sliding along the iron roofs, vanished, leaving no traces in the narrow gaps which separated the houses.

They were always large, and sometimes beautiful, these dwellings. Deformed people, ciphers, ran about like gray mice in the tortuous streets from morning till evening; and their eyes, full of covetousness, looked for bread or for some distraction; other men placed at the crossways watched with a vigilant and ferocious air, that the weak should, without murmuring, submit themselves to the strong. The strong were the rich: everyone believed that money alone gives power and liberty. All wanted power because all were slaves. The luxury of the rich begot the envy and hate of the poor; no one knew any finer music than the ring of gold; that is why each was the enemy of his neighbor, and cruelty reigned mistress.

Sometimes the sun shone over the city, but life therein was always wan, and the people like shadows. At night they lit a mass of joyous lights; and then famishing women went out into the streets to sell their caresses to the highest bidder. Everywhere floated an odor of victuals, and the sullen and voracious look of the people grew. Over the city hovered a groan of misery, stifled, without strength to make itself heard.

Everyone led an irksome, unquiet life; a general hostility was the rule. A few citizens only considered themselves just, but these were the most cruel, and their ferocity provoked that of the herd. All wanted to live; and no one

Translated from the French translation by S. Persky, published in *L'Aurore,* Paris.

knew or could follow freely the pathway of his desires; like an insatiable monster, the Present enveloped in its powerful and vigorous arms the man who marched toward the future, and in that slimy embrace sapped away his strength. Full of anguish and perplexity, the man paused, powerless before the hideous aspect of this life: with its thousands of eyes, infinitely sad in their expression, it looked into his heart, asking him for it knew not what—and then the radiant images of the future died in his soul; a groan out of the powerlessness of the man mingled in the discordant chorus of lamentations and tears from poor human creatures tormented by life.

Tedium and inquietude reigned everywhere, and sometimes terror. And the dull and somber city, the stone buildings atrociously lined one against the other, shutting in the temples, were for men a prison, rebuffing the rays of the sun. And the music of life was smothered by the cry of suffering and rage, by the whisper of dissimulated hate, by the threatening bark of cruelty, by the voluptuous cry of violence.

In the sullen agitation caused by trial and suffering, in the feverish struggle of misery, in the vile slime of egoism, in the subsoils of the houses wherein vegetated Poverty, the creator of Riches, solitary dreamers full of faith in Man, strangers to all, prophets of seditions, moved about like sparks issued from some far-off hearthstone of justice. Secretly they brought into these wretched holes tiny fertile seeds of a doctrine simple and grand—and sometimes rudely, with lightnings in their eyes, and sometimes mild and tender, they sowed this clear and burning truth in the somber hearts of these slaves, transformed into mute, blind instruments by the strength of the rapacious, by the will of the cruel. And these sullen beings, these oppressed ones, listened without much belief to the music of the new words—the music for which their hearts had long been waiting. Little by little they lifted up their heads and tore the meshes of the web of lies wherewith their oppressors had enwound them. In their existence, made up of silent and contained rage, in their hearts envenomed by numberless wrongs, in their consciences encumbered by the dupings of the wisdom of the strong, in this dark and laborious life, all penetrated with the bitterness of humiliation, had resounded a simple word:

Comrade.

It was not a new word; they had heard it and pronounced it themselves; but until then it had seemed to them void of sense, like all other words dulled by usage, and which one may forget without losing anything. But now this word, strong and clear, had another sound; a soul was singing in it—the facets of it shone brilliant as a diamond. The wretched accepted this word, and at first uttered it gently, cradling it in their hearts like a mother rocking her newborn child and admiring it. And the more they searched the luminous soul of the word, the more fascinating it seemed to them.

"Comrade," said they.

And they felt that this word had come to unite the whole world, to lift all men up to the summits of liberty and bind them with new ties, the strong ties of mutual respect, respect for the liberties of others in the name of one's own liberty.

When this word had engraved itself upon the hearts of the slaves, they ceased to be slaves; and one day they announced their transformation to the city in this great human formula:

I WILL NOT.

Then life was suspended, for it is they who are the motor force of life, they and no other. The water supply stopped, the fire went out, the city was plunged in darkness. The masters began to tremble like children. Fear invaded the hearts of the oppressors. Suffocating in the fumes of their own dejection, disconcerted and terrified by the strength of the revolt, they dissimulated the rage which they felt against it.

The phantom of Famine rose up before them, and their children wailed plaintively in the darkness. The houses and the temples, enveloped in shadow, melted into an inanimate chaos of iron and stone; a menacing silence filled the streets with a clamminess as of death; life ceased, for the force which created it had become conscious of itself; and enslaved humanity had found the magic and invincible word to express its will; it had enfranchised itself from the yoke; with its own eyes it had seen its might—the might of the creator.

These days were days of anguish to the rulers, to those who considered themselves the masters of life; each night was as long as thousands of nights, so thick was the gloom, so timidly shone the few fires scattered through the city. And then the monster city, created by the centuries, gorged with human blood, showed itself in all its shameful weakness; it was but a pitiable mass of stone and wood. The blind windows of the houses looked upon the street with a cold and sullen air, and out on the highway marched with valiant step the real masters of life. They, too, were hungry, more than the others perhaps; but they were used to it, and the suffering of their bodies was not so sharp as the suffering of the old masters of life; it did not extinguish the fire in their souls. They glowed with the consciousness of their own strength, the presentiment of victory sparkled in their eyes. They went about in the streets of the city which had been their narrow and somber prison, wherein they had been overwhelmed with contempt, wherein their souls had been loaded with abuse, and they saw the great importance of their work, and thus was unveiled to them the sacred right they had to become the masters of life, its creators and its lawgivers.

And the life-giving word of union presented itself to them with a new face, with a blinding clearness:

"Comrade."

There among lying words it rang out boldly, as the joyous harbinger of the time to come, of a new life open to all in the future—far or near? They felt that it depended upon them whether they advanced toward liberty or themselves deferred its coming.

The prostitute who, but the evening before, was but a hungry beast, sadly waiting on the muddy pavement to be accosted by someone who would buy her caresses, the prostitute, too, heard this word, but was undecided whether to repeat it. A man the like of whom she had never seen till then approached her, laid his hand upon her shoulder, and said to her in an affectionate tone, "Comrade." And she gave a little embarrassed smile, ready to cry with the joy her wounded heart experienced for the first time. Tears of pure gaiety shone in her eyes which, the night before, had looked at the world with a stupid and insolent expression of a starving animal. In all the streets of the city the outcasts celebrated the triumph of their reunion with the great family of workers of the entire world; and the dead eyes of the houses looked on with an air more and more cold and menacing.

The beggar to whom but the night before an obol was thrown, price of the compassion of the well-fed, the beggar also heard this word; and it was the first alms which aroused a feeling of gratitude in his poor heart, gnawed by misery.

A coachman, a great big fellow whose patrons struck him that their blows might be transmitted to his thin-flanked, weary horse, this man imbruted by the noise of wheels upon the pavement, said, smiling, to a passerby: "Well, Comrade!" He was frightened at his own words. He took the reins in his hands, ready to start, and looked at the passerby, the joyous smile not yet effaced from his big face. The other cast a friendly glance at him and answered, shaking his head: "Thanks, Comrade; I will go on foot; I am not going far."

"Ah, the fine fellow!" exclaimed the coachman enthusiastically, he stirred in his seat, winking his eyes gaily, and started off somewhere with a great clatter.

The people went in groups crowded together on the pavements, and the great word destined to unite the world burst out more and more often among them, like a spark: "Comrade." A policeman, bearded, fierce, and filled with the consciousness of his own importance, approached the crowd surrounding an old orator at the corner of a street, and, after having listened to the discourse, he said slowly: "Assemblages are interdicted . . . disperse . . ." And after a moment's silence, lowering his eyes, he added, in a lower tone, "Comrades."

The pride of young combatants was depicted in the faces of those who carried the word in their hearts, who had given it flesh and blood and the appeal to union; one felt that the strength they so generously poured into this living word was indestructible, inexhaustible.

Here and there blind troops of armed men, dressed in gray, gathered and formed ranks in silence: it was the fury of the oppressors preparing to repulse the wave of justice.

And in the narrow streets of the immense city, between the cold and silent walls raised by the hands of ignored creators, the noble belief in Man and in Fraternity grew and ripened.

"Comrade."—Sometimes in one corner, sometimes in another, the fire burst out. Soon this fire would become the conflagration destined to enkindle the earth with the ardent sentiment of kinship, uniting all its peoples; destined to consume and reduce to ashes the rage, hate, and cruelty by which we are mutilated; the conflagration which will embrace all hearts, melt them into one—the heart of the world, the heart of beings noble and just—into one united family of workers.

In the streets of the dead city, created by slaves, in the streets of the city where cruelty reigned, faith in humanity and in victory over self and over the evil of the world grew and ripened. And in the vague chaos of a dull and troubled existence, a simple word, profound as the heart, shone like a star, like a light guiding toward the future: COMRADE.

VOL. I, NO. 3, MAY 1906

Fifty Years of Bad Luck

By Sadakichi Hartmann

Sadakichi Hartmann was among the inner circle of Emma Goldman's friends that helped launch *Mother Earth*. An exotic-looking man of mixed German and Japanese parentage, his looks were matched by his eccentric behavior. Along with his drinking companion Hippolyte

Havel, he was a fixture at the Ferrer Center, where he was known for his finger plays, perfume concerts, recitations, and perpetually empty wallet. Hartmann was also a prolific and well-regarded writer, working in many fields and genres, and a regular contributor of photographic criticism to Alfred Stieglitz's *Camera Work*.

EVERY OCCUPANT OF THE RAMSHACKLE, old-fashioned studio building on Broadway knew old Melville, the landscape painter, who had roughed life within its dilapidated walls for more than a score of years. In former years the studio building had been quite fashionable and respectable; there is hardly a painter of reputation in New York today who has not, once in his life, occupied a room on the top floor. But in these days of "modern improvements," of running water and steam heat, of elevators and electric lights, it has lost its standing and is inhabited by a rather precarious and suspicious clan of pseudo-artists, mountebanks who vegetate on the outskirts of art; "buckeye painters," who turn out a dozen 20x30 canvases a day for the export trade to Africa and Australia; unscrupulous fabricators of Corots and Daubignys, picture drummers who make such rascality profitable, illustrators of advertising pamphlets, and so-called fresco painters, who ornament ceilings with sentimental clouds, with two or three cupids thrown in according to the price they extort from ignorant parvenus.

And yet, no matter on what byroads these soldiers of fortune wandered to earn their dubious livelihood, they all respected the white-bearded tenant, in his shabby gray suit, a suit which he wore at all seasons, and which time seemed to have treated just as unkindly as the bent and emaciated form of its wearer. Old Melville gave offense to nobody, and always had a pleasant word for everybody, but, as he was not talkative, and the other tenants were too busy to bother an old man painting, nobody knew much about his mode of living, the standard of his art, or his past history.

Very few had ever entered his studio—he had neither patrons nor intimate friends—and very likely they would not have enjoyed their visit. A peculiar gloomy atmosphere pervaded the room, almost sickening in its frugality, and as its skylight lay north, the sun never touched it. It had something chilly and uncanny about it even in summer. The floor was bare, furniture there was none, except an old worn-out kitchen table and chair, an easel, and an old box which served as a bookcase for a few ragged unbound volumes. The comfort of a bed was an unknown luxury to him;

he slept on the floor, on a mattress which in daytime was hidden with his scant wardrobe and cooking utensils in a corner, behind a gray faded curtain. His pictures, simple pieces of canvas with tattered edges, nailed to the four walls, leaving hardly an inch uncovered, were the only decoration and furnished a most peculiar wallpaper, which heightened the dreariness of the room.

There was after all a good deal of merit to old Melville's landscapes; on an average they were much better than many of those hung "on the line"; the only disagreeable quality was their sombreness of tone. He invariably got them hopelessly muddy in color, despite their resembling the color dreams of a young impressionist painter at the start. He worked at them so long until they became blurred and blotchy, dark like his life, a sad reflection of his unprofitable career.

It was nearly thirty years ago that he had left his native town and had come to New York as a boy of sixteen. He already knew something of life then; at an early age he had been obliged to help to support his family, and had served an apprenticeship as printer and sign painter. In New York he determined to become an artist: a landscape painter, who would paint sunshine as had never been done before; but many years elapsed before he could pursue his ambition. Any amount of obstacles were put in his way. He had married and had children, and could only paint in leisure hours, all his other time being taken up in the endeavor to provide for his family, by inferior work, inferior decoration, etc. Not before years of incessant vicissitudes, heartrending domestic troubles, and sorrow, not before his poor wife had died of consumption—that awful day when he had to run about all day in the rain to borrow money enough to bury her!—and his children had been put in a charitable institution, he took up painting as a profession. Then the hard times, which are proverbial with struggling artists without means, began; only they were easier to bear, as he was suffering alone. In days of dispossess and starvation he had at least his art to console him, and he remained true to her in all those years of misery, and never degraded himself again to "potboiling." In hours of despair, he also tried his hand at it, but simply "couldn't do it." Now and then he had a stroke of luck, a moderate success, but popularity and fame would not come. His pictures were steadily refused by the Academy. Every year he made a new effort, but in vain.

One day, when one of his large pictures was exhibited in the show window of a fashionable art store, a rich collector stepped out of his carriage and, entering the store, asked, "How much do you want for the Inness you have in the window?" The picture dealer answered, "It is no Inness, but just as good a piece of work." "No Inness!" ejaculated the man who wanted to buy a name, "then I don't want it," and abruptly left the store. This event, trifling as it was, threw a pale halo over old Melville's whole life and gave him strength to overcome many a severe trial. He hoped on, persevering in his grim fight for existence, despite failures and humiliation.

But the years passed by, and he still sat there in his studio, and in its emptiness, its walls covered with his dark and unsold pictures, whose tone seemed to grow darker with every year. He was one of those sensitive beings who continually suffer from the harsh realities of life, who are as naive as children, and therefore as easily disillusionized, and nevertheless cannot renounce their belief in the ideal. Not a day passed that he did not sit several hours before his easel, trying to paint sunshine as it really is. Nobody in this busy world, however, took notice of his efforts or comprehended the pathos of old Melville's life, those fifty years of bad luck. And yet such martyr-like devotion to art, such a glorious lifelong struggle against fate and circumstances, is so rare in modern times that one might expect the whole world to talk about it in astonished admiration.

And how did he manage to get along all this time, these twenty-five years or more, since "potboiling" had become an unpardonable crime to him? Now and then he borrowed a dollar or so, that lasted him for quite a while, as his wants were almost reduced to nothing. Of course he was always behind in the rent, but as he sometimes sold a sketch, he managed somehow to keep his studio. He did not eat more than once a day. "Too much eating is of no use," he consoled himself, and in this respect he had many colleagues in the fraternity of art, as more than one half of our artists do not manage to get enough to eat, which fact may explain why many paint so insipidly.

A few days before his sudden death, an old gentleman, a chance acquaintance, was talking with him about the muddy coloring of the pictures. Old Melville's eyes wandered over the four walls representing a life's work; at first he ardently argued in their favor, but finally gave in that they, perhaps, were a little bit too dark. "Why do you not take a studio where you can see real sunlight; there is one empty now with southern exposure, right in this building." Old Melville shook his head, murmuring some excuses of "can't afford it," of "being used so long to this one," but his visitor insisted, "he would pay the rent and fix matters with the landlord." The good soul did not understand much about painting, about tones and values, but merely wanted to get the old man into a more cheerful room.

It was difficult for old Melville to take leave of his studio, in which he had seen a quarter of a century roll by, which he had entered as a man in the best years of his life, and now left as an old man; but when he had moved into the new room, the walls of which were an agreeable gray, he exclaimed, "How nice and light!" After arranging his few earthly possessions, he brought out a new canvas, opened a side window, sat down once more before his easel, and gazed intently at the sunshine streaming in and playing on the newly painted and varnished floor.

For years he had wielded the brush every day, but on this day he somehow could not paint; he could not find the right harmony. He at first attributed it to a cold which he had contracted, but later on, irritated and somewhat frightened, he mumbled to himself, "I fear I can't paint in this room." And thus he sat musing at his easel with the blank canvas before him, blank as once his youth had been, full of possibilities of a successful career, when suddenly an inspiration came upon him. He saw before him the orchard of his father's little Canadian farm, with the old apple trees in bloom, bathed in the sweet and subtle sunlight of spring, a scene that for years had lain hidden among the faint, almost forgotten memories of his childhood days, but now by some trick of memory was conjured up with appalling distinctiveness. This he wished to realize in paint, and should he perish in the effort!

Feverishly he seized his palette and brushes, for hours and hours he painted—the sunlight had long vanished from his studio floor, a chill wind blew through the open window and played with his gray locks—and when the brush at last glided from his hand he had accomplished his lifelong aim—he had painted sunshine.

Slowly he sank back in his chair, the arms hanging limp at his sides, and his chin falling on his chest, an attitude a painter might adopt gazing at a masterpiece he had just accomplished—in this case old Melville's painting hours were over for evermore, his eyes could no longer see the colors of this world. Like a soldier he had died at his post of duty, and serene happiness over this final victory lay on his features. In every life some ideal happiness is hidden which may be found, and for which we should prospect all our days. Old Melville had attained his little bit of sunshine rather late in life, but he had called it his own, at least for however short a moment, while most of us others, whom life treats less scurvily, blinded by foolish and selfish desire, cannot even succeed in grasping material happiness, which crosses our roads quite often enough and stands at times right near us, without being recognized.

And the fate of old Melville's pictures? Who knows if they may not some day, when their colors have mellowed, be discovered in some garret, and reenter the art world in a more dignified manner? True enough, they will not set the world on fire, yet they may be at least appreciated as the sincere efforts of a man who loved his art above all else, and, despite deficiencies, had a keen understanding for nature and considerable ability to express it. Whatever their future may be, his work has not been in vain. It is the cruel law of human life that hundreds of men must drudge their whole lives away in order that one may succeed, not a bit better than they; in the same way in art, hundreds of talents must struggle and suffer in vain that one may reach the cloud-wrapped summit of popularity and fame. And that road is sure to lead over many corpses, and many of the nobler altruistic qualities of man have to be left far behind in the valley of unknown names.

Life was brutal to you, old Melville! But this way or that way, what is the difference?

VOL. 1, NO. 4, JUNE 1906

The Jungle

A Recension by Veritas

Upton Sinclair, a lifelong socialist and a muckraking journalist, sat on the Advisory Board of the Ferrer Center. His first novel, *The Jungle* (New York: Doubleday, Page, 1906), was in the realist literary vein so favored by the *Mother Earth* group. Mabel Dodge, in her memoirs, described the anarchists she met at Emma Goldman's apartment as "great meat eaters"; but whoever the reviewer "Veritas" was, he was apparently inclined to vegetarianism, at least after reading Sinclair's fictional account of Chicago's industrial meatpacking practices.

THE JUNGLE, A RECENT STORY BY Upton Sinclair, is a nightmare of horrors, of which the worst horror is that it is not a phantom of the night, but claims to be true history of one phase of our twentieth-century civilization. Nothing but the book itself could represent its own tragic power. In my opinion it is the most terrible book ever written.

It is for the most part a tale of the abattoirs, those unspeakable survivals in our Christendom in which man wreaks his savage and sensual will on the lesser animals; and indirectly it is a story of the moral abattoirs of politics, economics, society, religion, and the home, where the victims are of the species human, and where man's inhumanity to man is as selfish and relentless as his agelong cruelty to his brothers and sisters just behind him in the great procession.

Possibly the title is inappropriate. There is a "law of the pack," which is observed in the genuine jungle, but these human beasts appear to have all of the jungle's vices and few of its virtues. The author might have called his history, *The Slaughter House,* or, perhaps, plain Hell.

It is a common saying about a packinghouse, "We use all of the hog except the squeal." This author uses the squeal, or, rather, the wild death shrieks of agony of the ten millions of living creatures tortured to death every year in Chicago and the other tens of millions elsewhere, to pander to the old brutal, inhuman thirst of humanity for a diet of blood. The billions of the slain have found a voice at last, and if I mistake not, this cry of anguish from the "killing-beds" shall sound on until men, whose ancestors once were cannibals, shall cease to devour even the corpses of their murdered animal relatives. But while *The Jungle* will undoubtedly make more vegetarians, it would take more than the practice of universal vegetarianism to cause the book to fulfil its mission; for this is a story of Civilization's Inferno and of the crisis of the world, a recital of conditions for which, when once comprehended, there can be no remedy but the revolution of revolutions, the event toward which the ages ran, the establishment of a genuine political, industrial, and social democracy.*

If the story be dramatized and Mrs. Fiske take the part of Ona, her presentation will make Tess seem like a pastoral idyll in comparison.

The book is great even from a political standpoint.

But more than this, it is a great moral appeal. Not in Victor Hugo or Charles Dickens does the moral passion burn with purer or intenser light than in these pages.

I should not advise children or very delicately constituted women to read it.

I have said it is a book of horrors. I started to mark the passages of peculiar tragedy and found that I was marking every page, and yet it is a justifiable book and a necessary book.

---

*Genuine or not genuine: we live right now in a democracy. If, in spite of that, such diabolical crimes as Sinclair describes them are committed daily, then this only proves that democracy is no panacea for them. Why should it, if criminals of the Armour kind realize profits out of their wholesale poisoning of such dimensions that they can easily buy all the glory of the people's sovereignty. —Editor

The author tells as facts the story of "diseased meat," and worse, the preparation in the nighttime of the bodies of the cattle which have died from known and unknown causes before reaching the slaughter pens, and the distribution of the effects, with the rest of the intentional killing of the day; he describes the preparation of "embalmed beef" from cattle covered with boils; he even narrates the story of "men who fell into the vats," and "sometimes they would be overlooked for days till all but the bones of them had gone out to the world as Durham's Pure Leaf Lard"; he writes of the making of smoked sausage out of waste potatoes by the use of chemicals and out of spoiled meat as well; and he further speaks of rats which were "nuisances, and the packers would put poisoned bread out for them; they would die, and then rats, bread and meat would go into the hoppers together. This is no fairy story and no joke; the meat would be shovelled into carts and the man who did the shovelling would not trouble to lift out a rat even when he saw one—there were things which went into the sausage in comparison with which a poisoned rat was a tidbit."

But the worst of the story is a tale of the condition of the workers at Packingtown and elsewhere. It is the story of strong men who justly hated their work; of men, for no fault of their own, cast out in middle life to die; of weeping children driven with whips to their ignoble toil; of disease-producing conditions in winter, only surpassed by the deadly summer; of people working with their feet upon the ice and their heads enveloped in hot steam; of the perpetual stench which infested their nostrils, the sores which universally covered their bodies; of the terrible pace set by the continual "speeding up" of the pacemakers, goaded to a pitch of frenzy; of accidents commonplace in every family; of the garbage pile of refuse from the tables of more fortunate citizens, from which many were forced to satisfy their hunger; of the terrors of the blacklist, the shutdown, the strike, and the lockout; and of the universal swindle, whether a man bought a house, or doctored tea, coffee, sugar, or flour.

It is still further a story of the moral enormities and monstrosities of the almost universal graft, "the plants honeycombed with rottenness. The bosses grafted off the men and they grafted off each other, and some day the superintendent would find out about the boss, and then he would graft off the boss."

When the men were set to perform some peculiarly immoral act, they would say, "Now we are working for the church," referring to the benefactions of the proprietors to religious institutions.

It tells the story of the training of the children in vice, of girls forced into immorality, so that a girl without virtue would stand a better chance than a decent one. It is a tale of the terrible ending of old Antanas by saltpeter poisoning; of Jonas, no one knows how, possibly he fell into the vats; of little Kristoforas by convulsions; of little Antanas by falling into a pit before the door of his house; of Marija, in a house of shame; of Stanislovas, who was eaten by rats; and of beautiful little Ona, to the description of whose ending no other than the author's pen could do justice.

The book shows how men graft everywhere, not only in the packing-house, but how the slime of the serpent is over almost all of our modern commercial and political practices.

No one can justly hold the meat kings responsible for all of this.

Nothing less than a thorough reconstruction of our whole social organism will suffice. Palliative philanthropy is, as the author says, "like standing upon the brink of the pit of hell and throwing snow balls in to lower the temperature."

The Jungle is the boiling over of our social volcano and shows us what is in it. It is a danger signal!

We are all indicted and must stand our trial. There rests upon us the obligation to ascertain the facts. The author of *The Jungle* lived in Packing-town for months, and the eminently respectable publishers who are now issuing the book sent a shrewd lawyer to Chicago to report as to whether the statements in it were exaggerated, and his report confirmed the assertions of the author.

This book is a call to immediate action.

The Lithuanian hero found his solution of the problems suggested in Socialism. The solution lies either in that direction or in something better, and it behooves those who warn us against Socialistic experiments to tell us if they know of any other effective remedy. Surely all thoughtful men should study these theories of social redemption and learn why their advocates claim that putting them in practice would modify or abolish the evils of our modern conditions.

"The masters, lords and rulers of all lands," the thinkers and workers of our time must speedily give themselves to the understanding and application of some adequate remedy, or there will be blood, woe, and tears almost without end, "when this dumb terror shall reply to God, after the silence of the centuries."

VOL. I, NO. 7, SEPTEMBER 1906

Henrik Ibsen

By Georg Brandes

Emma Goldman and her circle were strong supporters of the new realist dramatists, among whom Henrik Ibsen held a prime place for his vividly expressed individualism. In her book *The Social Significance of Modern Drama* (1914), Emma Goldman called him an "uncompromising de-molisher of false idols and dynamiter of all social shams and hypocrisy," thereby elevating him to a near-heroic status among "the social icono-clasts of our time." The Danish critic Georg Brandes, himself a propo-nent of realism, placed Ibsen within a far wider literary and philosophical context. The two approaches to Ibsen were by no means incompatible. (Brandes' book-length work on Ibsen, published in 1916, first appeared in an English translation in 1964.)

A WRITER BORN IN A COUNTRY WHOSE language is not one of the principal languages of the world is generally at a great disadvantage. A talent of the third order that finds expression in one of the tongues that may be called universal achieves glory much more easily than a genius with whom the great nations cannot enjoy direct familiarity.

And yet it is impossible for another to produce anything whatever that is really artistic in any other than his native tongue. First of all, his fellow countrymen must recognize in his work the exact savor of the soil. There is nothing for him, then, but to bow to this alternative: either the savor in question will evaporate through translation, or else, by some masterstroke at the command of very few interpreters, it will persist; but in the latter case the work will preserve peculiar characteristics of a nature to render its dif-fusion slow and difficult.

If Henrik Ibsen has become known and admired in all countries in a minimum number of years, this is due, in the first place, to the fact that he wrote in prose. Everybody knows that prose is infinitely more easy to translate than poetry. Furthermore, he has no style, in the rhetorical sense of the word. He uses short, simple, clear phrases, whose shades lie in the content and not in the form.

On the other hand, his production has evolved steadily in the direction of the generalization, the universalization, of theses. After having written plays in which only the Scandinavian soul was faithfully reflected, he worked more and more for the world public. A detail here and there indicates this tendency in a remarkable fashion. Thus in a play written in the middle of his career he places in Norway a château (Rosmersholm) of a type very common in Germany, Scotland, and elsewhere, but utterly unknown in Scandinavia.

Finally, and especially, he has revolutionized the art form in which he expressed himself.

Efforts have been made to trace his work to the initiative of certain German dramatists—Friedrich Hebbel, for instance—but it has been impossible to deny that these were no more than precursors.

The French dramatists who dominated the European theater during Ibsen's youth belong to a category absolutely different from his own. We find in their works a special characteristic called intrigue, which Ibsen utilized only in the plays of his youth—which are not real Ibsen. Another peculiarity emphasizing the contrast between the French manner, classic or romantic, and Ibsen's manner is the development of the characters. In the French pieces the character is established almost from its first appearance, either by acts or by other external indications. But at an Ibsen play the spectator who would decipher an individuality is forced to the same efforts as in life. No more than in life, for instance, can he count on the aid of such childish expedients as the monologue and the aside.

The most happily conceived characters of modern French dramas are almost all one-sided, or in some other way incomplete. Émile Augier's Giboyer, which seems so lifelike, is lacking in complexity nevertheless, not only in comparison with kindred characters familiar to us in actual life, but in comparison with Rameau's nephew. In spite of everything, it is a symbol, and inspires within us no vibrant response.

How different with Solness! This character, too, is a symbol, but in his nature there are a number of individual peculiarities which create between him and ourselves close, firm, palpable ties—painful too, and thereby moving our passions.

And Ibsen has carried to such perfection this scenic realization of character and this thorough utilization of individual mental intrigue that it has become impossible to achieve theatrical success with plays of the sort that was triumphant in France and elsewhere twenty years ago.

Some of the most eminent *savants* of Scandinavia—Tycho Brahe, Linnaeus, Berzelius, Abel—and one sculptor, only one, Thorwaldsen, have won fame with some promptness beyond the confines of their own land. The number of writers who have had the same good fortune is limited. The novels of Tagner are esteemed in Germany and England; the fantastic tales of Andersen are popular in Germany, Poland, and France; Jacobsen has exercised a certain influence in Germany and Austria. This is all, or almost all; and the Danes, for instance, will never become resigned to the thought that the foreigner is unaware even of the existence of so profound and original a mind as Søren Kierkegaard.

This injustice, of which the rest of Europe is guilty toward most of the Scandinavian authors, and toward Kierkegaard in particular, has been of much service to Henrik Ibsen. He was the first Scandinavian to write for the universal public, and he worked a revolution in one branch of literature; it was commonly agreed that he was the greatest of all the writers ever born in the three countries of the north, and that, besides, he had no intellectual ancestry in his own race any more than in central, or western, or southern Europe.

One distinction must be noted. If the three Scandinavian literatures be considered from the absolute point of view; if account be taken only of the personal genius of the authors and of their national genius—that is, of their individual value and of the relations between this value and their environments, race, etc.—then several Norwegian, Danish, and Swedish writers are indisputably worthy to be ranked with Ibsen. But it is certain, on the other hand, that, if the first consideration is to be the influence exercised over universal intellectuality, Ibsen must be proclaimed the most powerful mind of Scandinavia up to the present time.

Henrik Ibsen began by producing plays whose subjects are borrowed from history or from legend. Then he gave to the stage works which fairly may be considered as purely polemical: *The Comedy of Love, Brand, Peer Gynt, The League of Youth.* But his glory rests on his twelve modern plays on which he worked during his maturity.

Of these twelve dramas six are devoted to social theses; these are: *The Pillars of Society, A Doll's House, Ghosts, An Enemy of the People, The Wild Duck,* and *Rosmersholm.* The six others are purely psychological developments, bearing principally upon the intellectual and sentimental relations between woman and man. It is possible, however, to view these also as pieces devoted to a thesis, for they seem written especially to establish the superiority of the feminine character. This cycle includes: *The Lady of the Sea, Hedda Gabler, The Master Builder, Little Eyolf, John Gabriel Borkman,* and *When We Dead Awaken.* This is a cycle of domestic and familiar plays—intimate, in short.

It is with these twelve plays that Ibsen has conquered one of the most eminent situations among the rare minds that guide the course of universal culture. And, to form an exact and precise idea of the importance and the nature of his influence, it is fitting to compare him with other directors of the contemporary conscience. Taine, Tolstoy, and Ibsen were born in the same year. Naturally, these three men possess several traits in common.

Taine, like Ibsen, began by being a rebellious mind; before the age of forty, he did his utmost to bring about a revolution of French intellectuality. And then, as the years passed, Taine, still like Ibsen, came to hate democracy more and more, looking upon it as a blind leveler. Both have taught that majorities always and everywhere group around the worst guides and the worst solutions.

Taine, however, is the more conservative of the two. His ideal is the British *régime.* Ibsen is no more indulgent for that *régime* than any other that rests on an *ensemble* of established principles. In his eyes doctrines scarcely count. It is not by the aid of new dogmas that society is to be ameliorated, but the transformation of individuals.

Tolstoy, so great in his feelings, but so narrow in his ideas, has failed to understand either Taine or Ibsen, and it is painful to hear him declare Ibsen unintelligible. He belongs nonetheless to the same family as the Scandinavian dramatist, the family of the great modern iconoclasts, who are also prophets. He, too, is working for the destruction of all prejudices, and announces the advent of a new order of things, which is born and develops without the aid of the State and even against its opposition. Like Ibsen, he is full of tenderness for all forms of insurrection against contemporary society—all, including Anarchism. Only he is impregnated with oriental fatalism, and of equality he has the most basely demagogical conception, the conception of a tramp—and of a Russian tramp at that! Whereas Ibsen is a furious aristocrat, who would tolerate only one form of leveling—a form whose plan should be indicated by the proudest of all souls. Tolstoy recommends the individual to dilute himself in evangelical love; Ibsen counsels him to disengage and fortify his autonomy.

We find in Ibsen certain of the fundamental ideas of Renan, who was his elder, and with whose works he seems to have been unfamiliar. When he writes: "I propound questions, knowing well that they will not be answered," do we not come in contact with a mentality substantially identical with that of Renan? The only difference to be seen sometimes between the two is that one attracts you by his charm, while the other lays hold of you in a manner that terrifies.

Count Prozor, moreover, has shown clearly the relationship existing between the conceptions set forth in a work of Ibsen's youth, *Brand,* and those developed by Renan in one of his early works, *The Future of Science.*

When Brand proclaims that the church should have no walls or any sort of limits, because the vault of heaven is the only roof befitting it, we recognize the same idea that Renan affirmed in declaring that the old church is to be succeeded by another vaster and more beautiful.

Among the great guides of conscience there is another whom we cannot help comparing with Ibsen. I mean Nietzsche, of whom, however, he had never read a line. Ibsen, Renan, Nietzsche, all three have claimed for truly noble individualities the right of escape from all social discipline. This is the favorite idea of Rosmer, and also that of Dr. Stockmann. Long before predicting the "overman" through the lips of Zarathustra, Nietzsche declared the formation of superior beings to be the essential aspiration of the race. The individualism of the three thinkers is of an ultra-aristocratic tendency.

Ibsen and Nietzsche meet also in the psychological domain. The latter loves life so passionately that truth seems to him precious only so far as it tends to the preservation of life. Falsehood, in his eyes, is reprehensible only because in general it exercises a pernicious influence upon life; when its influence becomes useful, then it is commendable.

In vain does Ibsen profess the worship of truth; he sometimes concludes, exactly like Nietzsche, in favor of the contingent legitimacy of falsehood. In *The Wild Duck* Dr. Relling pleads the necessity of certain simulations. In *Ghosts* the very thesis is the harm that truth may do. Madame Alving cannot and will not tell Oswald what his father really was. She refuses to destroy his ideal. For here Ibsen goes so far as to place the ideal in opposition with truth.

Madame Borkman lives on an illusion. She says to herself that Erhart will become capable of accomplishing great things and will make his family famous. "That is only a dream," another character tells her, "and you cling to it simply to avoid falling into despair." Borkman, for his part, dreams that a deputation is coming to offer him the management of a great bank. "If I were not certain that they will come," he cries, "that they must come, I would long ago have blown my brains out."

Says the sculptor Rubek: "When I created this masterpiece—for the 'Day of Resurrection' is surely a masterpiece, or was at the beginning. . . . no, it is still a masterpiece; it must, it absolutely must remain a masterpiece."

Ibsen and Nietzsche lived lives of grim solitude. It is difficult to solve the problem posited by Count Prozor—the question which of the two has best and most betrayed in his works the influence of this isolation. It would be still more difficult to decide which of the two makes the deeper impression on the reader, and which of the two will be the longer famous.

In Scandinavia, at any rate, Ibsen has founded no school. He seems really to have rendered the three kingdoms but one service—that of greatly contributing to draw the attention of the rest of the world to their literature.

In Germany, Ibsen was highly appreciated twenty years ago as a great naturalist, like Zola and Tolstoy. Nobody would hear a word of the idealism of Schiller, and it was thoroughly agreed that Ibsen was no idealist. Various groups began to be fond of him for diametrically opposite reasons. On account of the revolutionary current that runs, so to speak, through the depths of his works, and which is especially apparent in *The Pillars of Society*, the conservatives catalogued him among the Socialists. On account of his championship of the individual and his curses on majorities, the Socialists placed him, now in the category of reactionaries, now in that of Anarchists.

The contemporary German theater, especially that of Hauptmann—and Hauptmann is the greatest living German dramatist—reflects the influence of Ibsen even more than that of Tolstoy.

In France Ibsen was adored as the god of symbolism in the days when symbolism was the fashion. He won hearts by the Shakespearean character of his mystical discoveries—the white horses in *Rosmersholm*, the stranger in *The Lady of the Sea*. And they consecrated him Anarchist during the years when it was good form to pose in favor of Anarchism. The bomb-throwers, in their speeches in court, named him among their inspirers. On the other hand, his technique has made a school—witness, for example, François de Curel.

In England Ibsen has had scarcely any influence except on Bernard Shaw; and, in spite of the efforts of critics like Edmund Gosse and William Archer, his works are known to a very limited public. It is to be remarked that, in general, the English see in him the perfect materialist, but an admirable psychologist.

When everybody feels sure that he sees in the works of a genius a faithful reflection of the most diverse and contradictory mentalities, that genius must be very broad and very deep. The Norwegians have declared Ibsen a radical after having proclaimed him a conservative; elsewhere he has been dubbed by turns Socialist and Anarchist, idealist and materialist, and so on. He is all that, and he is nothing of all that; he is himself—that is, something as immense and manifold as humanity itself.

VOL. IV, NO. I, MARCH 1909

The Bomb

By Alexander Berkman

Frank Harris's first novel, *The Bomb* (London: J. Long, 1908; New York: Mitchell Kennerley, 1909), a fictional account of the Haymarket affair, opened with the deathbed confession, in Bavaria, of Rudolph Schnaubelt, who had fled the scene of the riot and was subsequently indicted for the bombing. ("I threw the bomb which killed eight policemen and wounded sixty in Chicago in 1886.") The real Schnaubelt, however, was still alive at the time of Harris's writing, having escaped first to England and then to Argentina, where he settled and raised a family; nor was there any evidence that he was the actual bomb thrower. In his review, Alexander Berkman skirted the question of Schnaubelt's identity in order to focus on the merits of Harris's book; though Max Baginski, writing several years later, affirmed in *Mother Earth* (September 1914) that Schnaubelt had never lived in Germany, was still alive, and was not the man who threw the bomb. Baginski's opinion very likely reflected that of other knowledgeable anarchists.

The reference to "Moyer, Haywood, and Pettibone" concerns the 1906 trial of union leaders Charles A. Moyer, William D. ("Big Bill") Haywood, and George A. Pettibone on trumped-up murder charges in the death of Frank Steunenberg, the former governor of Idaho. The men were defended by Clarence Darrow and acquitted.

I STOOD AT WALDHEIM AND GAZED UPON the graves of the dead. The golden rays of the setting sun were playing on the marble peaks and crosses, as if trying to warm the memory of those all but forgotten lives. Above, an azure sea, inlaid with tiny fleece, was softly flowing down the distant woods, that seemed to tremble expectant of the tender caress. And all was quiet around me, save for the low whisper of the leaves and the quickened breathing of the companion at my side.

I turned to look at her. In the bloom of mature womanhood her suppressed vitality seemed to palpitate for expression, every pore of her blithe figure eradiating the joy of living. How beautiful is life—I thought—with a beauty enhanced by the mystery of death, like the sun made more radiant by the thought of darkness. Ah, the sun! To live, like he, shedding sunshine, warmth, and cheer; to go one's way casting joyous life all around, and then slowly pass on, leaving sweet memories and buoyant hope.

The soft flutter of little wings suddenly recalled me to myself. The bird settled on a grave, and a volume of sweet tones poured forth from the tender throat. Was the life of those resting here such a joyous, sweet song? No strife to mar the peace and beauty of a glorious world, no hatred to embitter the sensitive soul, no thoughts of evil to pollute the spring of love, no sham or hypocrisy to deceive one's brother or oneself?

Ah, no! Those resting here knew never peace before. No sunshine poured on the paths clouded by black fear, no rays warmed the hearts chilled by malice, no joy filled the pale eyes of dread. Here they lie buried, the souls that never came to life for lack of inner sight, and thus they died unlived. And yonder in the great city, and all around and everywhere, men and women walk about, unburied yet dead, alive but not living, running and rushing, straining nerve and muscle, jostling and trampling each other in a mighty universal chaos. All dead in life.

All dead, buried beneath the weight of revered stupidity, stifled by self-imposed petty cares, held in eternal bondage by the bands of ignorance. Yet here before me rises, in all the majesty of conscious strength, the visible monument of the world's unthinkably brutal stupidity, the unsurpassed bestiality that has stifled the very voices which alone, out of numberless multitudes, dared to waken the dead, rouse them into life, and spread before them the feast of human brotherhood. Here they, too, lie buried, they who alone are still alive, and never can die. Here they lie buried, the eternal victims of power and darkness, Lingg and Parsons and Spies and Fischer and Engel. Ah, how vain to bury those that cannot die. . . . And there, above the immortal grave, stands the compelling figure that loving hands have reared upon the bleeding martyred hearts. Wistful of face she stands, the ever-longing Mother, confidently proud and unutterably sad: full of pitying kindness for her foolish, suffering children, ever crucifying themselves in their saviors, yet proudly looking with steadfast eye into the world, with a mother's noble pride in the brave sons who dared break the evil spell of night and boldly climbed the mountain, triumphantly crying, The light! The light!

And as I gazed upon the glorious figure, the sinking sun sped its last rays upon the beautiful sad face, the eyes became illumined amid the falling shades, and in their depths I could read shining Hope.

Over twenty years have passed since that Black Friday when five of the noblest of their race were foully murdered by legal process. But the eleventh of November, 1887, is not forgotten. Indeed, there are crimes so stupendous and horrible that no ocean of time could wash them off the memory of man. The hanging of our Chicago comrades was such a crime. The passage of years merely serves to accentuate the atrocity of the deed. Nor can time mellow the deep hatred of social conditions which continue their existence only by the systematic repetition of the injustice and barbarity which, in 1887, culminated in the death of our friends.

No drop of martyr's blood was ever shed in vain, however. The hurrying feet of Time are powerless to efface the footsteps of the Liberty's pioneers, and the voice in the wilderness ever finds an echo in suffering hearts. True, to the shame of America it must be said that it permitted the commission of an outrage rivaling feudal times. Especially the American proletariat must feel their cheeks burn at the mention of the Chicago Anarchists: the workingmen of this country can never be forgiven the cowardice of passively witnessing the legal murder of their most devoted champions. They could have most easily foiled the conspiracy of greed, as they did years later in the case of Moyer, Haywood, and Pettibone.

But though the plutocratic cabal was carried to completion, the protest against the legal murder quickly found expression in the erection of the Anarchist monument at Waldheim. And when the insane terror of the people, systematically fanned by a hireling press, somewhat subsided, there arose a man of compelling voice and courage who dared act the truth by liberating the three imprisoned Anarchists. Governor Altgeld gave the proof so dear to the American heart, the *legal* proof of our friends' innocence. And yet even his brave exposure of the capitalistic infamy was not sufficient to rouse the fair-play-loving American people to take a manly stand.

Indeed, poverty and political decapitation were the price Altgeld had to pay for challenging a hypocritical public opinion. The penny-a-liners of a prostitute press visited their paid wrath upon Altgeld, till he was driven from the political arena. To their eternal shame, and to that of American journalism generally, be it said that it remained for an Englishman, Frank Harris, to write the true story of the crime of 1887.

The Bomb, recently issued in this country by the publishing house of Mitchell Kennerley, is a very notable book. Chiefly, perhaps, because of its spirit of fairness and justice to an unpopular cause, all too rare in this day of commercialized journalism. The author is evidently a man of great moral courage, possessing the supreme strength of defying respectable shams and cant. To the same courage was due Harris' steadfastness in his friendship for Oscar Wilde, after the latter's release from prison—something that can be said to the credit of but very few of the poet's friends.

The story of *The Bomb* is told in the form of an autobiography of Rudolph Schnaubelt, the alleged thrower of the Haymarket bomb. The tale is smooth and vivid, at times very forcible. Its most prominent feature is the complete sincerity of the narrator, boldly and truthfully describing the events that culminated in the hanging of the Chicago Anarchists. The author gradually unfolds the movement for an eight-hour workday, led by Spies, Parsons, and their coworkers. He skillfully pictures the violent opposition of the manufacturers; the savage exploitation and resultant strikes, and the unspeakable brutality of the police in shooting down unarmed men and women at peaceful gatherings. Nor did Frank Harris neglect to castigate with a powerful pen the harlot American press that by lies and willful misrepresentation of the workingmen, especially of the foreign-born element, designedly encouraged the police to still greater outrages. The account of the events preceding the throwing of the bomb is pictured with historic accuracy. The conspiracy of the press and capital to inflame the popular mind against the strikers, the growing economic pressure and persecution, the desperate condition of the workers, and, finally, the spirit of human revolt culminating in the tragedy of the Haymarket—all these are told with convincing reality.

But *The Bomb* is by no means a mere photograph of men and events. It is a veritable human document, palpitating with the hopes and ambitions of the intelligent workingman, who bleeds at the degradation and oppression of his class and vainly seeks expression for his absorbing sympathies—vainly, because of our terrible social injustices and hypocritical cant.

The book is permeated by the spirit of profound sympathy with the ideal aspirations of the foreign-born workingmen in the large cities, who are shown to be the intellectual and revolutionary backbone of the American proletariat. It treats with rare appreciative understanding the exalted humanity of the Chicago Anarchists, though they are rather incorrectly classed by the author as Socialists. The heroic figure of Lingg dominates the greater part of the book, his remarkable personality pictured with great power, as well as the touching beauty of his relations with Ida, his sweetheart, the latter so different from, and yet so femininely akin to, the rather materialistic Elsie, the beloved of Rudolph.

Owing to the general excellence of the book, the presence of some inaccuracies is to be especially regretted. Among them, for instance, is the description of the English Socialist, Hyndman, as a Jew; the characterization of Lingg as the *only* Anarchist in the circle of Spies, Parsons, etc.; but, above all, the vital defect of imputing to Lingg the beliefs of a mere reformer who dreamed of a "State industrial army, uniformed and officered, employed in making roads and bridges, capitals and town halls, and people's parks, and all sorts of things for the common weal, and this army should be recruited from the unemployed. If the officers are good enough, believe me, in a year or two, service in the State army, at even a low rate of wages, would carry honor with it, as our army uniform does now."

Yet the descriptive power of Frank Harris is so compelling, his sympathies so wide and intimate, that the discrepancy of a pronounced Anarchist like Lingg, uttering such silly reformer talk, does not grate too unpleasantly on the ear.

We welcome *The Bomb* as a distinct service in the cause of humanity. It cannot fail to carry to all fair-minded men the realization of the terrible governmental crime of which our Chicago comrades were the victims. It must waken a serious interest in a cause that inspires its exponents with the high-mindedness of a Spies, the noble self-sacrifice of a Parsons, the uncompromising devotion and courage of a Lingg. It will, moreover, convince the unprejudiced mind that the Haymarket tragedy was the direct result of police brutality, press incitement, and the suppression of free speech. But, above all, it must prove a powerfully effective object lesson, revealing our economic and social barbarities in the very act of developing the most well-intentioned man into a desperate bomb-thrower.

The Haymarket bomb was ignited by the hand of greed, violence, and persecution. In the last analysis it is ever the exploiter and oppressor that are the men behind the bomb. The real and only criminal is that monster, Society, smooth and snug, upholding our Ishmaelitish system, while hiding behind respectable innocence and crying, "All is well!"

The effort of Frank Harris will not fail to contribute a goodly share to a clear understanding of the psychology of the situation, thus accomplishing a great and very necessary work.

VOL. IV, NO. 8, OCTOBER 1909

The Woman and the Poet

By Floyd Dell

Before the novelist, playwright, and critic Floyd Dell moved from
Chicago to New York in the fall of 1913, he was the editor of the influential *Friday Literary Review,* a supplement of the *Chicago Evening Post.*
In his memoirs, he described himself in those years as having "temperamental affinities" with anarchism, which clearly show in his romantic
fictional meditation on free love, "The Woman and the Poet." His literary circle included Margaret Anderson, Ben Hecht, Theodore Dreiser,
John Cowper Powys, and Sherwood Anderson, among others. In New
York, he became associate editor of Max Eastman's *The Masses,* the socialist counterpart to *Mother Earth.* He also was a founding member of
the Washington Square Players, often performing at the Ferrer Center's
Free Theatre.

THE WOMAN AT MY SIDE POINTED to one of the delicate vases that sat
clustered together where they had a few minutes before been brought
from the annealing furnace. "How beautiful it is!" she said.

One of the workmen, he under whose breath and hands we had just seen
take form one creation after another of shimmering grace, glanced keenly
at the vase as she spoke, and stopped for a single instant to take it up in his
fingers; then he smiled and said, "But it is flawed."

The glow from the furnaces that bathed us in its lucent flood touched
and caressed the condemned vase and lit up within its depths a thousand
fairy torches—fires that brought up from out the earth in cobalt and copper and gold invested with their own warmth the cold clear crystal in whose
embrace they were held fast, and made the whole tingle with seeming life;

it was the incarnation of some rare emotion. And yet he who knew said that it was flawed.

Certainly it was beautiful. It was as beautiful as the body of the woman beside me, her white gown grown in the light of the furnace like the petals of a crimson flower; beautiful as her soul, that was apparent to me of a sudden as she slowly turned her eyes to meet mine and bent her lips in a slight mysterious smile, in an exhalation like the flower's perfume, subtle, volatile, not to be seized upon.—But flawed!

"Come," she said, and pressed my arm, shivering in despite of the furnace's glow, as if with an intuitive perception of my thought. "Let us go." And as I went I thought of the chances of the molten stuff in its transformation under the hands of the workman, at the mercy of unseen forces beyond the reach of human skill in one process after another, from the whirling globe quivering at the end of the blowing-iron and yielding to the impress of pucellas and marver, to the final shape at rest in the quiescence of the annealing furnace, ready to come out into the shock and jostle of the world. Then I looked again at the woman at my side, as we passed from the door of the glasshouse into the coolness of the moonlit night, and whispered to myself, "But beautiful!"

I wondered if I would ever have the courage to take up this woman's soul in my fingers as the workman had that shapely thing of glass, and handling it tenderly even as a vase, admit to myself the justice of the sentence: "Flawed." We had entered a great park, through the shaded walks of which we passed slowly. I looked at her, a white shape in the dusk, an ethereal odor among the wind-blown perfumes of the night. I stopped, submerged by a wave of tenderness. "Kiss me!" I said.

She came close and pressed her mouth against mine; I drew her tightly against me and held her for a long time in the sheath of my arms, but we did not tremble nor grow faint; and at last I released her and walked on, clear-eyed. The kiss was confiding, comforting, complete; it held in it no throb of passion, no stinging sense of unfulfillment, nothing to allure or inspire, to make desperate or defiant of the gods. It opened up no new horizons, hinted of no hidden seas or undiscovered worlds. A poet it could not long content; for the poet is drawn by invisible golden threads toward the mellowest orchards in the garden of life, and may not linger long by the wayside for the bitter roots that grow among the wild grasses. The poet is doomed to the horror of silence unless he commune with equal souls. And this soul—beautiful and fragile and dear—was flawed.

We stopped, seating ourselves on a rustic bench. My arm was about her, and I could feel against my side the steady rise and fall of her bosom as she breathed. Her face was very white and sweet; but I was looking off to the whiter face of the moon, haloed about with a mystic effulgence and throned on a royal bank of clouds that hardly stirred under the touch of the breezes that swept faintly past us. I was forcing myself to be cruel—to tear up from their beds in the dark the pale-stemmed flowers of my lady's thoughts, the rare drooping blossoms of emotion, and look at them for what they were. Was there anything here that I could call love? Was there anything akin to generosity, daring, enthusiasm, sympathy?

"What are you thinking of?" she asked, a little troubled at my silence. "Of you," I said, and she smiled the pleased smile of a child.

What is the texture of my lady's soul? Is it richly woven cloth-of-gold, or fine-spun silk, or some rougher, cruder fabric—or perhaps the misty gossamer that clothes the fields at morn, to be torn and violated with a touch? Nevertheless, I said, I shall thrust in my hand and see.

"What are you thinking about me?" she asked, a little petulantly, turning to me a face like the face of a flower heavy with dew. "Is it nice?"

"I was wondering why you like me," I said. But even as I wondered, I knew; for the rise and fall of her bosom as it rested against my side, her happy breathing upon my cheek, had suddenly been transformed into the purring of a magnificent Persian cat, which had climbed upon my knee because I of all the world would soonest turn aside from my work to pet and caress it. For a moment the vision lasted, and then momentarily again I hated myself for my unkindness. But the truth stayed with me, was not to be destroyed or forgotten; and all the beautiful phrases that she might coin in a happier mood would never be able to blind me to the fact that it was not the essential I, the poet, the interpreter of the world to the minds of men, that my lady valued: only the lavisher of caresses, and words, and glances with the quality of a caress, the maker of sleek bright lies wherein to clothe her soul's nakedness, the bringer of tribute of rich, strange fruit of admiration and desire wherewith to feed her soul's hunger.

"You are not often like this," she said. "Perhaps that is one reason why I like you." In her voice I could discern sounding dully amidst the music of her words the note of jealousy—as though divining the import of my thoughts, she hated them, but with a hatred sunk in weariness and submission. It was a confession, a lowering of the battle-banner, a token of failure. I saw it all, knew it well, but it was not to my mind: so I turned again toward her beauty with an open heart, and clasped her head with its cloud of perfumed hair against my breast, hearing as for the first time intermixed with the ancient love song of the toads in the dim ponds behind us, the dim and tranquil passage of her breath. She seemed a part of the night, one with its immemorial sounds and odors, akin to its each faint color and mystic stillness. Beautiful she was: and I—did I love her?

The answer came in a moment: No—for I have sounded her depths; she has no deeper joy to yield, nothing to give me beyond this hour.

"Kiss me," she said.

As our lips met I demanded passionately of myself the proof of these charges that would make this kiss perhaps our last. Wherein lay her failure? I knew that she was, to me, sincere—in flash after flash of desperate or tender revealment she had opened to my gaze the utmost regions of her soul. But I knew, too, that there was something in her life that she herself dared not face, that she kept carefully hidden away from consciousness, before which when a word or look threatened its unveiling her spirit crouched in an agony of terror. The shamefulness of this something was not to be conveyed by any words of definition—at the utmost it could perhaps be stated as a sordid acquiescence in bondage; but it was to be known and understood from the poison which it spread through every vein of her life. Met and faced, it could have been only a sad and hateful fact, accepted because it seemed an absolute condition of existence; but flinched from and obscured, it repaid her dishonesty by dominating and obsessing her, by becoming an unforgettable subterranean horror.

Life itself had been infected by the taint: and from life as it became unbearably real she fled now and again to a dim place of dreams. Music and literature and art, all things I loved because of their deep and intimate relation to life, were to her the subtle wines with which she intoxicated herself so as to forget life.

Even her rebellion had partaken of the taint. Our kisses had from the first thrilled her with no quality within themselves—rather by virtue of an unrelated fact, the circumstance that they were secret and unallowed. I had told her of my desire because to me the yearning of my being to mix itself with hers was something fair and good; and she had listened, because the telling had for her a certain flavor of wickedness.

But most of all had the poison corroded her mind in regard to sex. There was for her nothing here of wonder and delight, nothing of loveliness frank and avowed; but only the muddy depths of mysterious vulgarity, lit up perhaps at times by a patch of light caught from the Sidonian moon.

"Where will you be tomorrow?" she asked suddenly. "I don't know," I answered. I thought inwardly—on the other side of the world. For the winds were calling, and the stars, and the song of the toads in the dim ponds behind us had changed to a low croon of farewell. I knew that a great happiness was in store for me somewhere, and I must go forth to meet it.

She rose. "Kiss me," she said, in a strange voice; "we may never see each other again."

A great flood of tenderness enveloped me. I clasped her close, so that I could feel the beating of her heart, and the blue veins in all her limbs kissed and stung me; then I pressed my mouth against hers, and drank its coolness in a long, long draught.

VOL. V, NO. 12, FEBRUARY 1910

Comstock Soliloquizes

By Don Marquis

The January 1910 issue of *Mother Earth* was held by the U.S. Post Office because of a complaint by its formidable special agent, Anthony Comstock, who objected to Emma Goldman's article "The White Slave Traffic." (see page 113). Comstock afterward publicly denied any responsibility for the Post Office's action, even though he had personally informed the editor, Alexander Berkman, that it was Goldman's piece which he found "unmailable." The issue was finally released on January 29. Berkman's detailed report on the episode of mail censorship, "Comstock and *Mother Earth,*" was the lead article for the February issue. It was followed by a bit of derisive light verse, "Comstock Soliloquizes," by the satirist Don Marquis, then a reporter for the *New York American* and the *Brooklyn Daily Eagle*. (Marquis in later years became well known for his "Archy and Mehitabel" series.) The pages of *Mother Earth* rarely made room for humor, but when it did, Comstock was a favored target. He was, after all, the man who in 1906 engineered a raid on the Art Students League to confiscate the paintings of nude figures.

WHAT, APHRODITE!
  Not even a nightie
Between you and Hades, my dear?
O Venus de Medici!
I can't stand for negligee,
Too negligee ladies, my dear!
And your sister of Milo
From her head to her heel, O,

Sets a perfectly horrid example;
Though she's minus her arms, O,
The rest of her charms, O,
Are extremely apparent—and ample.
And mercy upon us!
There's Billy Adonis
With such a décolleté gown
We'd welcome a freckle,
A wart or a speckle,
Tattoo marks, or even a frown!

Uncle Pete Phidias,
What perfectly hideous
Morals you must have possessed
To sculp ne'er a pimple,
An eyelash or dimple,
Let alone an occasional vest!
'Tis terribly plain, sir,
You'll wallow in pain, sir,
To the ultimate end of creation,
For you gave Aphrodite
Not even a nightie
Betwixt the poor thing and damnation.

VOL. V, NOS. 3–4, MAY–JUNE 1910

The Dominant Idea

By Voltairine de Cleyre

Voltairine de Cleyre's prescient essay "The Dominant Idea" is very much in the individualist tradition of Emerson and Thoreau. It is both a prophetic indictment of the shallow excesses of affluence and a ringing argument for the assertion of free will and personal responsibility. Leonard Abbott, looking back in 1949, called the essay a "radical classic." "The Dominant Idea" was published as a separate pamphlet in 1910 by the Mother Earth Publishing Association. A French edition appeared the following year and was twice reissued, in 1917 and 1933.

O N EVERYTHING THAT LIVES, if one looks searchingly, is limned the shadow line of an idea—an idea, dead or living, sometimes stronger when dead, with rigid, unswerving lines that mark the living embodiment with the stern, immobile cast of the nonliving. Daily we move among these unyielding shadows, less pierceable, more enduring than granite, with the blackness of ages in them, dominating living, changing bodies, with dead, unchanging souls. And we meet, also, living souls dominating dying bodies—living ideas regnant over decay and death. Do not imagine that I speak of human life alone. The stamp of persistent or of shifting Will is visible in the grass blade rooted in its clod of earth, as in the gossamer web of being that floats and swims far over our heads in the free world of air.

Regnant ideas, everywhere! Did you ever see a dead vine bloom? I have seen it. Last summer I trained some morning glory vines up over a second-story balcony; and every day they blew and curled in the wind, their white, purple-dashed faces winking at the sun, radiant with climbing life. Higher every day the green heads crept, carrying their train of spreading fans waving before the sun-seeking blossoms. Then all at once some mischance happened—some cutworm or some mischievous child tore one vine off below, the finest and most ambitious one, of course. In a few hours the leaves hung limp, the sappy stem wilted and began to wither; in a day it was dead—all but the top, which still clung longingly to its support, with bright head lifted. I mourned a little for the buds that could never open now, and pitied that proud vine whose work in the world was lost. But the next night there was a storm, a heavy, driving storm, with beating rain and blinding lightning. I rose to watch the flashes, and lo! the wonder of the world! In the blackness of the mid-NIGHT, in the fury of wind and rain, the dead vine had flowered. Five white, moon-faced blossoms blew gaily round the skeleton vine, shining back triumphant at the red lightning. I gazed at them in dumb wonder. Dear, dead vine, whose will had been so strong to bloom, that in the hour of its sudden cutoff from the feeding earth, it sent the last sap to its blossoms; and, not waiting for the morning, brought them forth in storm and flash, as white night glories, which should have been the children of the sun.

In the daylight we all came to look at the wonder, marveling much, and saying, "Surely these must be the last." But every day for three days the dead vine bloomed; and even a week after, when every leaf was dry and brown, and so thin you could see through it, one last bud, dwarfed, weak, a very baby of a blossom, but still white and delicate, with five purple flecks, like those on the live vine beside it, opened and waved at the stars, and waited for the early sun. Over death and decay the Dominant Idea smiled: the vine was in the world to bloom, to bear white trumpet blossoms dashed with purple; and it held its will beyond death.

Our modern teaching is that ideas are but attendant phenomena, impotent to determine the actions or relations of life, as the image in the glass which should say to the body it reflects: "*I* shall shape *thee.*" In truth we know that directly the body goes from before the mirror, the transient image is nothingness: but the real body has its being to live, and will live it, heedless of vanished phantoms of itself, in response to the ever-shifting pressure of things without it.

It is thus that the so-called Materialist Conception of History, the modern Socialists, and a positive majority of Anarchists would have us look upon the world of ideas—shifting, unreal reflections, having naught to do in the determination of Man's life, but so many mirror appearances of certain material relations, wholly powerless to act upon the course of material things. Mind to them is in itself a blank mirror, though in fact never wholly blank, because always facing the reality of the material and bound to reflect some shadow. Today I am somebody, tomorrow somebody else, if the scenes have shifted; my Ego is a gibbering phantom, pirouetting in the glass, gesticulating, transforming, hourly or momentarily, gleaming with the phosphor light of a deceptive unreality, melting like the mist upon the hills. Rocks, fields, woods, streams, houses, goods, flesh, blood, bone, sinew—these are realities, with definite parts to play, with essential characters that abide under all changes; but my Ego does not abide; it is manufactured afresh with every change of these.

I think this unqualified determinism of the material is a great and lamentable error in our modern progressive movement; and while I believe it was a wholesome antidote to the long-continued blunder of Middle Age theology, viz., that Mind was an utterly irresponsible entity making laws of its own after the manner of an Absolute Emperor, without logic, sequence, or relation, ruler over matter, and its own supreme determinant, not excepting God (who was himself the same sort of a mind writ large)—while I do believe that the modern reconception of Materialism has done a wholesome thing in pricking the bubble of such conceit and restoring man and his "soul" to its "place in nature," I nevertheless believe that to this also there is a limit; and that the absolute sway of Matter is quite as mischievous an error as the unrelated nature of Mind; even that in its direct action upon personal conduct, it has the more ill effect of the two. For if the doctrine of free will has raised up fanatics and persecutors, who assuming that men may be good under all conditions if they merely wish to be so, have sought to persuade other men's wills with threats, fines, imprisonments, torture, the spike, the wheel, the axe, the fagot, in order to make them good and save them against their obdurate wills; if the doctrine of Spiritualism, the soul supreme, has done this, the doctrine of Materialistic Determinism has produced shifting, self-excusing, worthless, parasitical characters, who are *this* now and *that* at some other time, and anything and nothing upon principle. "My conditions have made me so," they cry, and there is no more to be said; poor mirror ghosts! how could they help it! To be sure, the influence of such a character rarely reaches as far as that of the principled persecutor; but for every one of the latter there are a hundred of these easy, doughy characters, who will fit any baking tin, to whom determinist self-excusing appeals; so the balance of evil between the two doctrines is *about* maintained.

What we need is a true appraisement of the power and *rôle* of the Idea. I do not think I am able to give such a true appraisement: I do not think that any one—even *much* greater intellects than mine—will be able to do it for a long time to come. But I am at least able to suggest it, to show its necessity, to give a rude approximation of it.

And first, against the accepted formula of modern Materialism, "Men are what circumstances make them," I set the opposing declaration, "Circumstances are what men make them"; and I contend that both these things are true up to the point where the combating powers are equalized, or one is overthrown. In other words, my conception of mind, or character, is not that it is a powerless reflection of a momentary condition of stuff and form, but an active modifying agent, reacting on its environment and transforming circumstances sometimes slightly, sometimes greatly, sometimes, though not often, entirely.

All over the kingdom of life, I have said, one may see dominant ideas working, if one but trains his eyes to look for them and recognize them. In the human world there have been many dominant ideas. I cannot conceive that ever, at any time, the struggle of the body before dissolution can have been aught but agony. If the reasoning that insecurity of conditions, the expectation of suffering are circumstances which make the soul of man uneasy, shrinking, timid, what answer will you give to the challenge of old Ragnar Lodbrog, to that triumphant death song hurled out not by one cast to his death in the heat of battle, but under slow prison torture, bitten by serpents, and yet singing: "The goddesses of death invite me away—now end I my song. The hours of my life are run out. I shall smile when I die"? Nor can it be said that this is an exceptional instance, not to be accounted for by the usual operation of general law, for old King Lodbrog the Skalder did only what his fathers did, and his sons and his friends and his enemies, through long generations; they set the force of a dominant idea, the idea of the superascendant ego, against the force of torture and of death, ending life as they wished to end it, with a smile on their lips. But a few years ago, did we not read how the helpless Kaffirs, victimized by the English for the contumacy of the Boers, having been forced to dig the trenches wherein for pleasant sport they were to be shot, were lined up on the edge, and seeing death facing them, began to chant barbaric strains of triumph, smiling as they fell? Let us admit that such exultant defiance was owing to ignorance, to primitive beliefs in gods and hereafters; but let us admit also that it shows the power of an idea dominant.

Everywhere in the shells of dead societies, as in the shells of the seaslime, we shall see the force of purposive action, of intent *within* holding its purpose against obstacles *without*.

I think there is no one in the world who can look upon the steadfast, far-staring face of an Egyptian carving, or read a description of Egypt's monuments, or gaze upon the mummied clay of its old dead men without feeling that the dominant idea of that people in that age was to be enduring and to work enduring things, with the immobility of their great still sky upon them and the stare of the desert in them. One must feel that whatever other ideas animated them, and expressed themselves in their lives, this was the dominant idea. *That which was* must remain, no matter at what cost, even if it were to break the everlasting hills: an idea which made the live humanity, beneath it, born and nurtured in the coffins of caste, groan and writhe and gnaw its bandages till in the fullness of time it passed away: and still the granite mold of it stares with empty eyes out across the world, the stern old memory of the *Thing-that-was*.

I think no one can look upon the marbles wherein Greek genius wrought the figuring of its soul without feeling an apprehension that the things are going to leap and fly; that in a moment one is like to be set upon by heroes with spears in their hands, by serpents that will coil around him; to be trodden by horses that may trample and flee; to be smitten by these gods that have as little of the idea of stone in them as a dragonfly, one instant poised upon a wind-swayed petal edge. I think no one can look upon them without realizing at once that those figures came out of the boil of life; they seem like rising bubbles about to float into the air, but beneath them other bubbles rising, and others, and others—there will be no end of it. When one's eyes are upon one group, one feels that behind one, perhaps, a figure is uptoeing to seize the darts of the air and hurl them on one's head; one must keep whirling to face the miracle that appears about to be wrought— stone leaping! And this though nearly every one is minus some of the glory the old Greek wrought into it so long ago; even the broken stumps of arms and legs live. And the dominant idea is Activity, and the beauty and strength of it. Change, swift, ever-circling Change! The making of things and the casting of them away, as children cast away their toys, not interested that these shall endure, so that they themselves realize incessant activity. Full of creative power, what matter if the creature perished. So there was an endless procession of changing shapes in their schools, their philosophies, their dramas, their poems, till at last it wore itself to death. And the marvel passed away from the world. But still their marbles live to show what manner of thoughts dominated them.

And if we wish to know what master thought ruled the lives of men when the mediæval period had had time to ripen it, one has only at this day to stray into some quaint, out-of-the-way English village, where a strong old towered Church yet stands in the midst of little straw-thatched cottages, like a brooding mother hen surrounded by her chickens. Everywhere the greatening of God, and the lessening of Man: the Church so looming, the home so little. The search for the spirit, for the *enduring* thing (not the poor endurance of granite, which in the ages crumbles, but the eternal), the eternal—and contempt for the body which perishes, manifest in studied uncleanliness, in mortifications of the flesh, as if the spirit should have spat its scorn upon it.

Such was the dominant idea of that Middle Age which has been too much cursed by modernists. For the men who built the castles and the cathedrals were men of mighty works, though they made no books, and though their souls spread crippled wings, because of their very endeavors to soar too high. The spirit of voluntary subordination for the accomplishment of a great work, which proclaimed the aspiration of the common soul, that was the spirit wrought into the cathedral stones; and it is not wholly to be condemned.

In waking dream, when the shadow shapes of world ideas swim before the vision, one sees the Middle-Age Soul an ill-contorted, half-formless thing, with dragon wings and a great, dark, tense face, strained sunward with blind eyes.

If now we look around us to see what idea dominates our own civilization, I do not know that it is even as attractive as this piteous monster of the old darkness. The relativity of things has altered: Man has risen, and God has descended. The modern village has better homes and less pretentious churches. Also the conception of dirt and disease as much-sought afflictions, the patient suffering of which is a meet offering to win God's pardon, has given place to the emphatic promulgation of cleanliness. We have public school nurses notifying parents that "pediculosis capitis" is a very contagious and unpleasant disease; we have cancer associations gathering up such cancers as have attached themselves to impecunious persons and carefully experimenting with a view to cleaning them out of the human race; we have tuberculosis societies attempting the Herculean labor of clearing the Augean stables of our modern factories of the deadly bacillus, and they have got as far as spittoons with water in them in some factories; and others, and others, and others, which while not yet overwhelmingly successful in their avowed purposes are evidence sufficient that humanity no longer seeks dirt as a means of grace. We laugh at those old superstitions and talk much about exact experimental knowledge. We endeavor to galvanize the Greek corpse and pretend that we enjoy physical culture. We dabble in many things; but the one great real idea of our age, not copied from any other, not pretended, not raised to life by any conjuration, is the Much Making of Things—not the making of beautiful things, not the joy of spending living energy in creative work; rather the shameless, merciless driving and overdriving, wasting and draining of the last bit of energy, only to produce heaps and heaps of things—things ugly, things harmful, things useless, and at the best largely unnecessary. To what end are they produced? Mostly the producer does not know; still less does he care. But he is possessed with the idea that he *must* do it, everyone is doing it, and every year the making of things goes on more and faster; there are mountain ranges of things made and making, and still men go about desperately seeking to increase the list of created things, to start fresh heaps and to add to the existing heaps. And with what agony of body, under what stress and strain of danger and fear of danger, with what mutilations and maimings and lamings they struggle on, dashing themselves out against these rocks of wealth! Verily, if the vision of the Mediæval Soul is painful in its blind staring and pathetic striving, grotesque in its senseless tortures, the Soul of the Modern is most amazing with its restless, nervous eyes, ever searching the corners of the universe, its restless, nervous hands ever reaching and grasping for some useless toil.

And certainly the presence of things in abundance, things empty and things vulgar and things absurd, as well as things convenient and useful, has produced the desire for the possession of things, the exaltation of the possession of things. Go through the business street of any city, where the tilted edges of the strata of things are exposed to gaze, and look at the faces of the people as they pass—not at the hungry and smitten ones who fringe the sidewalks and plain dolefully for alms, but at the crowd—and see what idea is written on their faces. On those of the women, from the ladies of the horse shows to the shop girls out of the factory, there is a sickening vanity, a consciousness of their clothes, as of some jackdaw in borrowed feathers. Look for the pride and glory of the free, strong, beautiful body, lithe-moving and powerful. You will not see it. You will see mincing steps, bodies tilted to show the cut of a skirt, simpering, smirking faces, with eyes cast about seeking admiration for the gigantic bow of ribbon in the overdressed hair. In the caustic words of an acquaintance, to whom I once said, as we walked, "Look at the amount of vanity on all these women's faces," "No: look at the little bit of womanhood showing out of all that vanity!"

And on the faces of the men, coarseness! Coarse desires for coarse things, and lots of them: the stamp is set so unmistakably that "the wayfarer though a fool need not err therein." Even the frightful anxiety and restlessness begotten of the creation of all this are less distasteful than the abominable expression of lust for the things created.

Such is the dominant idea of the Western world, at least in these our days. You may see it wherever you look, impressed plainly on things and on men; very like if you look in the glass, you will see it there. And if some archæologist of a long future shall some day unbury the bones of our civilization, where ashes or flood shall have entombed it, he will see this frightful idea stamped on the factory walls he shall uncover, with their rows and rows of square lightholes, their tons upon tons of toothed steel, grinning out of the skull of this our life; its acres of silk and velvet, its square miles of tinsel and shoddy. No glorious marbles of nymphs and fawns, whose dead images are yet so sweet that one might wish to kiss them still; no majestic figures of winged horses, with men's faces and lions' paws casting their colossal symbolism in a mighty spell forward upon Time, as those old stone chimeras of Babylon yet do; but meaningless iron giants, of wheels and teeth, whose secret is forgotten, but whose business was to grind men up and spit them out as housefuls of woven stuffs, bazaars of trash, where-through other men might wade. The statues he shall find will bear no trace of mythic dream or mystic symbol; they will be statues of merchants and ironmasters and militiamen, in tailored coats and pantaloons and proper hats and shoes.

But the dominant idea of the age and land does not necessarily mean the dominant idea of any single life. I doubt not that in those long-gone days, far away by the banks of the still Nile, in the abiding shadow of the pyramids, under the heavy burden of other men's stolidity, there went to and fro restless, active, rebel souls who hated all that the ancient society stood for and with burning hearts sought to overthrow it.

I am sure that in the midst of all the agile Greek intellect created, there were those who went about with downbent eyes, caring nothing for it all, seeking some higher revelation, willing to abandon the joys of life, so that they drew near to some distant, unknown perfection their fellows knew not of. I am certain that in the Dark Ages, when most men prayed and cowered, and beat and bruised themselves, and sought afflictions, like that St. Teresa who said, "Let me suffer, or die," there were some, many, who looked on the world as a chance jest, who despised or pitied their ignorant comrades, and tried to compel the answers of the universe to their questionings, by the patient, quiet searching which came to be Modern Science. I am sure there were hundreds, thousands of them, of whom we have never heard.

And now, today, though the Society about us is dominated by Thing-Worship, and will stand so marked for all time, that is no reason any single soul should be. Because the one thing seemingly worth doing to my neighbor, to all my neighbors, is to pursue dollars, that is no reason I should pursue dollars. Because my neighbors conceive they need an inordinate heap of carpets, furniture, clocks, china, glass, tapestries, mirrors, clothes, jewels—and servants to care for them, and detectives to keep an eye on the servants, judges to try the thieves, and politicians to appoint the judges, jails to punish the culprits, and wardens to watch in the jails, and tax collectors to gather support for the wardens, and fees for the tax collectors, and strong houses to hold the fees, so that none but the guardians thereof can make off with it—and therefore, to keep this host of parasites, need other men to work for them and make the fees; because my neighbors want all this, is that any reason I should devote myself to such a barren folly? and bow my neck to serve to keep up the gaudy show?

Must we, because the Middle Age was dark and blind and brutal, throw away the one good thing it wrought into the fiber of Man, that the inside of a human being was worth more than the outside? that to conceive a higher thing than oneself and live toward that is the only way of living worthily? The goal strived for should, and must, be a very different one from that which led the mediæval fanatics to despise the body and belabor it with hourly crucifixions. But one can recognize the claims and the importance of the body without therefore sacrificing truth, honor, simplicity, and faith to the vulgar gauds of body service, whose very decorations debase the thing they might be supposed to exalt.

I have said before that the doctrine that men are nothing and circumstances all has been and is the bane of our modern social reform movements.

Our youth, themselves animated by the spirit of the old teachers who believed in the supremacy of ideas, even in the very hour of throwing away that teaching, look with burning eyes to the social East and believe that wonders of revolution are soon to be accomplished. In their enthusiasm they foreread the gospel of Circumstances to mean that very soon the pressure of material development must break down the social system—they give the rotten thing but a few years to last, and then they themselves shall witness the transformation, partake in its joys. The few years pass away and nothing happens; enthusiasm cools. Behold these same idealists then, successful businessmen, professionals, property owners, moneylenders, creeping into the social ranks they once despised, pitifully, contemptibly, at the skirts of some impecunious personage to whom they have lent money, or done some professional service gratis; behold them lying, cheating, tricking, flattering, buying and selling themselves for any frippery, any cheap little pretense. The Dominant Social Idea has seized them, their lives are swallowed up in it; and when you ask the reason why, they tell you that Circumstances compelled them so to do. If you quote their lies to them, they smile with calm complacency, assure you that when Circumstances demand lies, lies are a great deal better than truth; that tricks are sometimes more effective than honest dealing; that flattering and duping do not matter, if the end to be attained is desirable; and that under existing "Circumstances" life isn't possible without all this; that it is going to be possible whenever Circumstances have made truth-telling easier than lying, but till then a man must look out for himself by all means. And so the cancer goes on rotting away the moral fiber, and the man becomes a lump, a squash, a piece of slippery slime, taking all shapes and losing all shapes, according to what particular hole or corner he wishes to glide into—a disgusting embodiment of the moral bankruptcy begotten by Thing-Worship.

Had he been dominated by a less material conception of life, had his will not been rotted by the intellectual reasoning of it out of its existence, by its acceptance of its own nothingness, the unselfish aspirations of his earlier years would have grown and strengthened by exercise and habit; and his protest against the time might have been enduringly written, and to some purpose.

Will it be said that the Pilgrim fathers did not hew out of the New England ice and granite the idea which gathered them together out of their scattered and obscure English villages, and drove them in their frail ships over the Atlantic in midwinter, to cut their way against all opposing forces? Were they not common men, subject to the operation of common law? Will it be said that Circumstances aided them? When death, disease, hunger, and cold had done their worst, not one of those remaining was willing by an *easy lie* to return to material comfort and the possibility of long days.

Had our modern social revolutionists the vigorous and undaunted conception of their own powers that these had, our social movements would not be such pitiful abortions—core-rotten even before the outward flecks appear.

"Give a labor leader a political job, and the system becomes all right," laugh our enemies; and they point mockingly to Terence Powderly and his like; and they quote John Burns, who as soon as *he* went into Parliament declared: "The time of the agitator is past; the time of the legislator has come." "Let an Anarchist marry an heiress, and the country is safe," they sneer—and they have the right to sneer. But would they have that right, could they have it, if our lives were not in the first instance dominated by more insistent desires than those we would fain have others think we hold most dear?

It is the old story: "Aim at the stars, and you may hit the top of the gatepost; but aim at the ground and you will hit the ground."

It is not to be supposed that anyone will attain to the full realization of what he purposes, even when those purposes do not involve united action with others; he *will* fall short; he will in some measure be overcome by contending or inert opposition. But something he will attain, if he continues to aim high.

What, then, would I have? you ask. I would have men invest themselves with the dignity of an aim higher than the chase for wealth; choose a thing to do in life outside of the making of things, and keep it in mind—not for a day, nor a year, but for a lifetime. And then keep faith with themselves! Not be a light-o'-love, today professing this and tomorrow that, and easily reading oneself out of both whenever it becomes convenient; not advocating a thing today and tomorrow kissing its enemies' sleeve, with that weak, coward cry in the mouth, "Circumstances make me." Take a good look into yourself, and if you love Things and the power and the plenitude of Things better than you love your own dignity, human dignity, Oh say so, say so. Say it to yourself and abide by it. But do not blow hot and cold in one breath. Do not try to be a social reformer and a respected possessor of Things at the same time. Do not preach the straight and narrow way while going joyously upon the wide one. *Preach the wide one,* or do not preach at all; but do not fool yourself by saying you would like to help usher in a free society, but you cannot sacrifice an armchair for it. Say honestly, "I love armchairs better than free men, and pursue them because I choose; not because circumstances make me. I love hats, large, large hats, with many feathers and great bows; and I would rather have those hats than trouble myself about social dreams that will never be accomplished in my day. The world worships hats, and I wish to worship with them."

But if you choose the liberty and pride and strength of the single soul and the free fraternization of men as the purpose which your life is to make manifest, then do not sell it for tinsel. Think that your soul is strong and will hold its way, and slowly, through bitter struggle perhaps, the strength will grow. And the foregoing of possessions for which others barter the last possibility of freedom will become easy.

At the end of life you may close your eyes saying: "I have not been dominated by the Dominant Idea of my Age; I have chosen mine own allegiance, and served it. I have proved by a lifetime that there is that in man which saves him from the absolute tyranny of Circumstance, which in the end conquers and remolds Circumstance, the immortal fire of Individual Will, which is the salvation of the Future."

Let us have Men, Men who will say a word to their souls and keep it— keep it not when it is easy, but keep it when it is hard—keep it when the storm roars and there is a white-streaked sky and blue thunder before, and one's eyes are blinded and one's ears deafened with the war of opposing things; and keep it under the long leaden sky and the gray dreariness that never lifts. Hold unto the last: that is what it means to have a Dominant Idea, which Circumstance cannot break. And such men make and unmake Circumstance.

VOL. V, NO. 4, JUNE 1910

Martin Eden

By Hippolyte Havel

In his review of Jack London's largely autobiographical novel, *Martin Eden* (New York: Macmillan, 1909), Hippolyte Havel was all praise. London's relations with anarchism, however, were complex. Emma Goldman, for example, held him personally in high regard and greatly admired his realist fiction, calling *Martin Eden* "splendid"; yet at the same time, she considered him to be a "mechanical, bell-button socialist." London sat on the Advisory Board of the Ferrer Association and even contributed an introduction to Alexander Berkman's *Prison Memoirs of an Anarchist*. Berkman and Goldman, though, refused to print the introduction, which was written from a socialist stance they deemed inappropriate for so profoundly anarchist a work.

OUR AGE IS SYMBOLIZED BY THE PRINTED WORD. A veritable deluge of printed paper overwhelms us daily. The veriest witch sabbath celebrates its orgies on the book mart, and we are in danger of being suffocated by this literary high tide. The mind of the conscientious critic simply staggers beneath this oppressive burden. Where is the intellectual able to keep abreast of all this output in five or six modern languages? It fills one with weariness and disgust—disgust at the thousand and one papers, magazines, brochures, and books, at the interminable printed rubbish, the famous and infamous dime literature of literary vanity and commercialism.

Notwithstanding, one must read. Reading has become a part of our life, and I feel a certain mistrust towards people who do not read, a mistrust of their intellect, their depth and love. Books aid us to draw closer the lines separating man and man; they bring us nearer to the suffering, the disappointments and disillusions of our fellow beings; they are the bridges of human souls. There are days when one's heart just cries out for a book; a book that moves one to his depths, one in which the melodies of the heart find an answering echo, a book to live over again life's experiences; a book, in short, standing out from the literary rubbish heap, filling us with deep joy and forming new values.

Such a book Jack London has given us in *Martin Eden* (Macmillan Co., New York), a book of affecting tragedy and power.

Most men are inexpressibly distant and strange to each other. The soul, mirrored so clearly in the child's eyes, is soon hidden by fear, shame, and pride, and remains buried beneath the weight of its armor. Occasionally emboldened to show itself, it quickly shrinks back in affright, terrified by the suffocating air of conventionality, brutality, indifference, and lack of understanding.

The whole process of man's evolution consists in the struggle against this very conventionality and brutality, which in truth are synonymous. Conventionality and respectability are the means society employs to disguise the souls' differentiations and particular needs, endeavoring to cast them into molds of uniformity, that is, to level them to the insignificance of ciphers, for only thus similarity is possible. In this manner society paralyzes all upward striving, energy, and independence, robbing individuality of its best elements.

Yet, all these efforts are not entirely successful. At all times there have been souls who prized their independence so highly as to suffer everything for its sake. Such a nature London portrays in Martin Eden.

Martin Eden is an individuality which stands outside its environment, yet continually and ineffectually striving to touch the soul strings of that environment. A stranger to every one about him, Eden is known only to himself. The flight of his soul is on intimate heights, his language vibrates particular tones, his sympathies are full of distinctive nuances, and these mask him from those about him in spite of the candidness of his motives. The lack of understanding is the rock on which Martin Eden's soul is, must be, wrecked.

Eden is a personality which feels itself superior to formulated life, a nature affirming all that is wholesome, strong, and virile, seeking to free its creative artistic genius from all obstacles; a personality which sees in social manifestations merely the symbol of its unconscious powers. In a world of superficiality and inane incoherence such a personality must inevitably perish.

Jack London has undoubtedly portrayed much of his own life in this book. I am convinced that there is not another work in our autobiographic literature which in point of power and sincerity can compare with *Martin Eden*. It is a masterwork of psychologic perception. The characters are so vital and convincing that one almost feels himself in their actual presence, discussing the problems of life.

Martin Eden himself is a personality of tragic grandeur. The development of this character, his intellectual rise above his environment, finds no parallel in contemporary American literature. But this intimate delineation is not limited only to the central character; it is equally true of all the other characters in the work. With what a depth of appreciation and tenderness is Brissenden portrayed, the ingenious writer; Lizzie Connolly, the heart-genuine proletarian; and how clearly and pointedly Ruth Morse is drawn, the polished product of conventionality, and her bourgeois environment.

Some critics accuse Jack London of painting life in too brutal colors. What superficial criticism! London is not a writer for the matinée girl. His so-called brutality is in reality the virility of the great artist who portrays life as it actually is—too virile for a generation vitiated by a literature of mawkish sentimentality. All the works of London, true artist that he is, are characterized by a background symbolic of the New Life. His description of pity, for instance, as in the case of Gertrude Higginbotham, is not the superficial, passing, cold-hearted conventional philanthropy touched with pleasurable egotism; it is the sadness of deep-felt helplessness to lighten the heavy burden of a human soul. To some, pity is a kind of spiritual balm for their own little souls, gladdened by such expression of their high-minded generosity. I mistrust writers like Maeterlinck whose beautiful words of pity sound so profound and appear so deeply felt. They know nothing of the terrible soul anguish which such as Multatuli and Nietzsche experience.

London is by far the most virile writer in contemporary American literature. He personifies the wild beauty of the cruel, merciless, and yet magnificent life of our time, with all its disappointments, its rebellious iconoclasm, its uprising against the slavery and debasement of our existence. At a time when shrewd mediocrity gives the keynote to life, Jack London has struck a new chord, touched our innermost, and set in motion new vibrations. His distinctive quality is nobility of spirit.

VOL. VI, NO. 3, MAY 1911

The "American Sovereign"

[By Eugene O'Neill]

"The 'American Sovereign,'" unsigned, has been attributed to Eugene O'Neill (Winifred Frazer in *The Eugene O'Neill Newsletter,* May 1979), which makes the poem the playwright's first printed piece, predating his earliest published plays by three years. Although no radical activist, O'Neill was nevertheless on the periphery of the anarchist movement, which strongly influenced his work. He discovered anarchism as a college dropout in New York, attending occasional lectures and plays at the Ferrer Center and browsing in Benjamin Tucker's Unique Book Shop at 502 Sixth Avenue, where first he discovered *Mother Earth* and became an avid reader of the magazine. In time, he included among his friends Emma Goldman and Alexander Berkman as well as other members of the *Mother Earth* group, such as Hippolyte Havel, Goldman's niece Stella Comyn, Hutchins Hapgood, and Berkman's companion M. Eleanor Fitzgerald, who eventually became the manager of the Province-town Players. O'Neill corresponded with Goldman and Berkman long after their deportation in 1919, and his editor at Random House was Goldman's nephew Saxe Commins.

(With apologies to the literary executors of O. Khayyam)

INTO THE POLLING-PLACE, and why not knowing,
Nor whence, like water, willy-nilly, flowing,
  And out again, when he has made the Cross,
Back to his fruitless, ill-paid labor going.

He, in his youth, did eagerly frequent
Old party rallies, heard great argument,
   About the Robber Tariff, and the Trusts,
And came away, no wiser than he went.

With them the seed of Piffle did he sow,
In hopes of some cheap job, helped make it grow,
   And this is all the Working Class has reaped—
Their efforts help their leaders get the Dough.

VOL. VI, NO. 4, JUNE 1911

Freedom

By Lola Ridge

In her memoirs, Emma Goldman remembered Lola Ridge as "our gifted rebel poet." Ridge contributed two poems to *Mother Earth,* both intensely radical in tone, and was the first manager of the Ferrer Association. She remained a fervent activist all her life and in 1927 was arrested at the Massachusetts State House in Boston, along with many of her former Ferrer Center comrades, for demonstrating in support of the condemned anarchists Nicola Sacco and Bartolomeo Vanzetti. Ridge established a strong reputation with her first collection, *The Ghetto and Other Poems* (1918). Although no experimentalist herself, she was for a short while the editor of Alfred Kreymborg's *Others* magazine (1915–19), which counted among its contributors William Carlos Williams, Mina Loy, Wallace Stevens, Amy Lowell, and T. S. Eliot.

L ET MEN BE FREE!
All violence is but the agony
Of caged things fighting blindly for the right
To be and breathe and burn their little hour.
Bare spirits—not bedight
In smooth-set garments of philosophy;
But near earth forces, elemental, crude,
Scarce knowing their invincible, rude power;
Within the close of their primeval servitude
Half comatose.

Who, ravening for their depleted dower
Of so much sun and air and warmth and food,
And the same right to procreate and love
As the beasts have and the birds,
Strike wild—not having words
To parry with—at the cold force above.

Let men be free!
Hate is the price
Of servitude, paid covertly; and vice
But the unclean recoil of tortured flesh
Whipped through the centuries within a mesh
Spun out of priestly art.
Oh men, arise, be free!—Who breaks one bar
Of tyranny in this so bitter star
Has cleansed its bitterness in part.

VOL. VIII, NO. 12, FEBRUARY 1913

Prison Memoirs

By Bayard Boyesen

Emma Goldman, in her own memoirs, called Alexander Berkman's *Prison Memoirs of an Anarchist* (1912) "a document profoundly moving, a brilliant study of criminal psychology" and "the first great American study of a 'House of the Dead.'" It was that and more: an indictment of the brutalizing U.S. prison system; the story of an idealistic young immigrant's assimilation into the lower depths of the American working class; and a fascinating account of the waning of Russian revolutionary nihilism and the emergent anarchist movement in the United States. Yet Goldman was unable to find a publisher for the completed manuscript and had to bring it out under the imprint of the Mother Earth Publishing Association, with an introduction by Hutchins Hapgood. Bayard Boyesen, who reviewed the book for *Mother Earth,* was a former English instructor at Columbia whom Goldman had induced to leave the university to become the first director of the newly opened anarchist Ferrer School in January 1911.

IN HIS INTRODUCTION TO THE *Prison Memoirs of an Anarchist,* by Alexander Berkman, Mr. Hapgood says that he wishes "that everybody in the world would read this book," and adds, with characterictic optimism, that "the general and careful reading of it would definitely add to true civilization." Unquestionably many people will read it; but they will do so, I fear, because human beings relish the sufferings of their fellows and find fascination in watching the turns of pain. Of the broad nobility that breathes from it, of the lessons it should teach, how much will they see who spend their days in rehearsing ceremonies designed to blind themselves and in erecting institutions designed to blind their brothers?

If it serves to overcome in even a few people the prejudices they cherish it will do so not because of a careful reading or an open mind on their part, but because of the extraordinary literary power with which Mr. Berkman has presented his story. At the very beginning of the book one feels a movement, a rustle of spiritual and physical events that portends catastrophe. But in the great tragedies of literature and of life the essence of catastrophe lies in the fact that the spirit of the hero, in the final isolation of his material defeat, rises the nobler, unconquered still. So here, after the climactic deed has been accomplished, the protagonist maintains his attitude through all the years of suffering, accepts the catastrophe as a challenge, and overcomes it. If the author had been free to use his imagination only he could not have ordered the events to bring out more skillfully the spiritual significance of his deed.

These larger movements to which I have just referred, the movements of mind and emotion and spirit, are patterned with details of pathos and horror. Indeed, I know of few passages in literature more pathetic than that in which Mr. Berkman relates his meeting in jail with the Homestead striker. No one around has understood his motives; they have thought that he was concealing them or was crazy. But here at last is the man who can understand, one of the very men for whom the young Anarchist offered his life. So he explains to him. The striker says: "Some business misunderstanding, eh?"

Equally pathetic, though in a different way, are the incidents connected with the story of young Russell, whose character is the basis of some of the most beautiful passages in the book. Indeed, the characterization throughout is, if we judge from a literary viewpoint, the most remarkable thing about these remarkable Memoirs. No one who has met Russell, Wingie, Felipe, or the rest of the people portrayed will be likely to forget them. Something has been done to them that makes them more living than living beings; an imagination has touched them and bared them to our sight. I do not mean that they have been falsified by the author, or even added to; rather, that having been understood by that sort of an imagination that can put itself to the full in the places of other people, they are presented to us with such details as will convey the significance of their traits, the reality of their characters.

But the most interesting of all the characters is that of the author himself. In portraying it the author has used a method very different from that employed for the other characters. Instead of presenting outward detail, the details of the action, he emphasizes the motives, emotional and mental states, analyzes them, and lets what I have called outward detail fall in by way of illustration. Thus the other characters serve as a background to the deepest interest of the book, the reasons and motives of a human soul.

To follow out at length these reasons and motives is not the purpose of this review. I have merely sought to point out that here, from an Anarchist, is a book of rare power and beauty, majestic in its structure, filled with the truth of imagination and the truth of actuality, emphatic in its declarations and noble in its reach.

VOL. VIII, NO. 2, APRIL 1913

My Belovèd

By Mabel Dodge

Mabel Dodge held the first of her celebrated salon evenings, in her apartment at 23 Fifth Avenue, in May 1913. Her weekly gatherings brought together the "movers and shakers" in the arts, literature, and various radical causes. One evening in early 1914 was devoted to a "conversation" between proponents of direct action (such as Big Bill Haywood of the Industrial Workers of the World and Emma Goldman with her *Mother Earth* circle) and political action (such as the socialists William English Walling and Max Eastman of *The Masses* with his circle). It was Hutchins Hapgood who had introduced Dodge to Goldman. Dodge's enigmatic poem, "To My Belovèd," was dedicated to Hapgood, though they were not in fact lovers. She explained in her memoirs: ". . . Hutch and I were growing more and more attached to each other. Hutch, because I was such a perfect listener, so entirely understanding; I, because he was such a perfect listener and so entirely understanding. We told each other everything and we talked about our souls to our hearts' content. Each of us knew what the other meant. We sorrowed over each other and felt our mutual woe. We both felt like failures from the angle of worldly success, and we were proud of it, and we considered each other to be failures— and this drew us together into a luxurious, rich companionship."

I WENT FROM THE HOUSE to seek out my belovèd.
All along in the street in the dusk I sought after him,
And soon I knew that he surely was near me
From the old immemorial thrill in my heart.

All along in the street dark shadows moved by me,
And among their dim shapes I eagerly sought him.
In my passing a blind old cripple caught at my heart,
And turning, I found in his eyes my belovèd.

VOL. VIII, NO. 2, APRIL 1913

The Brothers Karamazov

By Hippolyte Havel

In writing of the work of Fyodor Dostoyevsky, Hippolyte Havel drew
upon the full range of his erudition. So complex a writer as Dostoyevsky,
himself an erstwhile revolutionist who had spent years in Siberian exile,
could present a problem for many political radicals. In his appreciative
review of Constance Garnett's translation of *The Brothers Karamazov*
(New York: Macmillan, 1912), Havel made it clear that literature must
be judged on its own terms, and not according to predetermined criteria,
anarchist or otherwise.

OF ALL THE GREAT RUSSIAN WRITERS of the last century, none
made so deep an impression upon his contemporaries as Fyodor
Mikhailovich Dostoyevsky. His popularity was immense. When he died,
forty thousand people followed his body to the grave. Turgenev and Tolstoy
had a great influence upon the artistic life of Western Europe, but the most
intellectual men of the time were fascinated by the brilliant genius of
Dostoyevsky. He is the father of the modern psychological novel. His influence one may detect in the works of all modern writers. Nietzsche calls him

"my great master." And while the popularity of many of his contemporaries is today on the wane, Dostoyevsky's fame is spreading from year to year, and his works find ever greater appreciation and understanding. The author who in his lifetime was labeled a Russian nationalist, even the apostle of Slavophilism, is now recognized as a cosmopolitan genius, the greatest analyst of the human soul.

To the English-reading public Dostoyevsky has so far remained a sealed book. To be sure, many are acquainted with *Crime and Punishment* and the *Memoirs from a Dead House;* but only in abridged and mutilated translations. Few people in this country are familiar with Vizetelly's series of Russian authors in which appeared *Injury and Insult, The Friend of the Family, The Idiot, Poor Folks, Uncle's Dream,* and *The Permanent Husband.* Like so many foreign writers, Dostoyevsky suffers much at the hands of translators. The English rendering is far inferior to those in the German language. Some of his works have been so distorted that they read more like dime novels than like psychological masterpieces.

It is praiseworthy, therefore, on the part of the Macmillan Company to have started the publication of Dostoyevsky's novels in their entirety, and it was a wise selection of the literary editor to choose *The Brothers Karamazov* as the first of the series. The novel, translated by Constance Garnett, appears in a complete, unabridged form.

If we consider that a translation of *The Brothers Karamazov* appeared in French as early as 1887 (the German translation even earlier), we see how long it takes the English-speaking public to get acquainted with the masterpieces of the world's literature. A synopsis of the novel was made for Pavel Orleneff several years ago by Miss Isabel Hapgood, and a French dramatization, made by J. Copeau and J. Croué appeared in 1911 in *L'Illustration Théatrale,* while the play was being produced at a Paris theater. Dostoyevsky planned *The Brothers Karamazov* when he lived in exile in Dresden, in the utmost misery, poverty, and sickness. The work was never finished. Dostoyevsky intended to write a novel of five volumes, but only two were completed. In the latter half of 1880 when he worked on the novel he was, as his friend Strakhov informs us, entirely exhausted. "He lived, it was plain, solely on his nerves. His body had become so frail that the first slight blow might destroy it." Yet his mental power was untiring.

Is *The Brothers Karamazov* a great novel, a novel which can be compared with *War and Peace* or *Fathers and Sons?* Opinions of the work vary considerably. The best critics of Russian literature disgree in their estimation. K. Waliszewski in his *Russian Literature* characterizes the novel as a "most invaluable treasury of information concerning the contemporary life of Russia, moral, intellectual, and social." Dmitri Mereshkovsky, in his essays on "Tolstoy and Dostoyevsky as Artists," says that "there is no doubt that *The Brothers Karamazov* is one of the greatest creations of Dostoyevsky, unlike anything else in the world's literature, a creation that has its roots in the inmost recesses of his consciousness and of his unconsciousness."

On the other hand, Peter Kropotkin in his *Russian Literature* finds the novel "so unnatural, so much fabricated for the purpose of introducing— here a bit of morals, there some abominable character taken from a psychopathic hospital, or again in order to analyze the feelings of some purely imaginary criminal, that a few good pages scattered here and there do not compensate the reader for the hard task of reading these two volumes." Melchier de Vogüé agrees with Kropotkin. In his *Russian Novelists* he finds many parts of the work "intolerably tedious. The plot amounts to nothing but a framework upon which to hang all the author's favorite theories, and display every type of his eccentric fancy."

How can we reconcile such diverse opinions, such diametrically opposed views? Is it overvaluation or underestimation; prejudice in favor of or against the author?

To me the criterion is simply this: does the book give one new values, a new view of life, does it disturb one's soul to the utmost depth? If it succeed in accomplishing this, it is a great book. I am convinced that the brothers Karamazov are a part of every one of us; we all are more or less either an Alyosha or Dmitri, an Ivan or a Smerdyakov. The brothers Karamazov live not only in Russia, but everywhere; we find them in every country, in every station of society. Their portrayal by Dostoyevsky is true and lifelike.

In making comparison between the art of Tolstoy and that of the author of *The Brothers Karamazov,* Mereshkovsky expresses the opinion that Dostoyevsky has no rival in the art of gradual tension, accumulation, increase, and alarming concentration of dramatic power. No doubt this characterization of Dostoyevsky's art is correct. The boundless picture which is enfolded in *The Brothers Karamazov* is condensed, if we do not count the intervals between the acts, into a few days. But even in one day, in one hour, and that almost on one and the same spot, the characters of the novel pass through experiences which ordinary mortals do not taste in a lifetime. Dostoyevsky has no need to describe the appearance of his characters, for by their peculiar form of language and tone of voice they themselves depict not only their thoughts and feelings, but their faces and bodies.

When the elder Karamazov, suddenly getting quite animated, addresses his sons thus: "Ah, you boys! You children, little sucking pigs, to my thinking. . . . I never thought a woman ugly in my life—that's been my rule! Can you understand that? How could you understand it? You've milk in your veins, not blood. You're not out of your shells yet. My rule has been that you can always find something devilishly interesting in every woman that you wouldn't find in any other. Only, one must know how to find it, that's the point! That's a talent! To my mind there are no ugly women. The very fact that she is a woman is half the battle . . . but how could you understand that? Even in *vielles filles,* even in them you may discover something that makes you simply wonder that men have been such fools as to let them grow old without noticing them. Barefooted girls or unattractive ones, you must take them by surprise. Didn't you know that? You must astound them till they're fascinated, upset, ashamed that such a gentleman should fall in love with such a little slut. It's a jolly good thing that there always are and will be masters and slaves in the world, so there always will be a little maid-of-all and her master, and you know that's all that's needed for happiness." We see the heart of the old man, and also his fat, shaking Adam's apple, and his moist, thin lips; the tiny, shamelessly piercing eyes, and his whole savage figure—the figure of an old Roman of the times of the decadence. When we learn that on a packet of money, sealed and tied with ribbon, there was also written in his own hand, "To my angel Grushenka, if she will come to me," and that three days later he added, "for my little chicken," he suddenly stands before us alive. We could not explain how, or why, but we feel that in this belated "for my little chicken" we have caught some subtle, sensual wrinkle on his face. It is just that last little touch which makes the portrait so lifelike, as if the painter, going beyond the bounds of his art, had created a portrait which is ever on the point of stirring and coming out of the frame like a specter or a ghost.

The wonderful portrait of the Grand Inquisitor will ever live in the world's literature. What a portrait!—Jesus appears again on earth at the time when heretics are daily being burned at the stake; he is recognized by the people—a deep offence to the Grand Inquisitor, who has Jesus arrested and brought before him. The admonition the Grand Inquisitor gives to Jesus is penetrating. Why has he come back to disturb the peace and the rule of the Church? "It is Thou? Thou? Don't answer, be silent. What canst Thou say, indeed? I know too well what Thou wouldst say. And Thou hast no right to add anything to what Thou hadst said of old. Why, then, art Thou come to hinder us? For Thou hast come to hinder us, and Thou knowest that. But dost Thou know what will be tomorrow? I know not who Thou art and care not to know whether it is Thou or only a semblance of Him, but tomorrow I shall condemn Thee and burn Thee at the stake as the worst of heretics. And the very people who have today kissed Thy feet, tomorrow at the faintest sign from me will rush to heap up the embers of Thy fire. Knowest Thou that?" The whole monologue of the Grand Inquisitor should be reprinted for the edification of the Church.

After all, the question whether *The Brothers Karamazov* is a masterpiece or whether it belongs to morbid literature stands and falls with the attitude one takes toward Dostoyevsky himself, his life and his philosophy. Estimates of *The Brothers Karamazov* differ as fundamentally as opinions concerning Dostoyevsky. Neither the judgment of the Englishman A. T. Lloyd, or of the German Julius Bierbaum, of the Frenchman André Gide, or the valuation of that universal connoisseur of literature, George Brandes—not to speak of the Russian critics—will help one to form a true estimate of Dostoyevsky. The problem is the same as with Schopenhauer. Those who understand and accept Schopenhauer will also understand and accept Dostoyevsky. To be sure, it would be as inappropriate to compare the political views of Schopenhauer with those of a Metternich as to draw a parallel between the philosophy of Dostoyevsky with the opinions of the Slavophiles Shcherbatov, Kireyevsky, Tchomykov, or the brothers Aksakov.

Dostoyevsky was considered a nationalist in the narrowest and most anti-European sense; in reality he was a cosmopolitan in the broadest conception. Throughout his life he preserved his feeling for universal culture ("omni-human" culture, he called it), the capacity to feel at home everywhere, to live the vital ideas of all ages and peoples. True, he believed the Russian genius to be more universal in its assimilative capacity and therefore superior to the genius of other nations, but in this respect Mereshkovsky says, "He, being next to Pushkin, the most Russian of Russian authors, was at the same time the greatest of our cosmopolitans."

Primarily he was, as no other writer before or since, the poet of the humiliated and the oppressed. He knew the people, felt and suffered with them. In his essay on the bourgeoisie, wherein he flays the superficial rationalism and the false sentiments of the middle class, he writes: "The theorists, burying themselves in their doctrinaire wisdom, not only fail to understand the people, but even despise them; not, be it understood, with evil intention, but almost instinctively. We are convinced that even the most intelligent among them believes that when occasion offered he would only have to talk ten minutes with the people in order to understand them thoroughly, while the people might probably not even be listening to what he was talking about."

Born in poverty, he died in poverty. The spirit of ownership, of detachment from the great mass of one's fellows seemed to Dostoyevsky the supreme sin. In his material and mental suffering he reminds one of another great analyst of the human soul, the Dutch writer Douwers Dekker-Multatuli.

1. Portrait of Emma Goldman by the Gerhard Sisters, St. Louis, 1912

Alexander Berkman

2. Alexander Berkman, frontispiece for *Prison Memoirs of an Anarchist*, 1912

3. Ben L. Reitman with Anna Baron in the *Mother Earth* office,
20 East 125th Street, *c.* 1916

4. Cover for the first issue of
Mother Earth, March 1906

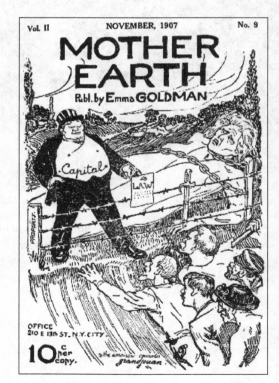

5. Cover for *Mother Earth* by Jules-Félix
Grandjouan, November 1907

6. Cover for *Mother Earth*,
memorial drawing of Francisco
Ferrer, November 1909

7. Cover for *Mother Earth*,
"San Diego Edition," June 1912

MOTHER EARTH

Vol. VII.   JULY, 1912   No. 5

VOLTAIRINE DE CLEYRE

8. Cover for *Mother Earth,* memorial
photograph of Voltairine de Cleyre, July 1912

MO
EA

K
J

C
A
HA
B

Vol. IX

MOTHER EARTH

Vol. VII.   ·DECEMBER, 1912   No. 10

PETER KROPOTKIN
Born December 9, 1842

9. Cover for *Mother Earth,* photograph
of Peter Kropotkin, December 1912

No. 5

10. Cover for *Mother Earth*
by Adolf Wolff, drawing of
his urn for those killed in the
July 4th Lexington Avenue
explosion, July 1914

11. Cover for *Mother Earth*
by Man Ray, August 1914

12. Cover for *Mother Earth* by
Man Ray, September 1914

13. Cover for *Mother Earth* by Robert Minor, "Billy Sunday Tango," May 1915

14. Cover for *Mother Earth*, marking the introduction of military conscription, June 1917

VOL. IX, NO. 1, MARCH 1914

The Feast of Belshazzar

By Voltairine de Cleyre

Among the regular contributors to *Mother Earth,* Voltairine de Cleyre was perhaps the most versatile, an accomplished poet as well as an essayist, short-story writer, and translator. A book of her early poems, *The Worm Turns,* was published in 1900. De Cleyre's work continued to appear in *Mother Earth* after her death in 1912. "The Feast of Belshazzar," drawn from the prophetic Book of Daniel, provided an especially apt image of complacent riches in contrast to her revolutionary asceticism.

HARK! LOW DOWN YOU WILL HEAR
    The storm in the underground!
Listen, Tyrants, and fear!
Quake at that muffled sound!

"Heavens, that mocked our dust,
Smile on, in your pitiless blue!
Silent as you are to us,
So silent are we to you!

"Churches that scourged our brains!
Priests that locked fast our hands!
We planted the torch in your chains:
Now gather the burning brands!

"States that have given us LAW,
When we asked for THE RIGHT TO EARN BREAD!

The Sword that Damocles saw
By a hair swings over your head!

"What ye have sown ye shall reap:
Teardrops, and Blood, and Hate,
Gaunt gather before your Seat,
And knock at your palace gate!

"There are murderers on your Thrones!
There are thieves in your Justice halls!
White Leprosy cancers their stones,
And gnaws at their worm-eaten walls!

"And the Hand of Belshazzar's Feast
Writes over, in flaming light,
Thought's Kingdom no more to the Priest;
Nor the Law of Right unto Might."

VOL. IX, NO. 5, JULY 1914

To Our Martyred Dead

by Adolf Wolff

The July 1914 issue of *Mother Earth* was a memorial to Arthur Caron, Carl Hanson, and Charles Berg, the three young anarchists who died in the July 4th Lexington Avenue explosion while preparing a bomb presumably intended for the Rockefeller estate in Tarrytown, New York (see Charles Robert Plunkett, "Dynamite!" page 75). On the magazine's cover was a drawing by the sculptor Adolf Wolff of the bronze urn he made for the men's ashes, shaped like a pyramid and topped with a fist clenched in the revolutionary salute (see Illustration 10, following page 220). Wolff's poem "To Our Martyred Dead" was the issue's lead piece.

Wolff, an immigrant from Belgium, was among the more fervent anarchist artists associated with the Ferrer Center, where he taught a children's art class at the Modern School. As a poet, he composed strong, impassioned polemics that were well regarded. His first book, *Songs, Sighs, and Curses,* was published as the inaugural issue of Alfred Kreymborg's magazine *The Glebe* (September 1913). The Boni brothers, Albert and Charles, brought out his second collection in 1914, *Songs of Rebellion, Songs of Life, Songs of Love.* He broke violently with the *Mother Earth* group and anarchism after America's entry into World War I, turning rabidly prowar and, in the course of time, becoming a member of the John Reed Club and a Communist sympathizer.

Arthur Caron, Charles Berg, and Carl Hanson

THE MAMMOTH BEAST WHOSE NAME IS IGNORANCE
And all its brood of venom-spitting cubs
In chorus hiss and howl their hellish glee
Over the death of our martyred comrades.

But in this world can greater glory be
Than to be hated by the powers of darkness?
To be misunderstood and crucified
Has ever been the fate of those who fought
The fight of light against the powers of darkness.

Ye hordes of knaves and fools, the day will come
When your descendants, shamed to call you sires,
Will raise a monument unto these men
Over whose torn remains you sneering gloat.

VOL. IX, NO. 8, OCTOBER 1914

Voltairine de Cleyre's Posthumous Book

By Leonard D. Abbott

For Alexander Berkman, editing Voltairine de Cleyre's posthumous *Selected Works* was a labor of love. The 500-page book, with a biographical sketch by Hippolyte Havel, was brought out in 1914 by the Mother Earth Publishing Association, two years after her death. A full-page advertisement in the magazine's issue for February 1914 read: "This volume of America's foremost literary rebel and Anarchist propagandist contains a choice selection of her poems, essays, sociological discourses, sketches and stories, which have proved a source of great inspiration to the revolutionary movement during the last twenty years."

THERE IS A FAMOUS PAINTING WHICH shows the Statue of Liberty looming up through the mists of New York Harbor. At the base of the statue ships are concealed by a fog. In the background, the skyscrapers of the metropolis are stained by a heavy and unwholesome atmosphere. The only sunlight in the picture falls on the head and the uplifted torch of the woman-symbol of Liberty. She is rising triumphant over commercialism, and her torch is strong and steadfast.

It is in some such way as this that I think of Voltairine de Cleyre, whose posthumous book (published by the Mother Earth Publishing Association) may be accurately termed an Anarchist classic. Voltairine de Cleyre was preëminently the standard-bearer of a libertarian gospel, and she struggled through every kind of conflict and poverty and sickness into a kind of sunlit immortality.

There are few, if any, books in the literature of Anarchism as lofty as these *Selected Works*. I have read Kropotkin and Elisée Reclus, and I know something of the writings of Bakunin and Proudhon and Stirner and Nietzsche and Tolstoy and Benjamin Tucker. But Voltairine de Cleyre stands alone. She has the individuality that only very great writers possess.

This book is divided by its editor, Alexander Berkman, into three sections—poetry, essays, and sketches and stories—and is prefaced by a biographical introduction from the pen of Hippolyte Havel. The introduction is not as inspired as the one that Havel wrote for Emma Goldman's *"Anarchism,"* but it is satisfactory as far as it goes. The poems cover seventy-five pages. They are remarkable for several reasons. I will confess that my first impression of this poetry, as a whole, was in the nature of a disappointment. We have heard much of the heights and depths of genius, and both are represented here. The really great poems of the collection were almost all printed, years ago, in a little pamphlet entitled *The Worm Turns,* and they are almost without exception poems of vengeance. They were born of the stormy period in which the Chicago Anarchists, Angiolillo, Vaillant, Henry, and Caserio died. They are crimson and black; they quiver with hatred; and I call them great because their expression is superb and their dramatic appeal is undeniable. But alongside of these historic poems, and others, such as "The Gods and the People" and "The Suicide's Defense," that are almost as great, appear a group that I can only call banal and that are of value merely because they trace moods and struggles in a soul's development. Think of Voltairine de Cleyre writing a Christian Science hymn! Yet she did it. And think of Voltairine de Cleyre writing "The Christian's Faith" and such lines as:

There's a love supreme in the great hereafter,
  The buds of earth are blooms in heaven;
The smiles of the world are ripples of laughter
  When back to its Aidenn the soul is given.

An immense gulf stretches between such sentiments as these and the uncompromising radicalism of the essays that follow. Voltairine de Cleyre's prose is a joy to read; it is so sincere, so clear, so simple, yet withal so warm and eloquent. She keeps to the main facts. She possesses, in a supreme degree, the faculty of separating the essential from the nonessential. Her note is American, yet she makes a universal appeal. This is not the first time that the statement of universal principles in distinctly national terms has been an important factor in creating the international fame of a writer.

Take the essay, "Anarchism and American Traditions." This is a memorable exposition of the truth that the spirit of Anarchism, so far from being a foreign importation, is rooted in our very soil. Voltairine de Cleyre bases Anarchism here in the colonization period of one hundred and seventy years from the settling of Jamestown to the outburst of the Revolution. She names as fundamental likeness between the Revolutionary Republicans and the Anarchists the recognition that the little must precede the great; that the local must be the basis of the general; that there can be a free federation only when there are free communities to federate. She reminds us that Thomas Jefferson, the author of the Declaration of Independence, declined a re-election to Congress in order to return to Virginia and do his work in his own local assembly, and that he said: "Let the general government be reduced to foreign concerns only, and let our affairs be disentangled from those of all other nations, except as to commerce, which the merchants will manage the better the more they are left free to manage for themselves, and the general government may be reduced to a very simple organization, and a very inexpensive one; a few plain duties to be performed by a few servants." And she also reminds us that that same formulator of our libertarian national charter wrote: "God forbid that we should ever be twenty years without a rebellion! . . . What country can preserve its liberties if its rulers are not warned from time to time that the people preserve the spirit of resistance? Let them take up arms. . . . The tree of liberty must be refreshed from time to time with the blood of patriots and tyrants. It is its natural manure."

"The Dominant Idea" and "Direct Action" are two of the strongest essays I know—as notable for their diction as for their arguments. "Crime and Punishment," in addition to its humanitarian thesis, conveys in its opening sentences an idea that Voltairine de Cleyre was fond of repeating and decorating—the idea, namely, that men are of three sorts: the "turn backs" (or conservatives), the "rush aheads" (or radicals), and the indifferents. Most people, she says, belong to the first and third types, yet "it is the radical who always wins at last." Noteworthy tributes may be found in these pages to three American contemporaries of Voltairine de Cleyre— Emma Goldman, Moses Harman, and Dyer D. Lum. Lum was Voltairine's teacher, confidant, and comrade. One of his favorite sayings was: "Events are the true schoolmasters." Voltairine de Cleyre, in speaking of his instinctive modesty, makes a remark that might be applied to herself: "The devotee of a cause is never the devotee of self." The Paris Commune and the Mexican Revolution are the subjects of masterly studies, while essays on Francisco Ferrer and on modern educational reform may be recommended to the careful attention of those who are trying to build up libertarian schools in America.

One of the most valuable features of the book is its clear definition, in several essays, of the meaning of Anarchism. Voltairine de Cleyre calls herself an Individualist-Anarchist, but she speaks of at least three other possible schools of Anarchism—namely, Anarchist Mutualists, Anarchist

Communists, and Anarchist Socialists. It would take too much space to explain in detail in this article her conception of these different schools. Suffice it to say that the point of agreement in all is: *no compulsion.* "For myself," she remarks, "I believe that all these and many more could be advantageously tried in different localities; I would see the instincts and habits of the people express themselves in a free choice in every community; and I am sure that distinct environments would call out distinct adaptations." She adds: "My ideal would be a condition in which all natural resources would be forever free to all, and the worker individually able to produce for himself sufficient for all his vital needs, if he so chose, so that he need not govern his working or not working by the times and seasons of his fellows. I think that time may come; but it will only be through the development of the modes of production and the taste of the people." Voltairine de Cleyre is as tolerant in her choice of methods as in her presentation of ideals. She speaks of nonresistance and of violent rebellion as both necessary, each in its time and place. She sees value in organization, education, agitation, and assassination. "Ask a method? Do you ask Spring her method? Which is more necessary, the sunshine or the rain? They are contradictory—yes; they destroy each other—yes, but from this destruction the flowers result. Each choose that method which expresses your selfhood best, and condemn no other man because he expresses his self otherwise."

In Voltairine de Cleyre's writings I find brain and emotion often at war. Like every great nature, she saw all around a subject, and her very breadth of view makes her seem inconsistent. She hesitates between love and hatred, and she exclaims: "No man is in himself a unit, and in every soul Jove still makes war with Christ." In 1902 she went so far as to say: "The spread of Tolstoy's *War and Peace* and *The Slavery of Our Times,* and the growth of the numerous Tolstoy clubs having for their purpose the dissemination of the literature of nonresistance, is an evidence that many receive the idea that it is easier to conquer war with peace. I am one of these. I can see no end of retaliation, unless some one ceases to retaliate." But a few years later found her throwing herself, with all her energy and enthusiasm, into the Mexican Revolution. She hesitates between action and her desire for seclusion. She hesitates between art and life, and finds a solace for life's disappointments in esthetic ecstasy and the inward vision. She hesitates between a coherent intellectual attitude and the sheer nihilism which makes it, at times, impossible for her to see life other than as "a vast scheme of mutual murder, with no justice anywhere, and no God in the soul or out of it."

Above all, she hesitates between life and death. Pessimism lurks below the surface of everything she has written, and she felt, at times, a strong inclination to give up the battle altogether. Her days were so unhappy that one is tempted to say of her, as of many another genius before her: "Her work was a success; her life was a failure." But, as she herself observed, "out of the blackest mire the whitest lily blooms." Her character became great through suffering and in spite of suffering. Voltairine de Cleyre failed to win happiness. But she won something that may be more precious—the satisfaction that comes from honest self-expression and from the exercise of rare intellectual gifts. Her writings will be an inspiration to humanity for generations to come, and her name will grow in fame and in honor as the ideals for which she fought are realized.

VOL. X, NO. 4, JUNE 1915

Flowers and Ashes

By Louise Bryant

Louise Bryant is best known for her marriage to the journalist John Reed, the author of the classic eyewitness account of the Bolshevik revolution, *Ten Days That Shook the World* (1919). Emma Goldman, on one of her national lecture tours, had met her in Portland, Oregon, before Bryant herself came to know Reed in the fall of 1915. Goldman thought Bryant's commitment to radicalism had no depth—an opinion shared by Reed's former lover Mabel Dodge—but softened her view after Reed's death in Moscow in 1920. When "Flowers and Ashes" appeared in *Mother Earth,* Bryant was still married to her first husband, Dr. Paul Trullinger, a Portland dentist (the poem was signed "Louise Bryant Trullinger"). Her own impressions of revolutionary Russia were published as *Six Red Months in Russia* (1918) and *Mirrors of Moscow* (1923).

T HE SWAYING STREETCAR bulged with human freight,
    A gust of sand blew up the narrow street
And caught it as it whirled with giddy gait.
    The souls within sighed wearily, the heat
Was so intense it hurt their tired feet,

Their tired eyes, and hands, and tired souls.
    It was the hour when the workers pause at last
And seek those murky, fetid, loathsome holes
    They call their homes; if thus their lot be cast.
Poor wrecks of lives! Poor ships with broken mast!

A woman sat beside me and her face
    Was lined with care and sorrow, as if the years
That she had lived and loved and kept her place
    Among the workers, had been a thing of tears;
A tragic life of agonies—and fears.

And in her hand she held some flowers,
    Old-fashioned flowers, like our grandames knew.
Their fragrance was so sweet, I minded distant hours.
    I touched their dear, soft faces for I knew
I'd think of other flowers wet with dew.

We jogged along street after street and then
    The woman spoke, "For my man's grave," she said
And then was silent. When I looked again
    On her pale cheek there burned a spot of red.
"For twenty years," she mused, "my man's been dead."

"Yes, I raise flowers for his grave. You see
    He loved the flowers and the soft green grass
And it is lonely where he sleeps and he . . .
    Must miss me, want me, so I always pass
The little plot at evening. . . . But alas!

Death comes so slow, with lagging steps . . . that pause . . .
    Before they reach me." "Why," I said, "it would seem
That you could find another love . . . another cause . . .
    To strive for . . . Do you have no babes . . . or dream
No dreams, nor see the future all agleam—

With promise?" She clutched the flowers, her thin form
    Shook with emotion. "Because I had two
When he fell off the painter's scaffold . . . and was torn . . .
    Right out of life . . . I knew not what to do . . .
I worked, I begged, I stole. And God, he knew,

I was so faint and sick in that foul air, . . .
    My babes were hungry and my life was dust.
. . . I gave my body for them . . . They were fair
    And young—with trustful eyes—I felt I must
Do all things for them, . . . even those of lust.

The law came down upon me with a din, . . .
    It took them both away—my babes—it said . . .
I was a thing of shame and marked with sin
    And babes were pure in heart and must be led
In whiter ways than mine, . . . who was not wed!

And I grow flowers in a little box
    High in a window in a dark old street . . .
Where children never come, to smile at phlox
    Or marigold or primrose. . . . There I meet
Only the wretched . . . still my heart does beat—

For Death must very old have grown, he does not
    Knock upon my battered door or lurk
Beside my flowers." We rode on.—Thus have you wrought,
    Oh, gloating *"men of God,"* who bow and smirk,
. . . Call you this *white* soul *black?* . . .
    Is this your holy work?

VOL. XII, NO. 3, MAY 1917

The Mob

By Ben Hecht

In 1917, Ben Hecht was a writer for the *Chicago Daily News,* to which he contributed sketches of everyday life in the city's streets, such as "The Mob." His work had already appeared in Margaret Anderson's *The Little Review.* "The Mob" catches the growing anarchist hysteria that was fed by America's entry into the European war and which would eventually lead to the country's first "red scare" in 1919–20 and the deportation to Soviet Russia of Emma Goldman and Alexander Berkman.

A CROWD GATHERED, SEEMING TO GROW out of the sidewalk. It was in front of a department store in State Street, the moving stream of men and women suddenly congealed.

Their mysterious and impenetrable energies were galvanized with an equal suddenness into a vacuous concentration.

The men edged each other and pried themselves into a great black knot. The women rose on tiptoes and stretched their necks.

Two policemen walked roughly into the throng, seeming to filter through the layers of thickly wedged spectators.

None knew exactly what had happened. In the center of the crowd, pressed against the wall of the store, stood two men and a woman. One of the men, well dressed, was bleeding from his nose.

The blood dripped over his clothes and spattered in bright stains on his shoes and the pavement. He paid no attention. His eyes were fastened on the other man, whose clothes were shabby. He regarded him viciously like a man whom sudden rage has robbed of thought. He stood breathing in gasps, his fists clenched and his mouth opened. For moments he remained speechless and then an inspiration struck him.

"You dirty Anarchist," he cried. The crowd thrilled. The men who heard the words repeated them in a whisper.

"Soak him," someone cried.

The police appeared suddenly in the center. One of them seized the man with the bloody nose.

The other seized his assailant, who was poorly dressed and who had been standing with his eyes to the ground and a listless expression on his face.

The woman, whose hat was awry and whose hair had become somewhat undone, suddenly screamed.

The crowd opened, and the five central figures passed through to the corner.

"I was walking along with her. She's my wife," the bloody nose began, "when this bum came up and struck me."

The policeman who was holding the bum shook him roughly and jerked him out of his tracks.

"What did yu hit him for?" he demanded.

"He was hitting the woman," said the bum, "I saw him pull her and slap her. I told him to stop, and he swore. So I hit him."

The policeman, who had inserted his hand under his collar, jerked him out of his tracks again.

"I was arguing with my wife," resumed the bloody nose, "and he came along and hit me. He butted right in and hit me. I was walking along peaceably minding my own business, and he came up and soaked me."

"What did yu do it for?" demanded the policeman for the second time.

The man lowered his eyes to the ground and stared and did not answer.

The crowd began to surge.

"Soak him," someone cried out again. "He's an Anarchist."

Those in the rear pressed forward. The man seemed oblivious. He kept his eyes lowered and his face remained blank. His features were thin, his skin smooth shaven. His hat had fallen off, and his long black hair lay uncombed on his head.

It made him look wild.

The policeman who was holding him unloosened his hand. The man bent forward to pick up his hat.

The policeman pounced on him and swung with his fist, landing a blow behind the man's ear. He fell to the ground.

The two policemen jerked him to his feet, shaking him into sudden consciousness.

"Yu will, will you," demanded the one who had struck the blow. "Yu'd better not try tu get away again."

The man stood looking dully at the ground.

"That's the idee," yelled someone in the crowd, "swat him again."

They pressed forward and several men nearest the group pushed violently against the "bum."

One of them shoved him with his hand. He staggered and fell against a short, stout man who gave him a shove back.

The policeman seized him by the collar and flung him toward the curbing.

"Stand still, will yu," he commanded, "or I'll fix yu good next time."

The man remained with his eyes fastened on the ground.

They were waiting for the patrol.

"I was walking along peaceably," resumed the bloody nose, "when he rushed up to me and banged me."

"How about it, lady," inquired the policeman, turning to the woman.

"Yes," said the woman. "He's my husband."

The man looked at her and repeated, "He was hitting the woman there when I saw him, and I told him to stop, and he swore. So I hit him."

"Well, what if he was hitting her?" demanded the policeman. "She's his wife, ain't she? What business have you got buttin' in and disturbin' the peace, eh?"

He jerked him again.

"Say, I have quarrels with my wife and so does everybody else. I guess yu'll keep yure hands tu yourself before yu're through with this."

"Why don't yu let the other fella poke him?" demanded a voice.

"He's a dirty Anarchist," howled someone in the rear.

"He's a bad one," whispered several. "Look at him."

The man stood with his eyes dully to the ground.

Moisse, the young dramatist, fought his way through the throng. In his slow progress he learned the nature of the disturbance.

A man had struck another whom he saw quarreling with a woman, one explained.

Another replied that it had been a cold-blooded assault. A third said the woman had been hit by the man.

Moisse arrived in the center in time to overhear the man's own explanation.

"Was yure husband hittin' yu?" asked the policeman of the woman.

"No," said the woman.

The man looked at her and remained silent. The patrol was in sight clattering down the street a block away.

Moisse, the young dramatist, stepped forward. He stood facing the man in the policeman's grasp.

"I want to shake hands with you," said Moisse in a loud voice. "You're a hero."

He extended his hand and seized the man's and shook it. The man kept his eyes dully on the ground.

"Anybody who will beat a woman is a damn cad and the man who will resent it shows a spark of chivalry worthy of a hero," he went on. "Let me shake your hand again."

He slapped the man on the back and dropped his hand.

"That's right," cried a voice, "he's right."

"The fella was hittin' a woman," cried another voice.

"He got what was comin' to him," said another.

A short, fat man stepped pompously forward.

"I want to shake your hand," he said to the culprit.

He seized the hand Moisse had dropped and shook it.

"Here, have a cigar," he added, and handing him a cigar, stepped back.

"That's the right idea," a voice cried.

"He did right," another added.

A third man suddenly detached himself from the ring around the central figures.

"Shake," he said brusquely.

The man kept his eyes dully on the ground.

"Have a cigar," he added.

As the patrol drew up a dozen men crowded around the culprit.

"Let him go, take the other man. He was hittin' a woman," cried voices. "Don't pinch him."

The man, his pockets suddenly stuffed with cigars, raised his eyes and looked vacantly at the crowd.

"We'll need him as a witness," explained the policeman.

"Hey you," he said, seizing the bloody nose, "get in there."

He shoved the bloody nose into the wagon.

"Yu'd better come along, too," he went on, pointing to the other.

The culprit stepped into the wagon. His eyes wandering over the crowd caught those of Moisse gazing at him.

The young dramatist winked, and the shabby one stared at him.

"Three cheers for the fellow who defended a woman's honor," cried the young dramatist, winking again at the shabby one.

The patrol started with a jerk.

The crowd broke into a cheer.

People passing on the other side of the street turned their heads. . . .

PART FOUR

CIVIL LIBERTIES

Liberty—the innate freedom to live and speak as one chooses, without the constraints of church and state—is central to all varieties of anarchism. Among radicals in the years that *Mother Earth* was being published, it was a sweeping concept, one that anticipated the contemporary idea of human rights and bore upon every aspect of the anarchist movement, but most pointedly the areas of women's rights (see "Part Two: The Woman Question"), free speech, education reform, and justice, the last including the related issues prisons and crime. "*Speak, speak, speak,*" heralded Voltairine de Cleyre, "and remember that whenever anyone's liberty to speak is denied, your liberty is denied also, and your place is there where the attack is."

Three Portraits of St. Anthony

The ever-vigilant Anthony Comstock, head of the New York Society for the Suppression of Vice and a special agent for the U.S. Post Office Department, was an object of loathing and ridicule in the pages of *Mother Earth*. There could be no kind words for the man on whose orders the magazine was periodically held up in the mail; who, during his persecution of Margaret Sanger over the issue of birth control, once promised immunity to William Sanger if he would betray his wife; and who, in the course of his career as America's quasi-official censor, confiscated 160 tons of "obscene" material (see Margaret Sanger, "Three Letters and a Vindication," page 126). (While Comstock found images of nudity to be morally corrupt, the Post Office, until 1908, was still routinely sending through the mail graphic picture postcards of lynchings in the South and elsewhere in the United States.) The satirical pieces that follow were published in 1906 and 1907, during the first year of *Mother Earth*'s existence. The earliest, "The Confiscated Picture," was unsigned but was probably written by the editor, Max Baginski, the author of the other two, "Anthony B. Comstock's Adventures" and "Recent Adventures of St. Anthony."

∞

VOL. I, NO. 5, JULY 1906

The Confiscated Picture

[Unsigned]

IT WAS QUITE A WHILE SINCE the agents of Comstock had made an important raid. No wonder the Royal Chamberlain of governmental morals of the United States felt irritated and annoyed.

As if the land were not always endangered by the immoral: like the devil, sneaking through the smallest keyhole, they steal into all circles of society and plant the poisonous seeds in the cornfields of the pious and virtuous.

Life in this world of nudity and shamelessness was hard indeed; it offered nothing but straw and thistles to goodness and chastity; whereas those that had neither conscience nor care feasted on rich wines and bathed in the glowing sun upon green meadows, full of sinful life's joys.

Sin, in all her voluptuousness, saturated the entire human race; she had but to intone the ancient song of love and passion, and all were enraptured. Young and old, regardless of station or wealth, worshiped at her shrine. It was sad that the Lord, in all His severity, could calmly look upon the triumphal march of indecent humanity . . .

Divine records prove that when His wrath was aroused He caused the entire human race to perish, saving only an old drunkard and his family. Why should not something similar be repeated? Has the Lord no courage, or has He lost all faith in the possible reformation of humanity by the help of the Young Men's and Young Women's Christian Associations?

Ah, if only I, Anthony B. Comstock, were the Lord, how different things would look! I should surround the entire universe, from dawn to sunset, with my emissaries, spies, and detectives.

Woe to the moon, if she dare to appear from behind the clouds without proper garments! Woe also to the sun, if he dare to rise without completing his toilet behind the heavenly screens!

In a corner of the office hung a picture which one of the agents had stolen on a raid. Its face was turned to the wall.

The Royal Chamberlain scrutinized it closely. It was a frightfully indecent affair; it represented the naked, voluptuous body of a woman. He frowned. The entire creation seemed a botched job to him. In vain he asked himself, again and again, why the Lord did not create men in the image of the seven lean years of Egypt. In vain, too, he asked himself, what one can possibly find to admire in a woman. Pink cheeks, tempting dimples, white arms, snowy breasts and legs—bah, is there really any truth in the theory that Nature knows no morality? In that case the entire scheme of the world is wrong, indecent, and in perverse contravention of the postal laws of the United States.

One who would blush at the nudity of a broomstick has no other course but suicide—a heroic death, indeed. All the newspapers would report that A. B. Comstock had committed suicide out of decency, and because he could endure the thought no longer that every human being stood naked in his boots.

He meditated a moment, and then concluded that, hateful as life seemed in these immoral days, he had to live, if only for the enemy's sake. In his imagination he could see long articles in publications like *Lucifer, The Truth Seeker, Liberty,* and Mother Earth heaping coals of fire upon his head. His terrified fantasy could actually see the mad cancan-dance of the letters. With wild eyes he followed their movements, and what he read threw him into convulsions.

"Anthony B. Comstock's suicide is a new argument for those optimists who forever seek for a redeeming feature in the greatest scoundrel. The mission of this man Comstock will remain an eternal blot upon the escutcheon of the Republic. Future generations will be unable to understand that the entire legislative body of America had not half a dozen honest and determined men in their midst to lay Comstock low. Men that, cowed by the conspiracy of hypocrites, swine, and eunuchs, dared not bring this national nuisance to account.

"However, we want to give the devil his due. Comstock has rendered the country a great service by his suicide. It is only to be regretted that he did not take this useful step twenty years ago.

"May his soul enter that heaven where angels are dressed in overalls, sweaters, and double-breasted coats!"

This sarcasm was too venomous. No, he could not die. He must remain and drink the bitter cup to the last drop. . . .

The world shall yet learn that he was a Hercules whose nose braved the odors of the Augean stables. Vice and indecency must be exterminated at all costs. If only his agents were not so deucedly stupid. More than once have they placed him in an embarrassing position. Why, only the other day one of them confiscated a little booklet named *Food for Pious Souls.* The agent thought it was a purposely misleading title; but he would not be fooled. In triumph he carried the booklet to his chief, in happy anticipation of the praise he would receive for his zeal. But his joy was of short duration. A few hours later one of the managers of a Bible Association stormed into the office and in loud, angry tones demanded to know whether Comstock and his staff had gone mad, that they dared lay sacrilegious hands on the Gospel. Oh, horrors! The confiscated booklet consisted of quotations from Holy Writ.

Comstock was furious. He was ready to strangle the whole office force, himself included. The very thought of it made his blood boil.

To regain his equanimity he decided to take a stroll through the streets. He knew that the devil was at work, doing mischief; and who but he himself could battle successfully with Satan?! He leisurely walked about, scrutinizing the windows of every book and picture store. In one of them he beheld an illustrated postal card that fairly made his hair rise. It represented a danseuse, her bodice cut low, shamelessly displaying faultless arms and tempting shoulders; her skirt was outrageously abbreviated, exposing charming, well-formed legs, and—her eyes! My, what glowing passion, what fatal seductiveness! . . .

In less than one second the Vandal of the twentieth century rushed into the store, seized the offending picture, and then hastened back to his office.

This case must be attended to at once, if the world is to continue.

Such damning evidence should suffice to send the best man to State's prison.

Our Torquemada quivered with the joy of anticipation. When he reached the office, he showed the confiscated card to his secretary; the latter scrutinized it closely; a malicious smile struggled on his face, as he pointed to the rift upon the neck of the danseuse. With one twist of his hand the secretary folded the face of the woman; behold! another face appeared. Horrors! It was the face of Anthony B. Comstock.

Unfortunate man, he had confiscated his own image!

VOL. I, NO. 7, SEPTEMBER 1906

Anthony B. Comstock's Adventures

By Max Baginski

NOT LONG AGO COMSTOCK was thrown into great excitement by the shocking news that a child was born in his neighborhood—perfectly naked.

To prevent scandalous possibilities he hurried to the scene of the motherly crime, armed with a pair of old trousers. There he found a most outrageous state of affairs—an infant born absolutely naked. But as it had not been delivered through the mails, it could not be confiscated.

Since that awful event Anthony B. is preparing a bill that will not permit babies to be born unless they come decently clothed.

Through the kindness of a detective Comstock heard of Zola's novel *At the Fireplace.* Immediately securing a copy, he sent an agent to locate the indecent author, determined to prosecute him for circulating immoral literature. However, the culprit could nowhere be found. For two weeks a staff of well-trained spies searched every nook and corner of the land, in quest of a man by the name of Zola. In one town a cheesemonger by that name was discovered, but he had never written any novels, much less *At the Fireplace.* In another town a Zola was seized, but had to be discharged—he was engaged in the legitimate sale of clay figures. Finally, through the wisdom of a newspaper, Comstock discovered that Zola had never lived in the United States and that, moreover, he has been dead for several years. Anthony's patriotic bosom expanded. "Is it not elevating to know," he remarked to one of his agents, "that our country has never produced such an author?!"

When Comstock first visited an Art Museum he was prostrated by the terrible display of nudity, the indecency of which made him quite ill. He realized that he must seek the safety of the retreat bearing the legend "For Men Only." There he meditated and prayed God to visit His vengeance upon these horrors. He was still young; his guardianship of public morals was in the dim future, but he keenly felt that something had to be done at once.

He sent in his card to the Director of the museum and requested an interview.

After a prolonged and serious consultation, Comstock framed a poster for the museum walls: "In the name of Decency all visitors are requested to examine the ladies and gentlemen of Greek mythology on the posterior side only."

The Director, however, must have been an immoralist in disguise. The posters were never placed on the walls.

Like all moralists, Comstock is subject to nightmares. One night he had a very severe attack. He felt as though a whole army of wild-looking creatures surrounded him, making indecent grimaces. He heard shrill laughter and felt himself a football in the hands of the hellish chorus.

Suddenly Venus stepped forward and pointing at Comstock she said, "Leave this man to me." The malicious wantonness of the lady exasperated Anthony. He wished a policeman were on hand to arrest her for disorderly conduct.

Soon the chorus withdrew. Venus approached Comstock. Her velvety, warm touch thrilled the saintly Anthony. Though fully conscious of his importance as the protector of his country's morals, he persuaded himself that he must make allowances for Venus—had she not for centuries past aroused the love ecstasies of young and old alike? . . . Besides, there were no witnesses . . .

He was about to embrace her, when he suddenly recollected that he was in his nightshirt. Blushingly he assured the divine seducer that he was a gentleman. He begged to be excused for a moment and soon returned in full dress.

Alas, the room was deserted. In the distance he heard the boisterous laughter of ridicule of the retreating Venus.

On one occasion Comstock surprised his wife in her bath. She greeted him with a smile. He frowned. "Scandalous! Had I ever suspected such depth of shamelessness, I should have never honored you as my wife."

"But Anthony, dear, have you not assured me last night that you loved my body as well as my soul, above everything under heaven?"

"To be sure, I did. We were in the dark, but it is broad daylight now."

VOL. I, NO. 12, FEBRUARY 1907

Recent Adventures of St. Anthony

By Max Baginski

HIS TERM OF SERVICE WAS AT AN END. His long years of activity as the Pinkerton of his country's morality brought a rich harvest. Patiently he had endured scorn, contempt, and contumely, but neither ridicule nor cowhiding succeeded in awakening his intelligence.

In art circles he was looked upon as a wild boar that, breaking through the brush, roots up the tender sprouts in order to destroy the young germinating life.

Writers of consequence were of the opinion that the postal censorship in his hands was equivalent to placing a sharp carving knife in the hands of a hydrocephalus with instructions for indiscriminate attack.

With the exception of Hearst's literary hacks, no one favored the objects of this nudity sniffer. His cause seemed on the decline. The government were glad to dispense with his services at the first opportunity.

St. Anthony grew still more pious and moral as this fear took possession of him. Possibly he would be even called upon to return the pictures and figures of nude women and the obscene literature he so zealously confiscated from the sinners against the postal censorship. He had grown so attached to those unclothed things and loved to scrutinize them in their minutest details.

Worriedly he gazed into the mirror. Oh, the contrariness of nature! Instead of giving him the aspect of a Saint, she had endowed him with the looks of an abortive faun. Again it was apparent that nature is a mean woman. And yet—murmured our hero—I wish I were a woman, that I might wear a veil to hide my ugly nudity.

His sorrow was soon changed into great joy. Postmaster General Cortelyou sent him a letter of congratulation and appreciation. "The services you have rendered the cause of morality have been very great. Your term of office will therefore be continued. The government has voted you a high salary—what do we care about public opinion!"

Cortelyou has fully grasped the mission of government. The latter needs patient subjects and submissive slaves. These are most successfully reared with the catechism, patriotic lies, and by moral preachers who extol moderation, submission, and resignation as the highest virtues.

The exposition of naked truth is dangerous to government, because it stimulates the love of life and the joy of the senses. The masses, however, must work rather than enjoy. Were they to grasp the depth and beauty of life, they would speedily cease their helot existence and turn their faces to the light of life.

The government must therefore acknowledge only untruthful art. The artist must market such pictures only which represent the prodigal son as feeding on husks, because he failed as a profitmaker, or as Roosevelt, storming the hill and thus saving the republic from destruction.

Such pictures stimulate virtue and patriotic murder.

"Oh, dear Cortelyou! You, at least, have not proved a disappointment to me"—thus spoke Anthony.

That night he was in high glee, and as he fell into the arms of Morpheus, he dreamed of his beautiful clay figures and the virtuous Diana.

Next morning he took a stroll through the town. On his way he remarked that all the canines made haste to escape at his approach. Be their object on the streetcorners ever so important, they lost no time as soon as they beheld our hero.

Highly surprised, he mused long over the strange phenomenon. At last he approached one of the streetcleaners. "Kindly tell me what is the matter with the dogs in your district," he asked. "Oh," came the reply, "our dogs are very intelligent. They know that Cortelyou has continued you in your position, and they fear lest you should reproach them with their naked legs."

Sabbath in the country! Though January, a soft breeze tenderly whispers among the leafless branches. The sun-kissed spots are as warm as spring. Puritanism reigns supreme through the length and breadth of the country. In the houses stupidity, gray and toothless, sits brooding, undisturbed by the Sunday city papers. If a god of joy created the world, he purposely punished the Puritans with the terrible Sunday ennui for their sacrilegious libel of life and ignorance of its joy.

Proceeding on his way, Anthony beholds a frog in the act of jumping into the brooklet. "Ashamed of his nakedness, in my presence," soliloquizes our saint. Moved to tears by such praiseworthy morality, Anthony exclaims, "There are only two beings in the whole wide world that understand me—Cortelyou and the frog."

VOL. I, NO. 6, AUGUST 1906

Prisons and Crime

By Alexander Berkman

Alexander Berkman served fourteen years in prison for his failed assassination of Henry Clay Frick (see Emma Goldman, "Alexander Berkman," page 14). "Prisons and Crime" appeared just three months after he regained his freedom. It was composed in a deliberate, analytical style that belied the emotional turmoil which Berkman suffered following his release, so extreme at times that Emma Goldman feared he might kill himself. His basic arguments, against incarceration and for abolishing the conditions that breed criminal behavior, are still debated today, when the United States maintains the largest prison population in the world. For anarchists, prisons were among the most brutal manifestations of state power, mocking the ideas of true justice and social reform.

MODERN PHILANTHROPY HAS ADDED A new rôle to the repertoire of penal institutions. While, formerly, the alleged necessity of prisons rested, solely, upon their penal and protective character, today a new function, claiming primary importance, has become embodied in these institutions—that of reformation.

Hence, three objects—reformative, penal, and protective—are now sought to be accomplished by means of enforced physical restraint, by incarceration of a more or less solitary character, for a specific or more or less indefinite period.

Seeking to promote its own safety, society debars certain elements, called criminals, from participation in social life, by means of imprisonment. This temporary isolation of the offender exhausts the protective rôle of prisons. Entirely negative in character, does this protection benefit society? Does it protect?

Let us study some of its results.

First, let us investigate the penal and reformative phases of the prison question.

Punishment, as a social institution, has its origin in two sources; first, in the assumption that man is a free moral agent and, consequently, responsible for his demeanor, so far as he is supposed to be *compos mentis;* and, second, in the spirit of revenge, the retaliation of injury. Waiving, for the present, the debatable question as to man's free agency, let us analyze the second source.

The spirit of revenge is a purely animal proclivity, primarily manifesting itself where comparative physical development is combined with a certain degree of intelligence. Primitive man is compelled, by the conditions of his environment, to take the law into his own hands, so to speak, in furtherance of his instinctive desire of self-assertion, or protection, in coping with the animal or human aggressor, who is wont to injure or jeopardize his person or his interests. This proclivity, born of the instinct of self-preservation and developed in the battle for existence and supremacy, has become, with uncivilized man, a second instinct, almost as potent in its vitality as the source it primarily developed from, and occasionally even transcending the same in its ferocity and conquering, for the moment, the dictates of self-preservation.

Even animals possess the spirit of revenge. The ingenious methods frequently adopted by elephants in captivity, in avenging themselves upon some particularly hectoring spectator, are well known. Dogs and various other animals also often manifest the spirit of revenge. But it is with man, at certain stages of his intellectual development, that the spirit of revenge reaches its most pronounced character. Among barbaric and semicivilized races the practice of personally avenging one's wrongs—actual or imaginary—plays an all-important rôle in the life of the individual. With them, revenge is a most vital matter, often attaining the character of religious fanaticism, the holy duty of avenging a particularly flagrant injury descending from father to son, from generation to generation, until the insult is extirpated with the blood of the offender or of his progeny. Whole tribes have often combined in assisting one of their members to avenge the death of a relative upon a hostile neighbor, and it is always the special privilege of the wronged to give the deathblow to the offender.

Even in certain European countries the old spirit of blood-revenge is still very strong. The semibarbarians of the Caucasus, the ignorant peasants of southern Italy, of Corsica and Sicily, still practice, this form of personal vengeance; some of them, as the Cherkess, for instance, quite openly; others, as the Corsicans, seeking safety in secrecy. Even in our so-called enlightened countries the spirit of personal revenge, of sworn, eternal enmity, still exists. What are the secret organizations of the Mafia type, so common in all South European lands, but the manifestations of this spirit?! And what is the underlying principle of duelling in its various forms—from the armed combat to the fistic encounter—but this spirit of direct vengeance, the desire to personally avenge an insult or an injury, fancied or real: to wipe out the same, even with the blood of the antagonist. It is this spirit that actuates the enraged husband in attempting the life of the "robber of his honor and happiness." It is this spirit that is at the bottom of all lynch law atrocities, the frenzied mob seeking to avenge the bereaved parent, the young widow, or the outraged child.

Social progress, however, tends to check and eliminate the practice of direct, personal revenge. In so-called civilized communities the individual does not, as a rule, personally avenge his wrongs. He has delegated his "rights" in that direction to the State, the government; and it is one of the "duties" of the latter to avenge the wrongs of its citizens by punishing the guilty parties. Thus we see that punishment, as a social institution, is but another form of revenge, with the State in the rôle of the sole legal avenger of the collective citizen—the same well-defined spirit of barbarism in disguise. The penal powers of the State rest, theoretically, on the principle that, in organized society, "an injury to one is the concern of all"; in the wronged citizen society as a whole is attacked. The culprit must be punished in order to avenge outraged society, that "the majesty of the Law be vindicated." The principle that the punishment must be adequate to the crime still further proves the real character of the institution of punishment: it reveals the Old Testamental spirit of "an eye for an eye, a tooth for a tooth"—a spirit still alive in almost all so-called civilized countries, as witness capital punishment: a life for a life. The "criminal" is not punished for his offence, as such, but rather according to the nature, circumstances, and character of the same, as viewed by society; in other words, the penalty is of a nature calculated to balance the intensity of the local spirit of revenge, aroused by the particular offence.

This, then, is the nature of punishment. Yet, strange to say—or naturally, perhaps—the results attained by penal institutions are the very opposite of the ends sought. The modern form of "civilized" revenge kills, figuratively speaking, the enemy of the individual citizen, but breeds in his place the enemy of society. The prisoner of the State no longer regards the person he injured as his particular enemy, as the barbarian does, fearing the wrath and revenge of the wronged one. Instead, he looks upon the State as his direct punisher; in the representatives of the law he sees his personal enemies. He nurtures his wrath, and wild thoughts of revenge fill his mind. His hate toward the persons, directly responsible, in his estimation, for his misfortune—the arresting officer, the jailer, the prosecuting attorney, judge and jury—gradually widens in scope, and the poor unfortunate becomes an enemy of society as a whole. Thus, while the penal institutions on the one hand protect society from the prisoner so long as he remains one, they cultivate, on the other hand, the germs of social hatred and enmity.

Deprived of his liberty, his rights, and the enjoyment of life; all his natural impulses, good and bad alike, suppressed; subjected to indignities and disciplined by harsh and often inhumanely severe methods, and generally maltreated and abused by official brutes whom he despises and hates, the young prisoner, utterly miserable, comes to curse the fact of his birth, the woman that bore him, and all those responsible, in his eyes, for his misery. He is brutalized by the treatment he receives and by the revolting sights he is forced to witness in prison. What manhood he may have possessed is soon eradicated by the "discipline." His impotent rage and bitterness are turned into hatred toward everything and everybody, growing in intensity as the years of misery come and go. He broods over his troubles, and the desire to revenge himself grows in intensity, his until then perhaps undefined inclinations are turned into strong antisocial desires, which gradually become a fixed determination. Society had made him an outcast; it is his natural enemy. Nobody had shown him either kindness or mercy; he will be merciless to the world.

Then he is released. His former friends spurn him; he is no more recognized by his acquaintances; society points its finger at the ex-convict; he is looked upon with scorn, derision, and disgust; he is distrusted and abused. He has no money, and there is no charity for the "moral leper." He finds himself a social Ishmael, with everybody's hand turned against him—and he turns his hand against everybody else.

The penal and protective functions of prisons thus defeat their own ends. Their work is not merely unprofitable, it is worse than useless; it is positively and absolutely detrimental to the best interests of society.

It is no better with the reformative phase of penal institutions. The penal character of all prisons—workhouses, penitentiaries, state prisons—excludes all possibility of a reformative nature. The promiscuous mingling of prisoners in the same institution, without regard to the relative criminality of the inmates, converts prisons into veritable schools of crime and immorality.

The same is true of reformatories. These institutions, specifically designed to reform, do as a rule produce the vilest degeneration. The reason is obvious. Reformatories, the same as ordinary prisons, use physical restraint and are purely penal institutions—the very idea of punishment precludes true reformation. Reformation that does not emanate from the voluntary impulse of the inmate, one which is the result of fear—the fear of consequences and of probable punishment—is no real reformation; it lacks the very essentials of the latter, and so soon as the fear has been conquered, or temporarily emancipated from, the influence of the pseudoreformation will vanish like smoke. *Kindness alone is truly reformative,* but this quality is an unknown quantity in the treatment of prisoners, both young and old.

Some time ago* I read the account of a boy, thirteen years old, who had been confined in chains, night and day, for three consecutive weeks, his particular offence being the terrible crime of an attempted escape from the Westchester, N. Y., Home for Indigent Children (Weeks case, Superintendent Pierce, Christmas, 1895). That was by no means an exceptional instance in that institution. Nor is the penal character of the latter exceptional. There is not a single prison or reformatory in the United States where either flogging and clubbing or the straightjacket, solitary confinement, and "reduced" diet (semistarvation) are not practiced upon the unfortunate inmates. And though reformatories do not, as a rule, use the "means of persuasion" of the notorious Brockway, of Elmira, N. Y., yet flogging is practiced in some, and starvation and the dungeon are a permanent institution in all of them.

Aside from the penal character of reformatories and the derogatory influence the deprivation of liberty and enjoyment exercise on the youthful mind, the associations in those institutions preclude, in the majority of cases, all reformation. Even in the reformatories no attempt is made to classify the inmates according to the comparative gravity of their offenses, necessitating different modes of treatment and suitable companionship. In the so-called reform schools and reformatories children of all ages—from five to twenty-five—are kept in the same institution, congregated for the several purposes of labor, learning, and religious service, and allowed to mingle on the playing grounds and associate in the dormitories. The inmates are often classified according to age or stature, but no attention is paid to their relative depravity. The absurdity of such methods is simply astounding. Pause and consider. The youthful culprit, who is such probably chiefly in consequence of bad associations, is put among the choicest assortment of viciousness and is expected to reform! And the fathers and mothers of the nation calmly look on and either directly further this species of insanity or by their silence approve and encourage the State's work of breeding criminals. But such is human nature—we swear it is daytime, though it be pitch-dark; the old spirit of *credo quia absurdum est.*

It is unnecessary, however, to enlarge further upon the debasing influence those steeped in crime exert over their more innocent companions. Nor is it necessary to discuss further the reformative claims of reformato-

* The above article is compiled from notes made by me in prison, in 1895. A. B.

ries. The fact that fully 60 percent of the male prison population of the United States are graduates of "reformatories" conclusively proves the reformative pretentions of the latter absolutely groundless. The rare cases of youthful prisoners having really reformed are in no sense due to the "beneficial" influence of imprisonment and of penal restraint, but rather to the innate powers of the individual himself.

Doubtless there exists no other institution among the diversified "achievements" of modern society which, while assuming a most important rôle in the destinies of mankind, has proven a more reprehensible failure in point of attainment than the penal institutions. Millions of dollars are annually expended throughout the "civilized" world for the maintenance of these institutions, and notwithstanding each successive year witnesses additional appropriations for their improvement, yet the results tend to retrograde rather than advance the purports of their founding.

The money annually expended for the maintenance of prisons could be invested, with as much profit and less injury, in government bonds of the planet Mars, or sunk in the Atlantic. No amount of punishment can obviate crime, so long as prevailing conditions, in and out of prison, drive men to it.

VOL. III, NO. 2, APRIL 1908

The Fight for Free Speech

By Ben L. Reitman

In April 1908, the name of Ben L. Reitman—the man who for the next
eight years would be Emma Goldman's tour manager and lover—made
its first appearance in *Mother Earth*. In "The Fight for Free Speech," he
recounted something of the circumstances of their meeting. The police
censorship of radical and even liberal speakers was a common practice of
the day, and when Goldman arrived in Chicago on March 5, she found
herself systematically barred from every lecture hall and public place of
gathering, on the orders of Police Chief George Shippy. The ostensible
reason was this. Two days earlier, an attempt was made on Shippy's life by
a certain Lazarus Averbuch, an obscure young immigrant who had been
beaten by the police at a demonstration of the unemployed in January.
Averbuch was shot and killed during his attack on Shippy and was, with
no corroborating evidence, immediately declared an anarchist follower of
Goldman's. Therefore, Goldman's free speech must be denied. The logic
and tactics Shippy employed were typical of police censorship in Chicago
and elsewhere. Such repeated violations of basic constitutional rights
helped galvanize a vigorous free speech movement that, in the course of
time, led to the founding of the American Civil Liberties Union by Roger
Baldwin, who always credited Goldman with inspiring him in his First
Amendment work.

(Correspondence)

"EMMA GOLDMAN CANNOT SPEAK," that's what Chief of Police Shippy
said. "All right," said Assistant Chief of Police Schuettler, "I will carry
out your orders." And he did. A two weeks' heroic effort to secure a hall for

Emma Goldman to speak in was unsuccessful. Many subterfuges were resorted to, but the police "always beat us to it." The Police Department publicly stated that they had no objection to Emma Goldman or any other Anarchists speaking in Chicago as long as they obeyed the law, but it was evident that they exercised the utmost vigilance in preventing her from speaking in Chicago.

The hall that was secured in the Masonic Temple for her first speech was the place where Anarchist meetings had been held for the last three years, without the least objection on the part of the landlord; but twenty-four hours before Miss Goldman was to speak, the chairman was notified by the proprietor that the police had been to his office and had given him strict orders not to let Emma Goldman speak, so he immediately canceled the lease. The police notified some six hundred hallkeepers in Chicago not to rent their halls for any meeting where Emma Goldman was to lecture. Mr. —, a saloonkeeper who had a hall on the North Side, told the police that he would rent his hall to anybody he chose; four hours later he was promptly arrested for selling liquor to minors.

Another hallkeeper who threatened to defy the police and rent his hall to Emma Goldman a few hours later was notified by the Building Department that he would have to put in a new fire escape, an alteration which would entail the cost of several thousand dollars.

I rented a store on Dearborn Street and made a public announcement that Emma Goldman was to speak there; at 12 o'clock the Building and the Health and Fire Departments had investigated the place, notifying me that everything was all right, but at 4 o'clock in the afternoon the police brought me word that no meeting could be held there because the store had been condemned by the Building Department as unsafe. I made inquiries and found that the place was condemned because the floor was unsafe and the door did not open outwardly. We offered to put in a new floor and to change the door, but the Building Department absolutely refused to consider our proposition.

At a meeting of the Literary Society at Workman's Hall Miss Goldman was on the program to speak; although the meeting was not publicly announced, the police got word of it through the treachery of a newspaper man and immediately filled the hall with about a hundred officers. When the chairman announced that after a clarinet solo Emma Goldman would speak, the police buckled up their belts, examined their guns, drew their clubs, and stood ready to charge. Miss Goldman came to the platform and said: "Ladies and gentlemen, I hope you will all remain quiet, no matter what happens," and immediately Captain Mahoney, a great, big pig-faced Irishman, weighing about two hundred and fifty pounds, rushed to the stage and without the slightest provocation dragged Miss Goldman from the platform and pulled and hauled her through the hall like a sack of flour, cursing and shoving her all the way. He used brute force, bad manners, and a language which is only characteristic of men who have spent many years in training. He wanted her to get out on the street without her coat and wrap, but finally, when Miss Goldman insisted on having her wraps, he said to a man: "Get the rags of this thing."

Why did he do this? She had not disobeyed any law, she had not uttered one word about Anarchism. Even Schuettler said that Mahoney "went a little too far, he ought not to have done that"; but he did it, and Mahoney bids fair to become an inspector some day.

One Sunday afternoon Miss Goldman went quietly to a meeting of the Anthropological Society to hear a friend of hers lecture. Immediately fifty stalwart guardians of the "peace" were sent to prevent her speaking.

Not only did the police suppress her lectures, but they did everything possible to annoy and make her uncomfortable. Schuettler sent two plain-clothesmen to trail her wherever she went. They did not even keep a respectful distance when Miss Goldman went visiting, or shopping, or walking; they were ever at her side. There was absolutely no sane reason why she should have been hounded by the police, except that Chief Shippy said, "Emma Goldman cannot speak"; and so the Constitution of the United States, the freedom of speech, decency, and a square deal have all been put aside because of the whim of Chief of Police Shippy. Yet with all the efforts that the Police Department made to hush the voice of Anarchy, Anarchism has taken a step forward such as it has not done in Chicago for many years.

During the three weeks that Miss Goldman was in Chicago the sale of Anarchist literature was greater than for the previous year. The Anarchist books at the public library were in constant demand. A large number of lectures and sermons was heard in the lecture halls, churches, and colleges in Chicago. Hundreds of letters from sane, rational, liberty-loving citizens were called forth, and absolutely every Anarchist plot which was started in the newspapers was proven to be a baseless fabrication.

Chicago realized for the first time that free speech and the privilege to assemble were interfered with by the Police Department without any rhyme or reason.

VOL. III, NO. 5, JULY 1908

The Philadelphia Farce

By Voltairine de Cleyre

In the winter of 1907–8, the United States was in the depths of a major depression. On February 20, Jewish and Italian anarchists in Philadelphia held a mass demonstration of the unemployed at the New Auditorium on South Third Street. Voltairine de Cleyre spoke briefly to the crowd of 2,000. Afterward, the demonstrators attempted to march to Broad Street but were blocked by club-wielding police. Dominick Donelli, an Italian anarchist, drew a pistol and fired it twice, hitting no one. Later in the day, police arrested de Cleyre at her home. She and an anarchist friend, Hyman Weinberg, were charged with inciting to riot. "The Philadelphia Farce," published in April, is de Cleyre's record of the prosecution's laughable ineptness in the conduct of their trial.

The "four men . . . in prison" mentioned at the end of the contribution were Michael Costello, Angelo Troi, Francesco Piszicallo, and Dominick Donelli, of whom only the last was an anarchist. They, too, had been arrested and charged with inciting to riot as well as assault and battery with intent to kill. Tried and convicted, they were given stiff sentences, Donelli receiving the harshest, a term of five years at hard labor. De Cleyre organized a defense committee on their behalf, raising money through appeals in such publications as *Mother Earth* and the Yiddish anarchist newspaper *Fraye Arbeter Shtime*. As a result of her efforts, Piszicallo was imprisoned for less than a year, both Costello and Troi were released before the end of 1909, and Donelli was freed in 1911. Joseph Cohen, referred to in the final paragraph, was prominent in the Jewish anarchist and Modern School movements and served from 1923 to 1932 as editor of *Fraye Arbeter Shtime*.

∞

AFTER THE LAPSE OF NEARLY FOUR months from "the riot" of last February, the case of the "Commonwealth of Pennsylvania vs. Hyman Weinberg and Voltairine de Cleyre" was called for trial on the 17th of June, the trial Judge being Mayer Sulzberger, a gentleman having the reputation of being somewhat more inclined to weigh the rights of citizens as against the attacks of the police than some other judges.

On the morning of the 17th, Weinberg and myself, the witnesses for the defense, and our respective lawyers were all ready in the court room. The State, however, was not ready; one of the arresting officers was not present.

Some very animated wrangling then took place between the Judge and the lawyers, in which the Judge, so far from upholding the dignity of office, presented, to me at least, the curious appearance of a scolding old woman; the effect was no doubt heightened by the black and somewhat out-of-date dress he wears. Under the regular rules of criminal court procedures, the case would then have gone over to the next term of court, but the result of the wrangling was that the case was continued to the next day. Accordingly, we appeared on the morning of June 18. The officer was now present, but the chief witness, in fact the only witness, was absent. The Prosecuting Attorney asked for a continuance of the case to search for the witness. The Judge ordered that the witness be called. The crier of the court holloed "John Ká-ret, John Ka-rét." No response. Another crier went down the hall and out into the corridor calling "John Ka-rét." John Karet did not appear.

The Judge asked if the State had Karet's sworn testimony at the hearing in the Magistrate's court. Upon the affidavit being produced, the Judge elected to "read it himself because it was easier." Having done so, he doubled the paper up with a rather disgusted face, remarking, "If that is all your evidence, we will 'submit the bill' to the jury."

A motion of our lawyers to dismiss the case (or some legal phraseology to that effect) was denied by the Judge; the prosecution said it had other witnesses.

At this point Attorney Nelson asked the Court to appoint a stenographer, which was refused by the Judge with the remark: "This Court is not here for the purpose of furnishing campaign literature to anybody."

We then engaged a stenographer on our own account; what follows is the verbatim report of the "trial."

| COMMONWEALTH
VS,
HYMAN WEINBERG and
VOLTAIRINE DE CLEYRE | } | Court of Quarter Sessions.
March Sessions, 1908ˈ
No. 18. |

Before HONORABLE MAYER SULZBERGER, P. J., and a Jury.

Philadelphia, June 18, 1908.

Present, of counsel:

MORRIS WOLF, Esq., Asst. District Attorney, for the Prosecution; and HENRY JOHN NELSON, Esq., and HENRY N. WESSEL, Esq., for the Defendants.

COMMONWEALTH'S EVIDENCE.
RALPH GOLD, called by Commonwealth, sworn.

By MR. WOLF:

Q. You are a special officer of the 33rd District?

A. Yes, sir.

Q. You arrested those defendants?

A. Yes, sir.

Q. When?

A. February 20th.

Q. 1908. Where?

A. I arrested Mr. Weinberg at Fifth and Lombard, in a restaurant, and also Mrs. de Cleyre at her home.

Q. Under what circumstances did you make the arrest?

By THE COURT:

Q. What do you know about them?

A. In fact, we know nothing; only the warrant sworn out by this Karat.

Q. What do you know about the case?

A. Nothing.

Q. Did they confess anything to you?

A. Nothing.

Q. Did they say anything to you?

A. Nothing at all.

By MR. WOLF:

Q. What did they say at the time you arrested them?

A. Nothing at all. I only placed them under arrest and said what it was for.

Q. They said nothing?

A. They said nothing; no, sir.

Q. Your first information was when this man Karat came to you?
A. He came to us and said these people were speaking.
Q. He said nothing in your presence?
A. Only at the hearing.
Q. You know nothing more about it?
A. No, sir.
(No cross-examination.)

JOSEPH VIGNOLA, called by Commonwealth, sworn.

By Mr. WOLF:
Q. You are a special officer?
A. Yes, sir; of the 33rd District.
Q. Did you participate in the arrest of these defendants?
A. No, sir.
Q. What do you know about this case?
A. I don't know anything about the case at all. I don't know how my name comes on the bill.
(No cross-examination.)

JOHN J. FOX, called by Commonwealth, sworn.

By Mr. WOLF:
Q. You are a special officer of the 2nd District?
A. Yes, sir.
Q. What do you know about the case?
A. All I know is information received from John Karat, who swore out the warrant for Voltairine de Cleyre, and we arrested her.
Q. Were you present at the meeting at which the statements were said to have been made?
A. No, sir.
Q. Did you have a conversation with either of the defendants?
A. Yes, sir.
Q. What did they say about it?
A. They didn't have anything to say.
Q. Did you have any conversation with Karat in the presence of the defendants?
A. Only at the hearing—that is, the hearing room.
Q. Do you know where Karat is now?
A. No, sir.
(No cross-examination.)

CHARLES PALMA, called by Commonwealth, sworn.

By MR. WOLF:
Q.   Do you know anything about the case?
A.   I don't know anything about this case.
Q.   Nothing at all?
A.   Nothing at all.
Q.   Nor about the defendants?
A.   I don't know anything about them.
Q.   Nor about Karat?
A.   Not a thing.
(No cross-examination.)

_____

LOUIS GREEN, called by Commonwealth, sworn.

By MR. WOLF:
Q.   You are a guard at City Hall?
A.   Yes, sir.
Q.   Do you know anything about the facts of this case?
A.   No, sir; nothing about the case.
Q.   Or about the defendants?
A.   No, sir.
Q.   Or about Karat?
A.   No, sir.
Q.   Do you know how your name got on the bill?
A.   At the time the arrest was made they brought me in to the hearing at Central Station. There was a couple of letters that was written in Yiddish that they give me, that I should read through a few lines—
Q.   You translated them?
A.   Yes.
Q.   To whom were those letters addressed?
A.   They were addressed to a little town in the State of New Jersey.
Q.   I mean to what person?
A.   It doesn't state. It doesn't state any person.
Q.   Who gave you the letters?
A.   The Assistant District Attorney, Mr. Rogers.
Q.   Have you them now or did he take them back?
A.   He took them with him.
(No cross-examination.)

_____

JEAN H. BENIAKOFF, called by Commonwealth, sworn.

By MR. WOLF:
Q.   You are an official interpreter in the Courts of Philadelphia?

A. I am; yes, sir.

Q. There were given to you certain letters.

A. Yes.

Q. Purporting to be addressed to whom?

A. To Mr. Weinberg.

Q. By whom were they given to you?

A. By Mr. Rogers, of the District Attorney's office.

Q. Did you translate those letters?

A. I read the letters.

Q. In what language are they?

A. In Yiddish.

Q. Have you them with you now?

A. I gave them to you a while ago.

Q. You showed them to me. I didn't know what they were. How many are there?

A. Ten letters. You have them.

Q. You say that you read them all?

A. Yes, sir.

Q. Is there anything in these letters which could be considered as at all inciting to Anarchy?

A. No, sir.

Q. Will you state what the substance of these letters was?

(Objected to by defendants.)

Q. Did Voltairine de Cleyre write them?

MR. WESSELS: No. They were written to Weinberg and were found in his possession. I object to the letters.

(Commonwealth rests.)

(Defendants move that, under the direction of the Court, the bill be submitted and verdicts of not guilty taken.)

THE COURT. Gentlemen of the Jury: Under the evidence produced by the Commonwealth, which is no evidence at all against the defendants, you are, of course, to find a verdict of not guilty.

Comment is unnecessary.

The court officers began hustling us out; but presently we were recalled. Mr. Wessel, attorney for Weinberg, was asking that the police return Mr. Weinberg's watch and letters which had been kept ever since the arrest. The Judge was endeavoring to be witty. "What!" said he to the police officer, "is there any law in the Commonwealth of Pennsylvania which says that because a man makes a fool of himself, the police should therefore take away his watch?" All the sycophants laughed. Personally, I think it was a gratuitous insult, since the Judge had no evidence whatever to suppose Weinberg had "made a fool of himself," and had just been saying he had not. Mr. Wessel arose with a smile, "But, your Honor, what we want now is the watch!"

"Oh give the man his watch," protested the Judge.

"And the letters."

More talk about the letters, and then the Judge, forgetting his former two-edged cut at the police and at Weinberg, remarked with judicial dignity, "When a man is put under arrest, he is searched, and his property taken charge of for his own protection!" . . .

And so, "for his own protection," the police had been holding Weinberg's watch for four months, while he was out on bail! This is the limit.

I wish to thank all contributors to our defense and to say that we have still work to do. Four men are in prison, under most rigorous and unjust sentences. We wish to do what can be done towards freeing these men or supporting their families till they are free.

Those who wish to assist in the work may communicate with Joseph Cohen, 859 N. 7th St., Philadelphia.

VOL. IV, NO. 5, JULY 1909;

REPRINTED, VOL. VII, NO. 5, JULY 1912

On Liberty

By Voltairine de Cleyre

Increasing police violations of First Amendment rights led to a mass meeting on June 30, 1909, at the Cooper Union in New York. It was organized by the National Free Speech Committee, a coalition of anarchists, socialists, and liberals that included, among others, Voltairine de Cleyre, Leonard Abbott, Eugene V. Debs, Clarence Darrow, and Jack

London. Recalling the event in her memoirs, Emma Goldman called de Cleyre's speech "the most brilliant" of the occasion. "On Liberty" was published in the pages of *Mother Earth* in July 1909, reprinted three years later in the special issue commemorating de Cleyre's death, and included in her posthumous *Selected Works* (1914).

∽

O NE OF THE SPEAKERS HAS SAID he is here in the interest of "good government"; so am I. But you know the brutal saying of some white man about Indians: "The only good Indian is a dead Indian." In my opinion, the only "good" government is a dead government.

I am in the habit of writing out what I have to say in advance; the reasons are several, but the principal one governing me in the present instance is that I am speaking not only to the people here, but before a censorship so ignorant that it can neither understand nor correctly report what it does understand; and in the event of my being called to account for what I did not say, I wish to be able to show in writing precisely what I did say. And in the event of my being pulled off the platform by the police before I have opened my mouth (as has happened to me before now), I may be able to say, "Here is what I would have said."

Alas, this censorship! This thing of large biceps, large necks, large stomachs, and pyramidal foreheads! It sits in judgment upon things spiritual, things moral, things social, things scientific, things artistic—laugh, O Muse of Comedy—all things which it knows nothing about. It sits and decides upon the iniquity of words which have not been spoken; out of the profundity of its nether stomach, declares that to be seditious which no man has yet heard. Ah, when Emma Goldman shall next lecture upon the Modern Drama, let her not forget this drama of the censorship, wherein avoirdupois is the hero and the people of America—if you please, the scientists, the artists, the teachers, the literateurs—are the pitiful clowns. Let us appreciate to the full the working of this fine sixth sense which has entered into the corporeality of the police, that spacious corporeality, permeating them with power to divine that what a man or a woman has not yet said *is going to be* dangerous to the order and welfare of society.

Anent this same censorship and its perspicacity, and information, I had

Speech delivered by Voltairine de Cleyre at the Cooper Union Meeting, June 30, 1909, held to protest against the suppression of free speech in New York and Philadelphia. The speech is characteristic of our departed Comrade's breadth of view and revolutionary spirit, and its republication is especially appropriate at this time.

an illustration some years ago, at the beginning of this wave of good-guard-ianship which we are now enjoying. The moral guardians of my city, who are every once in a while caught stealing and receiving stolen goods, con-ceived that it was important to protect the frequenters of a certain coopera-tive society against the sale of Anarchist literature. They paused therefore at the stand by the door and began the censoring task. Among the rest there lay on the desk the little booklet of verses which I have here, *The Worm Turns*. As its title would indicate to those not gifted with the sixth sense—the censorship sense, so to speak—it is a collection of rebel protests. The censor, however, looked it through—carefully—and laid it down. A second censor, a revisionary censor I presume, approached, picked it up, and in-quired, "What's this?" "Oh," said number one, "that's all right; that's some-thing about worms."

It happens that the first line of the first stanza of the first poem reads thus:

"Germinal! The field of Mars is ploughing—"

I presume the censor thought that Mr. Mars, some worthy Pennsylvania farmer, no doubt, having turned up a clod or so with his plough, had prob-ably discovered mischievous "worms" therein and set his wits to work to rid the field of them; and then to turn an honest penny by imparting to his fellow farmers the peculiar turning methods of the worms and how to cir-cumvent them.

Indeed, when we consider what liberty one time meant in America and what it means now; when we consider the ease with which our censors forbid anything at all which happens to come into their—sixth—sense, and the supineness with which the people in general accept these interfer-ences; when we see the terrorizing methods of the sixth-sensers in their determination to crush what little dignity there may be in hallkeepers, by threatening them with the arrest, not only of themselves, but of their wives and children, if they rent halls to whomsoever the police shall designate as under the ban, and the abject submission of the threatened; when we con-sider that the main activity in life, for the great majority of all the people, is grubbing and crawling and bending to get food and drink—perhaps—perhaps the censorship is right in thinking that the whole subject "is some-thing about worms." Verily, when I learned a short time ago that a man whose name has been identified with the cry of the "suffering ages" as one of the spokesmen of the disinherited had declined to sign the Demand of the Free Speech Committee, I felt that we were indeed dealing with annu-lates, not vertebrates—creatures with rings in their bodies instead of spines—and that the old religious phrase, "a worm of the dust," was no mock self-depreciation, but a bare fact; I felt the burning shame of Gerald Massey's words shoot through me like a flame:

Smitten stones will talk with fiery tongues,
  And the worm, when trodden, will turn;
But, cowards, ye cringe to the cruelest wrongs,
  And answer with never a spurn.

It is the people's fault far more than the fault of the police that these outrages upon the freedom of expression take place. I do not mean you here, who by coming and sitting here on this sweltering night have shown where your sympathies lie. But what are you in number compared to the millions of New York City?

If the people in the mass cared, the police would not have dared. If the suppression of a great fundamental freedom appealed to the mass as much as a baseball umpire's decision, there would be meetings from one end of the city to the other to make known the sentiment of the people in regard to these attacks upon liberty. The fact is there is but a handful which cares anything about the matter; and the question is, how far is this handful able to make itself heard? How determined are we, who do want free speech, to wring that right out of the rest?

There is but one way that free speech can ever be secured; and that is by persistent speaking. It is of no use to write things down on paper and put them away in a storeroom, even if that storeroom happens to be the Library at Washington and the thing written is that "Congress shall make no law abridging the freedom of speech." That's like anything else put away on a shelf and forgotten. *Speak, speak, speak,* and remember that whenever anyone's liberty to speak is denied, your liberty is denied also, and your place is there where the attack is.

Of late these attacks have centered upon one personality—that of Emma Goldman.

Emma Goldman is my friend and my comrade; and upon all large principles our thoughts are close kin. But were she as much my enemy as she is my friend, and were our thoughts as bitterly opposed as they are sympathetic, I should still say that an attack upon her freedom to speak was an attack on mine, and my business was to be there to resist.

Freedom of speech means nothing, if it does not mean the freedom for that to be said which we do not like. I have seen statements in reputable newspapers, such as the Philadelphia *Inquirer* and the *Press,* to the effect that the only proper place for an Anarchist is the end of a rope swung to a lamppost. Certainly I am not of that opinion; I think all hanging is brutal and barbaric; and I should naturally have a particular objection to its being applied to me; but those papers have a perfect right to say it, just as I have the right to say that the sayers have the souls of hangmen. And I will stand for their right.

There will come a time when with a lightning-like clarification the mass of the people *will* become conscious of this need of freedom. Just how, when, or why it will take place there can be no certainty; but it certainly will take place, just as it always has done in the past, when the measure of tyranny has gone overfull, and those who crept and crawled have suddenly realized that they had spines.

When the old iron tongue in Independence Hall clanged out from its brazen throat, "Proclaim liberty throughout the land to all the inhabitants thereof," oh, this wasn't the sort of thing they were dreaming of! Liberty was alive and awake then and quivering down to the fingertips in all the people. It sleeps now, a long, cold, dim sleep; but not forever. There will come a dawn, sharp and white, and liberty will be awake then—in that hour, when, in Kipling's phrase, "When the dawn comes up like thunder." It is at such periods that declarations of freedom are made, which afterward fall into disuse; nevertheless, some forward leap is taken which is never altogether lost. Until such time it must be the task of freedom lovers to carry a torch through the darkness; and this we will do, even if we have to carry it through dungeon stones. And we know what prisons mean: they mean broken-down body and spirit, degradation, consumption, insanity—we know it all; but if that is the price that we must pay, be sure that we shall pay it.

VOL. IV, NO. 9, NOVEMBER 1909

L'École Rénovée

By Francisco Ferrer

Francisco Ferrer, the Spanish education reformer and anarchist, founded his Escuela Moderna ("Modern School") at Barcelona in 1901. Eight years later, at the time of his execution by a government firing squad, there were well over a hundred independent secular schools in Spain that patterned themselves on Ferrer's model. Even before his death in October 1909, the influence of his education movement had spread beyond Spain. In 1908, he established in Paris the International League for the Rational Education of Children, with Anatole France as honorary president. In April, the first issue of the league's education review, *L'École Rénovée* ("The Renovated School"), was published in Brussels; it was relocated to Paris the following January. Ferrer himself edited and wrote for the periodical and in the two years of its existence published contributions by such European proponents of radical education reform as James Guillaume, Peter Kropotkin, Paul Robin (whose school in Cempuis, near Paris, was visited by Emma Goldman), and Fernando Tarrida del Mármol. The present article, "L'École Rénovée," was published in the November 1909 issue of *Mother Earth,* honoring the recently martyred Ferrer. The translator is unknown. The piece articulates the objectives of the League for the Rational Education of Children and its review, *L'École Rénovée,* which became the guiding motives of the anarchist Modern School movement in the United States. For anarchists, state- and church-controlled education, with its resultant intellectual constraints, made the dominant official schools instruments of social and economic injustice instead of places for the cultivation of a child's natural potentials. This stand was not mere polemics. It was because of his education reforms that Ferrer was silenced.

Literal translation of an article written by Francisco Ferrer for the L'École Rénovée, *the Paris review published in the interests of Modern Education.*

To THOSE WHO WISH TO RENOVATE the education of children two methods are open: To work for the transformation of the school by studying the child, so as to prove scientifically that the present organization of education is defective and to bring about progressive modification; or, to found new schools in which shall be directly applied those principles corresponding directly to the ideal of society and of its units, as held by those who eschew the conventionalities, prejudices, cruelties, trickeries, and falsehoods upon which modern society is based.

The first method certainly offers great advantages. It corresponds to that evolutionary conception which all men of science defend and which alone, according to them, can succeed.

In theory they are right, and we are quite ready to recognize it.

It is evident that experiments in psychology and physiology must lead to important changes in matters of education: that teachers, being better able to understand the child, will know better how to adapt their instruction to natural laws. I even grant that such evolution will be in the direction of liberty, for I am convinced that constraint arises only from ignorance and that the educator who is really worthy of the name will obtain his results through the spontaneous response of the child, whose desires he will learn to know and whose development he will try to further by giving it every possible gratification.

But in reality, I do not believe that those who struggle for human emancipation can expect much from this method. Governments have ever been careful to hold a high hand over the education of the people. They know, better than anyone else, that their power is based almost entirely on the school. Hence, they monopolize it more and more. The time is past when they opposed the diffusion of instruction and when they sought to restrain the education of the masses. These tactics were formerly possible, because the economic life of the nations allowed the prevalence of popular ignorance, that ignorance which renders mastery easy. But circumstances have changed. The progress of science, discoveries of all kinds, have revolutionized the conditions of labor and production. It is no longer possible for a people to remain ignorant: it must be educated in order that the economic situation of one country may hold its own and make headway against the universal competition. In consequence, governments want education; they want a more and more complete organization of the school, not because they hope for the renovation of society through education, but because they need individuals, workmen, perfected instruments of labor, to make their industrial enterprises and the capital employed in them profitable. And we have seen the most reactionary governments follow this movement; they have realized perfectly that their former tactics were becoming dangerous to the economic life of the nations and that it is necessary to adapt popular education to new necessities.

But it would be a great mistake to suppose that the directors have not foreseen the dangers which the intelligent development of the people might create for them and that it was necessary for them to change their methods of keeping the mastery. These methods have likewise been adapted to the new conditions of life, and they have labored to keep a hold over the evolution of ideas. At the same time that they seek to preserve the beliefs upon which social discipline was formerly based, they have sought to give to conceptions born of scientific effort a signification which could do no harm to established institutions. And to that end they took possession of the school. They who formerly left the priests in charge of the education of the people, because the priests were perfectly suited to the task, their instruction being at the service of authority, now took up everywhere the direction of scholarly education.

The danger, for them, lay in the awakening of human intelligence to the new outlook on life; the awakening, in the depths of men's consciousness, of a will towards emancipation. It would have been foolish to combat the evolving forces; they had to be driven into channels. That is the reason why, far from adhering to the old procedures of government, they adopted new ones, and evidently efficacious ones. It did not require great genius to find this solution; the simple pressure of facts led the men in power to understand what they must oppose to the apparent perils.

They founded schools, labored to spread education on all sides, and if there were those among them who at first resisted this impulse—for its diverse tendencies favored certain antagonistic political parties—all soon understood that it was better to yield to it, and that the best tactics were to assure the defense of their interests and their principles by new means. Forthwith began terrible struggles for the conquest of the School; in every country these struggles are still continuing with intensity; here, bourgeois republican society triumphs; there, clericalism. All sides know the importance of the game and recoil at no sacrifice to secure a victory. Everyone's cry is: "For and by the School." And the good people ought to be touched by so much solicitude! Everybody thirsts for their elevation by education, and by consequence—their happiness! Formerly some could say: "These others want to keep you in ignorance that they may the better exploit you:

we want to see you educated and free." Now that is no longer possible; they have built schools on every corner, for every sort of instruction.

It is in this unanimous change of ideas among the ruling classes in respect to the school that I find reason to be suspicious of their goodwill and the explanation of the facts which actuate my doubts as to the efficacy of the methods of renovation which certain reformers want to put in operation. These reformers are, moreover, very indifferent, generally speaking, to the social significance of education; they are men very ardent in the search of scientific truth, but who avoid all questions foreign to the object of their studies. They study patiently to know the child and will some day tell us— their science is young yet—what methods of education are most suitable for its integral development.

Now this, in some sort, professional indifference is very prejudicial, I think, to the cause they intend to serve.

I do not mean to say that they are unconscious of the realities of the social environment, and I know that they expect the best results for the general welfare from their task. They say: In trying to discover the secrets of the life of the human being, in seeking the processes of its normal physical and psychic development, we give education a form which cannot but be favorable to the liberation of energies. We do not wish to devote our attention directly to the liberation of the school: as savants moreover we cannot, for we are not yet able exactly to define what is to be done. We shall proceed by slow degrees, convinced that the school will be transformed just in proportion to our discoveries by the force of events themselves. If you ask us what are our hopes for mankind, we agree with you in foreseeing an evolution in the direction of a wide emancipation of the child and of humanity through science; but in that case again we are persuaded that our work must be directed entirely towards that end and will attain it by the most rapid and direct course.

This reasoning is apparently logical, and no one would dare to contradict it. And yet it is mixed considerably with illusion. Yes, if the governing powers had, as men, the same ideas as benevolent reformers, if they were really concerned for the continuous reorganization of society in the sense of the progressive disappearance of slavery, we might admit that scientific effort alone would improve the destiny of nations. But we should reckon without our host. We know too well that those who dispute for power have in view nothing but the defense of their own interests; that they busy themselves only with conquering what they want for themselves, for the satisfaction of their appetites. Long ago we ceased to believe in the words with which they mask their ambitions. Certain naïve persons still refuse to believe that there is not among them, all the same, some little sincerity and imagine that they, too, sometimes desire the happiness of their fellows. But these become fewer and fewer, and the positivism of the century has become far too cruel for us to deceive ourselves longer as to the intentions of those who govern us.

Just as they knew how to get out of the difficulty, when the necessity for education became evident, in such a way as to prevent that education from becoming a danger, just so they will know how to organize the school in accordance with the new discoveries of science that nothing may endanger their supremacy. These are ideas which are certainly not received without difficulty; but when one has seen, from close by, what takes place and how things are in reality arranged, one can no longer be caught by the whistling of words.

Oh, what have people not expected, what do they not expect still, from education! The majority of progressive men expect everything from it, and it is only in these later days that some begin to understand that it offers nothing but illusions. We perceive the utter uselessness of this learning acquired in the schools by the systems of education at present in practice; we see that we expected and hoped in vain. It is because the organization of the school, far from spreading the ideal which we imagined, has made education the most powerful means of enslavement in the hands of the governing powers today. Their teachers are only the conscious or unconscious instruments of these powers, modeled moreover according to their principles; they have from their youth up, and more than anyone else, been subjected to the discipline of their authority; few indeed are those who have escaped the influence of this domination; and these remain powerless, because the school organization constrains them so strongly that they cannot but obey it. It is not my purpose here to examine the nature of this organization. It is sufficiently well known for me to characterize it in one word: constraint. The school imprisons children physically, intellectually, and morally, in order to direct the development of their faculties in the paths desired. It deprives them of contact with nature in order to model them after its own pattern. And this is the explanation of all which I have here set forth: The care which governments have taken to direct the education of the people and the bankruptcy of the hopes of believers in liberty. The education of today is nothing more than drill. I refuse to believe that the systems employed have been combined with any exact design for bringing about the results desired. That would suppose genius. But things take place precisely as if this education responded to some vast entire conception in a manner really remarkable. It could not have been better done. What accomplished it was simply that the leading inspiration was the principle of discipline and of authority which guides social organizers at all times. They have but one clearly defined idea, one will, viz.: Children must be accustomed to obey, to believe, to think according to the social dogmas which govern us. Hence, education cannot be other than such as it is today. It is not a matter of seconding the spontaneous development of the faculties of the child, of leaving it free to satisfy its physical, intellectual, and moral needs; it is a matter of imposing ready-made ideas upon it; a matter even of preventing it from ever thinking otherwise than is willed for the maintenance of the institutions of this society; it is a matter of making it an individual strictly adapted to the social mechanism.

No one should be astonished that such an education has this evil influence upon human emancipation. I repeat, it is but a means of domination in the hands of the governing powers. They have never wanted the uplift of the individual, but his enslavement; and it is perfectly useless to hope anything from the school of today.

Now, what has been resulting up until today will continue to result in the future. There is no reason for governments to change their system. They have succeeded in making education serve for their advantage; they will likewise know how to make use of any improvements that may be proposed to their advantage.

It is sufficient that they maintain the spirit of the school, the authoritarian discipline which reigns therein, for all innovations to be turned to their profit. And they will watch their opportunity; be sure of that.

I would like to call the attention of my readers to this idea: All the value of education rests in respect for the physical, intellectual, and moral will of the child. Just as in science no demonstration is possible save by facts, just so there is no real education save that which is exempt from all dogmatism, which leaves to the child itself the direction of its effort and confines itself to the seconding of that effort. Now there is nothing easier than to alter this purpose, and nothing harder than to respect it. Education is always imposing, violating, constraining; the real educator is he who can best protect the child against his (the teacher's) own ideas, his peculiar whims; he who can best appeal to the child's own energies.

One may judge by this with what ease education receives the stamp they wish to put upon it and how easy is the task of those who wish to enslave the individual. The best of methods become in their hands only the more powerful and perfect instruments of domination. Our own ideal is certainly that of science, and we demand that we be given the power to educate the child by favoring its development through the satisfaction of all its needs in proportion as these arise and grow.

We are convinced that the education of the future will be of an entirely spontaneous nature; certainly we cannot as yet realize it, but the evolution of methods in the direction of a wider comprehension of the phenomena of life, and the fact that all advances toward perfection mean the overcoming of some constraint, all this indicates that we are in the right when we hope for the deliverance of the child through science.

Is this the ideal of those who control the present school organization? Is this what they, too, want to realize? and they, too, do they aspire to overcome restraint? Not at all. They will employ the newest and most effective means to the same end as now, that is to say, the formation of beings who will accept all the conventions, all the prejudices, all the lies upon which society is founded.

Let us not fear to say that we want men capable of evolving without stopping, capable of destroying and renewing their environments without cessation, of renewing themselves also; men whose intellectual independence will be their greatest force, who will attach themselves to nothing, always ready to accept what is best, happy in the triumph of new ideas, aspiring to live multiple lives in one life. Society fears such men; we must not then hope it will ever want an education able to give them to us.

What, then, is our own mission? What method are we going to choose to contribute to the renovation of the school?

We shall follow the labors of the scientists who study the child with the greatest attention, and we shall eagerly seek for means of applying their experience to the education we wish to build up, in the direction of an ever fuller liberation of the individual. But how can we attain our end? Shall it not be by putting ourselves directly to the work favoring the foundation of new schools, which shall be ruled as much as possible by this spirit of liberty, which we forefeel will dominate the entire work of education in the future.

A trial has been made which, for the present, has already given excellent results. We can destroy all which in the present school answers to the organization of constraint, the artificial surroundings by which the children are separated from nature and life, the intellectual and moral discipline made use of to impose ready-made ideas upon them, beliefs which deprave and annihilate natural bent. Without fear of deceiving ourselves, we can restore the child to the environment which entices it, the environment of nature in which he will be in contact with all that he loves and in which impressions of life will replace fastidious book learning. If we did no more than that, we should already have prepared in great part the deliverance of the child.

In such conditions we might already freely apply the data of science and labor most fruitfully.

I know very well that we could not thus realize all our hopes, that we should often be forced, for lack of knowledge, to employ undesirable methods; but a certitude would sustain us in our effort, namely, that even without reaching our aim completely we should do more and better in our still imperfect work than the present school accomplishes. I like the free spontaneity of a child who knows nothing, better than the word knowledge and intellectual deformity of a child who has been subjected to our present education.

What we have attempted at Barcelona others have attempted elsewhere, and we have all seen that the work is possible. And I think it should be begun without delay. We should not wait until the study of the child has been completed before undertaking the renovation of the school; if we must wait for that, we shall never do anything. We will apply what we do know and, progressively, all that we shall learn. Already, a complete plan of rational education is possible, and, in such schools as we conceive, children may develop, happy and free, according to their natural tendencies. We shall labor to perfect and extend it.

It is with this object in view that this Review has been founded, that the International League for the Rational Education of Children has been founded. We ask the aid of all those who desire, with us, the liberation of the child, who desire through it to contribute to the coming of a more beautiful, a stronger humanity. In this Review we shall confine ourselves to the discussion of a plan of rational education, such as it is possible to carry out in these days.

Moreover, as soon as circumstances permit, we shall take up again the work begun in Barcelona, we shall rebuild the schools destroyed by our adversaries. In the meantime, we shall labor to found a normal school in Barcelona for the training of teachers destined to second us later; we shall create a library of the modern school, in which such books will be published as will serve for the education of the educators as well as for that of the children. We shall also found a pedagogic museum, containing a collection of all the necessary materials for a renovated school.

Such are our plans. We are aware that their realization will be difficult. But we want to begin, convinced that we shall be aided in our task by those who are everywhere struggling for human liberation from dogmas and conventions which assure the support of the present iniquitous social organization.

The Need of Translating Ideals into Life

By Alexander Berkman

Within a year of Francisco Ferrer's death, the Ferrer Association had been organized in New York, a Modern Sunday School had been opened, and plans were afoot for a Francisco Ferrer Day School, all due largely to the efforts of Alexander Berkman. In "The Need of Translating Ideals into Life," the unrepentant would-be assassin of Henry Clay Frick made it clear that education, not violence, was the surest preparation for social revolution, and he criticized the anarchist movement for its martyrological tendency and for dwelling too much on utopian hopes for a brighter tomorrow.

ONE YEAR HAS PASSED SINCE THE DEATH of Francisco Ferrer. His martyrdom has called forth almost universal indignation against the cabal of priest and ruler that doomed a noble man to death. The thinking, progressive elements throughout the world have voiced their protest in no ambiguous manner. Everywhere sympathy has been manifested for Ferrer, the modern victim of the Spanish Inquisition, and deep appreciation expressed for his work and aims. In short, the death of Ferrer has succeeded—as probably no other martyrdom of recent history—in rousing the social conscience of man. It has clarified the eternally unchanging attitude of the Church as the enemy of progress; it has convincingly exposed the State as the crafty foe of popular advancement; it has, finally, roused deep interest in the destiny of the child and the necessity of rational education.

It would indeed be a pity if the intellectual and emotional energies thus wakened should exhaust themselves in mere indignation and unprofitable speculation concerning the unimportant details of Ferrer's personality and life. Protest meetings and anniversary commemorations are quite necessary and useful, in proper time and place. They have already accomplished, so far as the world at large is concerned, a great educational work. By means of these the social consciousness has been led to realize the enormity of the crime committed by the Church and State of Spain. But "the world at large" is not easily moved to action; it requires many terrible martyrdoms to disturb its equilibrium of dullness; and even when disturbed, it tends quickly to resume its wonted immobility. It is the thinking, radical elements which are, literally, the movers of the world, the intellectual and emotional disturbers of its stupid equanimity. They must never be suffered to become dormant, for they, too, are in danger of growing absorbed in mere adulation of the martyr and rhetorical admiration of his great work. As Ferrer himself has wisely cautioned us: "Idols are created when men are praised, and this is very bad for the future of the human race. The time devoted to the dead would be better employed in improving the condition of the living, most of whom stand in great need of this."

These words of Francisco Ferrer should be italicized in our minds. The radicals, especially—of whatever creed—have much to atone for in this respect. We have given too much time to the dead and not enough to the living. We have idealized our martyrs to the extent of neglecting the practical needs of the cause they died for. We have idealized our ideals to the exclusion of their application in actual life. The cause of it was an immature appreciation of our ideals. They were too sacred for everyday use. The result is evident, and rather discouraging. After a quarter of a century—and more—of radical propaganda, we can point to no very particular achievement. *Some* progress, no doubt, has been made; but by no means commensurate with the really tremendous efforts exerted. This comparative failure, in its turn, produces a further disillusioning effect: old-time radicals drop from the ranks, disheartened; the most active workers become indifferent, discouraged with lack of results.

It is this, the history of every world-revolutionizing idea of our times. But especially is it true of the Anarchist movement. Necessarily so, since by its very nature it is not a movement that can conquer immediate, tangible results, such as a political movement, for instance, can accomplish. It may be said that the difference between even the most advanced political movement, such as Socialism, and Anarchism is this: the one seeks the transformation of political and economic conditions, while the goal of the other includes a complete transvaluation of individual and social conceptions. Such a gigantic task is necessarily of slow progress; nor can its advancement be counted by noses or ballots. It is the failure to realize fully the enormity of the task that is partly responsible for the pessimism that so often overtakes the active spirits of the movement. To that is added the lack of clarity regarding the manner of social accoutrements.

The Old is to give birth to the New. How do such things happen? as little Wendla asks her mother in Wedekind's *Frühlings Erwachen.* We have outgrown the stork of Social Revolution that will deliver us the newborn child of ready-made equality, fraternity, and liberty. We now conceive of the coming social life as a condition rather than a system. A condition of mind, primarily; one based on solidarity of interests arising from social understanding and enlightened self-interest. A system can be organized, made. A condition must be developed. This development is determined by existing environment and the intellectual tendencies of the times. The causation of both is no doubt mutual and interdependent, but the factor of individual and propagandistic effort is not to be underestimated.

The social life of man is a center, as it were, whence radiate numerous intellectual tendencies, crossing and zigzagging, receding and approaching each other in interminable succession. The points of convergence create new centers, exerting varying influences upon the larger center, the general life of humanity. Thus new intellectual and ethical atmospheres are established, the degree of their influence depending, primarily, on the active enthusiasm of the adherents; ultimately, on the kinship between the new ideal and the requirements of human nature. Striking this true chord, the new ideal will affect ever more intellectual centers, which gradually begin interpreting themselves into life and transvaluing the values of the great general center, the social life of man.

Anarchism is such an intellectual and ethical atmosphere. With sure hand it has touched the heart of humanity, influencing the world's foremost minds in literature, art, and philosophy. It has resurrected the individual from the ruins of the social débacle. In the forefront of human advance, its progress is necessarily painfully slow: the leaden weight of ages of ignorance and superstition hangs heavily at its heels. But its slow progress should by no means prove discouraging. On the contrary: it evidences the necessity of greater effort, of solidifying existing libertarian centers, and of ceaseless activity to create new ones.

The immaturity of the past had blinded our vision to the true requirements of the situation. Anarchism was regarded, even by its adherents, as an ideal for the future. Its practical application to current life was entirely ignored. The propaganda was circumscribed by the hope of ushering in the Social Revolution. *Preparation* for the new social life was not considered necessary. The gradual development and growth of the coming day did not enter into revolutionary concepts. The dawn had been overlooked. A fatal error, for there is no day without dawn.

The martyrdom of Francisco Ferrer will not have been in vain if, through it, the Anarchists—as well as other radical elements—will realize that, in social as well as in individual life, conception precedes birth. The social conception which we need, and must have, is the creation of libertarian centers which shall radiate the atmosphere of the dawn into the life of humanity.

Many such centers are possible. But the most important of all is the young life, the growing generation. After all, it is they upon whom will devolve the task of carrying the work forward. Just in the proportion that the young generation grows more enlightened and libertarian, will we approach a freer society. Yet in this regard we have been, and still are, unpardonably negligent, we Anarchists, Socialists, and other radicals. Protesting against the superstition-breeding educational system, we nevertheless continue to subject our children to its baneful influence. We condemn the madness of war, yet we permit our offspring to be inculcated with the poison of patriotism. Ourselves more or less emancipated from false bourgeois standards, we still suffer our children to be corrupted by the hypocrisy of the established. Every such parent directly aids in the perpetuation of dominant ignorance and slavery. Can we indeed expect a generation reared in the atmosphere of the suppressive, authoritarian educational régime to form the cornerstone of a free, self-reliant humanity? Such parents are criminally guilty toward themselves and their children: they rear the ghost that will divide their house against itself and strengthen the bulwarks of darkness.

No intelligent radical can fail to realize the need of the rational education of the young. The rearing of the child must become a process of liberation by methods which shall not impose ready-made ideas, but which should aid the child's natural self-unfoldment. The purpose of such an education is not to force the child's adaptation to accepted concepts, but to give free play to his originality, initiative, and individuality. Only by freeing education from compulsion and restraint can we create the environment for the manifestation of the spontaneous interest and inner incentives on the part of the child. Only thus can we supply rational conditions favorable to the development of the child's natural tendencies and his latent emotional and mental faculties. Such methods of education, essentially aiding the child's imitative quality and ardor for knowledge, will develop a generation of healthy intellectual independence. It will produce men and women capable, in the words of Francisco Ferrer, "of evolving without stopping, of destroying and renewing their environment without cessation; of renewing themselves also; always ready to accept what is best, happy in the triumph of new ideas, aspiring to live multiple lives in one life."

Upon such men and women rests the hope of human progress. To them belongs the future. And it is, to a very considerable extent, in our own power to pave the way. The death of Francisco Ferrer were in vain, our indignation, sympathy, and admiration worthless, unless we translate the ideals of the martyred educator into practice and life and thus advance the human struggle for enlightenment and liberty.

A beginning has already been made. Several schools, along Ferrer lines, are being conducted in New York and Brooklyn; Philadelphia and Chicago are also about to open classes. At present the efforts are limited, for lack of aid and teachers, to Sunday schools. But they are the nucleus of grand, far-reaching potentiality. The radical elements of America, and chiefly the Francisco Ferrer Association, could rear no worthier nor more lasting monument to the memory of the martyred educator, Francisco Ferrer, than by a generous response to this appeal for the establishment of the first **Francisco Ferrer Day School in America.**

VOL. VII, NO. 4, JUNE 1912

The Respectable Mob

By Ben L. Reitman

One of the most celebrated free-speech fights took place in San Diego, where a vigilante committee in complicity with the police terrorized members of the Industrial Workers of the World (I.W.W.) in order to halt their union-organizing efforts. San Diego was on the itinerary of Emma Goldman's 1912 national lecture tour, even though she had been warned to stay away. When she and her tour manager, Ben L. Reitman, arrived in May, two Wobblies had already been murdered—Michael Hoey and Joseph Mikolasek—and many more brutalized. "The

Respectable Mob," Reitman's account of their hair-raising reception, was published in the special "San Diego Edition" of *Mother Earth* (June 1912). (See Illustration 7, following page 220.)

(CO

AFTER FOUR YEARS OF ACTIVE Anarchist propaganda, I am beginning to understand that which is difficult for every American to appreciate; namely, that there is only as much freedom in America as the authority and property interests are willing to grant. And it is very plain to me now that whenever the police permit "too much" free speech, the capitalist class will step in and take matters into its own hands. Our San Diego experience not only burned industrial unionism into my flesh, but also engraved on my heart and soul that this is a country of the master class, and that the latter controls free speech.

The San Diego mob that tried to tear us to pieces and kidnapped me was a typical respectable mob, made up of retired bankers, retired army officers, real estate men, lawyers, doctors, businessmen, and saloonkeepers. Most of the active vigilantes own an automobile and property. To the credit of the working class it can be stated that the few workingmen who were in the mob were there at the bidding of their masters and not on their own initiative. In relating my experience I want our readers to know that that which was done to me was done in a measure to 300 other men, mostly members of the I. W. W. When the manager of the U. S. Grant Hotel, in San Diego, came to our room and said, "the Chief of Police wants to see both of you," I at once became suspicious. When Miss Goldman and the hotel manager left the office to go into another room, I was left alone with six respectable citizens. As soon as the door was closed, they drew out six cold steel revolvers, that some workingmen had made, and pointed them at me. They said, "If you utter a sound, or make a move, we'll kill you." Then they gathered around me. One man took my right arm, the other the left; a third man grabbed the front of my coat, another the back, and I was taken out into the corridor, down the elevator to the main floor of the hotel, and out into the street past a uniformed policeman, and then thrown into an automobile. When the mob saw me in the automobile, they set up a howl of delight. The auto went slowly down the main street and was joined by another one containing seven law-abiding, respectable businessmen. This was about 10.30 P.M.

I wish I could describe the terror of that twenty-mile ride in the beautiful California moonlight. I was in an automobile with six men and a chauffeur, and as soon as we were out of the business district, these Christian gentlemen started cursing, kicking, and beating me. Each one seemed to vie with the other to get a blow at me. My long hair was a favorite spot for attack. They took turns at pulling it. These Christian patriots put their fingers into my eyes and nose; kicked, pounded, bit me, and subjected me to every cruel, diabolical, malicious torture that a God-fearing respectable businessman is capable of conceiving. Space will not permit me to make a detailed report of that ride, but there was not a second but what some new torture was inflicted upon me. In fact, so many different blows poured in on me, and impressions came so fast, that I was unable to register all of them in my mind. I must ask our readers to listen to a part of the conversation:

"Why did you come here, you damned Anarchist outlaw?"

"We telegraphed you and that woman to stay away from here."

"Don't break his nose. I promised the doctor in the other automobile that he could have this pleasure."

"Oh, we like this; it's a treat for us to get a dog like you; you are one of them editors, one of them leaders that have been sending these men here. We have been beating up those I. W. W. hobos, and now we've got you. We like to beat you."

"We could kill you and tear out your guts and no one would know who did it, but we promised the Chief of Police that we wouldn't kill you or beat up your face too much."

"Why did you come here, you dago, you ignorant foreigner? We don't want you here. This is our town. We own property here. We've got money in the bank. We are not workingmen; we are businessmen, doctors, and lawyers, and we've got the law and the police on our side; and even if we didn't, the businessmen in San Diego are able to keep out all the I. W. W. Anarchist outlaws."

"You thought we wouldn't hurt you, huh? You came here and you thought you'd get locked up and get free advertisement. But we are done locking men up. We arrested 300 of those I. W. W. outlaws, and we had every jail in the county full of them, and they wouldn't work while they were in jail. They sang songs, and they broke up the jail; so we ain't going to arrest anybody else; we're just going to club hell out of all who come here to take part in this free speech fight and we'll brand them."

"You won't kiss the American flag, eh? By God, we'll make you; we'll ram it down your throat. Now you — — — Anarchist, sing the 'Star Spangled Banner!' No, that ain't the way. Sing it with feeling. Now, you Anarchist editor; you go back East and you tell all the I. W. W. Anarchists and Socialists and agitators how we treated you. Tell them what to expect when they come here. We own this town, and we'll run it to suit ourselves, and there ain't none of your outlaws who can come here and interfere with our business. Understand?"

In the last twenty years I have traveled more than half a million miles; but that ride with the businessmen of San Diego on the night of May 14th, 1912, was the most excruciating in my not uneventful career. When we reached the county line, some twenty miles out of town, the two automobiles drove to a deserted spot, off the main road, and then they all got out of their machines and put the two automobiles together, so the lights from the auto lamps made a sickly stage light. Then these fourteen brave defenders of their country formed a ring around me and commanded me to undress. They tore my clothes from me, and in a minute I stood before them naked, and the naked stars looked painfully on "how men their brothers maim."

When I read of the horrors of the Spanish Inquisition I could hardly believe it was true, and when I was told about the barbaric treatment the Russian revolutionists were subjected to, I felt that these gruesome tales must be exaggerated. And so when I relate to the readers of Mother Earth the cruel and inhuman treatment I received at the hands of fourteen American citizens, who are not only businessmen but also loving husbands and kind fathers, many will question my statements.

At first I refused to kiss the American flag. I was knocked down and compelled to kiss the flag which I had been taught to love in my boyhood days. Once I joyfully sang, "My country 'tis of thee, Sweet land of liberty." Twenty-five years ago I was thrilled when I took part in a chorus which sang "Oh, the Star Spangled Banner, long may it wave." Now when I hear those songs I want to weep; to me they are hollow mockery—covering all the sins and crimes of a cowardly nation. I was taught to loathe my native flag, not by Anarchists, or by ignorant foreigners, but by law-abiding, respectable businessmen.

When I lay naked on the ground, my tormentors kicked and beat me until I was almost insensible. With a lighted cigar they burned I. W. W. on my buttocks; then they poured a can of tar over my head and body, and, in the absence of feathers, they rubbed handfuls of sagebrush on my body. One very gentle businessman, who is active in church work, deliberately attempted to push my cane into my rectum. One unassuming banker twisted my testicles. These and many other things they did to me, until I forgot "whether I had done a great or little thing." When these businessmen were tired of their fun, they gave me my underwear for fear I should meet some women. These respectable citizens are very considerate of their women. They also gave me back my vest, in order that I might carry my money, railroad ticket, and watch. The rest of my clothes they stole from me in highwayman fashion. I was ordered to make a speech, and then they commanded me to run the gauntlet. The fourteen vigilantes were lined up, and as I ran past them, each one, in a businesslike manner, gave me a parting blow or kick.

My suffering was terrible, but my greatest pain was anxiety about E. G. I took it for granted that she would leave San Diego on the 2.45 A.M. train, and I attempted to walk towards the next station, hoping to board the train which I supposed she would be on. I walked blindly, like one mad, over the hills and through the canyons, and finally when the sun came up at 5 A.M., I saw by a signpost that I was fifteen miles from the nearest railroad. At 7 A.M. I came to the village of Renando and, timidly going into a store, I bought a pair of overalls and a jumper, a large bottle of turpentine, and some tar soap. Under a bridge, knee deep in a soft running stream, I began the process of removing the evidence of the businessmen of San Diego. Turpentine and tar soap and two hours of hard work made me halfway presentable. I called up E. G., who had reached Los Angeles by this time, and notified her that I was alive. Then I walked to Escondido very cautiously. I was afraid of the businessmen of California. I caught the 2.30 P.M. train and arrived at Lost Angeles at 5.30 P.M.

All this happened in the year of Our Lord 1912, in the most beautiful and best organized State in America.

Many lessons can be drawn from our San Diego experience, but none more important than this: the businessmen and the property owners will *fight* for their "rights." The historian who analyzes the cause of the San Diego trouble will have to record that it was property, and the fear that it may be taken from them, that roused the savagery of the San Diego vigilantes.

Another lesson is that the business mob can always depend upon the police and the press to back them up. The most active men among the vigilantes is Harvey, a detective-sergeant, and Bierman, a newspaperman on the *San Diego Union*.

Comrade Joseph Mikolasek was wantonly killed by a policeman's bullet. Michael Hoey, an I. W. W. man, was knocked down by a stream of water and died soon after. An innocent child was washed out of the buggy by a hose held by the police and killed. Nearly four hundred men have been jailed on charges varying from vagrancy to murder. Practically all those men were innocent. Three hundred men have been beaten, kidnapped, and forced to undergo Spanish Inquisition tortures. The vigilantes and police have had a great deal of fun. None of them has been as much as slapped on the wrist. They proved to us that we were a lot of cowards, unable to protect ourselves. All that has been done in the way of retaliation has been to appeal to the government and the public for sympathy. We didn't even get that. The revolutionary movement of America has not justified its existence, at least so far as San Diego is concerned. For myself, I weep. I am ashamed that that great, big, strong giant, Labor, can be so readily bullied and beaten, and will not strike back.

A friend, whom I saw last week in San Quentin prison, asked me: "Why don't somebody do something?" I answered: "We are all cowards, I guess."

VOL. VIII, NO. 8, OCTOBER 1913

Prisons: Universities of Crime

By Peter Kropotkin

Like Alexander Berkman, Peter Kropotkin wrote of the relation of prisons to crime from firsthand experience. Active as a young man in the populist *narodnik* movement, he was arrested at St. Petersburg in 1874 and held for two years in the forbidding Peter-Paul Fortress while awaiting trial. He managed a daring escape from a prison hospital and fled to Western Europe, where he lived in exile until after the Russian Revolution. He was arrested again in 1883, this time in France, during a period of antianarchist hysteria, and spent three years in the prison at Clairvaux. His early writings on penology were collected in his *In Russian and French Prisons* (1887), and he vividly recounted his years of incarceration in his *Memoirs of a Revolutionist* (1899).

Paper read before the British Medical Association

LEAVING ASIDE THE GREAT QUESTION of "Crime and Punishment" which occupies now so many prominent lawyers and sociologists, I shall limit my remarks to the question: "Are prisons answering their purpose, which is that of diminishing the number of antisocial acts?"

To this question every unprejudiced person who has a knowledge of prisons from the inside will certainly answer by an emphatic *No*. On the contrary, a serious study of the subject will bring everyone to the conclusion that the prisons—the best as much as the worst—are breeding places of criminality; that they contribute to render the antisocial acts worse and worse; that they are, in a word, the High Schools, the Universities of what is known as Crime.

Of course, I do not mean that everyone who has been once in a prison will return to it. There are thousands of people sent every year to prison by mere accident. But I maintain that the effect of a couple of years of life in a prison—from the very fact of its being a prison—is to increase in the individual those defects which brought him before a law court. These causes, being the love of risk, the dislike of regular work (due in an immense majority of cases to the want of a thorough knowledge of a trade), the despise of society with its injustice and hypocrisy, the want of physical energy, and the lack of will—all these causes will be aggravated by detention in a jail.

Five-and-twenty years ago, when I developed this idea in a book, now out of print (*In Russian and French Prisons*), I supported it by an examination of the facts revealed in France by an inquest made as to the numbers of *récidivistes* (second offence prisoners). The result of this inquest was that from two fifths to one half of all persons brought before the assizes and two fifths of all brought before the police courts had already been kept once or twice in a jail. The very same figure of forty percent was found in this country; while, according to Michael Davitt, as much as ninety-five percent of all those who are kept in penal servitude have previously received prison education.

A little reflection will show that things cannot be otherwise. A prison has, and must have, a degrading effect on its inmates. Take a man freshly brought to a jail. The moment he enters the house he is no more a human being; he is "Number So and So." He must have no more a will of his own. They put him in a fool's dress to underline his degradation. They deprive him of every intercourse with those towards whom he may have an attachment and thus exclude the action of the only element which could have a good effect upon him.

Then he is put to labor, but not to a labor that might help to his moral improvement. Prison work is made to be an instrument of base revenge. What must the prisoner think of the intelligence of these "pillars of society" who pretend by such punishments to "reform" the prisoners?

In the French prisons the inmates are given some sort of useful and paid work. But even this work is paid at a ridiculously low scale, and, according to the prison authorities, it cannot be paid otherwise. Prison work, they say, is inferior slave work. The result is that the prisoner begins to hate his work, and finishes by saying, "The real thieves are not we, but those who keep us in."

The prisoner's brain is thus working over and over again upon the idea of the injustice of a society which pardons and often respects such swindlers as so many company promoters are, and wickedly punishes him, simply because he was not cunning enough. And the moment he is out he takes his revenge by some offence very often much graver than his first one. Revenge breeds revenge.

The revenge that was exercised upon him he exercises upon society. Every prison, because it is a prison, destroys the physical energy of its inmates. It acts upon them far worse than an Arctic wintering. The want of fresh air, the monotony of existence, especially the want of impressions, take all energy out of the prisoner and produce that craving for stimulants (alcohol, coffee) of which Miss Allen spoke so truthfully the other day at the Congress of the British Medical Association. And finally, while most antisocial acts can be traced to a weakness of will, the prison education is directed precisely towards killing every manifestation of will.

Worse than that. I seriously recommend to prison reformers the *Prison Memoirs* of Alexander Berkman, who was kept for fourteen years in an American jail and has told with great sincerity his experience. One will see from this book how every honest feeling must be suppressed by the prisoner, if he does not decide never to go out of this hell.

What can remain of a man's will and good intentions after five or six years of such an education? And where can he go after his release, unless he returns to the very same chums whose company has brought him to the jail? They are the only ones who will receive him as an equal. But when he joins them he is sure to return to the prison in a very few months. And so he does. The jailers know it well.

I am often asked—What reforms of prisons I should propose; but now, as twenty-five years ago, I really do not see how prisons could be reformed. They must be pulled down. I might say, of course: "Be less cruel, be more thoughtful of what you do." But that would come to this: "Nominate a Pestalozzi as Governor in each prison, and sixty Pestalozzis as warders," which would be absurd. But nothing short of that would help.

So the only thing I could say to some quite well-intentioned Massachusetts prison officials who came once to ask my advice was this: If you cannot obtain the abolition of the prison system, then—never accept a child or a youth in your prison. If you do so, it is manslaughter. And then, after having learned by experience what prisons are, refuse to be jailers and never be tired to say that prevention of crime is the only proper way to combat it.

Healthy municipal dwellings at cost price, education in the family and at school—of the parents as well as the children; the learning by every boy and girl of a trade; communal and professional cooperation; societies for all sorts of pursuits; and, above all, idealism developed in the youths; the longing after what is lifting human nature to higher interests. This will achieve what punishment is absolutely incapable to do.

VOL. IX, NO. 2, APRIL 1914

Tannenbaum before Pilate

By Alexander Berkman

In the winter of 1913–14, during a severe depression, a twenty-one-year-old anarchist and I.W.W. member named Frank Tannenbaum led unemployed workers into New York's churches, demanding food and shelter. Emma Goldman in her memoirs described Tannenbaum as "a vivid youth" who "spent much of his time in our office, reading and helping in the work of *Mother Earth*." The peaceful marches began on February 27, Tannenbaum bringing hundreds of the unemployed into such downtown churches as the Old Baptist Tabernacle, the Labor Temple, the First Presbyterian Church, and St. Mark's Episcopal Church, where they were generally well, if reluctantly, received. On the night of March 4, however, the rector of the Church of St. Alphonsus on West Broadway refused to let the men stay and called the police. As they were leaving, the sound of a newspaper photographer's exploding flash powder was mistaken for a gunshot, setting off a small police riot. For his exercise in direct action, Tannenbaum was arrested and sentenced to a year in jail on Blackwell's Island and fined $500. "Tannenbaum before Pilate" is Alexander Berkman's eyewitness report of the incident and the trial.

Tannenbaum's arrest and imprisonment received extensive newspaper coverage and triggered a series of demonstrations that lasted for months, organized largely by the indefatigable Berkman. Mabel Dodge devoted two whole chapters of her memoirs to Tannenbaum himself (he had attended one of her salon evenings, in Goldman's company) and the movement of the unemployed. Tannenbaum went on to become a leading authority on Latin America and a full professor of history at Columbia University. (See Berkman, "The Movement of the Unemployed," page 338.)

N O ONE FAMILIAR WITH THE circumstances can have the least doubt that Frank Tannenbaum has been made a victim of class justice and railroaded to prison on perjured evidence.

I speak as an eyewitness of the events that happened in St. Alphonsus Church at the time Tannenbaum and 189 other unemployed were arrested. I charge Detective Sergeant Geogan and "Father" Schneider with having deliberately perjured themselves for the purpose of securing the conviction of Tannenbaum and the other boys.

The facts in the case are these: When the unemployed army reached St. Alphonsus Church, Tannenbaum—accompanied by Detectives Geogan and Gilday—walked into the church, after he had requested the men to wait for him outside. In less than three minutes he reappeared.

"Boys," he said, "I am going in to the rectory next door to see the priest. Will you wait here and behave till I come?"

"Yes," the men replied, and Frank, still in the company of the detectives, entered the rectory.

We waited quietly a few minutes, when some reporters pushed through the crowd lining the sidewalk and the steps in front of the church. One of the newspapermen tried the door furthest north from the main entrance. It opened. The man entered, and after him filed in the crowd. So far as I could see there were no worshipers in the church at the time. All the men took off their hats and took seats. I think I was the only one to keep my hat on for a while, until I was seated. There was complete silence for at least five minutes, when a priest in the back of the church jumped noisily on a bench and shouted in much agitation something about "the presence of the holy ghost in this place."

At that moment Tannenbaum entered, the two detectives and several reporters at his side.

"Boys," he called, "we can't stay here. We are not wanted. Let's go to some other place."

The men began to file out. When more than half of the audience was already out, I, still keeping my seat, saw some plainclothes police roughly push some men toward the door. It was then that I heard a slight commotion, protests, and catcalls.

In a few minutes the whole assembly was out in the street. No arrests had been made, no uniformed police were in sight.

I remained on the sidewalk in front of the church for fully ten minutes, chatting with some acquaintances. The crowd was thinning. It was after eight in the evening, and as I had promised to attend the first meeting of the Conference of the Unemployed at 66 E. 4th Street, I went to the hall.

It was at least an hour later that some friends rushed into the place to inform us of the arrest of Tannenbaum and the other men. It appeared that by some trick the detectives succeeded in getting the people back into the church and locking the doors, meanwhile telephoning to the police.

These facts considered, the conviction of Frank Tannenbaum, D. Wisotsky, and several other men is a most dastardly frame-up on the part of the police and "Father" Schneider, of St. Alphonsus Church, all the witnesses for the prosecution perjuring themselves in the most infamous manner.

The beast of law and darkness thirsted for blood. Frank knew it. He knew that he had committed the worst of all crimes: he had preached a new gospel. What wonder, then, that in spite of the convincing evidence of the defense, Tannenbaum was convicted, the good Christian judge mollifying his hatred and revenge by dooming Frank to suffer the extreme penalty of the law: one year in the penitentiary at Blackwell's Island and $500.00 fine, signifying 500 additional prison days.

Tannenbaum, an intelligent and revolutionary worker, realized far better than his advisers that no justice is to be expected in the prostitute courts of capitalism. Unafraid and defiant, he threw this bold challenge into the teeth of the enemy:

"I'd like to say a few things, but if I do I suppose the newspapers will have me playing myself up as a martyr or a hero.

"There was once a person who said that a society would forgive every crime—murder, arson, theft, or rape—but that the one thing it will not forgive is the preaching of a new gospel. *That's* my crime. I was going about telling people that the jobless must be housed and fed, and for that I got locked up.

"I am accused of participating in an unlawful assembly. Well, I belong to the wage-slave class, and I don't know of any assembly on the part of *that* class that would be *lawful*. The assembly, being of slaves, was unlawful as a matter of course. And I participated in it. I don't deny that.

"There was no property destroyed, no people hurt, no violence used, no breach of the peace. But the papers wanted me arrested, the church people turned me over to the police, and the police turned me over to the court, the court over to the Grand Jury, and the Grand Jury again over to you. And you found me guilty!

"Somebody said I answered 'Yes' to a statement about bloodshed. Why all this nonsense about bloodshed? The capitalist class sheds more blood in one year than the working class does in five. We workers are being killed every day. We are killed in mines, in the factories, in buildings, and on the battlefield. There's never been a war in the interests of the workers, and yet it's the workers who die.

"Unlawful assembly, to be sure! We had gone to other churches and have been well received. Where they didn't give us food and shelter, they gave us money to get them. Dr. Duffy gave us $25.00, and this man Press calls it graft money. I don't believe the assistant district attorney has heart enough to be a dog catcher. Think of the injustice he does me in saying that the $25.00 given to feed the men I got was graft money! That money was given to Mr. Martin. We took 83 hungry and jobless men to a restaurant and fed them. Mr. Martin paid for those men's meals out of the money that was given to him. They talk about religion—praying to God—I think it was the most religious sight I ever saw—those starving men being fed. After we had arranged for their lodging there was ten cents left, and the assistant district attorney can have that if he wants it.

"The first time we were not well received was at Dr. Schneider's church. And from that we were not allowed to go away peaceably. For it is an absolute lie of Geogan's when he said that he did not call me back into the church.

"As to my attitude towards the priests, I want to say that by nature I am polite even to my enemies. And I tell you that Dr. Schneider, supposed to be a representative of Christ—the man who died on the cross for preaching a new gospel and whom the common people heard gladly—would be the first to crucify Christ if he came to us today.

"Before I was arrested I knew little or nothing about the police or courts. I was practically ignorant of all such things. But from what I have learned since—in this court and in the Tombs—*I have come to have no respect at all for the court and the law.*

"For several weeks I have lived with the fellows in jail, fellows who have been driven and kicked about from place to place. In my estimation they are as good as anybody else.

"The day that I was brought into the court justice flew out of the window and never came back. I didn't want this trial. I knew what I was going to get. But my friends prevailed on me to have a trial. And the result is exactly as I expected. If I am ever arrested again I will not have a trial. No more trials for me.

"As for the jury, they are all men who want to be rich. They are members of your class. They are capitalists in miniature. You couldn't get a jury of workingmen, of structural iron workers, for instance, to convict me.

"You jurymen fail to take into consideration the circumstances, the passions, the feelings of men. We boys who see and feel the misery of unemployment are more spontaneous, more human, I think, than other people. We can't adapt ourselves to this system, this rotten system which jails men for demanding a piece of bread. We don't believe in denying the right of hungry men to demand food. That was my crime—telling the producers of bread to get a bite of it for themselves. And I am willing to take the consequences."

VOL. X, NO. 7, SEPTEMBER 1915

A New Adventure in Arcadia

By Louise Bryant

The subject of birth control proved to be an easy excuse for police censorship and a continuing focus of free-speech fights on Emma Goldman's annual lecture tours. Louise Bryant, shortly before her move east with John Reed, reported one such episode in Portland, Oregon, when First Amendment justice actually prevailed. Goldman later wrote of Judge William Gatens's decision in her favor that "even judges sometimes progress" (see "The Social Aspects of Birth Control," page 134).

FOR ABOUT TWENTY YEARS Emma Goldman has been making an annual visit to what the boosters have chosen to name our "Rose City." There are certain ones of us in Portland who have acquired the habit of Emma Goldman, and it would be difficult, indeed, for us to go through a year without her, for like the Spring she always brings us new joy and life and inspiration. And as it would be tragic for any of us who live here where there are so many dismal, rainy days to miss the warm, sweet, healing incense of the Spring, so it would be just as hard to experience a summer without the usual inspirational messages which our good Arch-Anarchist annually brings us.

When we had settled down, as is our custom, to enjoy the course of lectures, we did not expect to be rudely interrupted either by the police or the ministers of the city. I say "settled down" because that is the way we do things in Portland, we do them comfortably and with dignity and poise or we do not do them at all. That is why Miss Goldman finds it so hard to lecture here. She said to me before one of her lectures, "My audiences are so dead!"

However, it remained for one little, frowsy-haired old woman, Mrs. Josephine Johnson, who was blighted by that deadly thing we call "provincialism," to get us all into a regular row and plunge Emma Goldman and Ben Reitman into such glaring headlines in the newspapers that for the time being Portland forgot the war in Europe or even that there were still loose about our merry land such men as Roosevelt and Billy Sunday. It was this little old lady, who has not been able to live up to the age, who swore to a complaint she knew nothing about and brought the majesty of the law down upon us all.

It came about thus: One evening when Miss Goldman was lecturing on Friedrich Nietzsche, someone distributed a few pamphlets giving methods of preventing conception. Miss Goldman really knew nothing about this distribution but, of course, she is so interested in the problem of birth control that she certainly approved of everything set forth in them. However, the point is that the lecture was not about birth control, and she had nothing to do with the pamphlet. Three nights later (August 6th), she was to deliver the birth control lecture, and just before that lecture, as she was making the first introductory remarks, both she and Dr. Reitman were arrested on the charge of distributing the pamphlet, *because that was the only excuse the police or any of the officials could find to break up the meeting!*

We have free speech in Portland, and we are very proud of it. Several times measures aiming at its destruction have been up before the voters, and these measures have been overwhelmingly defeated. With popular sentiment strongly in favor of free speech one might wonder why Miss Goldman could be notified on the afternoon of August 6th that she would not be allowed to speak anymore in Portland on any subject whatever. That is, one might if one did not know Portland and Portland's God-fearing Mayor.

Ever since Mayor Albee was elected three years ago he has put most of his problems into the hands of God. Personally, I feel that if God ever had anything to do with making the world he is so ashamed of it by this time that he does not like to be reminded. However, our Mayor always has a recourse if God does not help him out of his difficulties; he turns the affair over to his secretary, Mr. Warren.

Mr. C. E. S. Wood very wittily remarked in speaking of this case, "The Mayor is a good man filled with good intentions, in which he resembles hell, and the real power is exercised by his secretary, Mr. Warren, who is filled with bad intentions, in which he also resembles hell, and the difference is that the Mayor does not carry out his good intentions but Mr. Warren carries out his bad ones."

After Miss Goldman had received her notice from the police, Mr. Warren also told Ben Reitman that Miss Goldman would not be allowed to speak in Portland anymore and if Colonel Wood was with her on the platform he would be locked up too. That being the state of affairs, Colonel Wood, who is more influential and more loved and of more use in the world than any number of Mayor's secretaries, was very prompt to be on hand at the meeting. He was not arrested, but he was able that evening and later to help his friends not only with money but with his wide knowledge of the law, which is his profession.

The arrest was unique in many ways. The plainclothesman who arrested Miss Goldman and Dr. Reitman was made to read aloud the charge, while the erstwhile quiet audience hissed and stormed.

At ten-thirty at night the police refused to take Mr. Wood's personal check or anybody else's check or travelers' checks or any other bail except cash, and fixed the bail at $500 for each offender, making $1,000. This was, of course, contrary to all justice. At that hour of the night Mr. Wood was only able to raise $500, by going to one of the local hotels, so Dr. Reitman remained in jail.

At the trial, the next morning, the usual farce took place as far as justice was concerned. Judge Stadter, who was acting municipal judge during Judge Stevenson's vacation, fined our good friends $100 each.

This was promptly appealed, and this is where the real joy of the adventure in Arcadia came about and how Miss Goldman happened to meet a fair-minded judge.

The second trial was held in Dept. 5 of the Circuit Court, which is presided over by Judge Wm. N. Gatens. He is not the type of judge who "sit impassive high above the tears of women and the dull despair of men," but he is the type (alas! there are so few) who use the law as a real means of securing justice. He said some very good things at this trial, and he says some very good things at every trial where he presides, for he is very humane. Perhaps this is partly due to the fact that he has worked for his living since early childhood, when he was left an orphan. He really *knows* what hunger and despair and pain are like, he has not merely *heard* about them.

He dismissed the case because the offense brought no evidence to show that the defendants had anything to do with the pamphlets.

During the trial Judge Gatens made these remarks:

"The Court says the defendants are not here charged, as has been stated by the council, with creating anarchistic tendencies, or being anarchists; they are here to be tried for the offense set forth in the information and no other offense.

"Every person, when charged with a crime, should have the right to know the nature of the crime with which they are charged, meet the witnesses face to face, and be tried without prejudice, not to be tried on the ground that you don't like this person or that person because they have some view different from yours.

"Now it seems to me that the trouble with our people today is that there is too much prudery. Ignorance and prudery are the millstones about the necks of progress. Everyone knows that. We are all shocked by many things publicly stated that we know privately ourselves, but we haven't got the nerve to get up and admit it, and when some person brings to our attention something we already know, we feign modesty and we feel that the public has been outraged and decency has been shocked, and as a matter of fact we know all these things ourselves.

"I am a member of the Oregon Hygiene Association. We get out literature and place it in the toilets all over the State, telling people how to guard against the evils of venereal diseases, and so forth. We do that for the uplift of humanity, to protect society from all those things, and the public does not seem to be very much shocked about it."

Can you imagine anything more refreshing and hopeful than to hear a judge, talking thus openly and frankly in a case where Anarchists are being tried? If only such a clean-minded judge will preside over the trial of Margaret Sanger, what a fine thing for all mankind that will be!

There is little more to tell. Miss Goldman gave four more lectures after her arrest. One was at the Public Library. Hundreds were turned away.

The Case of Mooney and Billings

On July 22, 1916, amid increasing war fervor, a bomb exploded along the route of a "Preparedness Day" parade in San Francisco. Ten people were killed and forty injured. Two radical labor leaders, Thomas J. Mooney and Warren K. Billings, were arrested for the crime and tried and convicted by rigged juries on fabricated evidence and the contradictory testimony of perjured witnesses. Their innocence was clear, yet Mooney was sentenced to death on the gallows (later commuted to life behind bars) and Billings to life imprisonment. They were pardoned and released in 1939. Their frame-up is among the most egregious miscarriages of justice in the annals of U.S. labor history. Also arrested were Mooney's wife, Rena, and labor militants Israel Weinberg and Edward Nolan, but they were not convicted. The actual bomb thrower was never discovered.

At the time of the explosion, Alexander Berkman and his companion, M. Eleanor Fitzgerald, had moved to San Francisco, where they launched their own anarchist journal, *The Blast* (1916–17). On the very day of the parade bombing, Emma Goldman was in the city and gave a talk entitled "Preparedness, the Road to Universal Slaughter." The police naturally tried to implicate the three in the explosion and searched *The Blast* office for evidence. Berkman campaigned strenuously on behalf of Mooney and Billings, reporting on their cases in both *The Blast* and *Mother Earth*. Of the two articles that follow, the first was signed by him, while the second may very well have been from his pen. The quotation from *Organized Labor* is by the political cartoonist Robert Minor, whose work appeared in *The Blast* and *Mother Earth* as well as *The Masses*. Berkman's warning against "the constantly growing menace of reaction in the country" was no apparition, as rising support for war evolved into the ever more stringent political censorship and oppression that brought an end to *Mother Earth,* along with *The Blast* and *The Masses*.

VOL. XI, NO. 8, OCTOBER 1916

Legal Assassination

By Alexander Berkman

OUR WORST FEARS HAVE COME TRUE. Warren K. Billings has been found guilty by a professional and bitterly prejudiced jury. In spite of numerous reliable witnesses for the defense, in spite of the obviously bought testimony of the State, Billings was convicted on charge of murder in the first degree. The jury did as the District Attorney Brennan asked them: they brought in a verdict of guilty and fixed the penalty at life imprisonment. This was Brennan's masterstroke of villainy. He feared there might be at least *one* man on the jury who would object to hanging an innocent man. He therefore did not ask for the death penalty, but for a recommendation to life imprisonment, in order—in Brennan's own words— "to give Billings a chance to confess on the 'higher-ups.'"

And that is the key to the whole prosecution. It is some mysterious "higher-ups" that the Chamber of Commerce is planning "to get." District Attorney Fickert twice repeated in his address to the jury that there would be some lynchings unless the jury convict Billings. And Brennan made it clear that the conviction was wanted merely as "a stepping stone toward uncovering the greater conspiracy." That no doubt as to his meaning be left in the minds of the jury, Brennan reiterated that the real perpetrator of the bomb explosion of July 22nd was not just a man or men, but members of "*the class* opposed to preparedness." Brazenly and with low cunning he again and again reminded the jury that "the class opposed to preparedness is also opposed to our form of government" and that "such Anarchistic teachings are propagated by THE BLAST."

He waved the flag and appealed to the low prejudices of the jury to "save their accustomed comforts and not permit us to return to a state of savagery," by making an example of those who dared disagree with himself or criticize the hangmen of Labor.

In short, it was a worthy duplicate of the customary cheap Fourth of July oration. Brennan must have studied Grinnell's speech before the jury at the trial of our martyred Chicago comrades. He gave virtually a replica of it, only less intelligently. But it was effective enough for the jury of professional talesmen, every one of them dependent for his means of existence on the good will of the District Attorney. To think that the scales of justice are in the hands of such men! That these twelve men have in their hands the life or death of a real human being! That is the great tragedy of justice.

As to the case itself, the prosecution produced the very flimsiest evidence. Its witnesses contradicted each other over and again. They had Billings dressed in a black suit, a light suit, a dark-light suit, and a brown one, all at the same time. Also in as many different hats. According to several of the State's witnesses, Billings was on the roof of 721 Market Street at the very moment when other State witnesses saw him put the suitcase down at Steuart Street, a mile or more distant. They identified Billings as a man with a rash high up on his forehead, when they saw him only with his hat on—on the opposite sidewalk while the street was crowded with paraders. And in court it was proven that Billings indeed had a rash—on his knee.

The whole case of the prosecution was a veritable spider's web, as flimsy and treacherous, the threads woven by the promise of $21,000 reward, the pardoning of Mrs. Kidwell's husband from the penitentiary in payment for her daughter's—Estelle Smith's—perjury.

This Estelle Smith and a certain McDonald were the main stars of the prosecution. Estelle is a notorious *demimondaine*. She has an uncle who is serving a long term in the penitentiary, and her mother's second husband is doing time in Folsom prison for forgery. It might prove of educational interest for criminologists to investigate what relationship there may exist between forgery and perjury. Estelle Smith's testimony was of the most preposterous character; it bore inherent evidence of training and memorizing. But some of the jurymen declared, after the verdict was in, that they credited her testimony!

The other star witness of the State, John McDonald, is a man-about-town of the lowest character, a dope fiend who would sell his mother's womb for a smell of opium. Reputable witnesses for the defense proved that McDonald boasted he would convict the defendant and then return "on the cushions to Baltimore with plenty of coin." The prosecution admitted buying new clothes for him, paying his hotel bills, and otherwise "encouraging" him to do his "duty."

With entire impartiality it may be said that the State witnesses were a disreputable-looking lot, and that their evidence would not convict a louse that bit you, even if you, the bitten, were to sit in judgment.

But the jury of twelve men "honest and true" believed them. I had an opportunity to study that jury. I was in the courtroom and listened to the evidence. The witnesses for the defense—reputable citizens, veterans of the Civil War, a well-known member of the medical profession, men and women of probity and intelligence—made a splendid impression. Their appearance, their manner, and especially their intelligence and straightforwardness contrasted with the picture of the State witnesses. Friend and enemy alike felt this. The alibi of Billings was frank and convincing. The defense had such a good story that they not only completely discredited the State's witnesses and unmasked their commercial motives, but directly proved the innocence of Billings beyond the shadow of a doubt.

To everyone, even to the newspapermen originally antagonistic to the defense, the innocence of Billings was clear. To everyone—except the jury.

But when I looked at them, I knew the reason. I looked at them while the best testimony of the defense was being taken, and again when the defendant's Attorney, Maxwell McNutt, was addressing the jury. The courtroom was crowded, and I could not get a seat. A friendly attorney invited me into the railing, and I found a place directly facing the jury box. The witnesses for the defense were convincingly disproving, one after another, the testimony of the State. Conservative men and women, Grand Army men, members of the Sons of Veterans, believers in military preparedness and marchers in the parade endangered by the bomb explosion, who might reasonably be expected to feel some bitterness and prejudice against the accused—*they* were proving an alibi for Billings. The atmosphere of the courtroom was tense. The innocence of Billings was being established by reliable and absolutely disinterested witnesses, conservative law-worshiping citizens. You could feel the growing consciousness of the prisoner's innocence filling the courtroom. All eyes were turned on Billings. His tawny hair reflected the brightness of the sun stealing through the shaded windows. A frank, manly look lit up the young, intelligent face. You could feel the wave of sympathy streaming from spectators to the honest-faced boy in the prisoner's dock. The air vibrated with the assurance of a ringing "Not Guilty!"

I scrutinized the jurors. The one directly opposite me looked heavy, coarse and red-faced, with the peculiar earmarks of a detective. Next to him was a pale, anemic man that looked half wolf, half fox. An old man near him was drowsily nodding his head. I caught another surreptitiously smiling, apologetically and encouragingly, at the District Attorney.

My heart sank within me. I left the court convinced that the men in the jury box *were there to convict.*

I confided my suspicions and fears to a few friends. They ridiculed my pessimism. "We have established Billings' innocence," they told me, "even the newspapers had to change their hostile tone. All the prisoners will soon be at liberty."

"Do you really think that evidence counts in a case like this?" I persisted. "McNutt, sure of his case, hardly even examined the talesmen as to their formed beliefs, connections, and prejudices. I am afraid the jury is packed," I warned my friends of the defense. "Be easy," they said, "no jury on earth could help acquitting Billings on such evidence. Besides, Judge Dunne has been very fair; he would not stand for an unjust verdict."

The verdict of guilty stunned the friends of the accused. McNutt has hardly recovered yet. Even the great bulk of indifferent citizens were surprised. The majority looked for an acquittal. A disagreement was the very worst expected by the defense, the best hoped for by the prosecution. San Francisco is alive with the spirit of gamble. I heard bets made 10 to 1 in favor of Billings.

And now? The conviction of Billings, innocent as he is, means that the stage has been set for a repetition of the 11th of November, 1887. I do not want to make matters look darker than they are, but it is well for us to look the facts full in the face. Conversant with the local situation, I am absolutely convinced that the Chamber of Commerce of San Francisco—as its prototype, the Chicago Citizens' Alliance of 1886—has decreed the fate of the most intelligent and militant labor men on the Coast.

Innocence does not count in the courts of Mammon. Evidence is ignored. The dice are loaded against Labor, and the legal assassination of Mooney, Nolan et al. is but the prelude to the white terror campaign against Labor on the Coast.

In San Francisco, as in the iron districts of Minnesota and the coal regions of Pennsylvania, on the Atlantic coast as on the Pacific, the war of the classes is in full blast. We can't save the victims of the hydra-headed monster of Greed one by one; we can't save them individually. I see no hope anywhere, nowhere—except in the invincible arm of solidaric Labor.

But the Giant is blind and asleep, alive only in spots. Too long to wait for his awakening. Even the workers of San Francisco, aware of the terrible Chamber-of-Commerce conspiracy, remain indifferent, as a class. A few unions only have aided financially. Morally the workers are in the paralyzing grip of that worst of scourges, the labor politicians.

What remains, then? Only this: a united stand by all radicals, irrespective of philosophy, against the constantly growing menace of the reaction in this country. A united stand, and a direct, energetic campaign to rouse the social consciousness throughout the land.

VOL. XII, NO. I, MARCH 1917

A Lynch Jury in San Francisco Convicts Thomas Mooney

[Unsigned]

That is the consequence of being bribed to murder honest people in their sleep.

FIVE COURAGEOUS FIGHTERS FOR Labor's birthright of noble character and intellect, one of them a woman, are to be led to the gallows in San Francisco if the outrages committed in the trials of Billings and Mooney against truth, right, justice, find no redress. All the paraphernalia of that justice which serves the powerful and tramples the underdog into the mud has been on exhibition in the Mooney trial, ending with the death sentence.

The police, spies, detectives, who "collect" the evidence and "fix up" the material for the prosecution. Then the State and its attorneys, acting openly and brazenly as the servants of the wealthy classes, who furnish the money for the legal conspiracy and won't brook no organization, no resistance from the sons and daughters of toil.

Add to these instruments of justice false testimony, bribery, threats, perjuries, a polite—as far as technicalities go—obliging judge and a jury consisting of small, prejudiced, fossilized men, perhaps not averse in some cases to flattery, favors, and handshakes—and you have a pretty fair sample of justice as it is practiced against Labor in the law courts of our days.

However, in the Mooney trial right, truth, common sense were so strong and so obviously on the side of the defense that even with all the mentioned ghastly instruments of capitalistic justice, a verdict of guilty seemed impossible. But the prosecutors Cunha and Fickert triumphed with the help of Daniel Webster, whom Fickert plagiarized in order to obtain some catching phrases for his hell and damnation speech.

From an article written for *Organized Labor* by Bob Minor, who witnessed the shameful proceedings right on the spot, we quote the following passages:

Twenty-five witnesses swore to Mooney's alibi; seven photographs proved it. Three of these photos were those famous "alibi pictures" which had been faded out by the prosecutors so as not to show the time on the street clocks. Other photographs, newly discovered, showed the corner of Steuart and Market Streets at many intervals covering the period during which Oxman swore that the defendants were at that corner in Weinberg's jitney bus. These photographs flatly disproved Oxman's statement, the time shown on the Ferry clock in the pictures making the proof absolute.

Weinberg swore that Martin Swanson, private detective for the Pacific Gas and Electric Company, offered him on two occasions before the parade $5,000 to frame up Mooney. The prosecution did not put Swanson on the stand to deny this, although dared to do so by the defense.

The defense called attention to the fact that at the very outset false evidence was deliberately manufactured to fit Swanson's theory, showing that the photographs of the "scene of the explosion" which the prosecution palmed off on the jury were not photographs of the scene of the explosion, but of a hole in the sidewalk and wall deliberately manufactured with sledgehammer and crowbar in the presence of the District Attorney by a friend of his.

An expert was called to explain the detonation of dynamite by means of a dry-cell battery. Then a supposed "dry-cell battery coil" was brought out as "found at the scene." McNutt proved that it was *not* a dry-cell coil, but a *retarding coil from a telephone switchboard, "planted" at the scene two days after the tragedy!*

All of this was proven by the State's witnesses. The only photograph of the true scene of the explosion was introduced by the defense. All of the defendants were arrested before any evidence had been obtained. The defense attorney summarized the evidence of the State's police witnesses, as well as its corroboration by Weinberg, to prove that not one single person really identified any of the defendants. Oxman did not identify Mooney, but went to the jail register and got the number of his cell before even pretending to identify him, and then identified him simply by turning in the number of his cell. Mrs. Mooney was identified by the Edeaus and Oxman, being brought out and placed face to face with them, they being *told* who she was, and then *asked* who she was. Weinberg was forced to put on his hat and was addressed by name in the presence of the Edeaus and of Oxman, and then the "identifiers" were asked, "Is this Weinberg?" In not one single instance was a real identification made. It is the universal custom, wherever justice is pretended to be followed, to line up a prisoner with other prisoners and have the identifier pick him out of the crowd.

But all this was of no avail. A preconceived, carefully prearranged plan to send undesirable labor agitators to the scaffold, backed by all the powers of government and money, is hard to defeat. If Christ himself would have come to testify for Mooney the verdict would have still been the same.

Yet a new development in the case seemed to hold out some hope for at least a new trial.

Two affidavits were introduced after the jury's verdict, but before Judge Griffin had passed sentence, which strongly contradicted the testimony of Oxman, chief state witness against whom the police apparently hold some goods, the unpacking of which would embarrass him greatly.

The most important of these affidavits is that of Mrs. Charlotte La Posee, who swore that she knew Oxman in Oregon, that on the day of the preparedness parade bomb explosion she was standing with her little son Richard and her husband in front of the Phelan Building, O'Farrell and Market Streets, that she noticed Oxman standing right near her. She fixes the time at 1:45, the hour Oxman testified he was at Steuart and Market Streets, a mile away from the Phelan Building. In spite of this and other new aspects of the case Judge Griffin denied the motion for a new trial and sentenced Mooney to die on the gallows on the 17th of May.

The labor organizations of the country will have to come out immediately in full force and determination in behalf of Billings, Mooney, and the other three defendants—otherwise the infamous Chicago Haymarket trial, resulting in the legal murder of five of the bravest, kindest and most intelligent spokesmen of labor, will repeat itself.

The stage setting in California's metropolis resembles closely that of Chicago, only the intent to kill by hook or crook, law or no law, just or unjust, is yet more obvious and savagely outspoken.

The next to appear before court in this labor drama will be Israel Weinberg. His trial has been set for March 13th.

Besides the International Defense League, California's State Federation of Labor, the Molders' Union of San Francisco, and Chicago's Federation of Labor Unions, realizing that the whole energy and strength of the labor movement is necessary to rescue the brothers from the gallows, have taken the initiative. A powerful movement of protest and agitation from the Atlantic to the Pacific is contemplated, and it is to be hoped that neither the smallest nor the biggest labor organization will keep apart from it.

Also in New York mass meetings will be held, the halls and dates to be announced in time to give the organizations an opportunity to mobilize their membership

Friends and organizations in the West may communicate with the International Defense League, 210 Russ Building, San Francisco; those in the East with Alexander Berkman, 20 E. 125th Street, New York City.

PART FIVE

THE SOCIAL WAR

For revolutionary anarchists, the social war—the response to the social question and the precursor to the social revolution—presupposed the manifold powers of the state being organized to maintain the economic and social status quo, namely, capitalism, the exploitation for monetary profit of the laboring class by the class of owners. In this they differed fundamentally from socialists, who subscribed to the positive value of the state when in the proper hands, although the Marxists rather cryptically referred to its eventual "withering away." The war had many fronts, but the enemy was the same everywhere. As in every war, violence met with violence. There were strategic triumphs and mistakes, tactical victories and defeats, not to mention spies, defectors, and traitors to the cause. *Mother Earth* not only reported on the battles and skirmishes, but its publisher, editors, and contributors were often right there in the middle of the action.

Aim and Tactics of the Trade-Union Movement

By Max Baginski

The essential revolutionary character of organized labor was articulated in the preamble to the general rules of the First International (1864–76), to which both anarchists and socialists subscribed. Here in part is Mikhail Bakunin's paraphrase:

"*That the emancipation of the workers must be accomplished by the workers themselves;* . . .

"*That the emancipation of the workers is not simply a local or national problem—but* INTERNATIONAL."

For anarchists, however, the self-reliance of labor in carrying on the social war implied the total rejection of the state and the possibility of reform of economic conditions by legislative means. Max Baginski's "Aim and Tactics of the Trade-Union Movement" is a classic communist-anarchist analysis of American labor's betrayal of itself through its leaders' working hand in glove with government. A single phrase in his argument for a return to direct action with no compromise—labor's strongest weapon—recalls the revolutionary principles of the First International: "The human race must become its own liberator. . . ."

☙

TRADE UNIONISM REPRESENTS TO THE workingman the most natural form of association with his fellow brother. This medium became a necessity to him when he was confronted by modern industrialism and the power of capitalism. It dawned on him that the individual producer had not a shadow of a chance with the owner of the means of production, who, together with the economic power, enjoyed the protection of the State with its various weapons of warfare and coercion. In the face of such a giant master all the appeals of the workingman to the love of justice and common humanity went up into smoke.

The beginning of modern industry found the producer in abject slavery and without the understanding of an organized form of resistance. Exploitation reigned supreme, ever seeking to sap the last drop of strength of its victims. No mercy for the common man, nor any consideration shown for his life, his health, growth, and development. Capitalism's only aim was the accumulation of profits, of wealth and power, and to this Moloch everything else was ruthlessly sacrificed.

This spirit of accumulation did not admit of the right of the masses to think, feel, or demand; it merely considered them a class of coolies, specially created, as it were, for their masters' use.

This notion is still in vogue today, and if the conditions of the workers at this moment are somewhat better, somewhat more endurable, it is not thanks to the milk of human kindness of the money power. Whatsoever the workingmen have achieved in the way of better human conditions—a higher standard of living, or a partial recognition of their rights—they have wrenched from their enemies through a hard and bitter struggle that required great endurance, tremendous courage, and many sacrifices.

The tendency to treat the people as a herd of sheep the purpose of which is to serve as food for parasites is still very strong; but this tendency no longer goes unchallenged; it is being met with tremendous opposition; increased social knowledge and revolutionary ideas have taught the workingmen to unite their efforts against those who have been comfortably seated on their backs for centuries past.

The first unskilled attempt on the part of the people to gain a clear conception of their position brought out blind hatred against the technical methods of exploitation instead of hatred against the latter.

In England, for instance, the workingmen considered machinery their deadly foe, to be gotten rid of by all means. The simple axiom that machinery, factories, mines, land, together with every other means of production, if only in the hands of the entire community, would serve for the comfort and happiness of all, instead of being a curse, was a book of seven seals for the people in those days. And even at this late hour this simple truth is entertained by a comparative few, though more than one decade of socialistic and anarchistic enlightenment has passed.

The first trade-unionistic attempts have met with the same ferocious persecution that Anarchism is being met with today. Even as today capital avails itself of the strongest weapons of government in its attack upon labor. The authorities were not slow in passing laws against trade unionism, and every effort for organization was at that time considered high treason; organizers and all those who participated in strikes were considered aids and abettors of crime and conspiracy, punishable with long years of imprisonment and, in many cases, even with death.

At the behest of Money, the State sent human bloodhounds on the trail of the man who in any way was suspected in participating in the trade-union movement. The most villainous and brutal methods were employed to counteract the growth and success of labor organizations. The powers that be recognized the great force that is contained in organized labor as the means of the regeneration of society much quicker than the workingmen themselves. They felt this force hanging like a Damocles sword over their heads, which danger made them dread the future, and nothing was left undone to nip this force in the bud.

The fundamental principle of trade unionism is of a revolutionary character and, as such, it never was and never can be a mere palliative for the adjustment of Labor to Capital. Hence, it must aim at the social and economic reconstruction of society.

Many labor leaders in this country, who consider their duty performed when they sit themselves at the table of wealth and authority, trying to bring about peace and harmony between Capital and Labor, might greatly profit by the history of trade unionism and the various economic struggles it has fought.

Only ignorance can account for the birth of such superficial stuff on the labor question as the book of John Mitchell that has been launched upon the market through loud and vulgar advertisement. Nothing could have disproved the fitness of Mr. Mitchell for a labor leader so drastically as this book.

As already stated, the violent attempt to kill trade unionism or its organizations has proven futile. The swelling tide of the labor movement could not be stopped. The social and economic problem brought to light by modern industry demanded a hearing, produced various theories and an extensive literature on the subject—a literature that spoke with a tongue of fire of the awful existence of the oppressed millions, their trials, their tribulations, the uncertainty, the dangers surrounding them; it spoke of the terrible results of their conditions, of the lives crippled, of the hopes marred; a literature that demanded to know why it is that those who toil are condemned to want and poverty, while those who never produced were living in affluence and extravagance.

Well-meaning people have even attempted to prove that Capital and

Labor are twins, and that in order to maintain their common interests they ought to live in harmony; or that if Sister Labor had a grievance against its big brother it ought to be settled in a calm and peaceful way. Meanwhile the dear sister was fleeced and bled by Brother Capital, and every time the abused and slaved and outraged creature would turn to her brother for justice the dear fellow would whip the rebellious child into submission.

Along with the forcible subjection of organized labor, the minds of the people were confused and blurred by the sugarcoated promises of politicians who assured them that the trade unions ought to be organized by the law, and that all labor quarrels ought to be settled by political and legal means. Indeed, legislatures even discussed a few labor-protective laws that either never saw the light of day, or, if really enacted, were set aside or overridden by the possessing class as an obstacle to profit-making.

Every government, no matter what political basis it rests upon, acts in unison with wealth, and therefore it never passed any legislation in behalf of the producing element of the country that would seriously benefit the great bulk of the people or in any way aim at any change of wage-slaving or economic subjugation.

Every step of improvement the workingmen have made is due solely to their own economic efforts and not to any legal or political aid ever given them, and through their own endeavors only can ever come the reconstruction of the economic and social conditions of society. Just as little as the workingmen can expect from legislative methods can they gain from trade-unionistic efforts that attempt to better economic conditions along the basic lines of the present industrial system.

The cardinal fault of the trade-union movement of this country lies in the fact that its hopes and ideals rest upon the present social status; these ideals ever rotate in the same circle and, therefore, cannot bear intellectual and material fruit. Condemned to pasture in the lean meadows of capitalistic economy, trade unionism drags on a miserable existence, satisfied with the crumbs that fall from the heavily laden tables of their lordly masters.

True social science has amply proved the futility of a reconciliation between the two opposing forces; the existence of the one force representing possession, wealth, and power inevitably has a paralyzing effect upon its opposing force—Labor.

Trade-unionistic tactics of today unfortunately still travel the path marked out for Labor by the powers that be, while the majority of the labor leaders waste the time paid for by their organizations in listening to or discussing with capitalists sweet nothings in the form of arbitration or reconciliation, and are apparently unaware of the fundamental difference between the body they represent and the powers they bow to. And thus it happens that labor organizations are being brutally attacked, that the militia and soldiers are maiming their brothers in the various strike regions while the leaders are being dined and wined. The American Federation of Labor is lobbying in Washington, begging for legal protection, and in return venal Justice sends Winchester rifles and drunken militiamen into the disturbed labor districts. Recently the American Federation of Labor made an alleged radical step in deciding to put up labor candidates for Congress—an old and threadbare political move—thereby sacrificing whatever honest men and clear heads they may have in their ranks. Such tactics are not worth a single drop of sweat of the workingmen, since they are not only contradictory to the basic principles of trade unionism, but even useless and impractical.

Pity for and indignation against the workers fill one's soul at the spectacle of the ridiculous strike methods so often employed and that as often frustrate the possible success of every large labor war. Or is it not laughable, if it were not so deadly serious, that the producers publicly discuss for months in advance where and when they might strike, and therewith give the enemy a chance to prepare his means of combat. For months the papers of the money power bring long interviews with labor leaders, giving detailed descriptions of the ways and means of the proposed strikes, or the results of negotiations with this or that mine magnate. The more often these negotiations are reported, the more glory to the so-called leaders, for the more often their names appear in the papers; the more "reasonable" the utterances of these gentlemen (which means that they are neither fish nor flesh, neither warm nor cold), the surer they grow of the sympathy of the most reactionary element in the country or of an invitation to the White House to join the Chief Magistrate at dinner. Labor leaders of such caliber fail to consider that every strike is a labor event upon the success or failure of which thousands of lives depend; rather do they see in it an opportunity to push their own insignificant personalities into prominence. Instead of leading their organized hosts to victory, they disclose their superficiality in their zeal not to injure their reputation for "respectability."

The workingmen? Be it victory or defeat, they must take up the reins of every strike themselves; as it is, they play the dupes of the shrewd attorneys on both sides, unaware of the price the trickery and cunning of these men cost them.

As I said before, the unions negotiate strikes for days and weeks and months beforehand, even allowing their men to work overtime in order to produce all the commodities to continue business while the strike is going on.

The printers, for instance, worked late into the night on magazines that were being got ready four months in advance, and the miners who discussed the strike so long until every remnant of enthusiasm was gone.

What wonder, then, that strikes fail? As long as the employer is in a position to say, "Strike if you will; I do not need you; I can fill my orders; I know that hunger will drive *you* back into the mine and factory, *I* can wait," there is no hope for the success of the strike.

Such have been the results of the legal trade-union methods.

The history of the labor struggle of this country shows an incident that warrants the hope for an energetic, revolutionary trade-union agitation. That is the eight-hour movement of 1886 which culminated in the death of five labor leaders. That movement contained the true element of the proletarian and revolutionary spirit, the lack of which makes organized labor of today a ball in the hands of selfish aspirants, know-nothings, and politicians.

That which specifically characterized the event of 1886 as a revolutionary factor was the fact that the eight-hour workday could never be accomplished through lobbying with politicians, but through the direct and economic weapon, the General Strike.

The desire to demonstrate the efficacy of this weapon gave birth to the idea of celebrating the First of May as an appropriate day for Labor's festival. On that day the workingmen were to give the first practical demonstration of the power of the General Strike as an at least one-day protest against oppression and tyranny, and which day as gradually to become the means for the final overthrow of economic and social dependence.

One may suggest that the tragedy of the 11th of November of 1887 has stamped the General Strike as a futile method, but this is not true. The battle of liberation cannot be put a stop to by the brutality and rascality of the ruling powers. The vicious anger and the wild hatred that strangled our brothers in Chicago are the safest guarantee that their activity struck a potentially fatal blow to government and capital.

Neither Mr. Mitchell nor Mr. Gompers run the risk of dying upon the gallows of sacred capitalistic Justitia; her ladyship is not at all as blind as some suppose her to be; on the contrary, she has a very keen eye for all that may prove beneficial or dangerous to the society that draws its subsistence from the lives' blood of its people. She has quite made up her mind that the gentlemen in the ranks of Labor today lead the people about in a circle and never will urge them out into the open, towards liberation.

As I endeavored to prove in my article on this subject in the June number of MOTHER EARTH, trade unionism stood, from its very beginning, in extreme opposition to the existing political and economical powers. The latter not only suspected every labor organization of aiming to improve the condition of its members within the limits of the wage system, but they also looked upon the trade union as the deadly enemy of wage-slavery—and they were right. Every labor organization of sincere character must needs wage war upon the existing economic conditions, since the continuation of the same is synonymous with the exploitation and enslavement of labor.

The enmity of these antagonistic forces is so deeply rooted that the very organizations which were created for the purpose of stemming the tide of revolutionary ideas, sooner or later, became influenced by the latter. In France and Germany the Church organized labor unions to counteract the growth of Socialism and Anarchism. But these "yellow" organizations, as they were called, soon grew beyond the control of the clergy. They rapidly developed out of Christian prayer societies into proletarian fighting organizations. When confronted, during strikes and lockouts, with the necessity of either following the lead of the priests or joining forces with their brothers, their Christian foundation began to totter; they realized that their sympathies in the great economic struggle were not with the most benighted institution of all ages, the Church.

The clergy, too, learned a valuable lesson. They were like hens hatching duck eggs. When the young ones took to water, they realized, to their horror, that they had hatched not their own kind. The Church had hoped that Christian methods might drill the workingmen into servility under the banner of capitalism, but the spirit of discontent and revolt soon proved more powerful than the hope for the Hereafter. Much as economists may regret it, the workingman cannot continue to be a mere tool, a "hand"; the industrial and social pressure that rests so heavily upon him forces him to use his reason, to see and judge things for himself. A close examination of existing conditions will convince the workingmen that their liberation will never be effected in a society which treats the producer as a stepchild, as an inferior being.

The wealth that labor creates is labor's strongest fetters. Enslaved, robbed of its independence and liberty, deprived of all that makes life beautiful and joyous, its sole function is to accumulate riches for the masters.

Woe to the tool if it awaken to consciousness, if it attempt to show a sign of its own life! The entire machinery of government is brought to bear against it. Every attempt to secure better pay or shorter hours the law considers criminal. The same brutality that was employed to crush the slave uprising of ancient times is manifested today to crush strikes, to destroy them in the bud. Various labor massacres, as at Homestead, Hazelton, and at numerous other labor centers, are based on the notion that the workingman has no right to shape his own life, to decide for himself, or to manifest his desires in any manner whatever. The force that compels hundreds and thousands to continue their life of hell is by no means less severe, less cutting than the whip or cat-o'-nine-tails which was used to lash the slaves into submission. It is the force of hunger, of poverty.

Whenever poverty raises a threatening hand, government intervenes in favor of capital. It becomes the servant of the latter, the active enemy of labor. As if its only function were the subjection of the people to the arbitrary will of Mammon or to crush every murmur of discontent and to drown the faintest indication of rebellion in a bath of human blood.

Not that clearheaded men had not always insisted that the mission of the State is the destruction of human life, but they were always met with the assurance that it is the abuse of Government which is responsible for its crimes. "The mission of the State, however, is to bring about a just settlement between the contending elements in society and to see that justice and fair play be given to all."

A close study of the general history of Government disproves this assertion a thousandfold. Indeed, if one would take the trouble to make an examination of the various laws of the country, he would behold a chain of tremendous dimensions, every link of which was forged in the interest of the few, against the many. After all, law is but the legal form of conspiracy on the part of the possessing class against the nonpossessing, and the State is the right arm, the brutal fist of that conspiracy.

To what extent Government exerts its powers for the protection of the moneybags has been illustrated by Governor Gooding, of Idaho. He recently issued a proclamation to the bankers of Idaho and Colorado, calling upon them to raise a fund of $25,000 to aid the prosecution of Moyer, Haywood, and Pettibone. Just let us have enough money, and there will not be the slightest difficulty of sending these obnoxious labor leaders to the gallows. Is not this confession sufficiently frank? Do we need a more candid avowal as to the venal character of our courts? We are greatly indebted to Governor Gooding for his brutal frankness; he has torn the mask of Justice and honesty from the face of Authority, and has revealed the monster in all its damning nakedness—cold, hard, and shameless, ready to sell out to the highest bidder (or, ready to be prostituted for a respectable price).

In view of all this, what can the workingman expect from the State (government)? Nothing but treachery and deception; nothing but the cruelest injustice and inhuman brutality in its attitude toward labor and labor troubles.

The new conception of Right, which is not based upon the so-called equality before God, but which aims at social and economic equality on earth, is still to be conquered. It will not come down to us from heaven, nor need oppressed humanity hope to receive this right from Kings or Presidents, or from authority of any kind. The human race must become its own liberator; it must fight the good fight; and in that struggle for liberty one of the great factors will be a revolutionary trade-union movement, with uncompromising, revolutionary tactics. Such a movement must express the revolutionary spirit of the masses along economic lines; and eventually this revolutionary trade-union movement will become the arena where will be fought the battle for a new order of society—a society based upon the free expression of life in its deepest, richest form.

The work of the trade-union movement must, therefore, consist in the preparation of its members for that battle; it must cultivate in them strength, clearheadedness, and energy. No one disputes the utility and necessity of wrestling as much as possible for higher pay and shorter hours; but that should be considered in the light of merely preparatory exercises, as training for the final event, the Social Revolution and the overthrow of wage-slavery.

This aim, needless to mention, necessitates a radical change of present-day trade-union tactics. It were absurd to expect that those who stand for the continuation of the capitalistic and governmental régime should by some miracle assist in the overthrow of that régime. It is, therefore, neither logical nor consistent to hope for any real results through legislative means; nor can the workingman achieve anything by the way of arbitration with his masters. On the other hand, organized labor will find the most effective weapon in the method of Direct Action. Nothing wounds Capitalism so deeply as the discontinuation of work. So long as the workingmen are willing to negotiate and arbitrate; so long as they tolerate their leaders to be dined and wined, just so long Capitalism need have no fear. But when the toiler awakens to the realization that Direct Action will bring him closer to his own kind, will develop the spirit of solidarity, and at the same time give a fatal blow to the system of exploitation and robbery, he will have gained a weapon that nothing can equal in efficacy. In that case the workingman would no longer be in the stupid position of a client who submits to be fleeced by his lawyer because he knows naught of the tricks and machinations of the law. Once they should learn the methods of war, they would no longer be depended on the chance and whims of jurisprudence, but on their own fighting ability. A revolutionary trade union could never attack Capitalism upon legal grounds, realizing that the law has ever been in illicit relation with Mammon. These attacks must, therefore, be grounded in the solidarity which unites and strengthens those that stand for a common cause, a noble ideal—only this can equip man for a great struggle.

Though the very basis of trade unionism is solidarity, it has never yet been thoroughly understood nor practiced. True, the unions help their sister in distress; material aid is given in times of strikes, in time of storm. But this giving has always borne an artificial, forced, obligatory character, and consequently it produced only artificial results. The various unions, though affiliated, often possessed but little mutual understanding or sympathy. As a result, strikes could not—nor did they—bring about radical results; the enemy triumphed and labor succumbed to his whip.

The thing most sadly needed in the labor movement of this country is a proper understanding of the importance and value of work. The powers that be have recognized that long ago. No wonder they dread the possibility of Direct Action—the General Strike. They know that should Labor cease to produce, the entire structure of our society would crumble to ashes.

In Europe the workingmen have accomplished not only external improvements through the widespread practice of Direct Action and the General Strike, but they have also achieved moral victories since they were able to prove that organized labor can bring every function in society to a standstill. When the General Strike was inaugurated in Barcelona, crippling the entire life of the city, the authorities quickly conceded the most important demands of the strikers. This and similar tests have proven how quickly all values of capitalistic economy turn into waste paper. The most daring speculator on the Stock Exchange loses heart when he sees the moving spirit of bonds and stocks disappear. Indeed, the entire humbug of so-called values ceases to exist as soon as the sole, real value, the blood and nerves of the human system, stop their activity—labor.

The Russian revolutionary movement, for instance, has become a perilous menace to Russian autocracy; it has made the Russian Tsar tremble more violently since the workingmen and the peasants have awakened to the consciousness of their economic power than has been the case during the last fifty years. The numerous strikes, the peasant revolts, and the labor uprisings are fated to bring about the downfall of the barbaric Russian régime far quicker than all the efforts of the liberals can ever accomplish.

Witte was one of the first Russians to realize how far-reaching labor and its influence can be. No wonder he always hastened to assure the Russian creditors, whenever he went begging for a new loan, that the industrial conditions were in perfect order.

Labor supports society. If society is unwilling to assign to labor its proper place, the people have the right to withdraw their support and use their best efforts in an endeavor to create a new form of social life, where each man can find his sphere and his highest expression. A correct trade unionism will prove the most important factor in the fate of our social progress; Direct Action as well as the General Strike must be its methods of combat.

A Study of the General Strike in Philadelphia

By Voltairine de Cleyre

In June 1909, the trolleymen employed by the Philadelphia Rapid Transit Company (P.R.T.) went on strike. After a settlement was made that was apparently favorable to the workers, the company turned its back on the agreement and tried to break the union. Its efforts culminated in February 1910 with the mass firing of 600 men, which precipitated a walkout and talk of a general strike by the usually cautious union leaders. Voltairine de Cleyre reported on these events in the March issue of *Mother Earth* ("The Philadelphia General Strike") and a month later gave her judgment on labor's failures and successes in the fight against the P.R.T. Her discussion of the uselessness of playing by narrow trade-union rules is very much in accord with Max Baginski's views (see "Aim and Tactics of the Trade-Union Movement," page 297) and points to a future industrial unionism, international in scope, revolutionary in intent, and committed to the use of direct action.

A "CONDITION" IS ALWAYS MORE interesting than a "theory." The general strike of organized labor in Philadelphia has been the most interesting and instructive phenomenon in the economic struggle which any American city has offered since Chicago in 1885–86. It has revealed many things, both to its friends and its enemies, which no amount of theorizing could have foreseen. Its direct consequences, while considerable, have been insignificant compared with indirect results. As I wrote in my last month's article, it was called some ten days later than it should have been; it was fixed for Saturday morning, March 5th—Saturday being a blunder in itself, since most trades quit work at noon on Saturday anyhow. The general expectation was that the next Monday would be the test day, opponents contending it would collapse by Tuesday morning, while friends generally expected the manifestation of solidarity to be greatest on that day. Both, however, were mistaken. The number of organized workers out began with 50,000 on Saturday, rose to 60,000 or 70,000 on Monday, increased Tuesday and Wednesday, the ranks of the strikers swelling by appeals to the unorganized until 135,000 workers were out, according to the figures of the general strike committee, though some reports fixed the number at 160,000. The height of the strike was probably either Wednesday or Thursday, March 9–10. From then on the balance was about maintained by some going back and new ones going out for a week. Then the return tide generally set in, and at the end of three weeks the general strike was declared off.

Let us inquire what happened. The natural feeling, both on the part of friend and enemy, was that with the withdrawing of 100,000 people from the factories, the hostility of the city toward the car company would manifest itself in open demonstrations—car-smashing, scab-smashing, parading, demanding, etc. Unfortunately, the fatal policy of procrastination, which had originally delayed the calling of the general strike, had given the company and their agents at City Hall, the Mayor, the Director of Public Safety, the Superintendent of Police, and above all the courts which had been sentencing rioters to merciless punishments, an opportunity partially to denature the vital principle of the general strike, viz., active, open, and determined assertion of its demands.

Something, however, has to be said in extenuation, or at least in explanation, of this blunder of waiting. It was the policy of some of the participants in the car strike to play for public sympathy; to make it apparent to the half-awakes and the indifferents that they had no desire to inflict undue hardship upon anyone; that they waited as long as possible for the company to recede from its position; and that all blame for the general strike must rest with the P. R. T., which refused every overture for arbitration. It must be admitted that in this they succeeded. All newspapers, while attacking the principle of the general strike as tyranny and, of course (word of conjuration) "un-American," contended that right-thinking citizens must agree that the car men were right in the matter of being willing to arbitrate. That the support so gained was dearly bought by the devitalizing of the spirit of the people is probably apparent to them now. If not, they need the lesson again.

Another explanation, however, and even a more important one, is that,

"They didn't because they couldn't" call the strike sooner. At least officially. Herein lies the great and fundamental problem for organized labor: Is it to go on trying to meet the conditions of industrial warfare with the old inadequate weapon of the isolated union? Here was a case where the spirit of the people had gotten out of control of its narrow bonds, and human nature was clamoring to "go out with the car men"—ten or twelve days before. But the Central Labor Union had no power to make the declaration. Each union must vote on the question at its own special or regular meeting. And the days ran away. The police were clubbing and shooting. The cars were running. The generous spirit was already beginning to evaporate; men calculated. They said: "How can we afford to go on strike, when according to the Constitution of our Union it will be an illegal strike, and we shall receive no benefit from the international? We would believe in striking, if we could receive the support of our own treasury; but the consequence of striking in this way will be that those who cannot stand the financial strain will scab it; our own organization will be disrupted, there will be victimizations; men will suffer for years for the action of a few days; and no one will be benefited." Nevertheless, when the C. L. U. passed the resolutions calling for the strike, the wave swept up again. Ardent spirits talked, and careful spirits kept their mouths shut—which is a way careful spirits have, and then of blaming the other side for talking afterwards. Nevertheless, what the careful spirits foresaw is precisely what has happened. Within two weeks some of the most ardent strike-talkers were scabbing it—resting secure in the knowledge that any union man has a right to scab it in an illegal strike, and furthermore that the only way for them to atone to the bosses for their mischief-breeding talk was to get back to their jobs first. And a good many of the careful souls have been victimized along with the rest. From all of which two things must be apparent:

1.—That the unions must either break away from their old forms, to organize industrially; or they must devise some special means of responding to the call for the general strike in the future, by which they may order themselves out quickly and maintain their members while on strike.

2.—That wholesale enthusiasm is a straw fire which burns out quickly; therefore it must be utilized at once, if at all; *therefore,* those who seek to burn barriers away with it must direct it to the barriers at once.

Now, the fact is that those who called for the general strike had very much mixed ideas of what they were going to do with it after they got it. They *did* call for a mass meeting, having secured the Ball Park (private property) for the occasion. The police closed the Ball Park. The people then marched, 50,000 strong, down Broad Street. You would think this was an occasion to express their convictions concerning the P. R. T., the rights of the car men, the rights of union men, the rights of workingmen, the rights of people, their detestation of the "dummy mayor," the tsarism of Director Clay, the thuggery of "cop"-ism! Fifty thousand are a good many! But so little idea had anybody of saying or doing anything at all, that a few hundred cops (slightly more than were detailed to keep Emma Goldman from entering Odd Fellows' Temple last September) waded into the marchers with their clubs, drove them right and left, knocked some of them down, arrested a few more, and—"the ball was over." By the eternal gods, Dominick Donelli did better than that two years ago!

Strikers of Philadelphia! When the unemployed Italians marched to City Hall to ask for work, and received the club and the revolver, a lot of you said, "It served them right; they are dagos." When the Anarchists appealed to the Central Labor Union to support the right of free speech, denied by Director Clay to Emma Goldman, Ben Reitman, and Voltairine de Cleyre, you refused to protest against Clay's action, because we were Anarchists.

Have you had a lesson now? Do you know now that you are no more to Clay than the "dagos" and the Anarchists? Have you learned what a police club is for? Do you see whose "right of private property" is respected and protected? Do you know now who is allowed to hold meetings and march on the streets? Do you know now that your place is with him whose liberty is attacked, be he who he will?

Now, a glance at unorganized labor, and a feature of the strike which is more gratifying. From personal conversations with a number of unorganized workers who struck, I have learned that in the mass they struck very inconsciently. Supt. Vauclain, of Baldwin's Locomotive Works, where the most satisfactory strike of the unorganized element took place, was right when he said that "The men could hardly help striking—it was sort of in the air—they would come back in a few days." Unfortunately this was true, though not so much in his particular case. However deficient the unions, one thing is sure—a union strike has more stamina than a nonunion strike. Another reason to direct it *quickly.* People walked out of the shops with the sound of feet in their ears, pretty much as horses commence to mark time when they hear a band of music. Had they walked out with any definite purpose in their heads they might have accomplished it and remained heroes in their own eyes ever afterward. I suspect that the Bastille was taken by some such a sleepwalking crowd. However, these had no intentions, and three days afterward they went apologetically to the boss and told him they didn't know why they had quit; and now they will remain foolish in their own eyes ever afterward. And the boss's too.

Notwithstanding this, and as a splendid offset to occasional disruption and victimization, there has been a net gain of many thousands to the ranks of organized labor as a side result of the strike. The Committee of Ten reports it as 20,000. This may be figuring too high, but it is certain that it approaches that number. The organization of Baldwin's alone, with two thirds of its skilled employees enrolled, is a great piece of work. Moreover, one element of the unorganized has been attracted, of which I have not spoken: that class of workers who were not in the unions because they were superior to the unions; because the narrowness and meanness of the trade-union spirit disgusted them. Numerically, of course, these are few, but they are active and valuable spirits; and it was the sympathetic strike, the recognition of solidarity, which won them.

The failure of certain associations, such as the brewers, the typos, the musicians, and actors, to join in the strike, because of their contracts made through the national or international unions, puts another problem to labor men for settlement: How to modify the contract system so as to leave the local free in case of a local sympathetic strike? The bricklayers and builders stood by their class and broke their contracts: the brewers, etc., stood by their contracts and played traitor to their class. Of musicians and actors it was rather to be expected; they are, after all, hangers-on of the bourgeoisie; but the brewers and typos have disgraced themselves.

Well, Philadelphia has set the first example—a feeble example, lacking in purpose, wasting itself by reason thereof, and by reason of lack of organization and delay. However, it forced the company to the semblance of compromise; it made the Mayor and the City representative on the Board of the P. R. T. do what they had loudly proclaimed they would not do, confer with the officers of the car men; and while the terms were not accepted by the car men, as being deceptive and a mockery, and they are still out, there is no doubt that the enemy recognizes that the weapon of industrial warfare in the future will be the general strike—and dreads it.

Do they perceive, do *the workers* perceive, that it must be the strike which will *stay in* the factory, not *go out?* which will guard the machines and allow no scab to touch them? which will organize, not to inflict deprivation on itself, but on the enemy? which will take over industry and operate it for the workers, not for franchise holders, stockholders, and officeholders? Do they? Or will it take a few thousand more clubbings to knock it into their heads?

Philadelphia began a certain other fight one hundred and thirty-four years ago; she didn't win it on that 4th of July either. She was held by the British after that. But the fight went on, as this one will. What transportation company will be the next to precipitate the battle? *Six different companies in as many cities have raised the trolleymen's wages since this strike began.* Evidently they decline the battle and are more after immediate profits than crushing unions. But in a year or two some other city will have the fight. Let them profit by our mistakes.

VOL. VI, NO. 2, APRIL 1911

Everlasting Murder

By Max Baginski

At 4:30 P.M. on Saturday, March 25, 1911, a fire broke out at the Triangle Shirtwaist Company, housed on the upper stories of a factory building just east of New York City's Washington Square. The doors were locked; there were no sprinklers; the winding staircases were narrow; the fire escape tore away from the brick wall under the weight of the workers. In twenty minutes, the time it took to control the fire, 146 people were dead, most of them young Jewish and Italian immigrant women. It remains the worst industrial fire in the city's history and is to this day commemorated annually at the site of the tragedy. The event led to improved fire safety codes and the introduction of sweatshop reform regulations. It was also a turning point for organized labor in the needle trades, galvanizing support in particular for the International Ladies' Garment Workers' Union.

For outraged revolutionary anarchists like Max Baginski, the Triangle fire was yet another massacre—bound soon to be forgotten—in the continuing social war, to which the only proper response was "direct action and the general strike, and *sabotage*. . . ." Talk of government-inspired justice and reform was so much idle prattle; labor's salvation must come from labor's efforts alone.

WAR OR PEACE—THE SLAUGHTER CONTINUES, for the character of capitalist society is so inexorably murderous that no amount of moralizing can mitigate it.

Horrified we witness the carnival of death, fain to believe that these catastrophes are "accidental," exceptional, while in reality the destruction of human life, industrial murder because of greed and inhumanity, is an established institution. In a society where profit is paramount and the fate of the toilers a negligible quantity, what other result can be expected than the most cynical indifference to the lives of the workingmen.

The hundred and forty-five victims of the fire at the shirtwaist factory of Blanck & Harris, in Washington Square, New York, have been murdered by capitalism. The helpers and executioners in the massacre were the owners of the scab shop, the officials of the public safety department, the administration of the City of New York, and the government and legislature at Albany. These are the guilty. But as they control the machinery of "justice," they will acquit themselves. Within a few weeks the terrible crime will be all but forgotten and—the business of murder will continue.

May the terrible tragedy help to clarify our vision. Our grief is profound; may it bear emotions and resolves strong and effectual, worthy of our great sorrow.

With terrible clearness this crime has demonstrated how useless are the laws for the protection of the lives of the toilers. The laws are there; the rules and regulations are there; the highly paid officials are there; only the actual protection is not there. Government and officialdom are necessary, it is said, for the protection of life and property. In truth, they are capable of dooming the starving wretch to a few years' prison for stealing fifteen cents. They are indeed most faithful guardians of property. But when it concerns the effective protection of the workman's life against wholesale capitalist murder, the governmental Providence yawns and sleeps in the bureaus; or pretends to sleep, well knowing that it must not seem too watchful if it wishes to enjoy the sympathy and good will of the wealthy pillars of society. This officialdom is the "stall"* that decoys the capitalist victim. It is not its business to make such crimes as the Triangle fire impossible. Its duty is superficially to mask—by its laws, dignity, and authority—the plutocratic greed which is responsible for such holocausts.

In their simple trustfulness the "common people" believe that the governmental Providence is ever on the alert to prevent such accidents; meanwhile this good Providence is concerned mainly in removing the obstacles in the way of plutocratic exploitation and ensuring its own position and aggrandizement.

Heavy is the penalty for this error. Because the toilers believe that the government machinery is designed for their protection, they neglect them-

---

* Stall: the assistant of a pickpocket who jostles the passengers in the streetcar, or starts a fight, to give his partner an opportunity to rob the people.

selves to take steps to insure their safety. Hence official protection is not only useless; it is positively dangerous, often fatal.

May this be the first lesson to be learned from the murder of our comrades. And may we also realize that labor possesses the power, by means of united and direct action, forever to put a stop to the wholesale slaughter of capitalist greed. Henceforth let our motto be: Away with the deceptive hope for salvation from "representatives," politicians, and officeholders. Let us act for ourselves, on the spot: the control of the factories should be in the hands of those who work in them; the means: direct action and the general strike, and *sabotage,* which has accomplished such splendid results in the syndicalist movement of France and Italy.

It is the workers—not the landlords, manufacturers, or bosses; not the city or State authorities—that risk in the factories their health and life. It is therefore they who should also have the right to determine the conditions under which they will work and of taking such precautions as may be necessary to safeguard them, not only on paper, but in reality. Labor would indeed deserve to be charged with immaturity and lack of independent judgment if it will still longer continue to trust its fate to the plutocratic régime and its servants, and be persuaded to abstain from independent direct action. All too long the toilers have felt themselves mere "hands" and subjects. It is time to remember their rights as human beings and to realize their strength to assert these.

The power of labor seems weak only because it is never fully manifested. The workingmen still fail to realize their tremendous possibilities and the great tasks they could accomplish, because they do not dare to act for themselves, without go-betweens, politicians, and arbitration boards. It is these that paralyze independent action on the part of labor and strive to divert its every effort into channels profitable to capitalism.

Not merely fire escapes and safe exits can the workers secure by the exercise of their economic power, through direct action and general stoppage of work. They are also able—though naturally after a hard struggle —entirely to abolish the industrial system of wholesale slaughter and exploitation.

Upon this aim to concentrate our efforts, to work for it in the factories and shops, and finally to achieve this noble purpose be our vow at the grave of our hundred and forty-five murdered fellow workers.

VOL. VI, NO. 10, DECEMBER 1911

The Source of Violence

By Alexander Berkman

On October 1, 1910, amid a bitter dispute between structural steel work-ers and steel manufacturing interests, a dynamite explosion at the Los Angeles Times Building killed 21 people. The newspaper was taking a strong stand against labor. Two militant trade unionists, the brothers James and John McNamara, were arrested and tried. Liberals and leftist radicals of every persuasion rallied behind them, until their surprise con-fession on December 1, 1911, during their trial. The McNamaras were deserted by their former supporters, who felt betrayed, having believed in their innocence. *Mother Earth,* however, continued to speak on their be-half. In the issue for December, Emma Goldman wrote in a signed "Observations and Comments" editorial:

". . . MOTHER EARTH cries out against the slimy, creepy, cowardly renunciation of these two victims of a bitter, relentless, and inexorable social war.

"MOTHER EARTH cries out against the cheap and vulgar excuse: 'We were deceived, we thought the men innocent, we did not know.' Deceived in what? That there is a war? That there are two forces pitted against each other in a savage combat? Innocent of what? That the McNamaras did not stake their lives in behalf of their class, or that they had any choice between love and hate?

". . . No, the McNamaras are not Anarchists, nor do they understand Anarchism. But Anarchism understands them. It understands the terrible struggle of the disinherited, the soul of the worker exploited, harassed, humiliated, whipped into line, until finally driven to strike back with the only weapon his tormentors have left at hand.

"Anarchism knows that if guilt there be, it must be hurled, not at the McNamaras, but at all and every apologist of the system of organized crime and violence; at those who keep up the brazen lie that this system can be reformed, or that anything can be changed in its régime by senti-mental compromise or political wire pulling."

Alexander Berkman, in that same issue, picked up on the theme of justified violence, a subject that was never far from his mind. "I know that all life under capitalism is violence. . . . As long as the world is ruled by violence, violence will accomplish results."

THE MCNAMARAS HAVE PLEADED GUILTY. The whole country is swept by a whirlwind of denunciation. From capitalist to labor leader, from detective to Victor Berger, the whole pious crew shouts, "We don't believe in violence. Hang them!"

Not so fast, gentlemen. You all avow yourselves believers in law and order, which presumably represents all that is good and fine. With every one of you such staunch upholders of truth and justice, your lives no doubt mirror your lofty principles. Happy is the country of such citizenship; its politics are all that is pure and noble; its courts the acme of justice; its banks the depositories of honesty; its business the expression of probity; and its trusts the triumph of highest social welfare.

With each and every one of you such lovers of peace and goodwill to man, war and murder must be unknown in this happy land and crimes of violence unheard of.

Or is it *that* law you mean which enables you to sip the full goblet of life's wine, distilled from the blood and marrow of those who toil? Is it *that* order you sing the praises of which fills your coffers with wealth sweated from the miner in the bowels of the earth, pressed from the blood of the man at the furnace? Is it *that* order you cry protection for which enables your wives and mistresses to strut about in silks and laces, woven by the starved women and children in your sweatshops?

Away with your cursed law and order based on the hourly murder of the workers, on the oppression and robbery of widows and orphans. Away with your damned shams and cant! The McNamara brothers have committed murder and violence because *your* murder and violence have forced them to that extremity. *You* are the guilty ones, you who uphold the "law and order" founded on internecine strife, on tyranny and exploitation. As long as you defend and continue this murderous system, just so long will the violence of labor be inevitable. Away with the hypocritical horror on the part of capitalist, labor leader, and politician. The McNamaras had the courage of their convictions, while the Otises and Burnses, the Gomperses and Bergers have not. I am sick of all this rottenness and sham. I know that all life under capitalism is violence; that every instant of its existence spells murder and bloodshed. Every one of you who defends the present system knows it. Every one of you is guilty, openly and secretly, of violence and outrage in the protection of *his* interests. Well, then, since you have driven labor to this necessity, it defends *its* interests with the weapons *you* use against it, the weapons you force upon it.

In the duel with capitalism the McNamaras, whether consciously or unconsciously, fought for a principle—the lofty principle of emancipating labor both from exploitation and the need of violence. Never have the McNamara brothers been as truly the *martyrs of labor* as at this moment, forsaken on the cross, even as Christ. Thousands there are in the midst of the toilers who believe as the McNamaras; but they lack the courage of their convictions. Yet others there are who possess that courage. They will not be cowed by the yelping of curs, be it capitalist, labor leader, or Socialist politician. Nor will they be deceived by the jesuitic lie that violence is wrong in the struggle of labor. It is the gospel to keep the slave in submission. As long as the world is ruled by violence, violence will accomplish results. Unfortunately so, yet nevertheless true. Let history bear me witness. Did Great Britain gain her lordship over the seas by the Christian precept of loving her neighbors? Did the Colonies win their independence by crawling on their knees before the tyrant? Were the black slaves freed by imploring the good Lord to soften the hearts of their masters? Has a single step been made on the road of progress without violence and bloodshed? Has capital ever granted concessions without being forced to it? Has labor won aught but defeat and humiliation in the arena of legality? Away with deceit and cant! As long as you uphold the capitalist system of murder and robbery, just so long will labor resort to violence to wrest better terms. And the sooner we gain the courage to face the situation honestly, the speedier will come the day when the archcrime of the centuries—Capitalism—the source and breeder of all other crime and violence, will be abolished and the way cleared for a society based on solidarity of interests, where brotherhood and humanity will become a reality and violence disappear, because unnecessary.

VOL. VI, NOS. 10–12, DECEMBER 1911–FEBRUARY 1912

The Mexican Revolution

By *Voltairine de Cleyre*

Mexico's ten-year revolutionary period began with the November 1910 uprising against the longtime dictatorship of Porfirio Díaz by the liberal reformist Francisco Madero, whose book *La sucesión presidencial en 1910* ("The Presidential Succession in 1910"), opposing the reelection of Díaz, brought him into national prominence. Díaz resigned in May 1911, Madero assumed the presidency in November, but fighting continued nevertheless between government troops and various revolutionary militias. Voltairine de Cleyre in the last year of her life devoted her waning energies to writing, speaking, and raising money in behalf of the revolutionists, in particular the communist-anarchist Tierra y Libertad ("Land and Liberty") movement of Flores Magón in Baja California, which had initially supported Madero. Her first article on the subject in *Mother Earth,* "The Mexican Revolt" (Vol. VI, no. 6, August 1911), was reissued as a pamphlet by the Mother Earth Publishing Association. She wrote: "At last we see a genuine awakening of a people, not to political demands alone, but to economic ones—fundamentally economic ones." In a subsequent series of three articles on the Mexican Revolution, de Cleyre moved between the generalities of what revolution means to the economics of the Mexican situation, especially the question of reappropriation of the land. In the peasants' agrarian struggle, she placed her hopes on a latter-day Jeffersonian, albeit anarchist, democracy.

A lecture delivered in Chicago October 29, 1911.

THAT A NATION OF PEOPLE CONSIDERING themselves enlightened, informed, alert to the interests of the hour should be so generally and so profoundly ignorant of a revolution taking place in their backyard, so to speak, as the people of the United States are ignorant of the present revolution in Mexico, can be due only to profoundly and generally acting causes. That people of revolutionary principles and sympathies should be so, is inexcusable.

It is as one of such principles and sympathies that I address you—as one interested in every move the people make to throw off their chains, no matter where, no matter how—though naturally my interest is greatest where the move is such as appears to me to be most in consonance with the general course of progress, where the tyranny attacked is what appears to me the most fundamental, where the method followed is to my thinking most direct and unmistakable. And I add that those of you who have such principles and sympathies are in the logic of your own being bound first to inform yourselves concerning so great a matter as the revolt of millions of people—what they are struggling for, what they are struggling against, and how the struggle stands—from day to day, if possible, if not, from week to week, or month to month, as best you can; and second, to spread this knowledge among others, and endeavor to do what little you can to awaken the consciousness and sympathy of others.

One of the great reasons why the mass of the American people know nothing of the Revolution in Mexico is that they have altogether a wrong conception of what "revolution" means. Thus ninety-nine out of a hundred persons to whom you broach the subject will say, "Why, I thought that ended long ago. That ended last May"; and this week the papers, even the *Daily Socialist,* reports, "A *new* revolution in Mexico." It isn't a new revolution at all; it is the same Revolution, which did not begin with the armed rebellion of last May, which has been going on steadily ever since then, and before then, and is bound to go on for a long time to come, if the other nations keep their hands off and the Mexican people are allowed to work out their own destiny.

What is *a* revolution? and what is *this* revolution?

A revolution means some great and subversive change in the social institutions of a people, whether sexual, religious, political, or economic. The movement of the Reformation was a great religious revolution; a profound alteration in human thought—a refashioning of the human mind. The general movement towards political change in Europe and America about the close of the eighteenth century was a revolution. The American and the French revolutions were only prominent individual incidents in it, culminations of the teachings of the *Rights of Man.*

The present unrest of the world in its economic relations, as manifested from day to day in the opposing combinations of men and money, in strikes and bread-riots, in literature and movements of all kinds demanding a readjustment of the whole or of parts of our wealth-owning and wealth-distributing system—this unrest is the revolution of our time, the *economic revolution,* which is seeking social change and will go on until it is accomplished. We are in it; at any moment of our lives it may invade our own homes with its stern demand for self-sacrifice and suffering. Its more violent manifestations are in Liverpool and London today, in Barcelona and Vienna tomorrow, in New York and Chicago the day after. Humanity is a seething, heaving mass of unease, tumbling like surge over a slipping, sliding, shifting bottom; and there will never be any ease until a rock bottom of economic justice is reached.

The Mexican Revolution is one of the prominent manifestations of this worldwide economic revolt. It possibly holds as important a place in the present disruption and reconstruction of economic institutions as the great revolution of France held in the eighteenth-century movement. It did not begin with the odious government of Díaz, nor end with his downfall, any more than the revolution in France began with the coronation of Louis XVI or ended with his beheading. It began in the bitter and outraged hearts of the peasants, who for generations have suffered under a ready-made system of exploitation, imported and foisted upon them, by which they have been dispossessed of their homes, compelled to become slave-tenants of those who robbed them; and under Díaz, in case of rebellion to be deported to a distant province, a killing climate, and hellish labor. It will end only when that bitterness is assuaged by very great alteration in the land-holding system or until the people have been absolutely crushed into subjection by a strong military power, whether that power be a native or a foreign one.

Now the political overthrow of last May, which was followed by the substitution of one political manager for another, did not at all touch the economic situation. It promised, of course; politicians always promise. It promised to consider measures for altering conditions; in the meantime, proprietors are assured that the new government intends to respect the rights of landlords and capitalists, and exhorts the workers to be patient and—*frugal!*

Frugal! Yes, that was the exhortation in Madero's paper to men who, when they are able to get work, make twenty-five cents a day. A man owning 5,000,000 acres of land exhorts the disinherited workers of Mexico to be frugal!

The idea that such a condition can be dealt with by the immemorial remedy offered by tyrants to slaves is like the idea of sweeping out the sea with a broom. And unless that frugality, or in other words starvation, is forced upon the people by more bayonets and more strategy than appear to be at the government's command, the Mexican Revolution will go on to the solution of Mexico's land question with a rapidity and directness of purpose not witnessed in any previous upheaval.

For it must be understood that the main revolt is a revolt against the system of land tenure. The industrial revolution of the cities, while it is far from being silent, is not to compare with the agrarian revolt.

Let us understand why. Mexico consists of twenty-seven states, two territories, and a federal district about the capital city. Its population totals about 15,000,000. Of these, 4,000,000 are of unmixed Indian descent, people somewhat similar in character to the Pueblos of our own southwestern states, primitively agricultural for an immemorial period, communistic in many of their social customs, and like all Indians invincible haters of authority. These Indians are scattered throughout the rural districts of Mexico, one particularly well-known and much talked of tribe, the Yaquis, having had its fatherland in the rich northern state of Sonora, a very valuable agricultural country.

The Indian population—especially the Yaquis and the Moquis—have always disputed the usurpations of the invaders' government, from the days of the early conquest until now, and will undoubtedly continue to dispute them as long as there is an Indian left, or until their right to use the soil out of which they sprang *without paying tribute in any shape* is freely recognized.

The communistic customs of these people are very interesting, and very instructive, too; they have gone on practicing them all these hundreds of years, in spite of the foreign civilization that was being grafted upon Mexico (grafted in all senses of the word); and it was not until forty years ago (indeed the worst of it not till twenty-five years ago) that the increasing power of the government made it possible to destroy this ancient life of the people.

By them, the woods, the waters, and the lands were held in common. Anyone might cut wood from the forest to build his cabin, make use of the rivers to irrigate his field or garden patch (and this is a right whose acknowledgment none but those who know the aridity of the southwest can fully appreciate the imperative necessity for). Tillable lands were allotted by mutual agreement before sowing, and reverted to the tribe after harvesting, for reallotment. Pasturage, the right to collect fuel, were for all. The habits of mutual aid which always arise among sparsely settled communities are instinctive with them. Neighbor assisted neighbor to build his cabin, to plough his ground, to gather and store his crop.

No legal machinery existed—no tax-gatherer, no justice, no jailer. All that they had to do with the hated foreign civilization was to pay the periodical rent-collector and to get out of the way of the recruiting officer when he came around. Those two personages they regarded with spite and dread; but as the major portion of their lives was not in immediate contact with them, they could still keep on in their old way of life in the main.

With the development of the Díaz regime, which came into power in 1876 (and when I say the Díaz regime, I do not especially mean the man Díaz, for I think he has been both overcursed and overpraised, but the whole force which has steadily developed centralized power from then on and the whole policy of "civilizing Mexico," which was the Díaz boast), with its development, I say, this Indian life has been broken up, violated with as ruthless a hand as ever tore up a people by the roots and cast them out as weeds to wither in the sun.

Historians relate with horror the iron deeds of William the Conqueror who, in the eleventh century created the New Forest by laying waste the farms of England, destroying the homes of the people to make room for the deer. But his edicts were mercy compared with the action of the Mexican government toward the Indians. In order to introduce "progressive civilization" the Díaz régime granted away immense concessions of land to native and foreign capitalists—chiefly foreign, indeed, though there were enough of native sharks as well. Mostly these concessions were granted to capitalistic combinations, which were to build railroads (and in some cases did so in a most uncalled for and uneconomic way), "develop" mineral resources, or establish "modern industries."

The government took no note of the ancient tribal rights or customs, and those who received the concessions proceeded to enforce their property rights. They introduced the unheard-of crime of "trespass." They forbade the cutting of a tree, the breaking of a branch, the gathering of the fallen wood in the forests. They claimed the water courses, forbidding their free use to the people; and it was as if one had forbidden to us the rains of heaven. The unoccupied land was theirs; no hand might drive a plough into the soil without first obtaining permission from a distant master—a permission granted on the condition that the product be the landlord's, a small, pitifully small, wage, the worker's.

Nor was this enough: in 1894 was passed "The Law of Unappropriated Lands." By that law, not only were the great stretches of *vacant,* in the old time *common,* land appropriated, but the occupied lands themselves *to which the occupants could not show a legal title* were to be "denounced"; that is, the educated and the powerful, who were able to keep up with the doings of the government, went to the courts and said that there was no legal title to such and such land and put in a claim for it. And the usual hocus-pocus of legality being complied with (the actual occupant of the land being all the time blissfully unconscious of the law, in the innocence of his barbarism supposing that the working of the ground by his generations of forebears was title all-sufficient), one fine day the sheriff comes upon this hapless dweller on the heath and drives him from his ancient habitat to wander an outcast.

Such are the blessings of education. Mankind invents a written sign to aid its intercommunication, and forthwith all manner of miracles are wrought with the sign. Even such a miracle as that a part of the solid earth passes under the mastery of an impotent sheet of paper; and a distant bit of animated flesh which never even saw the ground acquires the power to expel hundreds, thousands, of like bits of flesh, though they grew upon that ground as the trees grow, labored it with their hands, and fertilized it with their bones for a thousand years.

"This law of unappropriated lands," says Wm. Archer, "has covered the country with Naboth's Vineyards." I think it would require a Biblical prophet to describe the "abomination of desolation" it has made.

It was to become lords of this desolation that the men who play the game—landlords who are at the same time governors and magistrates, enterprising capitalists seeking investments—connived at the iniquities of the Díaz régime; I will go further and say devised them.

The Madero family alone owns some 8,000 square miles of territory; more than the entire state of New Jersey. The Terrazas family, in the state of Chihuahua, owns 25,000 square miles; rather more than the entire state of West Virginia, nearly one half the size of Illinois. What was the plantation owning of our southern states in chattel slavery days compared with this? And the peon's share for his toil upon these great estates is hardly more than was the chattel slave's—wretched housing, wretched food, and wretched clothing.

It is to slaves like these that Madero appeals to be "frugal."

It is of men who have thus been disinherited that our complacent fellow citizens of Anglo-Saxon origin say: "Mexicans! What do you know about Mexicans? Their whole idea of life is to lean up against a fence and smoke cigarettes." And pray what idea of life should a people have whose means of life in their own way have been taken from them? Should they be so mighty anxious to convert their strength into wealth for some other man to loll in?

It reminds me very much of the answer given by a Negro employee on the works at Fortress Monroe to a companion of mine who questioned him good-humoredly on his easy idleness when the foreman's back was turned: "Ah ain't goin' to do no white man's work, fo' Ah don' get no white man's pay."

But for the Yaquis, there was worse than this. Not only were their lands seized, but they were ordered, a few years since, to be deported to Yucatan. Now Sonora, as I said, is a northern state, and Yucatan one of the southernmost. Yucatan hemp is famous, and so is Yucatan fever, and Yucatan slavery on the hemp plantations. It was to that fever and that slavery that the Yaquis were deported, in droves of hundreds at a time, men, women and children—droves like cattle droves, driven and beaten like cattle. They died there, like flies, as it was meant they should. Sonora was desolated of her rebellious people, and the land became "pacific" in the hands of the new landowners. Too pacific in spots. They had not left people enough to reap the harvests.

Then the government suspended the deportation act, but with the provision that for every crime committed by a Yaqui, five hundred of his people be deported. This statement is made in Madero's own book.

Now what in all conscience would anyone with decent human feeling expect a Yaqui to do? Fight! As long as there was powder and bullet to be begged, borrowed, or stolen; as long as there is a garden to plunder or a hole in the hills to hide in!

When the revolution burst out, the Yaquis and other Indian people said to the revolutionists: "Promise us our lands back, and we will fight with you." And they are keeping their word magnificently. All during the summer they have kept up the warfare. Early in September, the Chihuahua papers reported a band of 1,000 Yaquis in Sonora about to attack El Anil; a week later 500 Yaquis had seized the former quarters of the federal troops at Pitahaya. This week it is reported that federal troops are dispatched to Ponoitlan, a town in Jalisco, to quell the Indians who have risen in revolt again because their delusion that the Maderist government was to restore their land has been dispelled. Like reports from Sinaloa. In the terrible state of Yucatan, the Mayas are in active rebellion; the reports say that "The authorities and leading citizens of various towns" have been seized by the malcontents and put in prison. What is more interesting is that the peons have seized not only "the leading citizens," but still more to the purpose have seized the plantations, parceled them, and are already gathering the crops for themselves.

Of course, it is not the pure Indians alone who form the peon class of Mexico. Rather more than double the number of Indians are mixed breeds; that is, about 8,000,000, leaving less than 3,000,000 of pure white stock. This mestiza, or mixed breed population, have followed the communistic instincts and customs of their Indian forebears; while from the Latin side of their makeup, they have certain tendencies which work well together with their Indian hatred of authority.

The mestiza, as well as the Indians, are mostly ignorant in book knowledge, only about sixteen percent of the whole population of Mexico being able to read and write. It was not within the program of the "civilizing" régime to spend money in putting the weapon of learning in the people's hands. But to conclude that people are necessarily unintelligent because they are illiterate is in itself a rather unintelligent proceeding.

Moreover, a people habituated to the communal customs of an ancient agricultural life do not need books or papers to tell them that the soil is the source of wealth and they must "get back to the land"!—even if their intelligence is limited.

Accordingly, they have got back to the land. In the state of Morelos, which is a small, south-central state, but a very important one—being next to the Federal District, and by consequence to the City of Mexico—there has been a remarkable land revolution. General Zapata, whose name has figured elusively in newspaper reports now as having made peace with Madero, then as breaking faith, next wounded and killed, and again resurrected and in hiding, then anew on the warpath and proclaimed by the provisional government the arch-rebel who must surrender unconditionally and be tried by court martial; who has seized the strategic points on both the railroads running through Morelos, and who just a few days ago broke into the Federal District, sacked a town, fought successfully at two or three points with the federals, blew out two railroad bridges, and so frightened the deputies in Mexico City that they are all clamoring for all kinds of action; this Zapata, the fires of whose military camps are springing up now in Guerrero, Oaxaca, and Pueblo as well, is an Indian with a long score to pay and all an Indian's satisfaction in paying it. He appears to be a fighter of the style of our revolutionary Marion and Sumter; the country in which he is operating is mountainous and guerrilla bands are exceedingly difficult of capture; even when they are defeated, they have usually succeeded in inflicting more damage than they have received, and they always get away.

Zapata has divided up the great estates of Morelos from end to end, telling the peasants to take possession. They have done so. They are in possession and have already harvested their crops. (Morelos has a population of some 212,000.)

In Pueblo reports in September told us that eighty leading citizens had waited on the governor to protest against the taking possession of the land by the peasantry. The troops were deserting, taking horses and arms with them.

It is they, no doubt, who are now fighting with Zapata. In Chihuahua, one of the largest states, prisons have been thrown open and the prisoners recruited as rebels; a great hacienda was attacked and the horses run off, whereupon the peons rose and joined the attacking party.

In Sinaloa, a rich northern state—famous in the southwestern United States some years ago as the field of a great cooperative experiment in which Mr. C. B. Hoffman, one of the former editors of the *Chicago Daily Socialist,* was a leading spirit—this week's paper reports that the former revolutionary general Juan Banderas is heading an insurrection second in importance only to that led by Zapata.

In the southern border state of Chiapas, the taxes in many places could not be collected. Last week news items said that the present government had sent General Paz there, with federal troops, to remedy that state of affairs. In Tabasco, the peons refused to harvest the crops for their masters; let us hope they have imitated their brothers in Morelos and gathered them for themselves.

The Maderists have announced that a stiff repressive campaign will be inaugurated at once; if we are to believe the papers, we are to believe Madero guilty of the imbecility of saying, "Five days after my inauguration the rebellion will be crushed." Just why the crushing has to wait till five days after the inauguration does not appear. I conceive there must have been some snickering among the reactionary deputies, if such an announcement was really made; and some astonished query among his followers.

What are we to conclude from all these reports? That the Mexican people are satisfied? That it's all good and settled? What should we think if we read that the people, not of Lower but of Upper California had turned out the ranchowners, had started to gather in the field products for themselves, and that the Secretary of War had sent U. S. troops to attack some thousands of armed men (Zapata has had 3,000 under arms the whole summer, and that force is now greatly increased) who were defending that expropriation? If we read that in the state of Illinois the farmers had driven off the tax-collector? that the coast states were talking of secession and forming an independent combination? that in Pennsylvania a division of the federal army was to be dispatched to overpower a rebel force of fifteen hundred armed men doing guerrilla work from the mountains? that the prison doors of Maryland, within hailing distance of Washington City, were being thrown open by armed revoltees?

Should we call it a condition of peace? regard it as proof that the people were appeased? We would not: we would say the revolution was in full swing. And the reason you have thought it was all over in Mexico, from last May till now, is that the Chicago press, like the eastern, northern, and central press in general, has said nothing about this steady march of revolt. Even the *Daily Socialist* has been silent. Now that the flame has shot up more spectacularly for the moment, they call it "a new revolution."

That the papers pursue this course is partly due to the generally acting causes that produce our northern indifference, which I shall presently try to explain, and partly to the settled policy of capitalized interest in controlling its mouthpieces in such a manner as to give their present henchmen, the Maderists, a chance to pull their chestnuts out of the fire. They invested some $10,000,000 in this bunch, in the hope that they may be able to accomplish the double feat of keeping capitalist possessions intact and at the same time pacifying the people with specious promises. They want to lend them all the countenance they can, till the experiment is well tried; so they deliberately suppress revolutionary news.

Among the later items of interest reported by the *Los Angeles Times* are those which announce an influx of ex-officials and many-millioned landlords of Mexico, who are hereafter to be residents of Los Angeles. What is the meaning of it? Simply that life in Mexico is not such a safe and comfortable proposition as it was and that for the present they prefer to get such income as their agents can collect without themselves running the risk of actual residence.

Of course, it is understood that some of this notable efflux (the supporters of Reyes, for example, who have their own little rebellions in Tabasco and San Luis Potosí this week) are political reactionists, scheming to get back the political loaves and fishes into their own hands. But most are simply those who know that their property right is safe enough to be respected by the Maderist government, but that the said government is not strong enough to put down the innumerable manifestations of popular hatred which are likely to terminate fatally to themselves if they remain there.

Nor is all of this fighting revolutionary; not by any means. Some is reactionary, some probably the satisfaction of personal grudge, much no doubt the expression of general turbulency of a very unconscious nature. But granting all that may be thrown in the balance, the main thing, the mighty thing, the regenerative revolution is the REAPPROPRIATION OF THE LAND BY THE PEASANTS. Thousands upon thousands of them are doing it.

Ignorant peasants: peasants who know nothing about the jargon of land reformers or of Socialists. Yes: that's just the glory of it! Just the fact that it *is* done by ignorant people; that is, people ignorant of book theories; but *not* ignorant, not so ignorant by half, of life on the land, as the theory-spinners of the cities. Their minds are simple and direct; they act accordingly. For them, there is *one way* to "get back to the land": i.e., to ignore the machinery of paper landholding (in many instances they have burned the records of the title deeds) and proceed to plough the ground, to sow and plant and gather, and *keep the product themselves.*

Economists, of course, will say that these ignorant people, with their primitive institutions and methods, will not develop the agricultural resources of Mexico, and that they must give way before those who will so develop its resources; that such is the law of human development.

In the first place, the abominable political combination which gave away as recklessly as a handful of soap bubbles the agricultural resources of Mexico, gave them away to the millionaire speculators who were to *develop the country*—were the educated men of Mexico. And this is what they saw fit to do with their higher intelligence and education. So the ignorant may

well distrust the good intentions of educated men who talk about improvements in land development.

In the second place, capitalistic landownership, so far from developing
the land in such a manner as to support a denser population, has depopu-
lated whole districts, immense districts.

In the third place, what the economists do not say is that the only justification for intense cultivation of the land is that the product of such cultivation may build up the bodies of men (by consequence their souls) to
richer and fuller manhood. It is not merely to pile up figures of so many
million bushels of wheat and corn produced in a season; but that this wheat
and corn shall first go into the stomachs of those who planted it—and in
abundance; to build up the brawn and sinew of the arms that work the
ground, not meanly maintaining them in a half-starved condition. And
second, to build up the strength of the rest of the nation who are willing to
give needed labor in exchange. But never to increase the fortunes of idlers
who dissipate it. This is the purpose, and the only purpose, of tilling soil!
and the working of it for any other purpose is *waste,* waste both of land and
of men.

In the fourth place, no change ever was, or ever can be, worked out in
any society, except by the mass of the people. Theories may be propounded
by educated people, and set down in books, and discussed in libraries, sitting rooms, and lecture halls; but they will remain barren, unless the people
in mass work them out. If the change proposed is such that it is not adapt-
able to the minds of the people for whose ills it is supposed to be a remedy,
then it will remain what it was, a barren theory.

Now the conditions in Mexico have been and are so desperate that
some change is imperative. The action of the peasants proves it. Even if a
strong military dictator shall arise, he will have to allow some provision
going towards peasant proprietorships. These unlettered but determined
people must be dealt with *now;* there is no such thing as "waiting till they
are educated up to it." Therefore the wisdom of the economists is wisdom
out of place—rather, *relative unwisdom.* The people never *can* be educated
if their conditions are to remain what they were under the Díaz régime.
Bodies and minds are both too impoverished to be able to profit by a
spread of theoretical education, even if it did not require unavailable
money and indefinite time to prepare such a spread. Whatever economic
change is wrought, then, must be such as the people in their present state
of comprehension can understand and make use of. And we see by the
reports what they understand. They understand they have a right upon the
soil, a right to use it for themselves, a right to drive off the invader who has
robbed them, to destroy landmarks and title deeds, to ignore the tax-gatherer and his demands.

And however primitive their agricultural methods may be, one thing is sure: that they are more economical than any system which heaps up fortunes by destroying men.

Moreover, who is to say how they may develop their methods once they have a free opportunity to do so? It is a common belief of the Anglo-Saxon that the Indian is essentially lazy. The reasons for his thinking so are two: under the various tyrannies and robberies which white men in general, and Anglo-Saxons in particular (they have even gone beyond the Spaniard) have inflicted upon Indians, there is no possible reason why an Indian should want to work, save the idiotic one that work in itself is a virtuous and exalted thing, even if by it the worker increases the power of his tyrant. As Wm. Archer says: "If there are men, *and this is not denied,* who work for no wage, and with no prospect or hope of any reward, it would be curious to know by what motive other than the lash or the fear of the lash, they are induced to go forth to their labor in the morning." The second reason is that an Indian really has a different idea of what he is alive for than an Anglo-Saxon has. And so have the Latin peoples. This different idea is what I meant when I said that the mestiza have certain tendencies inherited from the Latin side of their makeup which work well together with their Indian hatred of authority. The Indian likes to *live;* to be his own master; to work when he pleases and stop when he pleases. He does not crave many things, but he craves the enjoyment of the things that he has. He feels himself more a part of nature than a white man does. All his legends are of wanderings with nature, of forests, fields, streams, plants, animals. He wants to live with the same liberty as the other children of earth. His philosophy of work is, Work so as to live carefree. This is not laziness; this is sense—to the person who has that sort of makeup.

Your Latin, on the other hand, also wants to live; and having artistic impulses in him, his idea of living is very much in gratifying them. He likes music and song and dance, picture-making, carving, and decorating. He doesn't like to be forced to create his fancies in a hurry; he likes to fashion them, and admire them, and improve and refashion them, and admire again; and all for the fun of it. If he is ordered to create a certain design or a number of objects at a fixed price in a given time, he loses his inspiration; the play becomes work, and hateful work. So he, too, does not want to work, except what is requisite to maintain himself in a position to do those things that he likes better.

Your Anglo-Saxon's idea of life, however, is to create the useful and the profitable—whether he has any use or profit out of it or not, and to keep busy, BUSY; to bestir himself "Like the devil in a holy water font." Like all other people, he makes a special virtue of his own natural tendencies and wants all the world to "get busy"; it doesn't so much matter to what end this business is to be conducted, provided the individual—scrabbles. Whenever a true Anglo-Saxon seeks to enjoy himself, he makes work out of that too, after the manner of a certain venerable English shopkeeper who, in company with his son, visited the Louvre. Being tired out with walking from room to room, consulting his catalogue, and reading artists' names, he dropped down to rest, but after a few moments rose resolutely and faced the next room, saying, "Well, Alfred, we'd better be getting through our work."

There is much question as to the origin of these various instincts. Most people have the impression that the chief source of variation lies in the difference in the amount of sunlight received in the native countries inhabited of the various races. Whatever the origin is, these are the broadly marked tendencies of the people. And "business" seems bent not only upon fulfilling its own foreordained destiny, but upon making all the others fulfill it too, which is both unjust and stupid. There is room enough in the world for the races to try out their several tendencies and make their independent contributions to the achievements of humanity, without imposing them on those who revolt at them.

Granting that the population of Mexico, if freed from this foreign "busy" idea which the government imported from the north and imposed on them with such severity in the last forty years, would not immediately adopt improved methods of cultivation, even when they should have free opportunity to do so, still we have no reason to conclude that they would not adopt so much of it as would fit their idea of what a man is alive for; and if that actually proved good, it would introduce still further development, so that there would be a natural and therefore solid economic growth which would stick; while a forced development of it, through the devastation of the people, is no true growth. The only way to make it go is to kill out the Indians altogether and transport the "busy" crowd there, and then keep on transporting for several generations to fill up the ravages the climate will make on such an imported population.

The Indian population of our states was, in fact, dealt with in this murderous manner. I do not know how grateful the reflection may be to those who materially profited by its extermination, but no one who looks forward to the final unification and liberation of man, to the incorporation of the several goodnesses of the various races in the one universal race, can ever read those pages of our history without burning shame and fathomless regret.

I have spoken of the meaning of revolution in general; of the meaning of the Mexican Revolution—chiefly an agrarian one; of its present condition. I think it should be apparent to you that in spite of the electoral victory of the now ruling power, it has not put an end even to the armed rebellion, and cannot until it proposes some plan of land restoration; and that it not only has no inward disposition to do, but probably would not dare to do, in view of the fact that immense capital financed it into power.

As to what amount of popular sentiment was actually voiced in the election, it is impossible to say. The dailies informed us that "in the Federal District where there are 1,000,000 voters, the actual vote was less than 450,000." They offered no explanation. It is impossible to explain it on the ground that we explain a light vote in our own communities, that the people are indifferent to public questions; for the people of Mexico are not now indifferent, whatever else they may be. Two explanations are possible; the first and most probable, that of governmental intimidation; the second, that the people are convinced of the uselessness of voting as a means of settling their troubles. In the less thickly populated agricultural states, this is very largely the case; they are relying upon direct revolutionary action. But although there was guerrilla warfare in the Federal District, even before the election, I find it very unlikely that more than half the voting population there abstained from voting out of conviction, though I should be glad to be able to believe they did. However, Madero and his aides are in, as was expected. The question is, how will they stay in? As Díaz did, and in no other way—if they succeed in developing Díaz's sometime ability, which so far they are wide from having done, though they are resorting to the most vindictive and spiteful tactics in their persecution of the genuine revolutionists wherever such come near their clutch.

To this whole turbulent situation, three outcomes are possible:

1. A military dictator must arise with sense enough to make some substantial concessions and ability enough to pursue the crushing policy ably; or

2. The United States must intervene in the interests of American capitalists and landholders, in case the peasant revolt is not put down by the Maderist power. And that will be the worst thing that can possibly happen, and against which every worker in the U. S. should protest with all his might; or

3. The Mexican peasantry will be successful and freedom in land become an actual fact. And that means the death knell of great landholding in this country also. For what people is going to see its neighbors enjoy so great a triumph and sit on tamely itself under landlordism.

Whatever the outcome be, one thing is certain, it is a great movement which all the people of the world should be eagerly watching. Yet, as I said at the beginning, the majority of our population know no more about it than of a revolt on the planet Jupiter. First, because they are so busy, they scarcely have time to look over the baseball score and the wrestling match; how could they read up on a revolution! Second, they are supremely egotistic and concerned in their own big country with its big deeds, such as divorce scandals, vice grafting, and auto races. Third, they do not read

Spanish and have an ancient hostility to all that smells Spanish. Fourth, from our cradles we were told that whatever happened in Mexico was a joke. Revolutions, or rather rebellions, came and went about like April showers, and they never meant anything serious. And in this indeed there was only too much truth; it was usually an excuse for one place-hunter to get another one's scalp. And lastly, as I have said, the majority of our people do not know that a revolution means a fundamental change in social life, and not a spectacular display of armies.

It is not much a few can do to remove this mountain of indifference; but to me it seems that every reformer, of whatever school, should wish to watch this movement with the most intense interest, as a practical manifestation of a wakening of the landworkers themselves to the recognition of what all schools of revolutionary economics admit to be the primal necessity—the social repossession of the land.

And whether they are victorious or defeated, I, for one, bow my head to those heroic strugglers, no matter how ignorant they are, who have raised the cry, Land and Liberty, and planted the blood-red banner on the burning soil of Mexico.

VOL. VII, NO. 3, MAY 1912

The Commune of Paris

By Peter Kropotkin

The Paris Commune of March–May 1871 continues to resonate in the history of the revolutionary left as the first mass working-class uprising in Europe. In this brief study of the Commune for *Mother Earth*, Peter Kropotkin sees in it the early affirmation of the international character of the coming revolution; it is also the event that clearly defined the schism in the First International between state socialism and anarchism, "the total abolition of the State, and social organization from the simple to the complex by means of the free federation of popular groups of producers and consumers." For Kropotkin, the philosopher of mutual aid, social revolution must be the inevitable outcome of social evolution. The defeat of the Commune and the terrible revenge that followed was thus the result not of misguided intentions but poor organization. As Kropotkin put it in his memoirs, "The Commune of Paris was a terrible example of an outbreak with insuffiently determined ideals."

O N THE 18TH OF MARCH, 1871, the people of Paris rose against a despised and detested Government and proclaimed the city independent, free, belonging to itself.

This overthrow of the central power took place without the usual stage effects of revolution, without the firing of guns, without the shedding of blood upon barricades. When the armed people came out into the streets, the rulers fled away, the troops evacuated the town, the civil functionaries hurriedly retreated to Versailles, carrying everything they could with them. The Government evaporated like a pond of stagnant water in a spring breeze, and on the 19th the great city of Paris found herself free from the impurity which had defiled her, with the loss of scarcely a drop of her children's blood.

Yet the change thus accomplished began a new era in that long series of revolutions whereby the peoples are marching from slavery to freedom. Under the name *Commune of Paris* a new idea was born, to become the starting-point for future revolutions.

As is always the case, this frutiful idea was not the product of some one individual's brain, of the conceptions of some philosopher; it was born of the collective spirit, it sprang from the heart of a whole community. But at first it was vague, and many of those who acted upon and gave their lives for it did not look at it in the light in which we see it today; they did not realize the full purport of the revolution they inaugurated or the fertility of the new principle they tried to put in practice. It was only after they had begun to apply it that its future bearing slowly dawned upon them; it was only afterwards, when the new principle came to be thought out, that it grew definite and precise and was seen in all its clearness, in all its beauty, its justice, the importance of its results.

During the five or six years that came before the Commune, Socialism had taken a new departure in the spread and rapid growth of the International Working Men's Association. In its local branches and general congresses the workers of Europe met together and took counsel with one another upon the social question as they had never done before. Amongst those who saw that social revolution was inevitable, and were actively busy in making ready for it, one problem above all others seemed to press for solution. "The existing development of industry will force a great economic revolution upon our society; this revolution will abolish private property, will put in common all the capital piled up by previous generations; but, what form of political grouping will be most suited to these changes in our economic system?"

"The grouping must not be merely national," answered the International Working Men's Association, "it must extend across all artificial frontiers and boundary lines." And soon this grand idea sunk into the hearts of the peoples and took fast hold of their minds. Though it has been hunted down ever since by the united efforts of every species of reactionary, it is alive nevertheless, and when the voice of the peoples in revolt shall melt the obstacles to its development, it will reappear stronger than ever before.

But when this vast idea of International Association had been struck out, it still remained to discover what should be the component parts of the federation of the world.

To this question two answers were given, each the expression of a distinct current of thought. One said, The Popular State; the other said, Anarchy.

The German Socialists advocated that the State should take possession of all accumulated wealth and give it over to associations of workers, and further, should organize production and exchange and generally watch over the life and activities of society.

To them the Socialists of the Latin race, strong in revolutionary experience, replied that it would be a miracle if such a State could ever exist; but if it could, it would surely be the worst of tyrannies. This ideal of the all-powerful and beneficent State is merely a copy from the past, they said; and they confronted it with a new ideal: An-archy, i. e., the total abolition of the State, and social organization from the simple to the complex by means of the free federation of popular groups of producers and consumers.

It was soon admitted, even by the more liberal-minded State Socialists, that Anarchy certainly represented a much better sort of organization than that aimed at by the popular State; but, they said, the Anarchist ideal is so far off that just now we cannot trouble about it.

At the same time, it was true that the Anarchist theory did need some short, clear mode of expression, some formula at once simple and practical, to show plainly its point of departure and embody its conceptions, to indicate how it was supported by an actually existing tendency amongst the people. A Federation of Workers' Unions and groups of consumers, regardless of frontiers and quite independent of existing States, seemed too vague; and, moreover, it was easy to see that it could not fully satisfy all the infinite variety of human requirements. A clearer formula was wanted, one more easily grasped, one which had a firm foundation in the realities of actual life.

If the question had merely been how best to elaborate a theory, we should have said, Theories, as theories, are not of so very much importance. But as long as a new idea has not found a clear, precise form of statement, growing naturally out of things as they actually exist, it does not take hold of men's minds, does not inspire them to enter upon a decisive struggle. The people do not fling themselves into the unknown without some positive and clearly formulated idea to serve them, as it were, for a springing-board when they reach the starting-point.

As for this starting-point, they must be led up to it by life itself.

For five whole months Paris had been isolated by the German besiegers; for five whole months she had lived as she listed and had learned to know the immense economic, intellectual, and moral strength which she possessed. She had caught a glimpse of her own force of initiative and realized what it meant. At the same time she had seen that the prating crew who took upon them to exercise authority had no idea how to organize either the defense of France or its internal development. She had seen the Central Government at cross-purposes with every manifestation of the intelligence of the mighty city. Finally, she had come to realize that any government must be powerless to guard against great disasters or to smooth the path of rapid evolution. During the Siege her defenders, her workers, had suffered the most frightful privations, whilst her idlers reveled in insolent luxury, and, thanks to the Central Government, she had seen the failure of every attempt to put an end to these scandals. Each time that her people had showed signs of a desire for a free scope, the Government had added weight to their chains. Naturally such experience gave birth to the idea that Paris must make herself an independent Commune, able to realize within her walls the wishes of her citizens.

And thus this word—*"The Commune"*—the freely federated Communes, instead of the State—became the general cry.

The Commune of 1871 could be nothing but a first attempt. Beginning at the close of a great war, hemmed in between two armies ready to join hands and crush the people, it dared not unhesitatingly set forth upon the path of economic revolution. It neither boldly declared itself Socialist nor proceeded to the expropriation of capital nor the organization of labor. It did not even take stock of the general resources of the city.

Nor did it break with the tradition of the State, of representative Government. It did not seek to effect *within* the Commune that very organization from the simple to the complex which it inaugurated *without*, by proclaiming the independence and free federation of Communes.

Yet it is certain that if the Commune of Paris could have lived a few months longer, it would have been inevitably driven by the force of circumstances towards both these revolutions. Let us not forget that the French middle class spent altogether four years, from 1789 to 1793, in revolutionary action before they changed a limited monarchy into a republic. Ought we then to be astonished that the people of Paris did not cross with one bound the space between an Anarchist Commune and the Government of the Spoilers. But let us also bear in mind that the next Revolution, which in France and Spain at least will be Communal, will take up the work of the Commune of Paris where it was interrupted by the massacres of the Versailles soldiery.

The Commune was defeated, and too well we know how the middle class avenged itself for the scare given it by the people when they shook their rulers' yoke loose upon their necks. It proved that there really are two classes in our modern society; on one side, the man who works and yields up to the monopolists of property more than half of what he produces and yet lightly passes over the wrong done him by his masters; on the other, the idler, the spoiler, hating his slave, ready to kill him like game, animated by the most savage instincts as soon as he is menaced in his possession.

After having shut in the people of Paris and closed all means of exit, the Versailles Government let loose soldiers upon them; soldiers brutalized by drink and barrack life, who had been publicly told to make short work of *"the wolves and their cubs."* To the people it was said:

"You shall perish, whatever you do! If you are taken with arms in your hands—death! If you use them—death! If you beg for mercy—death! Whichever way you turn, right, left, back, forward, up, down—death! You are not merely outside the law, you are outside humanity. Neither age nor sex shall save you and yours. You shall die, but first you shall taste the agony of your wife, your sister, your mother, your sons and daughters, even those in the cradle! Before your eyes the wounded man shall be taken out of the ambulance and hacked with bayonets or knocked down with the butt end of a rifle. He shall be dragged living by his broken leg or bleeding arm and flung like a suffering, groaning bundle of refuse into the gutter. Death! Death! Death!"

And after this mad orgy, these piles of corpses, this wholesale extermination, came the petty revenge, the cat-o'-nine tails, the irons in the ship's hold, the blows and insults of the warders, the semistarvation, all the refinements of cruelty. Can the people forget these doughty deeds?

Overthrown, but not conquered, the Commune in our days is born again. It is no longer a dream of the vanquished, caressing in imagination the lovely mirage of hope. No! the "Commune" of today is becoming the visible and definite aim of the Revolution rumbling beneath our feet. The idea is sinking deep into the masses, it is giving them a rallying cry. We count on the present generation to bring about the Social Revolution *within* the Commune, to put an end to the ignoble system of middle-class exploitation, to rid the people of the tutelage of the State, to inaugurate a new era of liberty, equality, solidarity in the evolution of the human race.

VOL. IX, NO. 2, APRIL 1914

The Movement of the Unemployed

By Alexander Berkman

Alexander Berkman's "The Movement of the Unemployed" appeared in
the same issue of *Mother Earth* as his "Tannenbaum before Pilate" (see
page 277) and placed Frank Tannenbaum's direct action within the context of the larger labor struggle. He detailed the divisions among anarchists, socialists, the I.W.W., and the ranks of organized labor over the
question of aiding the unemployed. After Tannenbaum's arrest, it was
Berkman and his immediate circle, mostly young men and women associated with the Ferrer Center and *Mother Earth,* who took up the cause
of the unemployed, in the face of growing resistance on the left and brutal overreaction by the police to public demonstrations.

Joseph Ettor and the poet and playwright Arturo Giovannitti, both
organizers for the I.W.W., were tried, but acquitted, on false murder charges in connection with the 1912 textile strike in Lawrence,
Massachusetts.

THE REAL SITUATION IN REGARD TO THE movement of the unemployed does not seem to be understood or appreciated even by some of
those who pretend to stand in the forefront of the proletarian struggle.

The movement sprang from the spontaneous need of the moment.
Thousands of men and women out of work, tramping the city in a vain
search for a job, many of them homeless and penniless—what more natural
than that such abject misery should crystallize itself in the cry for Bread.

To be sure, the demand was voiced by a small minority of the more intelligent and bolder spirits. *Was ever any demand* articulated first by the duller
majority, however dire their need? But there are always people so consti-

tuted that their first impulse is to belittle and condemn everything that is small in numbers, whatever its quality. There are others again who taboo everything not inspired by themselves, for their own greater glory or that of their party. These are the sane and safe ones who in their supreme wisdom and scientific foresight have irrevocably mapped out the path of human progress and who modestly insist on it that the "course of evolution" is inevitable and must proceed as mapped out. In their blind fanaticism they attempt to force every individual or social expression into the frame of their conception and denounce and obstruct every phenomenon that refuses to conform to their canned program.

This may help to explain the storm of abuse and condemnation that broke over the head of Frank Tannenbaum and his fellow-unemployed when their demand for bread began to take definite form. The masters denounced them; the good Christians called the wrath of God upon their heads; the police persecuted them; and the greater part of the Socialist press—to the shame of its decent supporters be it said—first ignored, then ridiculed and villified them.

And yet Tannenbaum's crusade against the churches was a most significant thing, from whatever standpoint considered. So far as the Christian element in the unemployed army is concerned, it was a convincing *argumentum ad hominem* that the starving man could expect no help from the religious institutions or the official followers of the poor Nazarene tramp. And as to the public at large—the manner in which the Protestant churches sought to avoid the issue, their begrudging aid forthcoming only because of their fear of the desperately hungry men, and the brazenly open repudiation of "the beloved of Christ" by the Catholic church—the Tannenbaum raids have accomplished more in tearing off the mask of religious hypocrisy than the yearlong propaganda of freethinkers.

Then came the trial of Frank Tannenbaum. It is sad, very sad to confess that those who style themselves the spokesmen of the oppressed kept a most shameful silence, where they did not directly condemn and ridicule Tannenbaum. Instead of starting a widespread agitation against his persecution, "the working class party" remained dumb. Not a finger was raised to rouse the public to the evident conspiracy on the part of the authorities and the invaded Catholic church to "make an example" of Frank Tannenbaum, as the menacing gesture of the depths.

Anyone familiar with the labor struggle knows the effect that an energetic public protest produces on the hand that holds the scales of capitalistic justice. Is it not sufficient to recall the cases of Moyer, Haywood, and Pettibone? of Ettor and Giovannitti? or the more recent instance of Alexander Salvanno, the Spanish marine fireman striker whom the multiple police charges threatened with imprisonment for life?

Not a word from the political party that allegedly exists only to further the interests of the downtrodden and disinherited. Indeed the conviction of Tannenbaum and the outrageous sentence imposed on him only called forth a malicious sneer against the victim in the columns of the *New York Call,* to the effect that Frank deserved a spanking.

After Tannenbaum's arrest it became evident that the Socialist party and certain prominent ones in the I. W. W. sought by every means to limit and paralyze the movement of the unemployed. Therefore the Conference of the Unemployed, consisting of delegates of various labor and radical organizations, decided to hold a mass meeting at Union Square, the date set being Saturday, March 21. The Socialist party and its locals absolutely refused to coöperate. Aye, even the I. W. W. declared itself bankrupt by declining to take part, as an organization, in the so vital mass movement. Orders were even given to individual members of the I. W. W. not to participate in the Union Square meeting. It was thought "wiser and more practical" by the official leaders—with one or two manly exceptions—to remain in the safe retirement of sex o'clock boudoirs.

Notwithstanding the misrepresentations of the capitalist and Socialist press, which insists on labeling the unemployed movement with the name of I. W. W., the fact is that but a small minority of I. W. W. boys are active therein, and that only as individuals, most of whom are disgusted with the weak-kneed passivity of the leaders of that organization. It has been charged that the movement of the unemployed is conducted largely by Anarchists. We plead guilty. But the Anarchists stepped in only after Tannenbaum's arrest, when neither Socialists nor official I. W. W. cared to risk their precious life and limb. Are not the Anarchists always the ones to face the fire when a situation becomes dangerous?

With tooth and nail the Socialist and I. W. W. officialdom opposed the mass meeting arranged for March 21. The *Call* even refused to print an advertisement of the planned meeting, to be inserted Saturday, March 21, though it had received payment and published the same ad on the day before. The animus of the Socialist politicians was so bitter that at their meeting at Cooper Union, March 19, arranged to discuss the unemployment problem, they refused the floor to the spokesmen of the unemployed, though the audience demanded to hear them. The treachery, but even more so the stupidity of the proceedings naturally resulted in disorder and the arrest of the intended speaker of the unemployed, Joe O'Carroll, subsequently discharged by the magistrate. The attitude of the priests of St. Alphonsus Church toward Tannenbaum and his men was duplicated by the Socialist high priests at Cooper Union.

The mass meeting at Union Square, March 21, was as inspiring as it was dignified. The condition of the unemployed was put up to the public of the city, squarely and tersely, mostly by the unemployed themselves, who emphasized the right of the starving to satisfy their hunger by any means.

The great meeting resolved itself into a parade up Fifth Avenue, a march of the disinherited whose very appearance was a challenge to the guilty conscience of the exploiters and well-fed idlers. For the first time in the history of this country did the black flag, symbol of starvation and desperate misery, flutter a menacing defiance in the face of parasitic contentment and self-righteous arrogance. The demonstration in Millionaire Avenue was permeated with the spirit of revolt that has fired the hearts of the downtrodden in every popular uprising. It gave full vent to the accumulated misery and suppressed rage against injustice and wrong, the parade continuing up to 107th Street, where it closed in the generously opened headquarters of the Francisco Ferrer Association with a substantial meal for the unemployed, who were also provided with tobacco and cigarettes and lodgings for the night.

The masters and their hireling press frothed at the mouth. What! The starvelings to be permitted to parade their naked misery, to threaten the moneychangers in their very temple? The black flag of hunger and destruction to wave so menacingly in the wealthiest and most exclusive section of the metropolis, the fearful cry of Revolution to thunder before the very doors of the mighty! That is too much!

The masters trembled. The hounds of capital—the press and police—were unleashed.

The movement of the unemployed continued on its way. In spite of repression and numerous arrests the agitation kept up. Meetings took place every evening at Rutgers Square, the Conference, representing the executive body of the unemployed, multiplying its efforts and daily carrying on large open air meetings at Franklin Statue ("Printers' Row"), on the East Side, and at various points in Harlem. At the same time the city was circularized with leaflets and pamphlets, enlightening the public as to the causes of the widespread unemployment and suggesting ways of immediate relief and the ultimate abolition of the conditions of economic exploitation and social injustice. The Conference further initiated another phase of its constructive work, an educational campaign in the labor unions, by means of circular letters and committees, to gain the solidarity and aid of the organized and employed for the unorganized and unemployed, on the basis of their common humanity and mutual interests.

It is from the army of the unemployed that the exploiters recruit the most dangerous foe of labor in times of strikes—scabs and blacklegs, and this point, among others, received special consideration and emphasis in our campaign in the labor unions.

The value of the agitational and educational propaganda resulting from the movement of the unemployed cannot be overestimated. Good seed has been sown in fertile soil, and the harvest will ripen in due time.

The second monster mass meeting of the unemployed was scheduled for Saturday, April 4, at Union Square. The spirit of the movement being thoroughly revolutionary, this meeting, like the preceding one, was not arranged with the kind permission of the master class and its armed hirelings. The unemployed workers do not beg; they *demand.* If they do not at present enforce all their demands, it is only because they don't as yet feel themselves strong enough to do so successfully. But in the matter of the mass meeting arranged for April 4, they were determined to assert their right of free speech, all the persecution and threats of the press and police notwithstanding.

I am confident that the determined attitude of the unemployed in refusing to call off their meeting at Union Square was the means of preventing bloodshed. The authorities faced a difficult dilemma; the executive Conference was not to be swayed from their position either by the threats of the enemy nor by the pleas of backboneless friends. Preparations for the mass meeting were energetically continued, when lo! the authorities hit upon a scheme to circumvent our meeting without the unpleasant necessity of an open conflict.

It was a Jesuitic cabal on the part of the heads of the police department and a few labor fakers representing the Central Federated Union. Two days before our meeting the newspapers suddenly announced that the C. F. U., through Ernest Bohm, its secretary, had secured a police permit to hold a mass meeting at Union Square on April 4, to be followed by a parade of the labor unions, to protest against the conditions in the copper mine strike region of Michigan. For the purpose of the parade Bohm was given seven different routes, covering practically the whole city of New York and thus excluding the possibility of any mass meeting or demonstration on the part of the unemployed.

The Executive of the Conference immediately communicated with various labor organizations, among them also the Women's Trade Union League. Not a single union was aware of any meeting or demonstration in which they were to participate; none had been either consulted or informed of the action of Ernest Bohm. The Executive of the Conference thereupon got in touch by telephone with Bohm, who asserted the authenticity of the press report concerning the C. F. U. mass meeting. We assured him that the unemployed, considering their cause solidaric with labor at large, were willing to coöperate with the C. F. U., or even postpone their much previously arranged mass meeting, in order not to conflict with the success of the labor protest against the masters' brutality in the copper strike. Mr. Bohm eagerly agreed to our proposal to coöperate, promising to give us final answer after his consultation with the visiting representative of the miners.

Failing to hear from Bohm at the appointed time, the Conference mailed to him a registered letter, repeating our offer either to coöperate in his meeting or to postpone ours. Copies of the letter were also sent to the press.

Receiving no reply from Bohm up to the last moment, we printed a special throwaway announcing the postponement of our meeting because of our solidarity with labor.

The result has been reported in the daily press. The Bohm C. F. U. mass meeting proved a fake. Not a single union knew anything about it; not a single union put in an appearance. The audience assembled at Union Square on April 4 came in response to the call of the Conference of the Unemployed, issued two weeks previously. It became patent to everyone that Ernest Bohm, in the name of the C. F. U., and backed by the authorities, had played the miserable role of a stool pigeon for the police, in order to prevent the unemployed from holding their meeting.

The police used the occasion to revenge themselves for our successful revolutionary demonstration of March 21, by a show of brutality equaled only by Russian Cossacks of the Red Sunday days. The mounted officers savagely attacked the peaceful gathering in the Square, the foot police wielding their clubs with fiendish glee. Many were injured by the hoofs of the police horses and riot sticks, but the most dastardly outrage was suffered by our Comrade Joe O'Carroll, against whom the uniformed pluguglies have a special grudge because of his tireless activity in the cause of the unemployed. Six detectives stealthily followed O'Carroll as he was leaving Union Square on his way home in the company of two women friends. When he was fully three blocks from the meeting place, they suddenly attacked him without the least provocation or warning, raining their clubs upon his head with murderous violence. According to impartial eye witnesses—passersby on the street—the brutality of the assault was inspired by such evident hatred and revenge that O'Carroll would have been clubbed to death were it not for the presence of mind and wonderful courage of one of the girls accompanying O'Carroll— Rebecca Edelsohn—who threw herself between the detectives and their victim, protecting O'Carroll with her own body till they ceased clubbing him.

Similarly brutal and utterly unprovoked assaults were committed by the police upon other men active in the unemployed agitation, among them Arthur Caron, Joe Gans, and G. Laricca. To justify their murderous assaults, the authorities arrested and brought charges against these and other prisoners, but the proof of police brutality was so overwhelming that the trial magistrate was moved to denounce the police scathingly, going even to the length of instructing counsel for the defense to prosecute the officers.

In the words of Joe O'Carroll, "They can't club me out of the movement." The agitation in the cause of the unemployed will continue. It will go on in spite of murderous police, in spite of persecution and imprisonment, in spite even of the dastardly denunciation by the Socialist *Call* in its editorial of April 7, so full of malice and venom that a staunch partisan like Ab Cahan, editor of the Socialist *Forward,* had to protest against the *Call's* infamy.

The agitation will go on, inculcating intelligent discontent, spreading broadcast the gospel of revolt, and fanning the fires of revolution that will strengthen the heart and mind of the proletariat to defy and destroy the law and order system of starvation and murder.

VOL. IX, NO. 3, MAY 1914

Remember Ludlow!

By Julia May Courtney

The massacre of striking miners and their wives and children at Ludlow, Colorado, ranks among the most horrific episodes in organized labor's bloody struggle for recognition and triggered protests nationwide against John D. Rockefeller, Jr., the principal shareholder in the Colorado Fuel and Iron Company. Although anarchists were not directly involved, the incident had a profound effect on the movement. Julia May Courtney, who wrote a gripping account of the April 20 confrontation for *Mother Earth,* was among Emma Goldman's loyal circle of comrades in Denver. The strike over working and living conditions had been in progress since the summer of 1913, with frequent skirmishes between the miners and hired guns. In September, the strikers and their families moved out of the company town and set up a tent colony at Ludlow. For Alexander Berkman, the situation in Colorado was a replay of the Homestead strike of 1892, with Rockefeller in the role of Henry Clay Frick. His attempts at holding peaceful rallies at Tarrytown, New York, near the Rockefeller estate of Pocantico Hills, resulted in violent clashes with both the police and local residents and jail for some of his followers. Ever more frustrated in their efforts, Berkman and his group turned away from public protest and to revenge, the consequence of which was the Lexington Avenue explosion on July 4, in which three anarchists were blown to bits when their bomb went off prematurely (see "Dynamite!" by Charles Plunkett, page 75, and "To Our Martyred Dead," by Adolf Wolff, page 212).

"REMEMBER LUDLOW!" the battle cry of the crushed, downtrodden, despised miners stifled at Calumet, in West Virginia, in Cripple Creek, has echoed from coal camp to coal camp in southern Colorado, and has served again to notify the world that Labor will not down.

Peaceful Colorado, slumbering in her eternal sunshine, has been rudely awakened. And her comfortable citizens, tremendously busy with their infinitely important little affairs, have been shocked into a mental state wavering between terror and hysteria. And the terrified and hysterical community, like the individual, has grabbed for safety at the nearest straw.

The federal troops are called to the strike zone in the vain hope that their presence would intimidate the striking miners into submission, and the first spasm of the acute attack has subsided. But the end is not yet.

In September the coal miners in the southern Colorado district went out on strike. Immediately the word went forth from No. 26 Broadway, the Rockefeller headquarters in New York City, and the thugs and gunmen of the Felts-Baldwin agency were shipped from the Virginia and Texas fields and sent by hundreds into the coal camps. With their wives and children the miners were evicted from their huts on the company's ground, and just as the heavy winter of the mountains settled down, the strikers put up their tents and prepared for the long siege. It was then that the puerile, weak-kneed Governor Ammons, fawning on the representatives of the coal companies, at the request of the Colorado Fuel & Iron Co., called out the militia to "keep order."

And the climax came when the first spring winds blew over the hills and the snows melted from the mountain sides. On the 20th of April the cry was heard "Remember Ludlow!"—the battle cry that every workingman in Colorado and in America will not forget. For on that day the men of the tent colony were shot in the back by soft-nosed bullets, and their women and children were offered in burning sacrifice on the field of Ludlow.

The militia had trained the machine guns on the miners' tent colony. At a ball game on Sunday between two teams of strikers the militia interfered, preventing the game; the miners resented, and the militia—with a sneer and a laugh—*fired the machine guns directly into the tents,* knowing at the time that the strikers' wives and children were in them. Charging the camp, they fired the two largest buildings—the strikers' stores—and going from tent to tent, poured oil on the flimsy structures, setting fire to them.

From the blazing tents rushed the women and children, only to be beaten back into the fire by the rain of bullets from the militia. The men rushed to the assistance of their families; and as they did so, they were dropped as the whirring messengers of death sped surely to the mark. Louis Tikas, leader of the Greek colony, fell a victim to the mine guards' fiendishness, being first clubbed, then shot in the back while he was their prisoner. Fifty-two bullets riddled his body.

Into the cellars—the pits of hell under their blazing tents—crept the women and children, less fearful of the smoke and flames than of the nameless horror of the spitting bullets. One man counted the bodies of nine little children, taken from one ashy pit, their tiny fingers burned away as they held to the edge in their struggle to escape. As the smoking ruins disclosed the charred and suffocated bodies of the victims of the holocaust, thugs in State uniform hacked at the lifeless forms, in some instances nearly cutting off heads and limbs to show their contempt for the strikers.

Fifty-five women and children perished in the fire of the Ludlow tent colony. Relief parties carrying the Red Cross flag were driven back by the gunmen, and for twenty-four hours the bodies lay crisping in the ashes, while rescuers vainly tried to cross the firing line. And the Militiamen and gunmen laughed when the miners petitioned "Czar Chase" and Governor Ammons for the right to erect their homes and live in them.

Then came reaction. Driven to desperation the miners attacked the mine guards at the Empire mine, at Forbes, at Aguilar. Everywhere they left destruction of property in their wake. Why should they not? Yet with this difference. When they had the power, when the strikers had captured the Empire mine, with thirty strikebreakers and guards as prisoners, with their women and children hiding in the tunnel—when by the touching of a match they could blow the entire mine and its human occupants into nothingness—they rescued the entombed men and protected the women and children!

Now they are fighting—fighting to the death—fighting as only men can fight who have nothing to lose and all to gain—and the hills of Walsenburg and Trinidad, of Louisville and Lafayette, of Forbes and Aguilar reecho with the conflict. For they are not fighting now to secure a fair day's wage for a fair day's work—nor the recognition of the union—nor the freedom from company stores—they are fighting to avenge the deaths of their loved ones at Ludlow!

And for the first time in the history of the labor war in America the people are with the strikers—they glory in their success. The trainmen have refused to carry the militia—entire companies of the National Guard have mutinied—nearly every union in the State has offered funds and support of men and arms to the strikers—and the governor has asked for federal troops.

The federal troops are here—the women who forced the governor to ask for them believe they have secured Peace—but it is a dead hope. For Peace can never be built on the foundation of Greed and Oppression. And the federal troops cannot change the system—only the strikers can do that. And though they may lay down their arms for a time—they will "Remember Ludlow!"

VOL. X, NO. 11, JANUARY 1916

Donald Vose: The Accursed

By Emma Goldman

Although the McNamara brothers, who admitted to the 1910 bombing of the Los Angeles Times Building, were not anarchists, two other men indicted with them were—David Caplan and Matthew Schmidt. Caplan and Schmidt went into hiding and were eventually betrayed by Donald Vose, a paid informer for the Burns Detective Agency and the son of Gertie Vose, a friend of Emma Goldman's at the Home Colony, an anarchist community near Tacoma, Washington. Caplan was sentenced to ten years in prison, Schmidt to a term for life. Goldman's outrage at Vose's treachery was volcanic. She had taken the young man in at his mother's request. He had spent a great deal of time in his spying at the *Mother Earth* office and with Goldman and her friends at her country retreat near Ossining, New York. Her denunciation appeared on the opening page of the magazine. An echo of the incident found its way into dramatic literature decades later, when Eugene O'Neill, in *The Iceman Cometh*, modeled the guilt-racked informer Don Parritt after Donald Vose. The other anarchists O'Neill had known who are portrayed in the play are his old drinking companions Hippolyte Havel ("Hugo Kalmar") and Terry Carlin ("Larry Slade"), who first introduced him to the *Mother Earth* group and the Ferrer Center.

EIGHTEEN YEARS AGO I MADE my second lecture tour to the Pacific Coast. While in Oregon I was invited to Scio, Oregon, a small hamlet. The comrade who arranged the meeting and with whom I stayed while in Scio was Gertie Vose.

I had heard of Gertie through the pages of *The Firebrand* and *Free Society*, from a number of friends, and a few letters exchanged with her. As a result I was eager to meet the woman who, in those days, was one of the few unusual American characters in the radical movement. I found Gertie to be even more than I had expected—a fighter, a defiant, strong personality, a tender hostess, and a devoted mother. She had with her at the time her six-year-old son, Donald Vose. Another child, a girl, lived with her father, a Mr. Meserve, from whom Gertie had separated.

The stress and travail of life interrupted a correspondence which was a great inspiration for a number of years after my visit. But I knew Gertie Vose had taken up land in the Home Colony at Lake Bay, Washington, and that her son was with her: that she continued to be the fighter when the occasion demanded. Between 1898 and 1907 I did not get to the Coast, and when I finally revisited the Home Colony about six years ago, Gertie Vose was away and so was her son.

In May 1914, while in Los Angeles, I was informed from MOTHER EARTH office that Donald Vose, the son of Gertie Vose, had come to our quarters with a letter from his mother begging that we befriend her boy, since he had no one else in New York. MOTHER EARTH was then installed in a large house, and as we rented out rooms, it was perfectly natural that our Comrade Berkman, in my absence, should have taken Donald Vose into the house. But even if we had lived in small quarters, we should have been willing to share them with a child of Gertie Vose; she who had been my friend for years; she who had been one of the greatest supporters to Berkman in his terrible prison days. How could we refuse her child?

In August of 1914, while in Seattle, I went over to the Home Colony and there was again entertained by Gertie Vose. We talked of the old days and old friends. There I learned how cruelly hard life had been with Gertie; how it had whipped her body, but her spirit was the same, though more mellowed by disappointment, by pain and sorrow. Her one great joy, however, was that her boy had finally gotten into the right atmosphere, that now he would become a man active in the movement. She told me of the glowing reports he was writing about Berk (as he called Berkman), the unemployed and antimilitary activities in New York at the time, and how interested Donald had become. Poor Gertie Vose! Like the last ray of the dying sun, clinging to the horizon, so Gertie—old, worn, bruised, beaten—clung to her son in the hope that he would fulfill her aspiration for humanity. How tragically blind motherhood is; how alien to the soul of its own creation!

I returned to New York, September 15th, 1914. I found confusion, entanglements, and burdens in MOTHER EARTH. To save the situation the house had to be given up and our whole life reorganized. The stress and strain of the situation absorbed me completely. I forgot even that the son of Gertie Vose was living in the house. I reproached myself for such neglect of him. One evening I went to his room and there for the first time in eighteen years saw the boy I had met as a child of six. My first impression of Donald Vose was not agreeable; perhaps because of his high-pitched, thin voice and shifting eyes. But he was Gertie's son, out of work, wretchedly clad, unhealthy in appearance. I stifled my aversion and told him that as I was about to give up the house, he might go to the little farm on the Hudson belonging to a friend of ours which I had been permitted to use for a number of years. (This farm, like a ghost, is traveling the country as E.G.'s estate.)

He said that as a matter of fact he had planned to leave for the Home Colony earlier in the summer, but at that time he was waiting for Berkman, who had contemplated a Western trip and was prevented from doing so through the antimilitary and unemployed agitation. Later Donald Vose lost his job as a chauffeur and was now expecting money to take him West. The main thing, however, which delayed his departure from New York, Donald said, was the message given to him by someone in Washington for M. A. Schmidt, the delivery of which was imperative.

Fate works inexorably. The last Saturday in September Matthew A. Schmidt called at the house to meet a few friends. Lincoln Steffens and Hutchins Hapgood, Alexander Berkman and Eleanor Fitzgerald made up the party of that afternoon. Matthew Schmidt was about to leave when Donald Vose returned to his room. With him was Terry Carlin. I told Schmidt that Donald Vose had a letter for him from a friend in Washington, whereupon Schmidt asked to see Donald and also Carlin, whom he had known in California. The meeting of the three men took place in the presence of the other guests and lasted not more than ten minutes. The conversation was general. Schmidt departed and nothing more was thought of his meeting with Vose.

A few days later we moved to 20 East 125th Street. Donald and Carlin went to the farm. I saw Donald Vose after that only when he would call for mail, as my time and energy were taken up with a new course of lectures and the daily grind of the readjustment to our new and hard mode of life. The third week in October I left on a lecture tour which brought me back to New York the 24th of December, 1914. From that time on persistent rumors came to me about Donald Vose spending a great deal of money on drink though he was not working. Yet he continued to look shabby and would often sit for a long time in the office "to warm up," as he stated. He did not even have an overcoat. When I asked him why he did not get warm clothing, he replied: "I am waiting for my check from Washington." Yet during all that time Donald Vose was dissipating with nearly everyone who was willing to carouse with him.

The situation became altogether too suspicious. I wrote to friends in Washington and after a long delay received a reply that no one was sending Donald money. A week later he left for the Coast. Shortly after that Matthew A. Schmidt and David Caplan were arrested. At once we realized that Donald Vose was the Judas Iscariot. Still so appalling is the thought of suspecting anyone of such a dastardly act that, even after the arrest, I hated myself for harboring such suspicions against the child of Gertie Vose.

Soon positive proofs came from the Coast. It was Donald Vose who cold-bloodedly, deliberately betrayed the two men. They who had been his friends; David Caplan who had shared his hearth, his bread, his all with him for two weeks; had betrayed Matthew A. Schmidt, who had befriended him in New York. The thing was altogether too awful. It was the most terrible blow in my public life of twenty-five years. Terrible because of the mother of that cur; terrible because he had grown up in a radical atmosphere, above all terrible that he had been under my roof and that he had met one of his innocent victims in my house.

It is of little consolation that it was utterly impossible to suspect a child of Gertie Vose, recommended by her and kindly spoken of by many people on the coast. For to do such a thing means to suspect one's own shadow. Nor could I console myself with the fact that if Wm. J. Burns had not found Donald, some other despicable tool would have lured our comrades into the net. All that cannot lessen the horror that was mine all year. At least I wanted it known through MOTHER EARTH that Donald Vose met M. A. Schmidt in my house and that it was Donald Vose who had sold him as well as David Caplan.

I shall not now describe my torture, agony, and disgust since the arrest of our comrades. Gladly would I give ten years of my life if Donald Vose had never stepped over my threshhold. But what did his victims do; Matthew A. Schmidt and David Caplan? They who have been described as murderers; Schmidt, who was convicted before he was tried! They begged me, yes, insisted, even as late as last month, that MOTHER EARTH should not expose Donald Vose. They had broken bread with him and they would not brand him for life as the sneak thief who had stolen into their hearts and then turned them over, sold them for a few peaces of silver.

Thus my hands were tied and MOTHER EARTH was gagged. But now that the spy himself has spoken, that he has brazenly taken the stand and face-to-face with Matthew A. Schmidt has testified in open court that since May 1914 he was in the employ of W. J. Burns, that he was sent by the latter to New York to trail Schmidt, that he was coached to pose as a radical and that under false pretense he obtained his mother's letter of introduction to Alexander Berkman and Emma Goldman. I must acquaint the readers of MOTHER EARTH with the fact that Donald Vose is the liar, traitor, spy who has deceived everyone, myself included, and has used everybody's credulity as a shield to cover his dastardly crime.

Donald Vose you are a liar, traitor, spy. You have lied away the liberty and life of our comrades. Yet not they but you will suffer the penalty. You will roam the earth accursed, shunned and hated; a burden unto yourself, with the shadow of M. A. Schmidt and David Caplan ever at your heels unto the last.

And you Gertie Vose, unfortunate mother of your ill-begotten son—? My heart goes out to you Gertie Vose. I know you are not to blame. What will you do? Will you excuse the inexcusable? Will you gloss over the heinous? Or will you be like the heroic figure in Gorky's *Mother*? Will you save the people from your traitor son? Be brave Gertie Vose, be brave!

VOL. XI, NO. 4, JUNE 1916

On the Death of James Connolly and Francis Sheehy-Skeffington

By Padraic Colum

The Irish Easter Rebellion of 1916 was brought about largely through the efforts of militant labor activists. Thus, for anarchists, it was not simply an isolated expression of national frustration against an imperial oppressor, but another battle in the international social war. James Connolly was a founder of the I.W.W., the organizer, with John Larkin, of the Irish National Transport and General Workers' Union, and the commander of the underground Irish Citizen Army. Francis Sheehy-Skeffington was a popular Dublin speaker, active in behalf of several causes, among them pacifism, socialism, feminism, vegetarianism, and temperance. The elegy on their deaths at the hands of the British that appeared in *Mother Earth* was by the Irish-American poet, playwright, and children's book writer, Padraic Colum.

WHEN THEY TOOK Francis Sheehy-Skeffington from the street, shot him to death in a barrackyard and buried him as gunmen bury their victim—when they took James Connolly out of his bed, and, propping him against a wall did the like by him, the British militarists in Ireland knew well what they were doing—they were killing the two men who were the coolest, the most intelligent, and the most resolute enemies of oppression alive in Ireland. And when they shot Connolly to death, it seemed as if they had shot the heart and brain out of the Irish proletariat.

James Connolly and Francis Sheehy-Skeffington had in the highest degree the quality of devotion—of heroic devotion. Skeffington had devoted himself to the idea of liberty—he was for the oppressed nationality, the oppressed class, the oppressed sex, the oppressed man. No Irishman fought the battle for liberty at so many points as did this eager, buoyant man. James Connolly was more exclusive in his devotion. He gave himself to the cause of the workers of the Irish cities. With a will and an intelligence that would have brought him to the easy chair and the good bank account, he refused to leave his comrades, the semiskilled workmen of Ireland. It was to show their position in the past and the present that he wrote his fine study in economics, *Labor in Irish History.* It was to help their cause that he returned from America. He put all his will and all his fine and trained intelligence into an effort to make a social order in which the Irish worker would have food and house-room, knowledge and fine thought, with some ease of mind for his wife and a happy growth for his children.

When an outsider called at the office of *The Irish Worker,* while James Connolly was in charge, he found there a heavy, earnest man who regarded him with deep-set eyes that had in them the shrewdness of the North-of-Ireland man. When this earnest heavy man stood up to speak to a crowd of impoverished Dublin workpeople, his deep-set eyes had flashes in them. The man was a fighter. All his blows were as shrewd as mother-wit and an intellectual training could make them. He spoke as one who had made all preparations, who had the resolution to go on, and who knew what terms would mean victory for his people. He spoke, as I always thought, like the Chief of a General Army Staff. I was not astonished when I saw that he had the command of the little Army of the Irish Republic.

He knew history and he knew economics, but he knew, too, that the militant force that was necessary in the Irish cities could not be built around abstractions. "This Union," he said, speaking of the Irish Transport Workers' Union, "has from its inception fought shy of all theorizing or philosophizing about history or tradition, but, addressing itself directly to the work nearest its hand, has fought to raise the standard of labor conditions in Dublin to at least an approximation to decent human conditions. To do this it has used as its inspiring battle cry, as the watchword of its members, as the key word of its message, the affirmation that 'An injury to one is the concern of all.'" The problem of the Irish workers had been shamefully neglected by the politicians. James Larkin and James Connolly created an organization that gave the workers solidarity—a thing difficult to do in Dublin, where there are few specialized industries and where general or unskilled labor bears a greater proportion to the whole body of workers than elsewhere, where the workers are often engaged in totally dissimilar industries. But the Irish Transport Workers' Union was created—a memorable thing in the history of Ireland. Then after the capitalists and the government authorities made a frontal attack upon the Union in 1913, James Connolly with another, a man of military experience, founded a defensive force for the Union—the Irish Citizen Army. In March last, when Irish nationalist journals were being suppressed and their type was being broken up by the authorities, the rifles of the Irish Citizen Army turned back the force that was sent to obliterate Connolly's paper, *The Worker's Republic.*

In James Connolly's household, between husband and wife, and father and children there was a wonderful comradeship. He had eight children, most of them girls, and all of them young. I knew one of his children— Nora—for a longer time than I knew Connolly himself. This child had been wisely and finely trained. She has the spirit of the Spartan with the mind of the Gael. She knows as much of song and story as the most fortunate peasant child; she knows what forces are in the way of freedom for her country and her people; she has all the spirit of class and national solidarity. With her bravery and her training she was well prepared to enter the combat.

Now that heavy, earnest man, that brave and clear-minded fighter has been shot to death, it is hard to think that the loss to Ireland is not irreparable. I find it difficult to believe that we will see in our time a man who will give the Irish workers such brave and disinterested service—who will give, as Connolly gave them, his mind, his heart, his life. He made a discovery in Irish history, and the workers of Ireland will be more and more influenced by what he wrote when he said "that the conquest of Ireland had meant the social and political servitude of the Irish masses, and therefore the re-conquest of Ireland must mean the social, as well as the political, independence from servitude of every man, woman and child in Ireland. In other words, the common ownership of all Ireland by *all* the Irish."

I shall remember Francis Sheehy-Skeffington as the happiest spirit I ever knew. He fought for enlightenment with a sort of angelic courage; austere, gay, uncompromising. Since he wrote his student pamphlet on Woman's Suffrage he was in the front of every liberalizing movement in Ireland. He was not a bearer of arms in the insurrection—he was a pacifist. But because they knew that his courage and his enlightenment made him a guide for the people, they took him on his way to his home where his wife and child were, and shot him in a barrackyard without even the form of court-martial. The matter will be inquired into, says Premier Asquith! But Skeffington is dead now, and the spiritual life of Ireland has been depleted by as much of the highest courage, the highest sincerity, the highest devotion as a single man could embody.

PART SIX

WAR AND PEACE

A shared internationalism and revolutionary vocabulary often blurred the differences between anarchists and socialists in matters of war and peace, but two momentous events underscored the deep divisions within the ranks of the left: World War I and the revolution in Russia. Even among anarchists themselves, the outbreak of the war in 1914 precipitated bitter disagreement, when the venerable Peter Kropotkin declared himself in favor of the Allies (including tsarist Russia), while the triumph of the state-socialist Bolsheviks in October 1917 put the libertarian supporters of the revolution to a severe test, engendering much wishful thinking and often strained apologias. It was, however, *Mother Earth*'s articulate and active stand against the war and conscription—and not its support of the Russian Revolution—that proved to be the immediate cause of the magazine's demise.

VOL. I, NO. I, MARCH 1906

National Atavism

By Internationalist

In its very first issue, *Mother Earth* announced the magazine's overriding internationalist view of even so provincial, yet emotionally fraught, a matter as Zionism. Although at the time the Zionism movement in the United States was still rather weak, a three-year wave of pogroms in Russia, starting with the Kishinev massacre of Easter 1903, had already caused many left-leaning Jews to reconsider their antinationalist, cosmopolitan assumptions. In the years before World War I, Jewish immigrants, most of them from Russia, were predominant in the American anarchist movement, especially in the industrial cities of the Northeast and the Midwest. Their Jewish identity was strong, their memories of Russia bitter, and they recognized the dangerous attraction of, in their eyes, a sentimental, idealistic cause counter to their own, which threatened defections from the ranks of social revolutionaries.

THE JEWISH CIRCLES IN New York, Boston, Philadelphia, and other cities of America are aroused over the visit of a specter called Nationalism, alias Territorialism. Like all specters, it is doing a lot of mischief and causing much confusion in the heads of the Jewish population.

The spirit of our ancestor, Abraham, has come to life again. Like Abraham, when Jehovah commanded him to go in quest of the promised land, the Jewish Nationalists make themselves and others believe that they long for the moment, when with wife and child and all possessions, they will migrate to that spot on earth, which will represent the Jewish State, where Jewish traits will have a chance to develop in idyllic peace.

Natural science calls retrogression of species, which shows signs of a former state already overcome, atavism. The same term may be applied to the advanced section of the Jewish population which has listened to the call of the Nationalists. They have retrogressed from a universal view of things to a philosophy fenced in by boundary lines; from the glorious conception that "the world is my country" to the conception of exclusiveness. They have abridged their wide vision and have made it narrow and superficial.

The Zionism of Max Nordau and his followers never was more than a sentimental sport for the well-to-do in the ranks of the Jews. The latter-day Nationalists, however, are bent on reaching those circles of the Jewish race that have so far followed the banner of Internationalism and Revolution; and this at a moment when revolutionists of all nationalities and races are most in need of unity and solidarity. Nothing could be more injurious to the Russian revolution, nothing prove a lack of confidence in its success, so much as the present nationalistic agitation.

The most encouraging and glorious feature of revolutions is that they purify the atmosphere from the thick, poisonous vapors of prejudices and superstition.

From time immemorial revolutions have been the only hope and refuge of all the oppressed from national and social yokes. The radical nationalistic elements seem to have forgotten that all their enthusiasm, their faith and hope in the power of a great social change, now falters before the question: Will it give us our own territory where we can surround ourselves with walls and watchtowers? Yes, the very people who once spoke with a divine fire of the beauty of the solidarity of all individuals and all peoples, now indulge in the shallow phrases that the Jew is powerless, that he is nowhere at home, and that he owns no place on earth where he can do justice to his nature, and that he must first obtain national rights, like all nations, ere he can go further.

These lamentations contain more fiction than truth, more sentimentality than logic.

The Poles have their own territory; still this fact does not hinder Russia from brutalizing Poland or from flogging and killing her children; neither does it hinder the Prussian government from maltreating her Polish subjects and forcibly obliterating the Polish language. And of what avail is native territory to the small nations of the Balkans, with Russian, Turkish, and Austrian influences keeping them in a helpless and dependent condition. Various raids and expeditions by the powerful neighboring states forced on them have proven what little protection their territorial independence has given them against brutal coercion. The independent existence of small peoples has ever served powerful states as a pretext for venomous attacks, pillage, and attempts at annexation. Nothing is left them but to bow before the superior powers or to be ever prepared for bitter wars that might, in a measure, temporarily loosen the tyrannical hold, but never end in a complete overthrow of the powerful enemy.

Switzerland is often cited as an example of a united nation which is able to maintain itself in peace and neutrality. It might be advisable to consider what circumstances have made this possible.

It is an indisputable fact that Switzerland acts as the executive agent of European powers, who consider her a foreign detective bureau which watches over, annoys, and persecutes refugees and the dissatisfied elements.

Italian, Russian, and German spies look upon Switzerland as a hunting ground, and the Swiss police are never so happy as when they can render constable service to the governments of surrounding states. It is nothing unusual for the Swiss police to carry out the order of Germany or Italy to arrest political refugees and forcibly take them across the frontier, where they are given over into the hands of the German or Italian gendarmes. A very enticing national independence, is it not?

Is it possible that former revolutionists and enthusiastic fighters for freedom, who are now in the nationalistic field, should long for similar conditions? Those who refuse to be carried away by nationalistic phrases and who would rather follow the broad path of Internationalism are accused of indifference to and lack of sympathy with the sufferings of the Jewish race. Rather is it far more likely that those who stand for the establishment of a Jewish nation show a serious lack of judgment.

Especially the radicals among the Nationalists seem to be altogether lost in the thicket of phrases. They are ashamed of the label "Nationalist" because it stands for so much retrogression, for so many memories of hatred, of savage wars and wild persecutions, that it is difficult for one who claims to be advanced and modern to adorn himself with the name. And who does not wish to appear advanced and modern? Therefore the name of Nationalist is rejected, and the name of Territorialist taken instead, as if that were not the same thing. True, the Territorialists will have nothing to do with an organized Jewish state; they aim for a free commune. But, if it is certain that small states are subordinated to great powers and merely endured by them, it is still more certain that free communes within powerful states, built on coercion and land robbery, have even less chance for a free existence. Such cuckoos' eggs the ruling powers will not have in their nests. A community in which exploitation and slavery do not reign would have the same effect on these powers as a red rag to a bull. It would stand an everlasting reproach, a nagging accusation, which would have to be destroyed as quickly as possible. Or is the national glory of the Jews to begin after the social revolution?

If we are to throw into the dustheap our hope that humanity will some-day reach a height from which difference of nationality and ancestry will appear but an insignificant speck on earth, well and good! Then let us be patriots and continue to nurse national characteristics; but we ought, at least, not to clothe ourselves in the mantle of Faust, in our pretentious sweep through space. We ought at least declare openly that the life of all peoples is never to be anything else but an outrageous mixture of stupid patriotism, national vanities, everlasting antagonism, and a ravenous greed for wealth and supremacy.

Might it not be advisable to consider how the idea of a national unity of the Jews can live in the face of the deep social abysses that exist between the various ranks within the Jewish race?

It is not at all a mere accident that the Bund, the strongest organization of the Jewish proletariat, will have nothing to do with the nationalistic agitation. The social and economic motives for concerted action or separation are of far more vital influence than the national.

The feeling of solidarity of the working people is bound to prove stronger than the nationalistic glue. As to the remainder of the adherents of the nationalistic movement, they are recruited from the ranks of the middle Jewish class.

The Jewish banker, for instance, feels much more drawn to the Christian or Mohammedan banker than to his Jewish factory worker or tenement house dweller. Equally so will the Jewish workingman, conscious of the revolutionizing effect of the daily struggle between labor and money power, find his brother in a fellow worker, and not in a Jewish banker.

True, the Jewish worker suffers twofold: he is exploited, oppressed, and robbed as one of suffering humanity, and despised, hated, trampled upon because he is a Jew; but he would look in vain toward the wealthy Jews for his friends and saviors. The latter have just as great an interest in the maintenance of a system that stands for wage slavery, social subordination, and the economic dependence of the great mass of mankind as the Christian employer and owner of wealth.

The Jewish population of the East Side has little in common with the dweller of a Fifth Avenue mansion. He has much more in common with the workingmen of other nationalities of the country—he has sorrows, struggles, indignation, and longings for freedom in common with them. His hope is the social reconstruction of society and not nationalistic scene shifting. His conditions can be ameliorated only through a union with his fellow sufferers, through human brotherhood, and not by means of separation and barriers. In his struggles against humiliating demands, inhuman treatment, economic pressure, he can depend on help from his non-Jewish comrades and not on the assistance of Jewish manufacturers and speculators. How then can he be expected to cooperate with them in the building of a Jewish commonwealth?

Certain it is that the battle which is to bring liberty, peace, and well-being to humanity is of a mental, social, economic nature and not of a nationalistic one. The former brightens and widens the horizon, the latter stupefies the reasoning faculties, cripples and stifles the emotions, and sows hatred and strife instead of love and tenderness in the human soul. All that is big and beautiful in the world has been created by thinkers and artists whose vision was far beyond the Lilliputian sphere of Nationalism. Only that which contains the life's pulse of mankind expands and liberates. That is why every attempt to establish a national art, a patriotic literature, a life's philosophy with the seal of the government attached thereto is bound to fall flat and to be insignificant.

It were well and wholesome if all works dealing with national glory and victory, with national courage and patriotic songs, could be used for bonfires. In their place we could have the poems of Shelley and Whitman, essays of Emerson or Thoreau, *The Life of the Bee,* by Maeterlinck, the music of Wagner, Beethoven, and Tchaikovsky, the wonderful art of Eleanore Duse.

I can deeply sympathize with the dread of massacres and persecutions of the Jewish people; and I consider it just and fair that they should strain every effort to put a stop to such atrocities as have been witnessed by the civilized world within a few years. But it must be borne in mind that it is the Russian government, the Russian reactionary party, including the Russian Church, and not the Russian people, that are responsible for the slaughter of the Jews.

Jewish Socialists and Anarchists, however, who have joined the ranks of the Nationalists and who have forgotten to emphasize the fundamental distinction between the people of Russia and the reactionary forces of that country, who have fought and are still fighting so bravely for their freedom and for the liberation of all who are oppressed, deserve severe censure. They have thrown the responsibility of the massacres upon the Russian people and have even blamed the Revolutionists for them, whereas it is an undisputed fact that the agitation against the Jews has been inaugurated and paid for by the ruling clique, in the hope that the hatred and discontent of the Russian people would turn from them, the real criminals, to the Jews. It is said, "We have no rights in Russia, we are being robbed, hounded, killed, let the Russian people take care of themselves, we will turn our backs on them."

Would it not show deeper insight into the condition of affairs if my Jewish brethren were to say, "Our people are being abused, insulted, ill-treated, and killed by the hirelings of Russian despotism. Let us strengthen our union with the Intellectuals, the peasants, the rebellious elements of the people for the overthrow of the abominable tyranny; and when we have accomplished that let us cooperate in the great work of building a social structure upon which neither the nation nor the race but Humanity can live and grow in beauty."

Prejudices are never overcome by one who shows himself equally narrow and bigoted. To confront one brutal outbreak of national sentiment with the demand for another form of national sentiment means only to lay the foundation for a new persecution that is bound to come sooner or later. Were the retrogressive ideas of the Jewish Nationalists ever to materialize, the world would witness, after a few years, that one Jew is being persecuted by another.

In one respect the Jews are really a "chosen people." Not chosen by the grace of God, nor by their national peculiarities, which with every people, as well as with the Jews, merely prove national narrowness. They are "chosen" by a necessity which has relieved them of many prejudices, a necessity which has prevented the development of many of those stupidities which have caused other nations great efforts to overcome. Repeated persecution has put the stamp of sorrow on the Jews; they have grown big in their endurance, in their comprehension of human suffering, and in their sympathy with the struggles and longings of the human soul.

Driven from country to country, they avenged themselves by producing great thinkers, able theoreticians, heroic leaders of progress. All governments lament the fact that the Jewish people have contributed the bravest fighters to the armies for every liberating war of mankind.

Owing to the lack of a country of their own, they developed, crystallized, and idealized their cosmopolitan reasoning faculty. True, they have not their own empire, but many of them are working for the great moment when the earth will become the home for all, without distinction of ancestry or race. That is certainly a greater, nobler, and sounder ideal to strive for than a petty nationality.

It is this ideal that is daily attracting larger numbers of Jews as well as Gentiles; and all attempts to hinder the realization thereof, like the present nationalistic movement, will be swept away by the storm that precedes the birth of the new era—mankind clasped in universal brotherhood.

VOL. II, NO. 7, SEPTEMBER 1907

Enough of Illusions!

By Peter Kropotkin

The revolutionary movement in Russia was a focus of continuing attention in the pages of *Mother Earth,* for it was seen as the harbinger of the coming international social revolution. When the first massive uprising in Russia, the Revolution of 1905, proved to be a hollow failure, it was no surprise to the anarchists, who had no expectations that the introduction of parliamentary government—the elected dumas—would solve the underlying causes of the upheaval. Peter Kropotkin, in "Enough of Illusions!" found the hopes of reformists naive, especially after the tsar's dissolution of the first and second dumas, the former having lasted only from April to June 1906, the latter from March to April of the following year. In an earlier contribution ("The Russian Revolution," July 1906), he had predicted the duma's impotence and concluded:

". . . the underground work, the slow work of maturing convictions and of grouping together, goes on all over Russia as a preparation to something infinitely more important than all the debates of the Duma.

"They don't even pronounce the name of this more important thing. Perhaps most of them don't know its name. But we know and we may tell it. *It is the Revolution: the only real remedy for the redress of wrongs.*"

THE DISMISSAL OF THE SECOND Duma terminated the first period of the Russian Revolution, the Period of Illusions. These illusions were born when Nicholas II, appalled by the general strike of October 1905, issued a manifesto promising to convoke the representatives of the people and to rule with their aid.

Everyone clearly recollects the circumstances under which these concessions were wrested. Industrial, commercial, and administrative activities came to a sudden stop. Neither revolutionists nor political parties instigated and organized this grand manifestation of the people's will. It originated in Moscow and rapidly spread over entire Russia, like those great elemental popular movements that occasionally seize upon millions, making them act in the same direction, with amazing unanimity, thereby performing miracles.

Mills and factories were closed, railroad traffic was interrupted; food products accumulated in huge masses on way stations and could not reach the towns where the populace were starving. Darkness and silence of the grave struck terror into the hearts of the rulers, who were ignorant of the happenings in the interior, as the strike had extended to the postal and telegraph service.

It was animal fear for himself and his own that forced Nicholas II to yield to Witte's exhortations and convoke the Duma. It was terror before the throng of 300,000 invading the streets of St. Petersburg and preparing to storm the prisons that compelled him to concede an amnesty.

It would seem that no faith should have been placed in the faint traces of constitutional liberties thus extorted. The experience of history, especially that of '48, has shown that constitutions granted from above were worthless, unless a substantial victory, won by the spilling of blood, converted the paper concessions into actual gains, and unless the people themselves widened their rights by commencing, of their own accord, a reconstruction along the lines of local autonomy.

The rulers, who had submitted on the spur of the moment, in such cases have usually allowed the heat and triumph of the people to subside, meanwhile preparing faithful troops, listing the agitators to be arrested or annihilated, and in a few months have repudiated their promises, and forcibly put down the people in revenge for the fear and humiliations they had to undergo.

Russia had suffered so much during the preceding half century of hunger and outrage and insolence of her masters; Russian cultured society was so exhausted by the long sanguinary and unequal struggle—that the first surrender of the treacherous Romanov was hailed as bona fide concession. Russia exultingly ushered in the Era of Liberty.

In a previous article we had pointed out that on the very day the October manifesto was signed, introducing a liberal régime, the wicked and treacherous Nicholas, with his consorts, instituted the secret government of Trepov in Peterhof, with the object of counteracting and paralyzing those reforms. In the first days of popular jubilations, when the people believed the Tsar, the gendarmerie, under the guidance of the secret government, hastily issued proclamations inciting to slaughter of Jews and intelligents, dispatched its agents to organize pogroms and raids. These agents gathered bands of hooligans, cut down intelligents in Tver and Tomsk, mowed down men, women, and children celebrating the advent of freedom, while Trepov—the right hand of the Tsar—issued the order "not to spare ammunition" in dispersing popular demonstrations.

The majority divined the source of the pogroms. But our radicals had committed their customary blunder. They were so little informed (and are yet today) as to the doings in the ruling circles that this double-faced policy of Nicholas was positively known only seven or eight months later when exposed by Urusov in the first Duma. Even then, prompted by Russian good nature, men still reiterated that it was not the Tsar's fault, but his advisers'. The Tsar, it was said, was too mild to be crafty. In reality—and it is now becoming a conviction—he is too malicious not to be treacherous.

While the secret government of Peterhof was thus organizing pogroms and massacres and turning loose upon the peasantry hordes of Cossacks brutalized in their police service, our radicals and Socialists had their dreams of "parliament," forming parliamentary parties, with their inevitable intrigues and factional dissensions, and imagined themselves in possession of the constitutional procedure that had taken England centuries to form.

The outlying provinces alone understood that, utilizing the discomfiture of the government caught unawares, it was necessary to rise at once, and, without consulting the abortive "autocratic constitution," to pull down the local institutions which are the mainstay of the government over the entire extent of Russia. Such risings broke out in Livonia, Guria, Western Grusia, and on the East Siberian railway. The Gurians and Letts set a fine example of a popular insurrection: their first step was to establish local revolutionary autonomy.

Unfortunately these revolts found no support either from their neighbors or from central Russia and Poland. And even where the villages revolted in central Russia they were not sustained by the cities and towns. Russia did not do what was done in July 1789, when the insurgent town populaces of eastern France abolished the crumbling-down municipalities and, acting from below, began with the organization of districts, ordering the town affairs without waiting for royal or parliamentary laws. Even the Moscow rising did not awaken active aid in the masses and failed to put forth the usual revolutionary expedient—an autonomous municipal commune.

Diligent inculcation of German ideals of imperial centralization, of party discipline, into the minds of Russian revolutionists bore fruit. Our revolutionaries heroically joined in the struggle, but failed to produce revolutionary mottoes. Even if they were vaguely surmised there was no one to formulate them definitely.

The individual revolts were crushed. Trains carrying the Semenov regiment were allowed to pass to Moscow while the revolutionaries were awaiting "directions" from some source. The punitive detachment led by Meller-Zokomelsky left Chelyabinsk and reached Chita unmolested: in spite of the strike on the Siberian railway it was permitted to proceed! The brutal inroads of Orlov raged in the Baltic provinces, but the Letts could elicit no help from the West and Poland. Guria was laid waste, and wherever the Russian peasants stirred the Cossacks beat them down with a ferocity like that of the Terrible Ivan's bodyguard.

In the meantime the naive—foolishly naive—faith in the Duma was still alive. Not that the Duma was regarded as a check to arbitrariness or capable in its narrow sphere of curbing the zeal of the Peterhofers. Oh no! The Duma was looked upon as the future citadel of legality. Why? "Because," reiterated our simpleminded intelligents, "autocracy cannot subsist without a loan, and foreign bankers will lend no money without the Duma's sanction." This was asserted at a time when the French and even the English governments were backing a new loan, not without guarantees to be sure, for it was desired to draw Russia into a contemplated conflict with Germany.*

Even the dismissal of the first Duma and the drumhead courts-martial did not sober our simplehearted politicians. They still believed in the magic power of the Duma and in the possibility of gaining a constitution through it. The character of the labors of both Dumas shows this.

There are words—"winged words"—that travel around the earth, inspire people, steel them to fight, to brave death. If the Duma did not pass a solitary law tending to renovate life, one might at least expect to hear such words. In a revolutionary epoch, when destructive work precedes constructive efforts, bursts of enthusiasm possess marvelous power. Words, mottoes are mightier than a passed law, for the latter is sure to be a compromise between the spirit of the Future and the decayed Past.

The Versailles House of 1789 lived in unison with Paris; they reacted upon each other. The poor of Paris would not have revolted on the 14th of July had not the Third Estate, three weeks before, uttered its pledge not to disperse until the entire order of things was altered. What if this oath were

---

*As if Turkey, ten times bankrupt, did not procure new loans, even for war purposes. As if the Western bankers do not exert themselves to reduce as many countries as possible to the condition of Greece and Egypt, wherein the bankers' trust, as a guarantee of debts, seize upon state revenues or state properties. As if the Russian looters would scruple to pawn state railways, mines, the liquor monopoly, etc.

theatrical; what if, as we now know, had not Paris risen, the deputies would have meekly departed, as did our Duma. Those were words, but they were words that inspired France, inspired the world. And when the House formulated and announced *The Rights of Man,* the revolutionary shock of the new Era thrilled the world.

Similarly we know now that the French King would have vetoed any law about the alienation, even with recompense, of the landlords' feudal rights; moreover, the House itself (like our Cadets) would not have passed it. What of that? Nevertheless, the House uttered a mighty summons in the first article of the declaration of principles on the 4th of August: "Feudal rights abolished!" In reality, it was mere verbal fireworks, but the peasants, consciously confounding declaration with law, refused to pay all feudal dues.

No doubt, those were mere words, but they stirred revolutions.

Finally, there was more than mere words, for, availing themselves of the government's perplexity, the French deputies boldly attacked the antiquated local institutions, substituting for the squires and magistrates communal and urban municipalities, which subsequently became the bulwarks of the revolution.

"Different times, different conditions," we are told. Indisputably so. But the illusions precluded a clear realization of the actual conditions in Russia. Our deputies and politicians were so hypnotized by the very words "popular representatives," and so far underestimated the strength of the old régime, that no one asked the pertinent question: "What must the Russian revolution be?" However, not only the believers in the magic power of the Duma were misguided. Our Anarchist comrades erred in assuming that the heroic efforts of a group of individuals would suffice to demolish the fortress of the old order reared by the centuries. Thousands of heroic exploits were performed, thousands of heroes perished, but the old régime has survived and still does its work of crushing the young and vigorous.

Yes, the era of illusions has terminated. The first attack is repulsed. The second attack should be prepared on a broader basis and with a fuller understanding of the foe's strength. There can be no revolution without the participation of the masses, and all efforts should be directed toward rousing the people who alone are capable of paralyzing the armies of the old world and capturing its strongholds.

We must forge ahead with this work in every part, nook, and corner of Russia. Enough of illusions, enough of reliance on the Duma or on a handful of heroic redeemers! It is necessary to put the masses forward directly for the great work of general reconstruction. But the masses will enter the struggle only in the name of their direct fundamental needs.

The land—to the tiller; the factories, mills, railways—to the worker;

everywhere, a free revolutionary commune working out its own salvation at home, not through representatives or officials in St. Petersburg.

Such should be the motive of the second period of the revolution upon which Russia is entering.

VOL. IV, NO. I, MARCH 1909

America and Russia

By Leo Tolstoy

Emma Goldman called Leo Tolstoy "the last true Christian." Max Baginski, writing in *Mother Earth* ("Tolstoy," January 1911), said of him: "He was an Anarchist; nay in spite of himself, even a rebel, and that notwithstanding his maxim that evil should not be resisted by force. Indeed, if his teachings would be applied, we should have the Social Revolution tomorrow." Voltairine de Cleyre, speaking of Peter Kropotkin, said he was "the greatest man, save Tolstoy alone, that Russia has produced." Although Tolstoy and his followers refused revolutionary activity on pacifist grounds, they rejected government by force as well, in ad- dition to empty parliamentarianism, while their vision of universal peace and brotherhood—the ultimate goal of internationalism—was one that anarchists who looked to Kropotkin could accept without reservation.

IF ONLY I HAD BEGUN TO PREACH LOVE and brotherhood when I first began to write stories, I should have accomplished more. It was Schopenhauer and the Bible that converted me.

I am an individualist and as such believe in free play for the psychological nature of man. For this reason I am claimed by the Anarchists. Even George Brandes declares that I am in philosophical harmony with the ideas of Prince Kropotkin.

The idea of Communism, and what it implies, refers to social conditions and their improvement. It would be senseless for me to demand that everyone should sleep as little as I do, eat the same food, wear the same clothes, or have the same feelings which are peculiar to me. A man is not a watch. Each is a world in himself. It is, therefore, an illusion to believe in materialistic economy as if it were a religion. It is foolish, therefore, to worship the idea of Socialism. I worship the soul of man, which is the only reality.

After all, it does seem as if the world likes to be deceived. If we did not have our illusions we could never find the truth. Through error we come to virtue, through ignorance to knowledge, through suffering to joy.

These opinions are naturally not popular with the Socialists, who therefore oppose me with bitterness. They love to spread broadcast the rumor that I am, instead of a doer of the word, a mere talker.

In my preachments of love and truth I am not partisan. I condemn both revolutionists and reactionaries. I loath the yoke of party; for I believe that all physical force is brutality.

My opposition to administrative power has often been interpreted into opposition to all government. This, however, is not true. I oppose only violence and the view that might makes right.

The only government in which I believe is that which exercises a moral authority. Moses, Buddha, Christ, these are the great lawgivers, the real autocrats, who ruled not by force, but by character, whose government was one of love, justice, and brotherhood.

I do not believe in a parliament as the final goal of social leadership, for instead of simplifying it only complicates human society. Parliament becomes an instrument to cheat the people, in that it deceives them into thinking that it truly represents them. They say, *"Vox populi, vox Dei,"* but that is never the case; for the greatest of illusions is that which supposes that society can be improved by law.

Just as I hate a hereditary potentate, so do I hate a cheap Duma. A government which relies on iron and explosives, which executes a murderer who is so because of insanity or of poverty, and which glorifies the butchery of innocent thousands, is the greatest instrument for wrong, the worst of oppressors.

Now I will explain why I criticize free America as severely as I do Russia. It is because it also is tending to the rule of force. The methods may differ, but the results are the same.

It is true that America does not exile one to Siberia or hang one on the gallows for protesting against the government. But nevertheless it has its lynchings, and, what is far worse, its judicial murders. It has its great railroad casualties by which thousands are killed by the criminal carelessness of the great corporations, and besides all this, it has the exploitation of the poor by the rich.

All this proves that government cannot improve the moral nature of man and that brute force always defeats its object. There can be no coercion of the soul. Every law must have the sanction of the free will.

Where America surpasses Europe is in its personal liberty, which is the heritage of a race of heroes. But this is doomed to be extinguished by the legislatures of a time-serving generation.

The greatest indictment against any country is the presence of capital punishment—which exists in such a form as if Christ had never been born. The judge who sentences a criminal to death is ten times more guilty himself. Oh, that ideas of humanity could end this tyranny, this black hypocrisy of legal procedure under which so many crimes are committed against humanity!

Yet the root of all the evils of civilization lies in the perverted teachings miscalled Christianity. The modern church is the greatest foe of man and the churchgoer a blind dupe.

Of course, my views are extremely unpleasant to the Russian Church, and often it has plotted to get rid of me. Many suppose that I have so far escaped imprisonment simply because of my prominence, but there may be another reason, which I am unable to explain.

I am not afraid of any punishment and would be happy if I might share it with the many martyrs who have suffered for truth and justice. Persecution gives freedom strength, and suffering ennobles and purifies.

Speaking of my past, I condemn myself unreservedly, for all my faults and errors were the natural result of my aristocratic birth and training, which is the worst thing that can befall a man, as it stifles every human instinct. Turgenev wrote to me: "You have tried for many years to become a peasant in conduct as well as in ideas, but you nevertheless are the same aristocrat. You are good-hearted and have a charming personality, but I have observed that in all your practical dealings with the peasants you remain the patronizing master who likes to be esteemed for his benefactions and to be considered the bounteous patriarch," in which he was very right.

I am not a lover of sports and athletics, for these I consider a misuse of energy, which might do much to relieve the poor. I am greatly in sympathy with the settlement work in America, but I do not believe in institutionalized charity or in mechanical philanthropy, but only in individual effort to relieve suffering.

War and the Anarchist Schism

A split among anarchists over World War I surfaced quickly as word went around that Peter Kropotkin was supporting the Allies against the Central Powers, instead of condemning both sides of the state- and capitalist-inspired conflict, on the grounds that German militarism threatened social-revolutionary progress in Western Europe and that the fall of kaiserdom would inevitably lead to the fall of tsardom. The November 1914 issue of *Mother Earth* included a letter by Kropotkin, previously published in the magazine *Freedom* (London), that clarified his stand, together with a brief rebuttal by Alexander Berkman. These were followed by the first chapter of Kropotkin's lengthy essay "Wars and Capitalism" (Chapter II appeared in the issue for December), on the assumption that "No better answer can be made to Kropotkin's attitude than his argument against war written in 1913. . . ." Few minds, however, were changed. Most anarchists continued to oppose the war, and it was not until after the Russian Revolution that the factions were reconciled.

VOL. IX, NO. 9, NOVEMBER 1914

Kropotkin on the Present War

By Peter Kropotkin

[*Various rumors have been circulating in regard to Peter Kropotkin's attitude toward the European War.* MOTHER EARTH *so far ignored the rumors, in expectation of direct expression of opinion from Kropotkin himself. We now reproduce from the London* FREEDOM *the letter written by Peter Kropotkin to the Swedish Professor Gustav Steffen—who had asked K. for his opinion—with the additions Kropotkin made in the three last paragraphs.*]

YOU ASK MY OPINION ABOUT THE WAR. I have expressed it on several occasions in France, and the present events, unfortunately, only reinforce it.

I consider that the duty of everyone who cherishes the ideals of human progress, and especially those that were inscribed by the European proletarians on the banner of the International Working Men's Association, is to do everything in one's power, according to one's capacities, to crush down the invasion of the Germans into Western Europe.

The cause of this war was *not* Russia's attitude towards the Austrian ultimatum, as the German Government, true to Bismarck's traditions, has tried to represent it. *Already on July 19* it was known among the West-European Continental statesmen that the German Government had definitely made up their mind to declare war. The Austrian ultimatum was the *consequence,* not the cause, of that decision. We thus had a repetition of Bismarck's well-known trick of 1870.*

The cause of the present war lies in *the consequences of the war of* 1870–71. These consequences were foreseen already in 1871 by Liebknecht and Bebel, when they protested against the annexation of Alsace and parts of Lorraine to the German Empire, for which protest they went to prison for

---

*I mean the falsified "Ems telegram," which he published to make people believe it was the French who were the cause of the war. Later on, he himself boasted of that trick.

two years. They foresaw that this annexation would be the cause of new wars, the growth of Prussian militarism, the militarization of all Europe, and the arrest of all social progress. The same was foreseen by Bakunin,* by Garibaldi, who came with his volunteers to fight for France as soon as the Republic was proclaimed, and, in fact, by all the representatives of advanced thought in Europe.

We, who have worked in the different factions, Social Democratic and Anarchist, of the great Socialist movement in Europe, know perfectly well how the menace of a German invasion paralyzed all advanced movements in Belgium, France, and Switzerland, as the workers knew that the moment an internal struggle should begin in these countries, German invasion would immediately follow. *Belgium had been warned of that.* France knew it perfectly well without warning.

The French knew that Metz, of which the Germans had made *not* a fortress for the defense of the territory they had appropriated, but *a fortified camp for aggressive purposes,* was within less than ten days' march from Paris, and that on the day of a declaration of war (or even before that day) an army of 250,000 men could march out of Metz against Paris, with all its artillery and train.

Under such conditions a country cannot be free, and France was not free in her development, just as Warsaw is not free under the guns of the Russian citadel and the surrounding fortresses, and Belgrade was not free under the Austrian guns of Zemlin.

Since 1871 Germany had become a standing menace to European progress. All countries were compelled to introduce obligatory military service on the lines it had been introduced in Germany and to keep immense standing armies. All were living under the menace of a sudden invasion.

More than that, for Eastern Europe, and especially for Russia, Germany was the chief support and protection of reaction. Prussian militarism, the mock institution of popular representation offered by the German Reichstag and the feudal Landtags of the separate portions of the German Empire, and the ill-treatment of the subdued nationalities in Alsace, and especially in Prussian Poland, where the Poles were treated lately as badly as in Russia—without protest from the advanced political parties—these fruits of German Imperialism were the lessons that modern Germany, the Germany of Bismarck, taught her neighbors and, above all, Russian absolutism. Would absolutism have maintained itself so long in Russia, and would that absolutism ever have dared to ill-treat Poland and Finland as

---

*In his "Lettres à un Français" and "L'Empire Knouto-Germanique, et la Révolution Sociale," published now in Vol. II. of his *Œuvres* (Paris) (P.-V. Stock).

it has ill-treated them, if it could not produce the example of "cultured Germany," and if it were not sure of Germany's protection?

Let us not be so forgetful of history as to forget the intimacy that existed between Alexander II and Wilhelm I, the common hatred they displayed for France, on account of her efforts to free Italy, and their opposition to the Italians themselves when in 1860 they sent away the Austrian rulers of Florence, Parma, and Modena, and Florence became the capital of Italy. Let us not forget the reactionary advices which Wilhelm I gave to Alexander III in 1881 and the support his son gave to Nicholas II in 1905. Let us not forget either that if France granted to the Russian autocracy the loan of 1906, it was because she saw that unless Russia succeeded in reforming her armies after the Manchurian defeat, she would be doomed to be torn to pieces by Germany, Italy, and Austria leagued against her. The events of the last few weeks have proved already how well-founded were these apprehensions.

The last forty-three years were a confirmation of what Bakunin wrote in 1871, namely, that if French influence disappeared from Europe, Europe would be thrown back in her development for half a century. And now it is self-evident that if the present invasion of Belgium and France is not beaten back by the common effort of all nations of Europe, we shall have another half-century or more of general reaction.

During the last forty years, a Franco-German war was all the time hanging over Europe. Bismarck was not satisfied with the crushing defeat inflicted upon France. He found that she was recovering too rapidly from her wounds. He regretted not having annexed the province of Champagne and not having taken an indemnity of fifteen thousand million francs instead of five thousand million. On three different occasions Alexander II and Alexander III had to interfere in order to prevent the German Imperialists from assailing France once more. And the moment they began to feel themselves strong as a sea power, the Germans took it into their heads to destroy the maritime power of Britain, to take a strong footing on the southern shores of the Channel, and to menace England with an invasion. The German "reptile press" is saying now that by sending their wild hordes to sack and burn the cities of Belgium and France they are fighting Russia; but I hope there is nobody stupid enough to believe this absurdity. They conquer Belgium and France, and they fight England.

Their purpose is, to force Holland to become part of the German Empire, so that the passages leading from the Indian Ocean into the Pacific, which are now held by the Dutch, should pass into German hands; to take possession of Antwerp and Calais; to annex the eastern portion of Belgium, as well as the French province of Champagne, so as to be within a couple of days only from the capital of France. This has been the dream of the German "Kaiserists" since the times of Bismarck, long before there was a *rapprochement* between France and Russia, and this remains their dream.

It was not to fight Russia that Germany in 1866 laid her hands upon Denmark and annexed the province of Schleswig-Holstein. It was not against Russia, but against France and England, that Germany has built her enormous navy; that she dug and fortified the Kiel Canal and established the military seaport of Wilhelmshafen, where an invasion of England or a raid upon Brest and Cherbourg can be prepared in full security and secrecy. The tale of fighting Russia on the plains of France and Belgium, which is now repeated by the German press, has been concocted for export to Sweden and the United States; but there is not a single intelligent man in Germany itself who does not know that the foes who were aimed at lately were Britain and France. The Germans themselves made no secrecy of it in their conversations and their works on the coming war.

The decision of declaring the present war was taken in Germany as soon as the works on the enlargement and the fortification of the Kiel Canal had been terminated in a great hurry this summer, on June 20. But the war nearly broke out in June 1911—we knew it well here. It would have broken out last summer, if Germany had been ready. Last February, the coming of the present war was so evident that, being at Bordighera, I told my French friends that it was foolish of them to oppose the three years' military law while Germany was busily preparing for war; and I advised my Russian friends not to remain too late in the German watering places, because war would begin as soon as the crops would be ready in France and in Russia. In fact, only those who buried their heads in the sand, like ostriches, could go on without seeing it themselves.

Now we have learned what Germany wants, how extensive are her pretensions, how immense and detailed were her preparations for this war, and what sort of "evolution" we have to expect from the Germans if they are victorious. What their dreams of conquest are we have been told by the German Emperor himself, his son, and his Chancellor. And now we have heard not only what a drunken German lieutenant or general can say to justify the atrocities committed in Belgium by the German hordes, but what a leader of the German Social Democratic Party, Dr. Sudekum, *delegated by his own party* to the workers of Sweden and Italy, had the impudence to say to excuse the barbarities committed by the German Huns in the Belgian villages and cities. They committed these atrocities because civilian inhabitants had fired upon the invaders in defense of their territory!! For a German Social Democrat this is quite enough! When Napoleon III gave the same excuse to account for the shooting of the Parisians on the day of his *coup d'état*, all Europe named him a scoundrel. Now the same excuse is produced to account for infinitely more abominable atrocities, by a German pupil of Marx!

This gives us the measure of the degradation of the nation during the last forty years.

And now let every one imagine for himself what would be the consequences if Germany came victorious out of this war.

Holland—compelled to join the German Empire, because she holds the passages from the Indian Ocean to the Pacific and "the Germans need them."

Most of Belgium annexed to Germany—*it is already annexed.* An immense, ruinous contribution levied, in addition to the already accomplished pillage.

Antwerp and Calais becoming military ports of Germany, in addition to Wilhelmshafen. Denmark—at the mercy of Germany, to be annexed the moment she would dare not to serve the aggressive plans of the Germans, which plans are bound to extend, as they have extended since the successes of 1871.

Eastern France—annexed to Germany, whose new fortresses will then be within two or three days' march from Paris. France will be thus at the mercy of Germany for the next fifty years. All French colonies—Morocco, Algiers, Tonkin—taken by Germany: "We have no colonies worth twopence: we must have them," said the elder son of Wilhelm the other day. It is so simple—and so candid!

Having opposite her shores a string of German military ports along the south coast of the Channel and the North Sea, what can be the life of the United Kingdom but a life entirely ruled by the idea of a new war to be fought in order to get rid of the standing menace of an invasion—an invasion being no longer impossible now, as the aggressor would have at his service big liners, submarine boats, and the aircraft.

Finland—becoming a German province. *Germany has been working at that since 1883,* and her first steps in the present campaign show where she is aiming at. Poland—compelled definitively to abandon all dreams of national independence. Are not the rulers of Germany now treating the Poles of Pozen as badly as, if not worse than, the Russian autocrat? And are not the German Social Democrats already considering the Polish dreams of national revival as stupid bosh! *Deutschland über Alles!* Germany above all!

But enough! Everyone who has any knowledge of European affairs and the turn they have taken during the last twenty years will himself complete the picture.

"But what about the danger of Russia?" my readers will probably ask.

To this question, every serious person will probably answer that when you are menaced by a great, very great danger, the first thing to do is to combat this danger, and then see to the next. Belgium and a good deal of France *are* conquered by Germany, and the whole civilization of Europe is menaced by its iron fist. Let us cope first with this danger.

As to the next, is there anybody who has not thought himself that the present war, in which all parties in Russia have risen unanimously against the common enemy, will render a return to the autocracy of old materially impossible? And then, those who have seriously followed the revolutionary movement of Russia in 1905 surely know what were the ideas which dominated in the First and Second, approximately freely elected, Dumas. They surely know that complete home rule for all the component parts of the Empire was a fundamental point of all the Liberal and Radical parties. More than that: Finland then actually *accomplished* her revolution in the form of a democratic autonomy, and the Duma approved it.

And finally, those who know Russia and her last movement certainly feel that *autocracy will never more be reestablished in the forms it had before 1905, and that a Russian Constitution could never take the Imperialist forms and spirit which Parliamentary rule has taken in Germany.* As to us, who know Russia from the inside, we are sure that the Russians never will be capable of becoming the aggressive, warlike nation Germany is. Not only the whole history of the Russians shows it, but with the Federation Russia is *bound* to become in the very near future, such a warlike spirit would be absolutely incompatible.

But even if I were wrong in all these previsions, although every intelligent Russian would confirm them—well, then there would be time to fight Russian Imperialism in the same way as all freedom-loving Europe is ready at this moment to combat that vile warlike spirit which has taken possession of Germany since it abandoned the traditions of its former civilization and adopted the tenets of the Bismarckian Imperialism.

It is certain that the present war will be a great lesson to all nations. It will have taught them that war cannot be combated by pacifist dreams and all sorts of nonsense about war being so murderous now that it will be impossible in the future. Nor can it be combated by that sort of antimilitarist propaganda which has been carried on till now. Something much deeper than that is required.

The causes of war must be attacked at the root. And we have a great hope that the present war will open the eyes of the masses of workers and of a number of men amidst the educated middle classes. They will see the part that Capital and State have played in bringing about the armed conflicts between nations.

But for the moment we must not lose sight of the main work of the day. *The territories of both France and Belgium* MUST *be freed of the invaders.* The German invasion *must* be repulsed—no matter how difficult this may be. All efforts must be directed that way.

VOL. IX, NO. 9, NOVEMBER 1914

In Reply to Kropotkin

by Alexander Berkman

W E COULD NOT AT FIRST CREDIT THE report that Peter Kropotkin, our old comrade and teacher, took sides in the war. It was tragic enough to witness the Socialists and other radicals of Europe swept off their feet by the murderous blast that is turning Europe into a human slaughter-house. But the attitude of the Social Democrats could at least be explained to some extent: they have remained good patriots and believers in the State and authority, with all the prejudices and narrow attitude of bourgeois morality and nationalism.

But Kropotkin—the clear Anarchist thinker, the uncompromising revolutionist and antigovernmentalist—he take sides in the European slaughter and give aid and encouragement to this or that government? Impossible! We could not believe it—till we read Kropotkin's own statement in the Jewish Anarchist weekly—the *Fraye Arbeter Shtime*—and the letter re-printed above.

It is a most painful shock to us to realize that even Kropotkin, clear thinker that he is, has in this instance fallen a victim to the war psychology now dominating Europe. His arguments are weak and superficial. In his letter to Gustav Steffen he has become so involved in the artificialities of "high politics" that he lost sight of the most elemental fact of the situation, namely that the war in Europe is not a war of nations, but a war of capitalist governments for power and markets. Kropotkin argues as if the German people are at war with the French, the Russian, or English people, when as a matter of fact it is only the ruling and capitalist cliques of those countries that are responsible for the war and alone stand to gain by its result.

Throughout his life Kropotkin has taught us that "the reason for modern war is always the competition for markets and the right to exploit nations backward in industry."* Is the *proletariat* of Germany, of France, or of Russia interested in new markets, in the exploitation of nations back-

* "Wars and Capitalism," Ch. I.

ward in industry? Have *they* anything to gain by this or any other capitalist war?

In the letter to Professor Steffen, Kropotkin strangely fails to mention the *working classes* of the contending powers. He speaks a great deal of the military ambitions of Prussia, of the menace of German invasion and similar governmental games. But where do the *workers* come in in all this? Are the economic interests of the working classes of Europe involved in this war, do *they* stand to profit in any way by whatever result there might be, and is international solidarity furthered by sending Russian and French workers to slaughter their brother workers in German uniform? Has not Kropotkin always taught us that the *solidarity* of labor throughout the world is the cornerstone of all true progress and that labor has no interest whatever in the quarrels of their governmental or industrial masters?

Kropotkin dwells on the menace of Prussian militarism and on the necessity of destroying it. But can Prussian militarism be destroyed by the militarism of the Allies? Does not the militarism of a country—of *any* country—ultimately rest on the consent of the people of that country, and has not Kropotkin always argued that the revolutionary consciousness and economic solidarity of the workers alone can force capital and government to terms and ultimately abolish both?

Surely Kropotkin will not claim that carnage, rapine, and destruction advance the civilization of one country as against that of another. He has always emphasized that real culture—in the sense of social liberty and economic well-being—rests with the people themselves and that there is no difference in the true character of government, whatever its particular form. Indeed, he has repeatedly said that the "liberal" governments are the more subtle and therefore the more dangerous enslavers of humanity.

We regret deeply, most deeply, Kropotkin's changed attitude. But not even the great European catastrophe can alter our position on the international brotherhood of man. We unconditionally condemn *all* capitalist wars, with whatever sophisms it may be sought to defend the one or the other set of pirates and exploiters as more "libertarian." We unalterably hold that war is the game of the masters, always at the expense of the duped workers. The workers have nothing to gain by the victory of the one or the other of the contending sides. Prussian militarism is no greater menace to life and liberty than Tsarist autocracy. Neither can be destroyed by the other. Both must and will be destroyed only by the social revolutionary power of the united international proletariat.

VOL. IX, NO. II, JANUARY 1915

VOL. X, NO. 7, SEPTEMBER 1915

Observations and Comments

[Unsigned]

Jews being an international people, the specter of anti-Semitism was naturally viewed in *Mother Earth* as a problem worldwide, though curiously no attempts were made to explain the prejudice beyond suggestions of cultural and historical backwardness. In benighted Russia, in 1911–13, Mendel Beilis, a Jewish bookkeeper from Odessa, was tried—but not convicted—for the medieval charge of ritual murder. In the benighted American South, on August 16, 1915, a Jew named Leo Frank was lynched and his body mutilated, after Governor John Slayton of Georgia commuted his death sentence to life imprisonment. Frank, a Northerner and the superintendent of a pencil factory in Atlanta, had been found guilty of the murder of an employee, the fourteen-year-old Mary Phagan, largely on the conflicting testimony of Jim Conley, the janitor who earlier had been under suspicion for the crime. The mob that abducted and killed Frank had been egged on by the populist, anti-Semitic Thomas Watson, owner of the misnamed weekly the *Jeffersonian*. The Beilis and Frank cases received extensive newspaper coverage, which to the writer of "Observations and Comments" boiled down to so many hypocritical "crocodile tears": murder by the state or by the mob were equal miscarriages of justice.

In the closing paragraph, "Lawson is sent away for life" refers to John Lawson, the strike leader during the Ludlow massacre, who was sentenced to life imprisonment (see Julia May Courtney, "Remember Ludlow!" page 344).

(C∾

L AST YEAR ALL OF EUROPE AND AMERICA was aroused over the Beilis case. It was believed that such black superstition, such barbarity which conspired against Beilis, was possible only in Russia. How many Europeans and even Americans know that a similar outrage has been perpetrated in Atlanta, Georgia, in the Frank case?

True, the ritual murder charge was not raised against Frank, though superstition will have it that since the Jewish religion forbids the outrage of Jewish women, Frank killed Mary Phagan for that purpose. But aside of the ritual spook, the Frank case is as vivid a repetition of the Beilis case as anything could possible be.

From the masterly report in *Collier's Weekly* by Connolly and Mr. Berry Benson of Georgia, in the Sunday *Times,* no one can doubt that Frank is a victim of "politics, perjury and prejudice," and that if he is to die it will be not because of his guilt, but because of the fact that he is a Jew and that Jew-baiting is beginning in the United States.

Everyone knew before this case that with all the opportunities offered the Jew in America, he is hated and discriminated against as much as he is all over Europe. There are any number of hotels and summer places where the Jews are not admitted, equally so is professional opportunity closed to the Jews. Under the circumstances it requires but a spark to kindle American anti-Semitism into a flame.

That this should come from the South is but natural, inasmuch as it is a hundred years behind the North and the latter is benighted enough. Besides, the South seems to be tired of "nigger" lynching; it needs a Jew for recreation.

The fact that Leo Frank was associated with employers of cheap labor ought not to blind the workers to the farcical procedure called justice, which has decreed that the man must die. We therefore hope that all liberal elements will unite in the demand that Frank be set free and thereby nip in the bud the contemptible method of Jew-baiting in America.

We are not among those who attempt to differentiate between murder committed by the State and murder committed without the sanction of legal murderers. We cannot see why the one is considered noble, honorable, moral, and just, while the other is merely criminal. Such distinctions are of value only to those who wish to monopolize the business of murder. The recent lynching of Leo Frank was not an illegal act; it was not an anarchistic act. It was the act of honorable, law-abiding, law-loving Georgians, whose defense must be that they were carrying out the decree of Georgia courts. They were embodying the spirit of the law, if they were not observing the letter of it. "Justice" in the Georgian sense had been miscarried by the individual and, from their point of view, anarchistic act of Slayton.

"The people rose and carried into effect the legal sentence," in the words of Thomas E. Watson. This in fact is the truth of the whole matter, in spite of the sentimental crocodile tears of the *New York Times* and other such sheets, which are the greatest champions of legal murder elsewhere. The real lesson of the Frank lynching is to be found in its revelation of the complete mastery of Prejudice, Stupidity, Ignorance, and Bloodthirstiness. These are the forces which control the courts, not only in Georgia but in every State of the Union. These are the forces which determine the activity of the State in all its departments. These are the powers of darkness which use the State to conduct the vicarious business of murder. There is no doubt in our mind that the chivalrous and honorable citizens who hanged Leo Frank to a tree would have objected to the Jew being murdered by the State. These lovers of justice wanted his blood. Therefore they were willing, in the words of Watson, to give him "a fair trial before an honest jury and a just judge"— merely as a preliminary and as the surest way of legitimatizing this murder. This "fair trial" has given an air of sanctity of respectability to the murder. Slayton's commutation of the sentence merely served to reveal, in the Marietta lynching, the forces that control the activities of the State, and which are not, as Slayton learned, in any crucial instance, to be opposed. Law and Order, in Georgia as elsewhere, are merely the thin veils which cloak the bloodthirstiness of respectable and law-abiding citizens.

Yet, on the other hand, how weak-kneed is the attempt of the conservative and respectable press elsewhere to protest against the lynching of Frank! Since when have these pimps of public opinion been the champions of decency and justice? They would throw dust in our eyes and try to make their readers believe that this mob murder is an exception in the annals of American courts. That is a lie. The same forces controlling the courts of Georgia are active elsewhere. The worm-eaten press does not say that, for it too is controlled in the same way. Mr. Rockefeller's lynchings, burnings, and massacres are commended. Lawson is sent away for life, but do these moral sheets protest? To give any idea of the injustice and the bloodthirstiness of the courts and the American press would fill volumes. The lynching of Frank is merely a bald instance of the fact that Law and Murder go hand in hand.

International Anarchist Manifesto on the War

The promulgation of the "International Anarchist Manifesto on the War" and its publication in *Mother Earth* were part of Emma Goldman's efforts to counter the influence of Peter Kropotkin's support of the Allies during World War I. The essence of the "Manifesto" is a classic expression of pure anarchism: "The truth is that the causes of wars, of that which at present stains with blood the plains of Europe, as of all wars that have preceded it, rests solely in the existence of the State, which is the political form of privilege." The signatories made up a miniature anarchist who's who on both sides of the Atlantic. One of them, Saul Yanovsky, was the editor of the Yiddish *Fraye Arbeter Shtime,* in whose pages Kropotkin had published an open letter stating his position on the war (see "Alexander Berkman, "In Reply to Kropotkin," page 380). Yanovsky allowed differing opinions on the matter to appear in the newspaper and by the end of 1914 himself went over to Kropotkin's side. Another who changed his mind as the war continued was Harry Kelly, a charter member of the Ferrer Association and a lifelong activist in the Modern School movement.

E UROPE IN A BLAZE, TWELVE MILLION MEN engaged in the most frightful butchery that history has ever recorded; millions of women and children in tears; the economic, intellectual, and moral life of seven great peoples brutally suspended, and the menace becoming every day more pregnant with new military complications—such is, for seven months, the painful, agonizing, and hateful spectacle presented by the civilized world.

But a spectacle not unexpected—at least, by the Anarchists, since for them there never has been nor is there any doubt—the terrible events of today strengthen this conviction—that war is permanently fostered by the present social system. Armed conflict, restricted or widespread, colonial or European, is the natural consequence and the inevitable and fatal outcome of a society that is founded on the exploitation of the workers, rests on the savage struggle of the classes, and compels Labor to submit to the domination of a minority of parasites who hold both political and economic power.

The war was inevitable. Wherever it originated, it had to come. It is not in vain that for half a century there has been a feverish preparation of the most formidable armaments and a ceaseless increase in the budgets of death. It is not by constantly improving the weapons of war and by concentrating the mind and the will of all upon the better organization of the military machine that people work for peace.

Therefore, it is foolish and childish, after having multiplied the causes and occasions of conflict, to seek to fix the responsibility on this or that government. No possible distinction can be drawn between offensive and defensive wars. In the present conflict, the governments of Berlin and Vienna have sought to justify themselves by documents not less authentic than those of the governments of Paris and Petrograd. Each does its very best to produce the most indisputable and the most decisive documents in order to establish its good faith and to present itself as the immaculate defender of right and liberty and the champion of civilization.

Civilization? Who, then, represents it just now? Is it the German State, with its formidable militarism, and so powerful that it has stifled every disposition to revolt? Is it the Russian State, to whom the knout, the gibbet, and Siberia are the sole means of persuasion? Is it the French State, with its *Biribi,* its bloody conquests in Tonkin, Madagascar, Morocco, and its compulsory enlistment of black troops? France, that detains in its prisons, for years, comrades guilty only of having written and spoken against war? Is it the English State, which exploits, divides, and oppresses the populations of its immense colonial Empire?

No; none of the belligerents is entitled to invoke the name of civilization or to declare itself in a state of legitimate defense.

The truth is that the cause of wars, of that which at present stains with blood the plains of Europe, as of all wars that have preceded it, rests solely in the existence of the State, which is the political form of privilege.

The State has arisen out of military force, it has developed through the use of military force, and it is still on military force that it must logically rest in order to maintain its omnipotence. Whatever the form it may assume, the State is nothing but organized oppression for the advantage of a privileged minority. The present conflict illustrates this in the most striking manner. All forms of the State are engaged in the present war; absolutism with Russia, absolutism softened by Parliamentary institutions with Germany, the State ruling over peoples of quite different races with Austria, a democratic constitutional régime with England, and a democratic Republican régime with France.

The misfortune of the peoples, who were deeply attached to peace, is that, in order to avoid war, they placed their confidence in the State with its intriguing diplomatists, in democracy, and in political parties (not excluding those in opposition, like Parliamentary Socialism). This confidence has been deliberately betrayed, and continues to be so, when governments, with the aid of the whole of their press, persuade their respective peoples that this war is a war of liberation.

We are resolutely against all wars between peoples, and in neutral countries, like Italy, where the governments seek to throw fresh peoples into the fiery furnace of war, our comrades have been, are, and ever will be most energetically opposed to war.

The role of the Anarchists in the present tragedy, whatever may be the place or the situation in which they find themselves, is to continue to proclaim that there is but one war of liberation: that which in all countries is waged by the oppressed against the oppressors, by the exploited against the exploiters. Our part is to summon the slaves to revolt against their masters.

Anarchist action and propaganda should assiduously and perseveringly aim at weakening and dissolving the various States, at cultivating the spirit of revolt, and arousing discontent in peoples and armies.

To all the soldiers of all countries who believe they are fighting for justice and liberty, we have to declare that their heroism and their valor will but serve to perpetuate hatred, tyranny, and misery.

To the workers in factory and mine it is necessary to recall that the rifles they now have in their hands have been used against them in the days of strike and of revolt and that later on they will be again used against them in order to compel them to undergo and endure capitalist exploitation.

To the workers on farm and field it is necessary to show that after the war they will be obliged once more to bend beneath the yoke and to continue to cultivate the lands of their lords and to feed the rich.

To all the outcasts, that they should not part with their arms until they have settled accounts with their oppressors, until they have taken land and factory and workshop for themselves.

To mothers, wives, and daughters, the victims of increased misery and privation, let us show who are the ones really responsible for their sorrows and for the massacre of their fathers, sons, and husbands.

We must take advantage of all the movements of revolt, of all the discontent, in order to foment insurrection, and to organize the revolution to which we look to put an end to all social wrongs.

No despondency, even before a calamity like the present war. It is in periods thus troubled, in which many thousands of men heroically give their lives for an idea, that we must show these men the generosity, greatness, and beauty of the Anarchist ideal: Social justice realized through the free organization of producers; war and militarism done away with forever; and complete freedom won, by the abolition of the State and its organs of destruction.

Signed by—Leonard D. Abbott, Alexander Berkman, L. Bertoni, L. Bersani, G. Bernard, G. Barrett, A. Bernardo, E. Boudot, A. Calzitta, Joseph J. Cohen, Henry Combes, Nestor Ciele van Diepen, F. W. Dunn, Ch. Frigerio, Emma Goldman, V. Garcia, Hippolyte Havel, T. H. Keell, Harry Kelly, J. Lemaire, E. Malatesta, H. Marques, F. Domela Nieuwenhuis, Noel Panavich, E. Recchioni, G. Rijnders, I. Rochtchine, A. Savioli, A. Schapiro, William Shatoff, V. J. C. Schermerhorn, C. Trombetti, P. Vallina, G. Vignati, Lillian G. Woolf, S. Yanovsky.

This manifesto is published by the International Anarchist movement and will be printed in several languages and issued in leaflet form.

London, 1915.

VOL. X, NO. 5, JULY 1915

Italy Also!

By Errico Malatesta

One of the signatories of the "International Anarchist Manifesto on the War" (see page 385) was the by then legendary Italian anarchist, Errico Malatesta. Like Bakunin before him, Malatesta was a personification of the stormy international revolutionary, living most of his life in exile, in prison, or in hiding, seeming to appear wherever there was word of insurrection. The term "propaganda by deed"—that is, direct action in violent form, usually taken to mean assassination—was said to be his invention. Malatesta spent the war years in London, having left Italy in June 1914 after the collapse of "Red Week," a general strike that had begun, with his encouragement, in the province of Ancona on the Adriatic coast and quickly spread to other parts of Italy. From exile he viewed Italy's entry into the war in May 1915 with despair—but with some hope and pride, too, in the anarchist movement of his native land and its continued opposition to the European slaughter.

(∞)

WE HAD HOPED THAT THE ITALIAN WORKERS would be able to resist the governing classes and affirm to the last their brotherhood with the workers of all countries and their resolution to persevere in the struggle against the exploiters and oppressors, for the real emancipation of mankind. The fact that the great majority of Socialists and Syndicalists, and all the Anarchists (except a very few) were solid against war, added to the evident general disposition of the masses, gave us this hope that Italy would escape the massacre and keep all her forces for the works of peace and civilization.

But, alas! no. Italy, too, has been dragged into the slaughter. The same Italians who were oppressed and famished in the country of their birth and were compelled very often to go and earn their bread in faroff lands; the same Italians who tomorrow will be famished and compelled to emigrate again are now killing and being killed in defense of the interests and ambitions of those who deny them the right to work and live a decent life.

It is astonishing and humiliating to see how easily the masses can be deceived by the coarsest lies!

All these dreary months the Italian capitalists have been enriching themselves by selling at enhanced prices to Germany and Austria an immense quantity of things useful for the war. The Italian Government has been trying to sell to the Central Empires Italian neutrality in exchange for more additions to the dominions of the Savoyan King. And now, because they could not obtain all they wanted, and have found it more advantageous to cast in their lot with the Allies, they speak, with brazen face, as if they were disinterested knights-errant, of the defense of civilization and the vindication of "poor Belgium." Yet their mask is very transparent. They say that they go to war for the liberation of the peoples from foreign domination, and they try to inflame the young men with the glories of the Italian struggle against the Austrian tyranny; but they try to crush into submission the

Arabs of Tripoli, they want to keep the Greek islands "provisionally" occupied at the time of the war with Turkey, they ask for territories and privileges in Asia Minor, they occupy a part of Albania, which certainly is not Italian in any sense of the word, and pretend to annex Dalmatia, where the Italians are only a small percentage of the population. Really, they pretend to have a claim on every country which they have, or think they have, the power to take and keep. One place ought to belong to Italy because it was once conquered by the Romans of yore, another because there was a Venetian countinghouse there, another because it is inhabited by many Italian immigrants, another because it is necessary for military security; and every other place in the world because it may be useful to the development of Italian commerce.

But there is nothing astonishing in this: Governments and the dominating classes in every country have always invoked international justice when they were weak; but as soon as they are, or think they are, strong enough, they begin to dream of universal domination. They protest now against the domineering spirit of the Germans, but as a matter of fact they are all "Germans."

What seems less natural, and is more disheartening, in Italy is the conduct of the Republicans. They affected to put above all the question of the form of government; for them the first, the all-important question was the abolition of the Monarchy. But it has been sufficient to appeal to their national passions, and all their desire of liberty, all their hatred against the House of Savoy, has disappeared. They have done their utmost to resuscitate in the masses the old ideal of patriotism, which was developed in the time when national independence seemed to be the means for attaining emancipation from poverty and bondage, and which had decayed in consequence of the experience that a national government is as bad as a foreign one. They have raised the cry "War or Revolution," and when the King, perhaps to save himself from the revolution, has declared war, they have put themselves in the mass at the service of the King. What, then, about the Republic? Many of them still say that they want war in order to facilitate the revolution; but what nonsense! If Italy is victorious, certainly it will be to the exclusive advantage of the Monarchy; and, on the other hand, we cannot conceive that the Republicans would be capable of the infamy of pushing the people into war with the secret hope that they would be beaten and their country invaded and devastated.

We do not know, for want of reliable information, the present situation in Italy, and what are the true factors that have determined so quick a change in her attitude. But one redeeming feature is revealed by the news received in London.

The Italian Government has felt that it was not safe to make war without suppressing every liberty and putting in prison a great number of Anarchists.

This means that the Anarchists remain loyal to their flag to the last and, what is more important, that the Government fears their influence on the masses.

This gives us the assurance that as soon as the war fever has calmed down we will be able to begin again our own war—the war for human liberty, equality, and brotherhood—and in better conditions than before, because the people will have had another experience, and what a terrible one! That from the Government can be expected only injustice, misery, and oppression, and then, as a change, slaughterings on a colossal scale; that patriotism, nationalism, racial rivalry are only means for enslaving the workers, and that their salvation lies in the abolition of Government and Capitalism.

The War at Home

As the United States moved closer and closer to joining the European conflict, despite President Woodrow Wilson's recent reelection on a peace platform ("He Kept Us Out of War"), antiwar activists stepped up their efforts and were met with ever-increasing governmental resistance. There is a noticeable desperation, born of anger and frustration, in Emma Goldman's voice in "The Promoters of the War Mania," published in March 1917, the month before the president declared the country at war.

The effect of the war at home was politically devastating, initiating a period of unparalleled repression of First Amendment rights that would be unthinkable today, even under similar circumstances. On May 18, the Selective Service Act established universal military conscription, to go into effect on June 5. From mid-May to mid-June, Goldman and others associated with *Mother Earth* held a series of mass rallies protesting the draft, drawing as many as 10,000 people, and formed a No-Conscription League. The meetings were discontinued in the face of harassment by heavily armed police and violent hecklers bent on provoking the audience and when it was realized that young men were being searched and arrested for not carrying draft registration cards.

On June 15, Wilson signed the Espionage Act, which established penalties of up to twenty years' imprisonment and fines as high as $10,000 for interfering with conscription, encouraging disloyalty among the armed forces, as well as aiding the enemy, and also authorized the Post Office Department to confiscate any written matter that advocated treason, insurrection, or forcible resistance to federal law. Emma Goldman and Alexander Berkman were arrested that very day.

The all-type cover for *Mother Earth* in June 1917 proclaimed: "JUNE 5TH IN MEMORIAM AMERICAN DEMOCRACY" (see Illustration 14, following page 220). That same issue included Emma Goldman's program for the ill-fated No-Conscription League. *Mother Earth* itself, because of its acts of "espionage" under the broad definition of the law, survived only two more issues and was succeeded by the truncated and short-lived *Mother Earth Bulletin*.

VOL. XII, NO. I, MARCH 1917

The Promoters of the War Mania

By Emma Goldman

A T THIS MOST CRITICAL MOMENT IT BECOMES imperative for every liberty-loving person to voice a fiery protest against the participation of this country in the European mass murder. If the opponents of war, from the Atlantic to the Pacific, would immediately join their voices into a thunderous No!, then the horror that now menaces America might yet be averted. Unfortunately it is only too true that the people in our so-called Democracy are to a large extent a dumb, suffering herd rather than thinking beings who dare to give expression to a frank, earnest opinion.

Yet it is unthinkable that the American people should really want war. During the last thirty months they have had ample opportunity to watch the frightful carnage in the warring countries. They have seen universal murder, like a devastating pestilence, eat into the very heart of the peoples of Europe. They saw cities destroyed, entire countries wiped off the map, hosts of dead, millions of wounded and maimed. The American people could not help witnessing the spread of insane, motiveless hatred among the peoples of Europe. They must realize the extent of the famine, the suffering and anguish gripping the war-stricken countries. They know, too, that while the men were killed off like vermin, the women and children, the old and the decrepit remained behind in helpless and tragic despair. Why then, in the name of all that is reasonable and humane, should the American people desire the same horrors, the same destruction and devastation upon American soil?

We are told that the "freedom of the seas" is at stake and that "American honor" demands that we protect that precious freedom. What a farce! How much freedom of the seas can the masses of toilers or the disinherited and the unemployed ever enjoy? Would it not be well to look into this magic thing, "the freedom of the seas," before we sing patriotic songs and shout hurrah?

The only ones that have benefitted by the "freedom of the seas" are the exploiters, the dealers in munition and food supplies. The "freedom of the seas" has served these unscrupulous American robbers and monopolists as a pretext to pilfer the unfortunate people of both Europe and America. Out of international carnage they have made billions; out of the misery of the people and the agony of women and children the American financiers and industrial magnates have coined huge fortunes.

Ask young Morgan. Will he dare admit his tremendous pecuniary gain from the export of munition and food supplies? Of course not. But the truth will out, sometimes. Thus a financial expert recently proved that even old Pierpont Morgan would be astounded could he see the dazzling profits gathered in by his son through war speculations. And, incidentally, do not let us forget that it is this speculation in murder and destruction which is responsible for the criminal increase in the cost of living in our own land. War, famine, and the capitalist class are the only gainers in the hideous drama called nationalism, patriotism, national honor, and freedom of the seas. Instead of putting a stop to such monstrous crimes, war in America would only increase the opportunities of the profit mongers. That and only that will be the result if the American people will consent to thrust the United States into the abyss of war.

President Wilson and other officials of the administration assure us that they want peace. If that claim held even one grain of truth, the government would have long ago carried out the suggestion of many true lovers of peace to put a stop to the export of munition and food stuffs. Had this shameful trade with the implements of slaughter been stopped at the beginning of the war, the good results for peace would have been manifold.

First, the war in Europe would have been starved out through the stoppage of food exports. Indeed, it is no exaggeration when I say that the war would have been at an end long ago had the American financiers been prevented from investing billions in war loans and had the American munition clique and food speculators not been given the opportunity to supply warring Europe with the means to keep up the slaughter.

Second, an embargo on exports would have automatically taken out American ships from the war and submarine zones and would have thus eliminated the much discussed "reason" for war with Germany.

Third, and most important of all, the brazen, artificial increase in the cost of living, which condemns the toiling masses of America to semistarvation, would be an impossibility were not the great bulk of American products shipped to Europe to feed the fires of war.

Peace meetings and peace protests have no meaning whatever unless the government is challenged to stop the continuance of exports. If for no other reason, this ought to be insisted upon, be it only to prove that Washington is capable of nice phrases, but that it has never made a single determined step for peace. That will help to demonstrate to the American people that the government represents only the capitalists, the International War and Preparedness Trust, and not the workers. Are then the people of America good enough only to pull the chestnuts out of the fire for the thieving trusts? That is all this wild clamor for war means as far as the masses are concerned.

The attempt to light the torch of the furies of war is the more monstrous when one bears in mind that the people of America are cosmopolitan. If anything, America should be the soil for international under- standing, for the growth of friendship between all races. Here, all narrow, stifling national prejudices should be eradicated. Instead, the people are to be thrown into the madness and confusion of war, of racial antagonism and hatred.

True, there never was much love wasted in this country on the unfortunate foreigner, but what about the boast that the Goddess of Liberty holds high the beacon to all oppressed nations? What about America as the haven of welcome? Should all this now become the symbol of national persecution? What can result from it but the pollution of all social relationship? Think of it, war in this country is at present only a possibility, and already the Germans and the Austrians are being deprived of employment, ostracized, and spied upon, persecuted and hounded by the jingoes. And that is only a small beginning of what war would bring in its wake.

I do not have to emphasize that I entertain not a particle of sympathy with the Germany of the Höhenzollern or the Austria of the Hapsburgs. But what have the Germans and the Austrians in America—or in their own country, for that matter—to do with the diplomacy and politics of Berlin or Vienna? It is nothing but blind, cruel national and patriotic madness which would make these people, who have lived, toiled, and suffered in this country, pay for the criminal plans and intrigues in Berlin and Vienna palaces.

These millions of Germans and Austrians, who have contributed more to the real culture and growth of America than all the Morgans and Rockefellers, are now to be treated like enemy aliens, just because Wall Street feels itself checked in its unlimited use of the seas for plunder, robbery, and theft from suffering America and bleeding Europe.

Militarism and reaction are now more rampant in Europe than ever before. Conscription and censorship have destroyed every vestige of liberty. Everywhere the governments have used the situation to tighten the militaristic noose around the necks of the people. Everywhere discipline has been the knout to whip the masses into slavery and blind obedience. And the pathos of it all is that the people at large have submitted without a murmur, though every country has shown its quota of brave men that would not be deluded.

The same is bound to take place in America should the dogs of war be let loose here. Already the poisonous seed has been planted. All the reactionary riffraff, propagandists of jingoism and preparedness, all the beneficiaries of exploitation represented in the Merchants and Manufacturers' Association, the Chambers of Commerce, the munition cliques, etc., etc., have come to the fore with all sorts of plans and schemes to chain and gag labor, to make it more helpless and dumb than ever before.

These respectable criminals no longer make a secret of their demand for compulsory military training. Taft, the spokesman of Wall Street, expressed it cynically enough that now, in face of the war danger, the time has come to demand the introduction of compulsory militarism. Subserviently echoing the slogan, principals and superintendents of our schools and colleges are hastening to poison the minds of their pupils with national "ideals" and patriotic forgeries of history to prepare the young generation for "the protection of national honor," which really means the "glory" of bleeding to death for the crooked transactions of a gang of legalized, cowardly thieves. Mr. Murray Butler, the lickspittle of Wall Street, is in the lead, and many others like him are crawling before the golden calf of their masters. Talk about prostitution! Why, the unfortunate girl in the street is purity itself compared with such mental degeneration.

Added to this process of poisoning are the huge appropriations rushed through by Congress and the state legislatures for the national murder machinery. Sums reaching into the hundreds of millions for the Army and Navy fly through the air within such enticing reach that the Steel Trust and other corporations manufacturing ammunition and war supplies are dissolving in patriotic sentiment and enthusiasm and have already offered their generous services to the country.

Hand in hand with this military preparedness and war mania goes the increased persecution of the workers and their organizations. Labor went wild with enthusiasm and gratitude to the President for his supposed humanity in proclaiming the eight-hour law before election, and now it develops that the law was merely a bait for votes and a shackle for labor. It denies the right to strike and introduces compulsory arbitration. Of course it is common knowledge that strikes have long since been made ineffective by antipicketing injunctions and the prosecution of strikers, but the federal eight-hour law is the worst parody on the right to organize and to strike, and it is going to prove an additional fetter on labor. In connection with this arbitrary measure goes the proposition to give the President full power in case of war to take control of the railroads and their employees, which would mean nothing less than absolute subserviency and industrial militarism for the workers.

Then there is the systematic, barbarous persecution of radical and revolutionary elements throughout the land. The horrors in Everett, the conspiracy against labor in San Francisco, with Billings and Mooney already sacrificed—are they mere coincidences? Or do they not rather signify the true character of the war which the American ruling class has been waging against labor?

The workers must learn that they have nothing to expect from their masters. The latter, in America as well as in Europe, hesitate not a moment to send hundred thousands of the people to their death if their interests demand it. They are ever ready that their misguided slaves should have the national and patriotic banner over burning cities, over devastated countrysides, over homeless and starving humanity, just as long as they can find enough unfortunate victims to be drilled into mankillers, ready at the bidding of their masters to perform the ghastly task of bloodshed and carnage.

Valuable as the work of the Women's Peace Party and other earnest pacifists may be, it is folly to petition the President for peace. The workers, they alone, can avert the impending war; in fact, all wars, if they will refuse to be a party to them. The determined antimilitarist is the only pacifist. The ordinary pacifist merely moralizes; the antimilitarist acts; he refuses to be ordered to kill his brothers. His slogan is: "I will not kill, nor will I lend myself to be killed."

It is this slogan which we must spread among the workers and carry into the labor organizations. They need to realize that it is monstrously criminal to voluntarily engage in the hideous business of killing. It is terrible enough to kill in anger, in a moment of frenzy, but it is still more so to blindly obey the command of your military superiors to commit murder. The time must come when slaughter and carnage through blind obedience will not only not receive rewards, monuments, pensions, and eulogies, but will be considered the greatest horror and shame of a barbaric, bloodthirsty, greed-obsessed age; a dark, hideous blotch upon civilization.

Let us understand this most valuable truth: A man has the power to act voluntarily only as long as he does not wear the uniform. Once you have donned the garb of obedience, the "voluntary" soldier becomes as much a part of the slaughter machine as his brother who was forced into military service. It is still time in our land to decide against militarism and war, to hold out determinately against compulsory military service for the murder of your fellow men. After all, America is not yet like Germany, Russia, France, or England in the throes of a military regime with the mark of a Cain upon her brow. The determined stand which the workers can take individually, in groups and organizations against war, will still meet with ready and enthusiastic response. It would arouse the people all over the land. As a matter of fact, they want no war. The cry for it comes from the military cliques, the munition manufacturers, and their mouthpiece, the press, this most degenerate criminal of all criminals. They all stand by the flag. Oh, yes; it's a profitable emblem that covers a multitude of sins.

It is still time to stem the bloody tide of war by word of mouth and pen and action. The promoters of war realize that we have looked into their cards and that we know their crooked, criminal game. We know they want war to increase their profits. Very well, let them fight their own wars. We, the people of America, will not do it for them. Do you think war would then come or be kept up? Oh, I know it is difficult to arouse the workers, to make them see the truth back of the nationalistic, patriotic lie. Still we must do our share. At least we shall be free from blame should the terrible avalanche overtake us in spite of our efforts.

I for one will speak against war so long as my voice will last, now and during war. A thousand times rather would I die calling to the people of America to refuse to be obedient, to refuse military service, to refuse to murder their brothers, than I should ever give my voice in justification of war, except the one war of all the peoples against their despots and exploiters—the Social Revolution.

VOL. XII, NO. 4, JUNE 1917

The No-Conscription League

By Emma Goldman

CONSCRIPTION HAS NOW BECOME A FACT in this country. It took England fully 18 months after she engaged in war to impose compulsory military service on her people. It was left to free America to pass a conscription bill six weeks after war was declared.

What becomes of the patriotic boast of America to have entered the European war in behalf of the principle of democracy? But that is not all. Every country in Europe has recognized the right of conscientious objectors—of men who refuse to engage in war on the ground that they are opposed to taking life.

Yet this democratic country makes no such provision for those who will not commit murder at the behest of the profiteers through human sacrifice. Thus the "land of the free and the home of the brave" is ready to coerce free men into the military yoke.

Liberty of conscience is the most fundamental of all human rights, the pivot of all progress. No human being may be deprived of it without losing every vestige of freedom of thought and action. In these days when every principle and conception of democracy and individual liberty is being cast overboard under the pretext of democratizing Germany, it behooves every liberty-loving man and woman to insist on his or her right of individual choice in the ordering of his life or action.

The NO-CONSCRIPTION LEAGUE has been formed for the purpose of encouraging conscientious objectors to affirm their liberty of conscience and to translate their objection to human slaughter by refusing to participate in the killing of their fellow men. The NO-CONSCRIPTION LEAGUE is to be the voice of protest against war and against the coercion of conscientious objectors to participate in the war. Our platform may be summarized as follows:

We oppose conscription because we are internationalists, antimilitarists, and opposed to all wars waged by capitalistic governments.

We will fight for what we choose to fight for: we will never fight simply because we are ordered to fight.

We believe that the militarization of America is an evil that far out-weighs, in its antisocial and antilibertarian effects, any good that may come from America's participation in the war.

We will resist conscription by every means in our power, and we will sustain those who, for similar reasons, refuse to be conscripted.

The first important public activity of the NO-CONSCRIPTION LEAGUE took the form of a large mass-meeting on May 18th, attended by 8,000 people. The enthusiasm was so great that the uniformed patriots who came to break up the meeting soon slunk courageously away. A Mothers' No-Conscription meeting has been arranged for June 4th. Besides, 100,000 No-Conscription manifestos have been circulated broadcast.

We are not unmindful of the difficulties in our way. But we have resolved to go ahead and spare no effort to make the voice of protest a moral force in the life of this country. The initial efforts of the conscientious objectors in England were fraught with many hardships and danger, but finally the government of Great Britain was forced to give heed to the steadily increasing volume of public protest against the coercion of conscientious objectors. So we, too, in America will doubtless meet the full severity of the government and the condemnation of the patriotic jingoes, but we are nevertheless determined to go ahead. We feel confident in bringing out thousands of people who are conscientious objectors to the murder of their fellow men and to whom a principle represents the most vital thing in life.

Will you help us in this great undertaking? Will you enable us to carry on the fight? Send your contribution to me at once, to 20 E. 125th St., New York. Send for manifestos.

VOL. XII, NO. 6, AUGUST 1917

Speaking of Democracy

By Martha Gruening

Emma Goldman and Alexander Berkman were tried in New York between June 27 and July 9, 1917, for conspiracy to violate the Selective
Service Act (see Appendix, page 413). They conducted their own defense
very ably, but were found guilty. Each was sentenced to two years' imprisonment and fined $10,000, and the judge recommended their deporta-
tion after the prison terms were finished. In their absence, *Mother Earth,*
and after its demise the *Mother Earth Bulletin,* was edited by Goldman's
niece Stella Comyn and M. Eleanor Fitzgerald, joint editor with Berkman
of *The Blast,* which had relocated from San Francisco to New York.

One of the witnesses appearing in Goldman and Berkman's defense
was Martha Gruening, who had been active in the No-Conscription
League from its start. For what proved to be the last issue of *Mother Earth*
(August 1917), she contributed an account of the East St. Louis race riot
of July 2, one of the worst in U.S. history. Reported casualty figures vary,
but 39 to 200 blacks and 8 or 9 whites were killed. Hundreds of houses
were destroyed, and as many as 6,000 blacks were driven from their
homes—many of them recent immigrants from the South, with their
wives and children, come to work in factories with government contracts
for the war effort. Police and the state militia stood by while local union
leaders urged, "East St. Louis must remain a white man's town." One
Jewish observer likened the riot to a Russian pogrom. "East St. Louis,"
commented Gruening, "is an example of that democracy we are to spread
over the world. . . . That is why I want the world made unsafe for it." The
August issue of *Mother Earth* was deemed unmailable by the U.S. Post
Office and confiscated.

FRANK BROWN, WHO LAY TERRIBLY BURNED in the hospital at East St. Louis, told me he had never meant to jump from the second story of his blazing house. He did so only when the flames were all about him and he "just couldn't stand it" any longer. The instinct which overcame his prudence in this instance was not that of self-preservation. He was impelled to leap and brave the "frightfulness" of the white Americans simply by his overwhelming desire to escape the torture of the flames and very much against his better judgment. He was at a loss to understand how he had been saved, and he spoke of it reverently as the "will of God," but as I looked at him and recalled all I had seen and heard in East St. Louis, I could only believe that the mob must have thought him too far gone to make it worthwhile to molest him further. One comes away from East St. Louis believing in this sort of cruelty—the supreme and deadly cruelty of the white race asserting its superiority.

This superiority has now been established in East St. Louis, once and for all time. That the "insolence" of the "nigger" who comes North made it necessary was of course "deplorable" (so I was sometimes told by white East St. Louis). But necessary it clearly was, for "Too many 'niggers' were coming in here—there were thousands of them taking white men's jobs. They vote and ride in streetcars next to white women. They pass remarks about white women. You see, once they get away from the South where they know how to treat them, they get insolent. They think they're as good as white people, and of course, that makes trouble." If this explanation does not seem adequate to you, you are woefully deficient in the race consciousness natural and becoming in a white person; while if you can contemplate "being shoved off the sidewalk by a buck 'nigger'" (I am quoting the exact words used to me by three white editors on as many separate occasions) without instant recourse to your hip pocket, you are disqualified at the outset from understanding a race riot. To the initiated it is at once clear that the wholesale slaughter of his people is the only answer to be made to the "buck" in question.

All of this is thoroughly understood by the A. F. of L. Its constitution decrees that members shall not be discriminated against because of "race, creed, or color," but its membership is largely composed of loyal nigger-hating Americans, who know that when black men in large numbers escape from the intolerable conditions of the South and attain an economic foothold in the North, something has to be done. Accordingly, on May 23, 1917, a call was sent out to the delegates to the Central Trades and Labor Union of East St. Louis, signed by its secretary, Edward F. Mason, to a meeting to take "drastic action" on the immigration of Negroes and to "devise a way to get rid of a certain portion of those already here." With characteristic efficiency these members of the superior race accomplished their ends in little more than a month's time by slaughtering several hundred Negro men, women, and children, burning nearly two hundred and fifty Negro homes, and driving out the majority of the survivors.

The meeting to which these delegates were called took place on May 28. Its immediate result was a riot in which a number of Negroes and some white men were injured, and much Negro property destroyed and damaged. It was after this riot that Mayor Mollman, with the wisdom of his kind, decided that the way to preserve peace was to prevent the sale of firearms to Negroes. An ordinance to that effect was passed and, unlike most ordinances passed in East St. Louis, was rigidly enforced. At the three bridges between St. Louis and East St. Louis, detectives were stationed who stopped and searched all colored people and if they found weapons in their possession, disarmed them. No white man was stopped. Negro homes were also visited and searched for arms. The reason for this, as explained to me by the local District Attorney, Hubert Schaumleffel, and others, was the necessity of foiling a wicked Negro plot to massacre the white population on the Fourth of July. No need to waste any sympathy on the "niggers"— they got just what they deserved and what they would have done themselves had they gotten the chance. But the Negroes are an inferior race —when not "insolent" they are "just children," and they can't even pull off a decent massacre. Twenty thousand strong, with arms being furnished to them by "German gold" and "agitators" of their own race, they still allowed themselves to be killed, maimed, and tortured by the justly aroused white population. As I have said, on the authority of white East St. Louis, the Negroes thought they were as good as white people—yet there is not one instance of their having during the riots burned a white woman or child, shot an unarmed fugitive, or kicked a wounded man to death. Most of them couldn't even kill an innocent man in cold blood, as is attested by the story of the white physician connected with one of the big industrial plants of East St. Louis. He and his wife were driving along one of the main streets when they were stopped by a mob of "bad niggers" who still retained their arms and who told him they would kill him. The white man was able to reason with them and presently was recognized as a "good white man" by one Negro whom he had treated and who persuaded the others to let him go.

When the militia was sent in to restore order, further proof of white superiority was given—if indeed any was needed. The boys of the Illinois militia understood that order could not exist as long as both races did, and so they proceeded to help both actively and passively in wiping out the black race. This was a natural and correct assumption on their part, for most of them came from small towns in southern Illinois where "they don't tolerate niggers" and whose railroad stations bear the sign "Nigger, don't let the sun set on you." With the spread of our democratic ideals, we may hope shortly to see translations of this sign in the railroad stations of Paris and Petrograd. We may also hope, perhaps, to establish an atrocity record which even the Germans will envy when southern Illinois furnishes its quota of men to be sent to the trenches. German eyewitnesses will doubtless be able to tell many stories such as the following told me by a white woman, a member of the Volunteers of America:

"I saw a crowd of white women grab a colored woman's baby and fling it into a blazing house. The woman was then shot while these women held her, and they threw her body in, too. They (the other women) were screaming like wild and tearing her clothes off her. I was thankful when she was shot. I saw them shooting into burning houses so that the people who were inside, who were wounded, couldn't get out and were roasted alive. Down by the Free Bridge I saw them behead a man with a butcher's knife. They threw his head over one side and his body over the other. They dragged trolley cars from the tracks, and then they'd make the people inside stick up their hands to show if they were black or white. If they were black, they dragged them out and killed them—how? Oh, any way—with knives and bottles, and stones, and iron pokers and crowbars. There wasn't any kind of weapon they didn't have in that crowd. I saw some with steel rods they tore off the railroad tracks. 'Long about five o'clock, a car of miners came in from Belleville. They had their dinner pails and pickaxes. They started into the crowd with their pickaxes hitting the niggers on the head with them. I saw them dropping all around and their blood and brains running out on the streets. I saw one of those miners afterwards with his pickaxe on his shoulder dripping blood all down his back. I saw the crowd close in on a woman. She was kneeling by the car track beside her little girl who had fainted—about twelve she looked like. When I saw her again she was down with a hole as big as your fist in her head. I saw them kick the wounded to death and heave rocks at them—big paving blocks. None of them would have lived to see the ambulances if the crowd could have helped it. I saw a dozen white men dragging an old nigger they wanted to hang by a rope about his neck. The first fire I saw was set by a young white girl. She came along Fourth Street, and the curtain blew out of the window of a nigger house. She just set fire to it and walked away. Nobody said anything to her. The next day I came along, and there were some white women hacking away at what was left of a man's body. They said they wanted a souvenir. I said, "Here, how do you know that's what you want? He's burned so you can't tell whether he's black or white." And that stopped them.

Yes, I believe the Germans will have many such stories to tell before the war is over. Stories like that of Frank Brown who thought the flames more merciful than the white man; like that of Lulu Cole, who was shot three times by the mob which broke into her house, whose twelve-year-old son was shot dead before her eyes, and whose husband "must be dead. I guess. He's never turned up since he went to work that Monday morning"; like that of Minnie Grey who was shot on her way to work on the morning after the riot by a soldier and a policeman. "They must have been done it," she told me, "they were the only ones on the street, and it happened right after I passed them." Stories like those of the seven Negroes who, as two militiamen told me humorously, were thrown into Cahokia Creek and "rocked every time they came up till they were all drowned"; like those of the Negro fugitives who, stripped of their weapons, ran to the soldiers for protection, only to be bayoneted back into the hands of the mob; like that of the Negro woman who ran upon the porch of a white woman's house with a mob in pursuit to find the door slammed and held against her; like that of the wounded old Negro woman who escaped with her life by hiding all night in a sewer pipe; and like those of the hundreds of refugees more tragic than those of Belgium who are still seeking for missing husbands, wives, and brothers, whose entire families have been wiped out or scattered, and whose homes were looted and laid waste.

East St. Louis is an example of that democracy we are to spread over the world—the democracy of caste and race oppression, of unspeakable cruelty and intolerance, of hideous injustices. It is the democracy of President Wilson and Mr. Gompers. The former has carefully refrained from making any public statement disapproving the massacre, while the latter is its open and shameless apologist. I have seen this democracy at close range, and I know what it means. That is why I want the world made unsafe for it.

The Russian Revolution

No single event at the start of the twentieth century so electrified the American left as the Russian Revolution. Partisan rivalries were put aside in March 1917 at the grand spectacle of a successful and long hoped-for people's revolution that overthrew the vast and reactionary empire of the tsars. In November, when the moderate provisional government of Aleksandr Kerensky fell following the Bolshevik coup d'état, social revolutionaries the world over rightly expected the leaders of the new Marxist state, Vladimir Lenin and Leon Trotsky, to make peace with the Central Powers and bring the eastern front of the war to a close. In America, it was rumored that both the Bolsheviks abroad and the antiwar activists at home were in the pay of the kaiser. Emma Goldman and Alexander Berkman were among those who put their trust in the Bolsheviks, optimistic that the overwhelming fact of the revolution would bridge the bitter fifty-year divide between anarchists and Marxists, and early representations to that effect by Lenin and Trotsky seemed to point in that direction. The Russian Revolution looked to be the great unifier of the left—especially in the face of hostility from the Allies.

Goldman and Berkman, after serving a brief part of their prison sentences for conspiracy (see "The War at Home," page 391), were released on bail in the summer of 1917 and thus able to publish their thoughts on the Russian situation in the pages of the *Mother Earth Bulletin*. Their spelling of *Boylshevik* was an attempt to approximate in English the original Russian pronunciation of the word. Goldman can hardly contain her exuberance in "The Russian Revolution." Berkman, in "The Trotsky Idea" and "The Surgeon's Duty," is characteristically more analytical in offering reasons why anarchists should now support a government, and a Marxist government at that. There is a sad irony in his confidence in Trotsky. Three years later, after having been deported to Russia, it was Trotsky's bloody suppression of the Kronstadt rebellion that drove Berkman and Goldman to make their final, irreparable break with the Soviets and live in exile for the rest of their lives.

Mother Earth Bulletin, VOL. I, NO. 3, DECEMBER 1917

The Russian Revolution

By Emma Goldman

SHORTLY AFTER THE EUROPEAN CATACLYSM swept over the world, American correspondents and magazine writers told glowing stories about the marvelous unity which existed in Russia between the people and the Tsar. They would have the world believe that the struggle of well-nigh one hundred years against Tsarism had ceased overnight, to give way to perfect harmony between the Russian autocracy and the people. They told marvelous tales about the kindness and humanity of the Russian officers to soldiers who had hitherto known nothing but the knout from their superiors. They described in glowing colors how the persecuted, exploited workers, and the flogged, famished peasants were as one with their government, imbued with one passion in the great war.

Barely three years after these shameful lies of the war unity in Russia, the Revolution swept Tsarism into the gutter and dispelled the myth that the Russian people wanted the war, that they were eager to die in the trenches for their Batiushka. In one mighty voice the people thundered from every nook and corner of Russia for peace, for fraternization with the people of Germany and with all their oppressed and disinherited brothers. That was their reply to the willful misrepresentations which had been sent broadcast to Western Europe and America about the unity of the people with their governing class.

To understand the Revolution one must trace its beginnings to the heroic movement which had for nearly a hundred years carried on an incessant battle against the dark forces of Russian autocracy. During that period the blood of the Russian martyrs had nurtured the seed of idealism and rebellion in the womb of the Russian soil. The hosts that had been done to death in the Peter and Paul Fortress, in Schlüsselburg, in Siberia, by the knout and the scaffold, have come to life in the Russian Revolution. The message of the men and women with the white hands—the intellectuals— the Petrashevskys and Chernyshevskys, the Sofia Perovskayas and Helfmans, the Alexander Herzens, Vera Figners, Spiridonovas, Babushkas, and thousands of others, had borne fruit. Their message was: Death to tyranny and Life to the people. Human brotherhood and social well-being was their slogan.

Through a slow and painful process, and at the expense of the best and finest of the Russian generations, this message was carried to the hearts and minds of the people, the peasants, the workers. It became their hope, their dream, their paean song. In the face of the great sacrifice the people often despaired of realizing their dream. Then new forces were sent into the villages to reassure the people, to strengthen their faith, to inspire them with new hope, for no message conceived in pain and nourished by blood and tears can ever be lost.

On the very eve of Russia's entry into the war, she was seething with revolution. The General Strike spread like wildfire in the industrial centers. Discontent and rebellion imbued the slow peasant and rejuvenated him to action. It is not at all unlikely that war was welcomed by autocracy as a check on the rising revolutionary tide.

Blind to the tendencies of the time, autocracy, even as all other governments, coerced the people into the war, but it was stupid to assume that they would submit very long: that they would so easily betray their martyrs who had died for universal peace and social brotherhood, that they would forget the tortures inflicted upon them, the sufferings and horrors endured at home, and rush off, bayonet in hand, to make Germany safe for democracy.

The Russian Revolution was the culminating expression of all the accumulated longings of the Russian people. It was the breaking point of the hatred for the old regime, and the realization of the great dream, cherished by the people for so long. Coming from the very depths of the Russian soul and spirit, how could anything so deep-rooted, so overpowering content itself with the overthrow of the Tsar, and his replacement by some cheap liberal regime, embodied in a Milyukov, a Lvov, or even a Kerensky.

Kerensky's regime was a compromise between political Socialism and economic liberalism, both contrary to the Revolution and its promise. It seems to have been Kerensky's dream to see "law and order" triumph, while leaving intact the social conditions which the Revolution purported to change. Kerensky's regime played the same role as all provisional governments temporarily washed in by a revolutionary tide. From the very first day of their appearance, they proclaim the end of the revolution. They take possession of power; but power, like all gods, can tolerate no other god beside it. Starting from this autocratic premise, the provisional government in Russia inevitably became reactionary, a new despotism, ready to strangle the Revolution before it had made a decisive step.

The powerful revolutionary consciousness of the Russian people could not be stayed by the command of a renegade. The Revolution would not stop because the provisional government attempted to check its march. It only struck deeper and went on in its persistent demand. The Revolution which managed to overcome the age-long despotic regime of the Tsar was not likely to collapse because of the obstacles placed in its way by politicians à la Kerensky. The Russian Revolution has triumphed over prisons, Siberia, and scaffolds. Pogroms have failed to slay it. The knout, cutting deep into its flesh, has been unable to stifle its spirit. How, then, was it to be dominated by a few upstarts of the moment?

To the Russian people the Revolution means a fundamental change in the political and economic arrangements of life. Primarily it means the confiscation of the land and the sources of production from those who had grown rich upon them while keeping the people in poverty. The Russians have begun to realize that mere political liberties are not lasting; that nothing is gained unless a fundamental change has been brought about to sustain the newly achieved political advantages.

All preceding revolutions were in this respect a warning and instructive example for the Russian Revolution. They never went much beyond the change of government. The people shed their blood, but received as reward nothing save the old despotism hidden under a new mask of hypocritical liberalism. How easily such a mask can be worn the Russian people had ample opportunity to learn from the modern bourgeois republics of Europe and America. Yes, even easier than under a monarchy has it proven in republics to enslave the people, mentally and physically.

The new phase, the Boylsheviki Revolution, lifts Russia out of the paralyzing position of a merely political machine into a virile, active economic force. Verily, this new phase shows how inexhaustible the Russian Revolution is. How many times she has already been buried, and yet how many times she has arisen! Nor is it the end, but rather the beginning of the real Social Revolution.

The very fact that such an extreme Marxian as Lenin and revolutionists like Trotsky and Kollontai can work together with the vast number of Russians who will not continue to shed their blood and waste their lives for the perpetuation of the world war proves that they are actuated, not by German money, but by the inner psychic necessity of the Russian Revolution to proclaim the ultimatum of "Universal Peace and the Land to the People" to the rest of the world. Great as the Lenins, the Trotskys, and the others may be, they are but the pulse-beat of the people who, as Lincoln Steffens justly said, are the only heroes in Russia. They are worn and weary with everlasting strife and bloodshed. They want peace as a means of getting back to themselves, of getting back to their land, of reconstructing their beloved Matushka Rossiya.

In the midst of the confusion and horrors of war, the Russian Revolution raises in its mighty arm the torch to illumine the horizon for all the peoples of the world. What irony that the light of real liberty and justice should emanate from a people who until very recently were considered the most primitive, uneducated, and uncultured, a half-Asiatic race. Yet it is well for the Russian Revolution that her people have remained primitive. That is why they can face life and life's problems in a simple, unspoiled, and uncorrupted state of mind, with true feeling and sound judgment. After all, true intelligence is primitive because it originates within man. It is not brought about through external, mechanical methods of education. It is well for the Revolution that her people are uncultured, uneducated. That means not yet drilled into blind obedience, into automata, into cringing slaves. It were desirable that the peoples of other countries had remained as primitive and uneducated. They would then have the courage for independent thinking and the seal of independent revolutionary action.

The demand of the people for universal peace, as the only basis for the working out of the fulfillment of the Revolution, is the greatest victory of modern times, a victory which will satisfy the yearning not only of the Russian people, but of the people of the rest of the world. Out of it we must drink new hope and strength for the overthrow of the tyranny and oppression which have ruled humanity so long. Out of it must come the new hope of a brotherhood which shall put an end to war and militarism and give to the world freedom of mind and body, freedom of life, and the joys which come from social harmony and a mutual understanding of the peoples of the earth.

Mother Earth Bulletin, VOL. I, NO. 4, JANUARY 1918

The Trotsky Idea

By Alexander Berkman

ONLY A FEW WEEKS AGO THE AMERICAN press and jingo intellectuals were unanimous in denouncing Lenin and Trotsky as the agents and spies of the Kaiser. The Boylsheviki were branded as the tools of Prussian militarism, and anyone who dared to protest in this country against that infamous misrepresentation was himself considered guilty of sedition.

All of a sudden the tune has changed. Quite unblushingly the *New York Times,* heretofore foaming at the mouth at the very mention of the Boylsheviki, now writes: "The reactionary press (in England) has misrepresented Trotsky as an agent of Germany." It would be rather interesting to know what peculiar kind of journalism the ultrachauvinist *Times* regards as reactionary.

Wilson himself, in his latest peace message, was moved to acknowledge that "the Russian people," whose spokesmen now are the Boylsheviki, "will not yield either in principle or in action. Their conception of what is right, of what is humane and honorable for them to accept, has been stated with a frankness, a largeness of view, a generosity of spirit and a universal human sympathy which must challenge the admiration of every friend of mankind."

This tribute to Trotsky, though somewhat belated, is at least indicative of some understanding of the soul of Russia. No doubt it is a bitter pill for certain quarters, but it may lead the American people to revise their newspaper-made opinion of the Lenins and Trotskys and help them to appreciate the true character of the Russian Revolution.

Trotsky—for the time being personifying the spirit of revolutionary Russia—has in two short months done more for peace and humanity than all the diplomats and politicians of the combined governments of the world. He has torn the mask off diplomacy and shown to the world that diplomacy itself is one of the chief causes of the war. He proved that revolutionary consciousness and frankness of purpose are a veritable David to the diplomatic Goliath. The undiplomatic honesty of Trotsky has wiped diplomacy off the map. There is a grave menace to ALL government in such smashing of the sacrosanct.

By far the greatest significance of Trotsky is the effect of his peace negotiations on the German people themselves. He has done more to discredit Prussian Junkerism in Germany than all the military activities of the allies. Moreover, it is only too evident that the German government is more afraid of the Trotsky propaganda among German forces than of Allied artillery. Prussian militarists know that revolutionary IDEAS are more fatal to autocracy than the armed legions of the Entente. That is the true reason why Germany is loath to continue the peace parleys with Russia.

The world diplomats have entirely missed the mark. They fear a separate peace between Russia and Germany. Yet a separate peace may prove the undoing of Kaisertum. A general peace, on the contrary, will enable Prussian militarism, with the aid of its armies, to hold its own against an uprising at home. But with the necessity of keeping up the war against the

Allies, a separate peace with Russia would prove a terrible menace to German militarism at home.

The original idea of Trotsky was a GENERAL peace, with the initiative taken by Russia. But the Allies failing to join in his efforts, he may work for a separate peace—a proletarian peace—fully aware of the moral debacle it involves for Prussian autocracy and militarism.

Mother Earth Bulletin, VOL. I, NO. 4, JANUARY 1918

The Surgeon's Duty

By Alexander Berkman

"HOW CAN YOU ANARCHISTS APPROVE of Trotsky and support the Russian Boylsheviki?" a pacifist friend recently asked me. "Most of the Boylsheviki are Social Democrats," he added; "believers in government. Moreover, Trotsky has resorted to methods of suppression, as in the dispersal of the Constituent Assembly. Can you explain why you support him?"

I shall try. As Anarchists we believe neither in government nor in violence, both of which are indeed synonymous in our philosophy. And no doubt we, the Anarchists, would be the first to oppose the Socialist Boylsheviki should they attempt to establish themselves as a PERMANENT government with the power to impose its authority upon the people. We believe, however, that the Russian Boylsheviki—consisting as they do of Social Democrats, Social Revolutionists, Syndicalists, and Anarchists —do not represent the narrowminded Socialist type whose ideal is a strongly centralized Socialist government. On the contrary, we have reason to believe that the Boylsheviki in Russia are the expression of the most fundamental longing of the human soul that demands fullest individual liberty within the greatest social well-being. That is why they have become, and are permitted to remain, the public voice of revolutionary Russia.

As to the Boylshevik activities at the present moment, and the immediate program of Lenin and Trotsky—I can only say that an extraordinary situation may demand extraordinary measures.

It is most unfair to judge Trotsky and his coworkers on the basis of actions forced upon them by the stress of a most momentous crisis. Take, for instance, the suppression of the Constituent Assembly. We know Trotsky and his views. We know that Trotsky does NOT believe in the limitation of the freedom of press and assembly or indeed in suppression of any kind. But Russia is in the midst of a revolution, the greatest socioeconomic upheaval of all times. A revolution is not a pacifist pink tea affair. A revolution is the reaction against the oppression of ages, and a violent reaction at that. As such it involves, necessarily, force and violence. It will be the great marvel of the future that this most momentous of all revolutions has been accomplished with comparatively so little violence, but has, on the contrary, been characterized by the greatest forbearance toward the hereditary tyrants, the most wonderful tolerance and kindliest humanity.

It is capitalist atrocities and governmental tyranny that produce crime and violence in time of peace, wholesale slaughter in war, and culminate in violent revolutions. Revolution is inherent in every social system based on slavery, and only the abolition of the system itself will usher in an era where force and violence will be things of the past.

Those that pretend to loathe violence, and yet permit present conditions to continue, are in reality directly responsible for the perpetuation of the evil.

Russia is now by no means in a normal condition where our heart's desire of universal peace and brotherhood can actually be practiced. The great passion to make the world fit for such conditions, to clear the way for them, is the supreme justification of the Lenins and Trotskys and is at the same time the explanation of our support.

The proletariat of Russia has suffered and bled for centuries. At last they have overthrown Tsarism and got rid of their tyrants. Shall they now meekly submit to a new set of bloodsuckers fastening themselves on their vitals? The Constituent Assembly was the saddle of the bourgeois exploiters eager to climb upon the back of the Russian proletariat. Away with the saddle!

"But two wrongs don't make a right," exclaims the nonresistant.

Oh, my good man, when the patient's life is in grave danger, the surgeon is justified—nay, it is his sacred duty—to perform an operation.

VOL. XII, NO. 5, JULY 1917

Appendix

The Trial and Conviction of
Emma Goldman and Alexander Berkman

By Leonard D. Abbott

Half of the july 1917 issue of Mother Earth was given over to Leonard Abbott's condensed presentation of the events that led to Goldman and Berkman's final imprisonment and subsequent exile. It appeared only a few days after the proceedings and reads with the immediacy of an on-the-scene report. Rushed to trial for conspiring against military conscription, given less than a week to prepare their case, and without access to their personal papers, which were seized at the time of their arrest, they neverthess held forth eloquently and cogently not only in their own defense but that of anarchism and the rights of free speech and assembly as well. They were both seasoned extempore speakers, and with considerable irony the two political conscientious objectors addressed the extraneous charge of inciting violence amid the government drumbeats of war. The freshness of Abbott's transcription catches their complementary rhetorical styles: Berkman's precise thinking underscored by wry humor; Goldman's passion rising quickly to soaring sarcasm.

The lines by Whitman on page 414 are from "To a Foil'd European Revolutionaire"; Berkman's "greatest philospher of modern times" (page 424) is Nietszche; the "Cruger case" that Goldman cites on page 432 refers to the gruesome murder that previous winter of Ruth Cruger, an eighteen-year-old girl of working-class background. In the hurried circumstances of the trial and preparation, it is remarkable that in matters of fact the defendants made so few errors, as when Goldman slightly misquotes the Gospel of John (page 435) and Luther (page 438) and identifies Camille Desmoulins, instead of Joseph Rouget de Lisle, as the writer of the "Marsellaise"—minutiae that in no way whatsoever undermine their splendid defense.

"TELL ALL FRIENDS that we will not waver, that we will not compromise, and that if the worst comes, we shall go to prison in the proud consciousness that we have remained faithful to the spirit of internationalism and to the solidarity of all the people of the world."

So Emma Goldman wrote in the days when she and Alexander Berkman were fighting for their liberty in the sweltering court room in the Federal Building in New York. In this spirit she still greets, from behind the bars of the federal prison in Jefferson City, Mo., the thousands of friends who will read this record in *Mother Earth*.

When Emma Goldman and Berkman, charged with conspiracy to defeat military registration under the conscription law, were sentenced by Judge Julius M. Mayer, on July 9, to serve two years in prison, to pay fines of $10,000 each, and to be probably deported to Russia at the expiration of their prison terms, United States Marshal McCarthy said: "This marks the beginning of the end of Anarchism in New York." But Mr. McCarthy is mistaken. The end of Anarchism will only be in sight when Liberty itself is dead or dying, and Liberty, as Walt Whitman wrote in one of his greatest poems, is not the first to go, nor the second or third to go—"it waits for all the rest to go, it is the last."

> When there are no more memories of heroes and martyrs,
> And when all life and all the souls of men and women are discharged
>   from any part of the earth,
> Then only shall liberty or the idea of liberty be discharged from
>   that part of the earth,
> And the infidel come into full possession.

THE ARREST

Emma Goldman and Berkman were arrested on June 15, at 20 East 125th Street, New York. At the time of the arrival of the marshal and of his minions, late in the afternoon, Miss Goldman was in the room which served as the office of the No-Conscription League and of *Mother Earth*. Berkman was upstairs in the office of *The Blast*. A number of helpers were in the building at the time, including M. Eleanor Fitzgerald, Carl Newlander, Walter Merchant; and W. P. Bales. Mr. Bales, a young man, was arrested without a warrant. The raiding party included, besides Marshal McCarthy, Assistant Unites States District Attorney E. M. Stanton, Lieutenant Barnitz, of the so-called "Bomb Squad," Deputy Marshals Doran, Hearne, and Meade, and Detectives Murphy and Kiely of the police department.

"I have a warrant for your arrest," Marshal McCarthy said to Emma Goldman.

"I am not surprised, yet I would like to know what the warrant is based on," Emma Goldman replied.

Marshal McCarthy answered by producing a copy of *Mother Earth* containing an article on the No-Conscription League, signed "Emma Goldman."

"Did you write that?" asked the marshal.

Miss Goldman replied that she had written the article, and in answer to another question said she stood for everything in *Mother Earth*, because, she added, she was the sole owner of the publication.

A few minutes later, officers mounted the stairs and arrested Alexander Berkman.

In the meantime, policemen were busy searching both offices. They found books and pamphlets written by Kropotkin, Malatesta, Voltairine de Cleyre, Max Stirner, Frank Harris, C. E. S. Wood, Charles T. Sprading, Gorky, Andreyev, Strindberg, William Morris, George Bernard Shaw, and many other writers. They seized everything they could lay their hands on, including a card index, bank- and checkbooks, and thousands of copies of *Mother Earth* and *The Blast*, held up by the Post Office. *The Blast*, which was solemnly pronounced by the newspapers "one of the vilest things ever sent through the United States mails," contained, in addition to Berkman's writings, quotations from Victor Hugo and Edward Carpenter, and articles written by Leonard Abbott and Robert Minor.

After the police had rifled the contents of both offices, the three prisoners were taken down to the street and rushed to the Federal Building. They were joined by the radical attorney Harry Weinberger. There was no opportunity for arraignment that evening, and the prisoners were locked up in The Tombs.

THE ARRAIGNMENT

On the morning of June 16, Emma Goldman and Berkman were brought before United States Commissioner Hitchcock. Assistant United States District Attorney Harold A. Content appeared as prosecutor. "These two Anarchists," he said, "are the leading spirits in this country in a countrywide conspiracy to spread antiregistration propaganda." Mr. Weinberger, attorney for the defendants, made a motion for dismissal on the ground that advising anybody not to register is not a violation of law. "Failing to register, no doubt is a crime," said Weinberger, "but telling people not to do so is certainly not a violation of the law." The commissioner is old and gray; he looked like a relic of the Dark Ages. He held the prisoners in $25,000 bail each. Weinberger protested against the bail as excessive, but was not able to change the decision. Later, when Weinberger and Leonard Abbott approached Marshal McCarthy and when Abbott protested against the holding of the young man Bales without warrant or charge, the marshal became violently abusive and ordered the ejection of Abbott from the Federal Building.

THE GRAND JURY INDICTS

The prisoners were held in The Tombs practically incommunicado; it was only with the greatest difficulty that they were able to communicate with any of their friends. Gross unfairness was shown in the matter of the bail. When more than enough property was offered to cover the necessary sum, it was refused by Attorney Content on the ground of petty technicalities. Many friends offered money. By June 21, Emma Goldman was free. Four days later, Berkman was released. In the meantime, the federal grand jury had framed a formal indictment.

OPENING OF THE TRIAL

The trial began before Judge Mayer on June 27. Judge Mayer is a German, and he has the Prussian type of face. It occurred to more than one spectator that the defendants, charged with the "crime" of fighting Prussianism in America, were being tried before a Prussian judge. They announced, at the outset, that they had decided to conduct their own cases. They made it clear that this decision was not in any way to be construed as a reflection upon their lawyer. Mr. Weinberger, indeed, had consecrated himself to this case with conspicuous idealism, and was still giving advice and suggestions. But they had decided that, as Anarchists, it would be more consistent to go into court without a lawyer.

The defendants asked for a postponement on the ground that they had so recently been released from prison that they had had no opportunity to summon witnesses and to familiarize themselves with their cases. They also asked for a postponement on the ground of Berkman's physical condition. He had sprained his leg, prior to his arrest, and appeared in court on crutches. Both of these requests were denied by the judge. He insisted upon an immediate trial. Emma Goldman and Berkman were at first so incensed by the injustice of this decision that they declined to take part in the proceedings. The trial, as Emma Goldman put it, was "a farce." Later, however, the defendants consented to examine the talesmen.

For three days the examination proceeded. It is certain that never before in a court of "justice" has there been such a questioning of talesmen, and it is to be hoped that some of those who listened or answered learned something about *real* justice and social ideals. Alexander Berkman, who took the lead in the questioning, created an atmosphere that was libertarian and antimilitarist. Among the questions asked were:

"Do you believe in free speech?"

"Do you believe in the right to criticize laws?"

"Do you believe that the majority in a community is necessarily right?"

"Would you be biased against the defendants because they had been active in the labor movement?"

"Would you be biased because they had fought conscription?"

"Do you feel that you would be unable to render a just verdict because the defendants are antimilitarists, or Anarchists?"

"Do you know what Socialism and Anarchism mean?"

"Have you read any Socialist or Anarchist books?"

"Have you attended any Socialist or Anarchist meetings?"

Incidentally, Emma Goldman and Berkman managed to convey a great deal of information bearing on the libertarian struggle in many countries. Robert Emmet was mentioned, and George Washington. The birth control movement came in for discussion. The courtroom was packed. Stella Comyn sat directly behind Emma Goldman and offered suggestions from time to time. Anna Sloan was also in court. Many friends of the defendants were excluded. Some were roughly handled. June 27, it happened, was Emma Goldman's birthday, and, during the lunch hour, Marie Yuster, Rose Yuster, Puck Durant, and others brought her a bouquet of red roses.

A MESSAGE FROM C. E. S. WOOD

On June 29, just as the jury was selected, the following telegram was received from Charles Erskine Scott Wood, of Portland, Oregon. Mr. Wood is a Single-Taxer, poet, and art connoisseur, and was at one time colonel in the United States army.

"I have wired the judge and attorney general and prosecuting attorney, and please say to Emma I can be quoted as believing with her that conscription utterly belies democracy, and punishment for criticizing the government marks an autocracy in spirit, no matter what the form. Thousands here share this view."

THE CASE OF THE PROSECUTION

On Monday morning, July 2, Prosecutor Content opened his case. He said he would show that the two defendants, whom he characterized as "disturbers of law and order," had both tried in their writings and in their public addresses to influence the ignorant amongst the men of military age not to register. The first witness that he put on the stand was Miss Fitzgerald. He questioned her regarding the No-Conscription League and the "profits" of *The Blast*. She answered him that she and her colleagues had worked for the sake of principle and not for profits. Mr. Content went to the trouble of presenting newspaper reporters, printers, binders, etc., to testify as to the contents, printing, and binding of *Mother Earth, The Blast* and No-Conscription literature; but all this, as the defendants pointed out, was superfluous. They admitted the authorship of the writings which were the basis of the government's case. Berkman looked the student, the intellectual, with his black-rimmed eyeglasses. Emma Goldman was constantly on her feet, parrying unfair questions, elucidating doubtful points.

"WE BELIEVE IN VIOLENCE AND WE WILL USE VIOLENCE"

One of the witnesses that Mr. Content put on the stand was a police stenographer who testified that in her speech at Harlem River Casino on May 18, Emma Goldman used the words that stand at the head of this paragraph. But Emma Goldman denied ever having used any such words, and she was able to call many witnesses who corroborated her statement. This led to lengthy discussion of the entire question of violence and of violent methods as a means of advancing Anarchist propaganda. Emma Goldman and Berkman read to the jury extracts from articles on this subject, appearing in *Mother Earth*. The stenographer who reported the Harlem River Casino meeting was shown to be untrustworthy. Another stenographer testified, incidentally, that Emma Goldman was the best speaker he had ever heard. The proprietor of the Harlem River Casino, called by the prosecution, gave testimony favorable to the defendants. He said that the meeting of May 18 had been perfectly orderly, in spite of the fact that a group of soldiers, carrying a flag, had tried to make trouble. A sergeant of the Coast Guard, appearing on the witness stand in uniform, confirmed this testimony.

During the examination of several of these witnesses, a military band was playing beneath the open windows, and patriotic speeches, punctuated by applause, could be heard. In the street below, a recruiting station had been established. By a curious irony of fate, militarism and antimilitarism, each in its most dramatic phase, had been set in juxtaposition.

BERKMAN OUTLINES THE CASE OF THE DEFENDANTS

Alexander Berkman, when he came to present to the jury the line of argument on which he proposed to build his case, said in substance: "We admit that we are opposed to militarism and to conscription. We have been carrying on an antimilitarist propaganda for twenty-five or thirty years. But we did not conspire, and we did not advise people not to register. The No-Conscription League refused to commit itself to a policy of definitely advising young men not to register. We decided to leave the matter to the conscience of each individual." All this was substantiated by the testimony of a "conscientious objector" who declared that he had gone to the office of the league for definite counsel and had been unable to get such counsel. It was further confirmed by a letter of Emma Goldman's, referred to by Miss Fitzgerald. In this letter Miss Goldman said that so long as she was not in danger of arrest under the registration law, she would not advise young men not to register; she added that, as a matter of principle, she would not tell a man to do a thing or not to do a thing, "because if I would have to tell him what to do, he would have no strength of character and courage to stand by what he is doing." The position of Emma Goldman and of others connected with the league was: "Each man must decide the issue for himself. As a conscientious objector, he has to decide for himself." Anna Sloan, Helen Boardman, Rebecca Shelly, and Nina Liederman all testified that they had never heard Miss Goldman urge violence or nonregistration.

THE MYSTERIOUS $3,000

When the offices of the No-Conscription League were raided by the police, a newspaper published an account of a mysterious bank deposit of $3,000. It was hinted that the money had come from pro-German sources. On July 5, James Hallbeck, eighty years old and a native of Sweden, testified that he had given Emma Goldman a check for $3,000 as a contribution to her work. So the "pro-German" bubble was pricked.

REED, STEFFENS, HALL

John Reed and Lincoln Steffens, magazine writers, testified that they had known Emma Goldman and Berkman for many years, and that they did not regard either as "violent." Bolton Hall, Single-Taxer and writer, said that he was a member of the Free Speech League. Asked by the judge what the principles of the league are, he said:

"It believes in activities tending to promote liberty, and particularly free speech. We have long fought for free speech. We do not believe in putting any restraint on it. We hold that limiting free expression of opinion is the best way to foster insurrection. We are never afraid to listen to any expression, even if we believe it wrong, but we have decided that the individual must bear the consequences for anything he utters."

"Does that mean that you permit free speech even when it is opposed to law?" queried Judge Mayer.

"We believe the constitutional guarantee of free speech makes free speech of every kind permissible," said Hall.

"In other words, the league permits free speech though it may be contrary to existing statutes," the judge again asked.

"I think that is free speech," Hall retorted.

Hall asserted he had always known Emma Goldman believed in educational work, and in benefiting people through educational activities. He said he had never known her to advocate violence, or to deny any principle which she preached.

LEONARD D. ABBOTT TESTIFIES

Leonard Abbott, chairman of the Ferrer Association and president of the Free Speech League, was sure that Emma Goldman had not urged violence at the Harlem River Casino meeting. He said that he had expected she would take a more extreme attitude than she did take. Questioned by Berkman in relation to the educational work of the Ferrer Association, in which both Emma Goldman and Berkman had had a share, Abbott spoke at some length of the Children's School in Stelton, New Jersey, created as a memorial to the Spanish martyr, Francisco Ferrer.

"Does the Ferrer School teach children to disobey the laws of the country?" Mr. Abbott was asked.

"It teaches them," he replied, "to criticize all laws and to prepare themselves for a free society."

"When you speak of criticizing laws, do you include the laws of this government?" Judge Mayer asked the witness.

"Yes," was the reply.

"Why was Francisco Ferrer executed by the Spanish government?" the judge asked the witness.

"He was executed because he loved liberty and human rights," said Abbott.

"Wasn't he executed upon false testimony?" asked Miss Goldman, springing to her feet.

"Yes," was the reply.

MARTIAL MUSIC GIVES COLOR TO THE TRIAL

Revolutionary and patriotic music clashed toward the end of the trial. At one moment the clear strains of the "Marseillaise" floated in through the open windows from bands accompanying the Russian Mission, which was marching past City Hall with its streaming red banners. This happened just as Miss Goldman read from her writings passages to the effect that war was only in the interests of the working class when it aimed at the overthrow of the capitalist system. When she read her "new declaration of independence," setting forth the right of the masses to overthrow a tyrannous and iniquitous government, the band suddenly burst forth with the "Marche Militaire," France's new song of revolution and freedom.

Twice the bands played "The Star-Spangled Banner." Everybody was ordered to rise. The first time, a young girl refused to do so and was ejected by court attendants. The second time Stephen Kerr and another man were led from the room for refusal to stand, whereupon the judge said: "Any man who refuses to stand will be taken from the room, and will not be permitted to come back." Emma Goldman and Berkman remained seated.

CLOSING SCENES OF THE TRIAL

The trial occupied eight days and came to an end on Monday, July 9. Alexander Berkman spoke for two hours. Emma Goldman then spoke for something over an hour. Mr. Content summed up for the government in a speech not quite an hour long.

ALEXANDER BERKMAN'S SPEECH

The gist of Alexander Berkman's speech is contained in the following passages:

GENTLEMEN OF THE JURY: It is the first time that I rise to address a jury. It was a new experience for Miss Goldman and myself to examine the talesmen, and it is a new experience to conduct a trial without the presence of counsel. It is more than probable and quite natural that we did not follow the usual procedure. It is also very likely that we have neglected many points and circumstances that a trained lawyer would have used in behalf of the defense. But, as indicated in our introductory statement, it is a matter of principle on our part to dispense with counsel and to address the jury face-to-face and enable the jury to judge for themselves as to the quality and the character and motives of the defendants. No doubt we could have had the services of brilliant lawyers, and I am not sure but even the best legal talent of the country could have been at our disposal. We believe that the fact that we have dispensed with lawyers is to a considerable extent to our detriment. But for the sake of the opportunity to speak to you as I have indicated face-to-face, we are willing to take that disadvantage, because after all the standing up for our principles in the expression of our ideas for ourselves is more important, more vital to us than the mere question of liberty or even of life.

Gentlemen, if in the examination of the talesmen we have asked perhaps inappropriate questions, or if in the excitement of the unusual experience we have been guilty of some discourtesy, we wish now to express to you our deepest regret and apology. I am sure that you will not hold our inexperience against us.

And now to the case. The charge against us, as you know from the indictment, is that we conspired to advise and to urge men of conscriptable age not to register. Remember, gentlemen, the indictment is in regard to a conspiracy to urge people not to register. If you look through the indictment you will not find a single word about conscription. I want you gentlemen to bear it in mind that the indictment sets forth a conspiracy and overt acts alleged to be connected, in order to induce young men not to register. The question now is, Did the prosecution prove the alleged conspiracy? Did the prosecution prove that we urged people not to register? Did it prove any overt acts in furtherance of that alleged conspiracy? Did it even attempt to prove or to demonstrate that we are guilty as charged? Oh no. The prosecution felt its case so weak that it had to drag in a thousand and one issues that have nothing to do with the charge in question. It had to drag in the question of Anarchism, of violence, of the Ferrer Modern School, of mass meetings held three years ago under some special circumstances, of protest meetings held in this city about four years ago with regard to the Colorado miners' strike, of protest meetings held in connection with the Rockefeller treatment of the Ludlow miners. It had to drag in a thousand and one questions that had as much relation to this case as a lion is related to a jackass.

Why were those irrelevant issues dragged in by the prosecution? Was it not because the prosecution hopes to obscure the issue in this case? Was it not because the prosecution hoped to prejudice you jurymen if possible, perhaps to frighten you, if that were possible, in order to set you up against the defendants because there was no evidence whatever to prove the charges of this indictment? The prosecution so far as these defendants are concerned is perfectly welcome to its professional subterfuges to becloud the issue before it. We don't evade any issue. But the bare fact that the prosecution is compelled to resort to such doubtful tactics ought to be sufficient for any intelligent man to realize that there is absolutely no foundation for that charge and that we stand here indicted for a charge never mentioned in the indictment itself. We stand here accused of being Anarchists. A vain accusation! We are Anarchists, and I for one am proud of being an Anarchist, and I am sure I may say the same for my codefendant, Miss Goldman.

You have heard a good deal here about Anarchism and about violence and similar matters unrelated to this indictment. Now, once for all, what is all this talk about violence in relation to Anarchism? I think it is time to explain and to make this matter clear. I am tired of hearing Anarchism confused with violence, the explanation of a thing confused with the cause of the thing. I am tired of all that, and I am glad of the opportunity—whatever it may cost—to speak to you gentlemen and to tell you just what Anarchism is to Anarchists—not to the enemies of Anarchism, but what Anarchism is to us and what our position is on violence. There will be no evasion in this on any matter, on any imaginable matter mentioned in any of those things read. Now there is talk about violence. Gentlemen, there is too much humbug in the alleged attitude of the average man about violence. You speak to the average man, the unthinking man, and ask him does he believe in violence and he will hold up his hands in horror. "No!" he will shout. And yet you know it is the most unthinking statement an intelligent man could make. I am sure each and every one of you gentlemen is a law-abiding, peaceful citizen. You believe in peace rather than violence. And yet you are all concerned and involved in the present war. You all support the war, which is nothing but wholesale violence. And therefore it will appeal to your common ordinary sense that this general statement of violence or belief in violence or even disbelief in violence is the statement of an unthinking person. We all believe in violence, and we all disbelieve in violence; it all depends upon the circumstances. Under ordinary circumstances no one wants violence, no one wants bloodshed; and yet certain circumstances arise when violence seems to be necessary in order perhaps to combat greater violence, in order to combat a greater evil that may menace humanity. You all therefore and each of you do not believe in violence, and yet you support the government of the United States today, you support it in the war, a war that means the greatest possible violence. But you have your own good reasons to support that war. I personally do not believe in this war. I do not believe in any war of that character. I believe the war is merely for the purpose of furthering capitalistic interests. I believe the people have nothing to gain from this war, neither the people of Europe nor the people of America. I believe in universal peace. But I am not a pacifist. I am a fighter, and all my life I have been fighting for liberty. I am not a pacifist. I want that emphasized. I believe in war under certain circumstances. I believe in fighting. And so when an expression of violence is picked out here and there perhaps from a mass meeting held three years ago, an expression used by people who may be dead now for all I know— yet I am ready to stand as the editor of that magazine for any expression used there. And all I want is to explain, explain the meaning of such phrases.

Now, what is the relation of this particular point to Anarchism itself? Of course, gentlemen of the jury, you know that Anarchism is a new idea, comparatively speaking. It takes thousands and thousands of years to elucidate and explain and make a new idea popular, especially a new idea that runs contrary to all the accepted notions, all old prejudices, all our old superstitions. An idea is new, radically new, new in the sense that it has changed or wants to change the values we have accepted, the false values. Anarchism wants to change the false values of hatred, of strife, of brother murdering brother, the false values of exploitation and robbery, of tyranny, of oppression. We want to change these false values and give humanity new values; in the words of the great, perhaps the greatest philosopher of modern times, we want to transvalue all human values, to give them a new meaning, a new foundation, with the hope and the necessary results of a different and better society. Anarchism has been misrepresented. Naturally so. As many past philosophies have been misrepresented that you have accepted today. What is the matter with Christianity itself? You remember the early Christians in the time of the Roman Caesar, the Christians who stood for an ideal then as we stand for an ideal of brotherhood today. What did they do with those Christians, Mr. District Attorney? They put them in the arena to be torn by wild beasts. They crucified them on the streets of Rome, because crucifixion then was the customary method of capital punishment. And if we had crucifixion today I am sure that these defendants would be crucified also. What did they do with the Huguenots, the conscientious objectors of their time? You know. They slaughtered the Huguenots by the hundreds of thousands all through France. And what did they do with this Garibaldi that the city of New York has been celebrating in honor of a few days ago? There is his statue. What did they do with this Garibaldi, the liberator of Italy from the yoke of the foreign oppressor? They put him in prison. What did they do to Mazzini and the other great liberators of Italy? They put them in prison. And you have celebrated here the other day. What did they do with Bruno, who propagated a new and strange and unpopular theory and philosophy? They burned Bruno at the stake. And I am sure that there are men today who would burn the modern Brunos at the stake. And a thousand years hence their descendants would build monuments for them, as you have built a monument there for Garibaldi.

We do not need to go back very far in history. We do not need to go back with oppressions. What is the matter with the Russian revolutionists? Their commission is honored by your city right now at this very moment. I say that their commission honors your city. The representatives of the Russian Revolution, the revolution fought by them against the tyranny of the Tsar, the revolution whose great gospel is liberty for all, well-being for each, happiness for humanity, that revolution has today its representatives in your midst and you are honoring them. And who are these revolutionists? They have returned from Siberia, from the dungeons of the Peter and Paul Fortress, they have returned from Schlüsselburg, from the mines of Kara, from Vladivostok, from the places where revolutionists were sent by the Tsar and governors of Russia for a hundred years. These rebels against tyranny, these lovers of humanity have come back from Siberia, and today they are at the helm of the destinies of Russia. You celebrate them today in the presence of their representatives, and we are here being tried for what? For loving humanity.

I said it would be interesting to know on this occasion, especially because it is in the evidence, what relation has violence to Anarchism. You have heard the word Anarchism mentioned many times, but perhaps you have not heard what it really means. It comes from two Greek words, and very simple they are. "Arche" means power or violence. And "an," a prefix, means without. "Anarche" in Greek. Anarchy in English, which means without violence. The very philosophy of Anarchism is the negation of violence. The very opposition of violence. The very translation of the word means absence of violence and absence of government as represented in the organized form of violence. And yet this stupid man, the ignorant man opposite me, dares say Anarchism means violence, when the very meaning of the word Anarchism stands for the negation of all forms of violence and force. I have tried to call your attention, gentlemen, to the fact that Anarchism, which stands for human brotherhood, for the constructive tendencies of man, seeks an opportunity only, an opportunity to develop these tendencies of man, these constructive tendencies as against the destructive tendencies; an opportunity to develop them first, of course, by enlightening the people, by telling the people what Anarchism really means, by doing away with all those misrepresentations of Anarchism and by doing away with all those false notions about Anarchism our enemies have inculcated into the minds of the people. Misrepresentations—and when was there a time when a new idea was not misrepresented? Why, some of you perhaps remember the Abolitionist days in this country. Did not the ordinary stupid citizen consider an Abolitionist a murderer? Why? Because those who were their enemies, those who were opposed to their ideas misrepresented the Abolitionists, misrepresented the philosophy and vilified the champions of that philosophy. And what did the Abolitionists want? Oh, today they are heroes. But what did they want? They wanted the emancipation of the black man. Today it is a fact. They were successful finally. We have not been successful yet. But before they were successful what happened to the greatest, to the noblest representatives of abolition? What happened to Garrison, William Lloyd Garrison, who was dragged in the streets of Boston, dragged by a mob and almost lynched because he stood for a bigger conception of human love, because he stood for a greater conception of brotherhood, because he said "No country can be free when halfway free and halfway slave." And we, gentlemen of the jury, say the same thing today. No country is free, halfway free and halfway slave. We are in the position of Garrison and Wendell Phillips and John Brown. But we say not only the black slave must be emancipated but also the white wage slave of the factory. We say in these things we are the emancipators of humanity.

The district attorney has proven that we are Anarchists, and I want you to know what we Anarchists stand for. What else has the district attorney proved? He was to prove two things, gentlemen. He was to prove that there was a conspiracy between these defendants, a conspiracy to advise and urge conscriptable men not to register; and he was to prove that overt acts had been committed by us in pursuance of that conspiracy. Has he proved either one of these two propositions? He has not proved a single thing about either one, neither the conspiracy nor the overt act. And when I go ahead to analyze his testimony and our testimony I think I can convince you, gentlemen, beyond a reasonable doubt that we have proved our case instead of the district attorney proving his. You have heard here, gentlemen, that on your oaths you cannot convict unless you are absolutely certain in your own hearts and consciences that the district attorney has proven his case beyond a reasonable doubt. But I say the defense has proved its case beyond a reasonable doubt and the district attorney's case has not a leg to stand on. Now I will proceed to examine the evidence submitted by the district attorney and let us see what he has proved and how he has proved it.

His case was so strong that he had immediately to lay his strongest proof here before you by producing here a printer and a bookbinder, an express-man and a telephone man. And he actually proved, gentlemen of the jury, that *Mother Earth* was printed at a printer's. He actually proved that *The Blast* was also printed at a printer's. He proved that *Mother Earth* was bound in a bindery. He proved that *The Blast* was bound in a bindery. He proved that an expressman actually delivered packages of *Mother Earth* to the *Mother Earth* office. He proved that packages of *The Blast* were delivered to *The Blast* office. Do you think a paper is printed without a printer, without an electrotyper to make electros from the pictures and illustrations? Do you think we do not need an expressman to deliver all those packages? Why did the district attorney waste your time and patience by proving these things? Because he can prove nothing else. All those things were admitted by the defense. Ridiculous even to submit such things in evidence! And lo and behold, we get a new Sherlock Holmes upon the scene, Harold A. Content! He discovers a tremendous secret and submits it to you as his chief piece of evidence. What is that big discovery of our great detective? The No-Conscription Manifesto, the No-Conscription Manifesto that was sent out in 50,000 copies all over the country. The No-Conscription Manifesto that was read by millions of people in this country. Some secret! By millions of people—because practically every big paper in New York and Chicago and in all the other cities reprinted the manifesto, some in whole, some in excerpts. Millions of people have read it. Fifty thousand copies were sent out through the mails of the federal government. It required the great Sherlock Holmes to demonstrate here the tremendous secret, the existence of a No-Conscription Manifesto. I think, gentlemen of the jury, the very fact that the district attorney had to submit such inadequate, irrelevant, absolute useless facts as proof is an insult to your intelligence as jurymen. And when we come to the No-Conscription Manifesto, what do you find there? The word registration is never mentioned. And here is his own charge about registration. The whole charge, the indictment of conspiracy to induce people not to register is based practically on this manifesto; and this manifesto never mentions the word registration. Some detective. Some proof. Some foundation for this ridiculous charge! Now let me just read to you just one more passage to tell you the real meaning of this manifesto, what it is for. The essence of the whole thing. And here it is: The No-Conscription Manifesto, the very title of it, No-Conscription, not "No-Registration." Do you think if I wanted a No-Registration pamphlet I would issue a No-Conscription pamphlet? Have I ever hidden my meaning? Have I not always been frank to express it and perfectly free to express my views? Why, the very purpose of my life is to express my views. They say we published a No-Conscription Manifesto when we meant No-Registration—we who have been only too frank all through this trial; who mean to be frank the rest of our lives; who have been frank all through the past, beginning with Russia, and suffered for it, too. We have said No-Conscription when we meant No-Registration! And what does this No-Conscription Manifesto say in essence? "Liberty of conscience is the most fundamental of all human rights, the pivot of all progress. No man may be deprived of it without losing every vestige of freedom of thought and action. In these days when every principle and conception of democracy and of liberty is being cast overboard under the pretext of democratizing Germany, it behooves every liberty-loving man and woman to insist on his or her rights of individual choice in the ordering of his life and actions." And here is again a passage that gives the very gist of the matter in one sentence: "The No-Conscription League is to be the voice of protest against war and against the coercion of the conscientious objectors to participate in the war." The whole gist of the whole No-Conscription movement in one pamphlet. That whole No-Conscription movement in this country and all through the country was and is for the purpose of giving voices of protest, expressing the opinions of the conscientious objectors who do not want to participate in the war, their reasons for objecting to the war; people who are opposed to bearing arms for reasons of conscience. That was the purpose of the No-Conscription movement. That was the purpose of the No-Conscription Manifesto. Here it is expressed in the plainest, simplest language. And only a district attorney could misunderstand it and try to impose upon you that this means no registration; it does not mean no registration at all. It does not mean that; it means something else. Because it was necessary to use subterfuge and such professional tricks to support the impossible, the ridiculous position of the district attorney on this charge.

As absolutely unsuccessful and impossible as it was for the district attorney to prove a conspiracy, impossible because it did not exist, just as unsuccessful was the district attorney in proving any overt acts. As a matter of fact, perhaps if I were a lawyer I would stop right here, because since he did not prove any conspiracy the whole charge falls; and even if there had been any overt acts the charge falls, because we are charged with conspiracy and I have proved, I think, and I believe the intelligence of the jurors themselves will convince them, that the very suggestion of a conspiracy is ridiculous, preposterous, taking into consideration the facts of the prosecution, taking into consideration the very character of the work we have been doing for the past thirty years. The conspiracy not proved—but I am not satisfied merely to show you that the district attorney did not prove his case. Far from having proved his case beyond a reasonable doubt, I want to show you that he did not begin to prove his case but that the defendants did prove their case beyond a reasonable doubt. They are not expected to prove that. They do not need to prove that. But I shall not be satisfied in my own conscience until I show that to you. And I know I can. I say that the district attorney proved neither conspiracy nor any overt acts in furtherance of any imaginary conspiracy. Now, what are the overt acts that he is charging us with?

He talks about the May 18 meeting. Miss Goldman and I had a conspiracy there, he says, and he quotes the false words of her speech. But why didn't he quote the words of my speech?

I defy them to introduce in evidence that either I or Miss Goldman ever said in public speeches or in *Mother Earth* or in *The Blast* "Don't register," or "You don't register," or "You should not register." And we are people who tell just what we feel like saying, just what we believe is right for us to say.

I will tell you why we refused to advise young men not to register.

I would never advise anyone to do a thing which does not endanger me. I am willing to resist tyranny. If I were willing and ready to resist tyranny I may advise others to resist tyranny, because I myself would do it. I would be with them and take the responsibility. But I was excepted from that registration business. I did not have to register. I was beyond the age. I was not in danger. And would I advise anyone to do the thing which does not put me in danger? I would advise people once in a while if I thought it necessary to do things, dangerous things; but I would be with them. Never would I advise anybody to do a thing that is dangerous and I not be there or I not be in danger, because the registration law excludes me. That is why I did not advise people not to register.

Gentlemen of the jury, I think that I should not use any more time with regard to the evidence. I believe it is absolutely demonstrated here that the district attorney has no case. I believe that it is absolutely demonstrated here that he did not begin to prove a conspiracy. They did not prove any overt acts. And it is further demonstrated that such a conspiracy could not possibly exist, that all the previous acts alone of enlightening propaganda and agitation and all the ideals of Miss Goldman and myself are inherently opposed to any such thing as a dark conspiracy, and that some other things which I have cited here made it impossible for me to incite people not to register. I think I have sufficiently proved beyond any reasonable doubt that the defense or defendants never advised or urged anyone not to register and that there was no such conspiracy. I think I have said enough about that. If I argue this point, gentlemen, before I conclude, I want you to know that I am not arguing to keep myself from going to prison. I am not afraid of prison. I am willing to suffer for my ideas in prison if necessary. Life is dear, but not so dear that I should be at liberty without self-respect. I would rather be in prison with my ideals, with my convictions, true to myself than be outside with my soul damned in my own estimation. So I am not pleading to save ourselves

from prison. Ourselves, I say, because I know that Miss Goldman shares my
views and my feelings in this matter. No, it is not a question of prison with
me. It is a question of whether we stand here indicted as guilty of conspiracy
to induce people not to register, or whether it has been planted upon your
prejudice by the prosecution, whether he tried to arouse your passions and
opposition against us as Anarchists. That is the question. And it is really
Anarchism that is on trial here, and I am glad it is, because it is well for you
to know what Anarchism is, since we are Anarchists. Gentlemen of the jury,
this is an important, a solemn moment in your lives, much more your lives,
much more than in mine. A solemn moment, because the eyes of the whole
country, indeed the eyes of the world are upon you. This is no petty question
of telling someone not to register. That is not the question here. The question
here is, have we got free speech and liberty of expression in this country, or
not? That is the real question at issue, over and above this indictment, over
and above all these things that have been quoted by the district attorney. And
it is up to you as representatives just now of the American people, it is up to
you as the jury in this case to tell the world by your verdict whether you believe that free speech is necessary, whether you believe that free speech is a
good thing, whether you believe that the grandfathers, the founders of this
republic, sacrificed their lives in vain, whether free speech should be permitted, whether we should throw on the dungheap all those things for which
they fought, for which people have bled, for which the martyrs of all countries have bled: free speech and liberty of expression and freedom of conscience. That is, that will be the meaning of your verdict. It will not be a
question of a few years in prison. It will not be a question of conspiracy or
registration. It will be a question whether you say by your verdict that people
shall not talk in this country, that people shall not think, that people shall not
dare express an opinion. And if you say, "We have war," I say to you because
of the war it is necessary for you to show that we do have liberty, that we do
have some democracy here. Why, yes, the war you say is for the very purpose
of carrying democracy and liberty to Europe; and we want the world to know
that you who carry liberty and democracy to Europe have no liberty here,
that you who are fighting for democracy according to your own lights in
Europe suppress democracy right here in New York, in the United States. Are
you going to suppress free speech and liberty in this country, and still pretend
that you love liberty so much that you will fight for it five thousand miles
away? Charity begins at home, gentlemen of the jury. Liberty begins at home.
That is where you begin right now, today, to show that you stand for liberty.
We have to speak for liberty all our lives. Now you are put to the test as men
who believe in liberty, you are put to the test. It is for you to show whether
you believe in liberty. And let me tell you, whether you think that we are right
or we are wrong, one thing we know: that the spirit that animates this woman,

the spirit that animates these defendants is the spirit that has in the past emancipated the slaves. It is the spirit that will in the future emancipate the slave from his slavery, from his tyranny, emancipate the whole country, abolish war, make us all brothers of one family, without all these evils and crimes, without all this oppression and monopoly in the world, and make the world a fit place to live in, with a real motto, actually applied: Liberty for all, wellbeing for everyone, and happiness for humanity.

EMMA GOLDMAN'S SPEECH

Emma Goldman spoke, substantially, as follows:

GENTLEMEN OF THE JURY: On the day after our arrest it was given out by the marshal's office and the district attorney's office that the two "big fish" of the No-Conscription activities were now in the hands of the authorities, that there would be no more troublemakers and dangerous disturbers, that the government will be able to go on in the highly democratic method of conscripting American manhood for European slaughter. It is a great pity, it seems to me, that the marshal and the district attorney have used such a flimsy net to make their catch. The moment they attempted to land the fish on shore the net broke. Indeed the net proved that it was not able and strong enough to hold the fish. The sensational arrest of the defendants and the raid of the defendants' offices would have satisfied the famous circus men, Barnum & Bailey. Imagine, if you can, a dozen stalwart warriors rushing up two flights of stairs to find the two defendants, Alexander Berkman and Emma Goldman, in their separate offices quietly seated at their desks, wielding not the gun or the bomb or the club or the sword, but only such a simple and insignificant thing as a pen. As a matter of fact two officers equipped with a warrant would have sufficed to arrest us two, for I take it that we are well known to the police department and the police department will bear me out that at no time have we run away or attempted to run away, that at no time have we offered any resistance to an arrest, that at no time did we keep in hiding under the bed. We have always frankly and squarely faced the issue. But it was necessary to stage a sensational arrest so that Marshal McCarthy and the attorney should go down to posterity and receive immortality. It was necessary to raid the offices of *The Blast* and the No-Conscription League and *Mother Earth,* although without a search warrant, which was never shown to us. I ask you, gentlemen of the jury, should it be customary from the point of view of law to discriminate in the case of people merely because they have opinions which do not appeal to you? What is a scrap of paper in the form of a search warrant, when it is a question of raiding the offices of Anarchists or arresting Anarchists?

Would the gentlemen who came with Marshal McCarthy have dared to go into the offices of Morgan or of Rockefeller or any of these men without a search warrant? They never showed us the search warrant, although we asked them for it. Nevertheless, they turned our office into a battlefield, so that when they were through with it it looked like invaded Belgium, with only the distinction that the invaders were not Prussian barbarians but good patriots who were trying to make New York safe for democracy.

The first act of this marvelous comedy having been properly staged by carrying off the villains in a madly rushing automobile which came near crushing life in its way, merely because Marshal McCarthy said, "I am the marshal of the United States," he even reprimanding officers on the beat who lived up to their duty and called attention to the fact that the automobile should not have rushed at such violent speed—I say the first act having been finished by locking the villains up, the second act appeared on the scene. And the second act, gentlemen of the jury, consisted not in prosecution but in persecution. Here are two people arrested, known to the police department, having lived in New York City for nearly 30 years, never having offered resistance to an arrest, always facing the issue. And yet we were placed under $50,000 bail, although the principal witness in the Cruger case is held only in $7,000 bail. Why were we placed under $50,000 bail? Because the district attorney knew that it would be difficult to raise that bail and therefore out of personal spite made us stay in The Tombs instead of enjoying our liberty. And furthermore, not only did the district attorney and the prosecution insist upon $50,000 bail, but when we produced a man whose property is rated at $300,000 in this city his real estate was refused. Why? Because the district attorney suddenly remembered that he needed 48 hours to look into the man's reputation—knowing perfectly well that we were to go to trial on Wednesday, and yet not permitting the defendant, Alexander Berkman, to get out, although we had relied on an authentic and absolutely secure bail. So that I say that the second act, gentlemen of the jury, demonstrated that it was not only to be a case of prosecution, that it was also to be a case of persecution.

And finally the third act which was played in this court and which you, gentlemen of the jury, witnessed last week. I may say here that it is to be regretted indeed that the district attorney knows nothing of dramatic construction, otherwise he would have supplied himself with better dramatic material, he would have used better acts in the play to sustain the continuity of the comedy. But the district attorney is not supposed to know anything about modern drama or the construction of modern drama.

Now then, you have already been told and I am sure you will be charged by His Honor that the indictment against us is, having conspired and having used overt acts to carry out the conspiracy to induce men of conscriptable age not to register. That is the indictment and you cannot and you may not render a verdict for anything else, no matter what material came up in this court during the last week or ten days. As to the conspiracy: imagine, if you please, people engaged along similar lines for nearly 30 years, always standing out against war, whether that war was in China or Japan or Russia or England or Germany or America, always insisting with the great essayist Carlyle, that all wars are wars among thieves who are too cowardly to fight and who therefore induce the young manhood of the whole world to do the fighting for them—that is our standing; we have proved it by evidence, we have proved it by witnesses, we have proved it by our own position, that always and forever we have stood up against war, because we say that the war going on in the world is for the further enslavement of the people, for the further placing of them under the yoke of a military tyranny; imagine also people who for 30 years in succession have stood out against militarism, who claim militarism is costly and useless and brutalizing to every country; imagine us standing for years, and especially since conscription was declared in England and the fight began in Australia and conscription was there defeated by the brave and determined and courageous position of the Australian people; imagine that since that time we have been against conscription, then say how there can possibly be a conspiracy when people merely continue in their work which they have carried on for 30 years and for which they have spoken in different meetings and by letters! What kind of conspiracy is that? Was there any need of a conspiracy if we really had wanted to tell young men not to register? I insist that the prosecution has failed utterly, has failed miserably to prove the charge on the indictment of a conspiracy.

As to the meeting of May 18: it was dragged in here only for reasons known to the prosecution, otherwise I can't understand why that meeting played such an important part. No matter what we would have said at that meeting, no matter what language we would have used, that meeting cannot constitute an overt act, because although it is true that the draft law was passed on the 18th, it is equally true that it was not made a law until the president of the United States signed that law. And the president of the United States did not sign it until late that evening, at the time when we had the meeting and couldn't have any idea or knowledge as to whether he was going to sign it. So the meeting of the 18th is utterly irrelevant. But since the meeting came in it is necessary to emphasize one or two points. And I mean to do so, because it concerns the defendant Emma Goldman. The main thing upon which evidently the prosecution concentrated is that the reporter credited the defendant Emma Goldman with saying, "We believe in violence and we will use violence." Gentlemen of the jury, if there were no other proof to absolutely discredit this particular line and sentence and expression, there would yet be the following reasons: In the first place, I have been on the public platform for 27 years and one of the things that

I am particularly careful of in my speeches is that they shall be coherent and shall be logical. The speeches delivered on that evening, on May 18, absolutely excluded the necessity of using the expression "We believe in violence and we will use violence." I couldn't have used it, as an experienced speaker, because it would merely have made the whole speech nonsensical, it would have dragged in something which was irrelevant to the body of the speech or the material used. That is one of the reasons why I never at that meeting said "We believe in violence and we will use violence."

I am a social student. It is my business in life to ascertain the cause of our social evils and of our social difficulties. As a student of social wrongs it is my business to diagnose a wrong. To simply condemn the man who has committed an act of political violence, in order to save my own skin, would be just as pardonable as it would be on the part of the physician who is called to diagnose a case, to condemn the patient because the patient had tuberculosis or cancer or any other disease. The honest, earnest, sincere physician diagnoses a case, he does not only prescribe medicine, he tries to find out the cause of the disease. And if the patient is at all capable as to means, he will tell the patient, "Get out of this putrid air, get out of the factory, get out of the place where your lungs are being infected." He will not merely give him medicines. He will tell him the cause of the disease. And that is precisely my position in regard to violence. That is what I have said on all platforms. I have attempted to explain the cause and the reason for acts of political violence.

And what is the cause? Is it conditioned in the individual who commits an act of individual violence? It is not. An act of political violence at the bottom is the culminating result of organized violence on top. It is the result of violence which expresses itself in war, which expresses itself in capital punishment, which expresses itself in courts, which expresses itself in prisons, which expresses itself in kicking and hounding people for the only crime they are guilty of: of having been born poor. So that after all, when we come to consider an act of political violence committed by an individual, I take it, gentlemen of the jury, that you are conversant with history and that you know that not only a stray Anarchist here and there, but rebels of every movement in Ireland, in France, in Russia, in Italy, in Spain, all over the world, even in passive India, the country which has the most wonderful civilization and rests upon passive resistance—even in that country, men were driven to acts of violence by organized violence on top. So, as I said in one of the evidences we have given, we say with the greatest psychologist living, Havelock Ellis, that an act of political violence committed by an individual is the result of social wrong and social injustice and political oppression. Wherever there is political liberty—and I can demonstrate it in the Scandinavian countries: has there been any act of violence committed in Norway, in Sweden, in Denmark, in Holland—why are there no acts of violence there? Because the government doesn't only preach free speech and free press and assembly, but lives up to it. There was no need to be driven into acts of violence. So, gentlemen, I say with Havelock Ellis that the political offender or the "political criminal," as you choose to call him, is so not because of criminal tendency, not because of personal gain, not because of personal aggrandizement, but because he loves humanity too well; because he cannot face wrong and injustice and because he cannot enjoy his meal when he knows that America is getting rich on two million wage-slave children who are ground into dust and into money and power.

And so, gentlemen, I have explained the act. I have explained the act. Does that mean advocating the act? If that is your version—and I can't believe that it will be—I say, gentlemen of the jury, that you might as well condemn Jesus for having defended the prostitute Mary Magdalene, you might as well say that he advocated prostitution because he said to the mob on that occasion: "Let him among you that is without sin cast the first stone." I refuse to cast the stone at the "political criminal," if he may be called so. I take his place with him because he has been driven to revolt, because his life-breath has been choked up. And if I am to pay with prison for that, if I am to pay with my life-breath for that, gentlemen of the jury, I shall be ready at any time to take the consequences. But I refuse to be tried on trumped-up charges, and I refuse to be convicted by perjured testimony for something which I haven't said, when it had absolutely no relation whatever to the indictment as stated, that we conspired and agreed to con-spire and used overt acts to tell people not to register.

Gentlemen of the jury, the meeting of May 18 was called for an express purpose and for that purpose only. It was called to voice the position of the conscientious objector who, as far as America is concerned, was a new type of humanity. Oh I know that we should be expected to call the conscientious objector, just as he is being called by the papers, a "slacker," a "coward," a "shirker." These are cheap names, gentlemen of the jury. To call a man a name proves nothing whatever. What is the conscientious objector? I am a consci-entious objector. What is he? He is impelled by what President Wilson said in his speech on the 3rd of February, 1917; he is impelled by the force of righteous passion for justice, which is the bulwark and mainstay and basis of all our existence and of all our liberty. That is the force which impels the conscientious objector: a righteous passion for justice. The conscientious ob-jector, rightly or wrongly—that is a thing which you will have to argue with him—does not believe in war, not because he is a coward or a shirker, not because he doesn't want to stand responsible, but because he insists that, be-longing to the people whence he has come and to whom he owes life, it is his place to stand on the side of the people, for the people, and by the people, and not on the side of the governing classes. And that is what we did at that particular meeting. We voiced the position of the conscientious objector. But I reiterate once more, so you may not overlook it: that whatever we said on the 18th of May has no bearing whatever on the indictment for conspiracy, because that meeting took place before the president signed that bill.

Gentlemen of the jury, when we examined talesmen we asked whether you would be prejudiced against us when it was proved that we were engaged in an agitation for unpopular ideas. You were instructed by the court to say, "If they were within the law." But there was one thing I am sorry that the court did not tell you. It is this: that there has never been any ideal—though ever so humane and peaceful—introduced for human betterment which in its place and in its time was considered within the law. I know that many of you believe in the teachings of Jesus. I want to call your attention to the act that Jesus was put to death because he was not within the law. I know that all of you are Americans and patriots. Please bear in mind that those who fought and bled for whatever liberty you have, those who established the Declaration of Independence, those who established the constitutional right of free speech—that they were not within the law; that they were the Anarchists of their time; that they wrote a famous document known as the Declaration of Independence, a document indeed so great that it is evidently considered dangerous to this day, because a boy was given 90 days in a New York court for distributing a leaflet of quotations from the Declaration of Independence. They were not within the law. Those men were the rebels and the Anarchists. And what is more important, they not only believed in violence, but they used violence when they threw the tea into Boston harbor.

Furthermore, your country and in a measure my country—my country out of choice—is now allied with France. Need I call your attention to the fact that the French republic is due to the men who were not within the law? Why, friends, even the man who is responsible for the stirring music of the "Marseillaise," which unfortunately has been deteriorating into a war tune—even Camille Desmoulins was not within the law, was considered a criminal. And finally, gentlemen, on the very day when we are tried for a conspiracy, when we are tried for overt acts, our city and its representatives were receiving with festivities and with music the Russian Commission. Every one of the Russian commissioners is what you would choose to call an ex-political criminal. Every one of them had been in exile or in prison. As a matter of fact, gentlemen, the tree of Russian liberty is watered with the blood of Russian martyrs.

So no great idea in its beginning can ever be within the law. How can it be within the law? The law is stationary. The law is fixed. The law is a chariot wheel which binds us all regardless of conditions or circumstances or place or time. The law does not even make an attempt to go into the complexity of the human soul which drives a man to despair or to insanity, out of hunger or out of indignation, into a political act. But progress is ever changing, progress is ever renewing, progress has nothing to do with fixity. And in its place and in its time every great ideal for human reconstruction, for a reconstruction of society and the regeneration of the race—every great idea was considered extralegal, illegal, in its time and place. And so I must refer to Havelock Ellis when he said that the political criminal is the hero and the martyr and the saint of the new era. Hence the country that locks up men and women who will stand up for an ideal—what chance is there for that country and for the future and for the young generation, a country that has not in her midst dangerous disturbers and troublemakers who can see further than their time and propagate a new idea?

Well, gentlemen, I take it that perhaps the prosecution will say that that means propagating dangerous and seditious ideas in this time of war and patriotism. Maybe it does, gentlemen of the jury. But that doesn't prove that we are responsible for the existence of such ideas. You might as well condemn the very stars that are hanging in the heavens eternally and inalienably and unchangeably for all time, as to accuse us or find us guilty because we propagate certain ideas. Gentlemen of the jury, I wish to say right here, we respect your patriotism. We wouldn't, even if we could, want you to change one single iota of what patriotism means to you. But may there not be two kinds of patriotism, just as there are two interpretations of liberty, the kind of liberty which is real liberty in action, and the kind which has been placed on a document and is dug out once a year on the Fourth of July and is not allowed to exist for the rest of the year? And so, gentlemen, I wish to emphasize this very important fact, because I know how you feel on the war, I know what patriotism means to you: that the mere accident of birth or the mere fact that you have taken out citizens' papers does not make a man necessarily a patriot. Who is the real patriot, or rather what is the kind of patriotism that we represent? The kind of patriotism we represent is the kind of patriotism which loves America with open eyes. Our relation toward America is the same as the relation of a man who loves a woman, who is enchanted by her beauty and yet who cannot be blind to her defects. And so I wish to state here, in my own behalf and in behalf of hundreds of thousands whom you decry and state to be antipatriotic, that we love America, we love her beauty, we love her riches, we love her mountains and her forests, and above all we love the people who have produced her wealth and riches, who have created all her beauty, we love the dreamers and the philosophers and the thinkers who are giving America liberty. But that must not make us blind to the social faults of America. That cannot make us deaf to the discords in America. That cannot compel us to be inarticulate to the terrible wrongs committed in the name of patriotism and in the name of the country.

We simply insist, regardless of all protests to the contrary, that this war is not a war for democracy. If it were a war for the purpose of making democracy safe for the world, we would say that democracy must first be safe for America before it can be safe for the world. So in a measure I say, gentlemen, that we are greater patriots than those who shoot off firecrackers and say that democracy should be given to the world. By all means let us give democracy to the world. But for the present we are very poor in democracy. Free speech is suppressed. Free assemblies are broken up by uniformed gangsters, one after another. Women and girls at meetings are insulted by soldiers under this "democracy." And therefore we say that we are woefully poor in democracy at home. How can we be generous in giving democracy to the world? So we say, gentlemen of the jury, our crime, if crime there be, is not having in any way conspired to tell young men not to register, or having committed overt acts. Our crime, if crime there be, consists in pointing out the real cause of the present war.

I wish to state to you here that whatever your verdict is going to be it cannot have a possible effect upon the tremendous storm brewing in the United States. And the storm has not been created by two people, Alexander Berkman and Emma Goldman. You credit us with too much power altogether. That storm was created by the conditions themselves, by the fact that the people before election were promised that they would be kept out of war and after election they were dragged into war. Gentlemen of the jury, your verdict cannot affect the growing discontent of the American people. Neither can it affect the conscientious objector to whom human life is sacred and who would rather be shot than take the life of another human being. Of course your verdict is going to affect us. It will affect us only temporarily. And it will affect us physically; it cannot affect our spirit, gentlemen of the jury, whether we are found guilty or whether we are placed in jail. Nothing will be changed in our spirit. Nothing will be changed in our ideas. For ever if we were convicted and found guilty and the penalty were, to be placed against a wall and shot dead, I should nevertheless cry out with the great Luther: "Here I am and here I stand and I cannot do otherwise."

And so, gentlemen, in conclusion let me tell you that my codefendant, Mr. Berkman, was right when he said the eyes of America are upon you. And they are upon you not because of sympathy for us or agreement with Anarchism. They are upon you because it must be decided sooner or later. Are we justified in telling people that we will give them democracy in Europe when we have no democracy here? Shall free speech and free assemblage, shall criticism and opinion, which even the espionage bill did not include—shall that be destroyed? Shall it be a shadow of the past, the great historic American past? Shall it be trampled underfoot by any detective, any policeman, anyone who decides upon it? Or shall free speech and free press and free assemblage continue to be the heritage of the American people? And so, gentlemen of the jury, whatever your verdict will be, as far as we are concerned, nothing will be changed. I have held ideas all my life. I have publicly held my ideas for 27 years. Nothing on earth would ever make me change my ideas except one thing; and that is, if you will prove to me that our position is wrong, untenable, or lacking in historic fact. But never would I change my ideas because I am found guilty. I may say in the great words of two great Americans, undoubtedly not unknown to you gentlemen of the jury, and that is Ralph Waldo Emerson and Henry David Thoreau: when Henry David Thoreau was placed in prison for refusing to pay taxes, he was visited by Ralph Waldo Emerson, and Emerson said: "David, what are you doing in jail?" and Thoreau said: "Ralph, what are you doing outside, when people are in jail for their ideals?" And so, gentlemen of the jury, I do not wish to influence you. I do not wish to appeal to your passions. I do not wish to influence you by the fact that I am a woman. I have no such desires and no such designs. I take it that you are sincere enough and honest enough and brave enough to render a verdict according to your convictions, beyond the shadow of a reasonable doubt.

Please forget that we are Anarchists. Forget that we said that we propagated violence. Forget that something appeared in *Mother Earth* when I was thousands of miles away three years ago. Forget all that. And merely consider the evidence. Have we been engaged in a conspiracy? Has that conspiracy been proved; have we committed overt acts; have those overt acts been proved? We for the defense say they have not been proved. And therefore your verdict must be not guilty.

THE VERDICT OF THE JURY

After listening to the speeches of Alexander Berkman and Emma Goldman, the members of the jury filed out of the courtroom. They deliberated for thirty-nine minutes. It was late afternoon. Judge Mayer came into the courtroom at 6 o'clock. The clerk called the roll of the jury, and then turned to Frank M. White, the foreman, and asked him if a verdict had been agreed upon. Mr. White replied that the jury had agreed.

"What is your verdict?" the Clerk asked.

"Guilty," the foreman replied, in a voice that could be heard in the corridors.

Emma Goldman was immediately on her feet.

"I move," she said, "that this verdict be set aside as absolutely contrary to the evidence."

"Denied," replied Judge Mayer.

"I then ask that sentence be deferred for a few days, and that bail be continued in the sum already fixed in our case," Miss Goldman added.

"Motion denied," said the judge.

The clerk then took the pedigrees of the defendants. Berkman said he was born in Petrograd about forty-eight years ago, that he was single, and not a citizen of the United States. Miss Goldman said she was born in Kovno, Russia, in 1869, was single, and that she was not a citizen by application, although, she added, her father had died an American citizen.

THE PRISONERS SENTENCED

Judge Mayer announced that he was about to impose sentence and asked the defendants if they know of any reason why sentence should be deferred.

"I think it only fair to suspend sentence and give us a chance to clear up our affairs," Berkman said. "We have been convicted simply because we are Anarchists, and the proceeding has been very unjust." Emma Goldman also protested against the way in which they were being railroaded to prison.

Then came the sentence. Judge Mayer stood, while the defendants remained seated.

"In the conduct of this case," said Judge Mayer, "the defendants have shown remarkable ability, an ability which might have been utilized for the great benefit of this country, had they seen fit to employ themselves in behalf of it rather than against it. In this country of ours, we regard as enemies those who advocate the abolition of our government, and those who counsel disobedience of our laws by those of minds less strong. American liberty was won by the forefathers, it was maintained by the civil war, and today there are the thousands who have already gone, or are getting ready to go, to foreign lands to represent their country in the battle for liberty. For such people as these, who would destroy our government and nullify its laws, we have no place in our country. In the United States law is an imperishable thing, and in a case such as this I can but inflect the maximum sentence which is permitted by our laws."

The judge imposed a penalty of two years in prison, with a fine of $10,000 in each case. He instructed Mr. Content to communicate the record of the conviction to the immigration authorities for such action as those authorities might see fit to take when the prisoners had served their terms. Under a new federal law an alien, twice convicted of a crime, may be deported by the government to the country from whence he came.

As the judge finished pronouncing sentence he declared the court adjourned and started to leave the bench. Emma Goldman at once arose.

"One moment, please," she shouted. Judge Mayer turned and faced her.

"Are we to be spirited away in a speedy manner? If so, we want to know now, right now," she said.

"You have ninety days in which to file an appeal," replied the judge.

"Well, how about the next hour or so?" Miss Goldman demanded.

"The prisoners are in the custody of the United States marshal," Judge Mayer quietly answered, and for a second time he started to leave the room.

"One more word," Miss Goldman said. "I want to thank Your Honor for your marvelous fairness in this trial. Also I want to thank Your Honor for refusing us the two days which are given even to the most heinous of criminals. Again I thank Your Honor."

RUSHED TO JAIL

The prisoners were spirited away, by midnight trains and with indecent haste. Emma Goldman was taken to Jefferson City, Mo.; Alexander Berkman, to Atlanta, Ga.

The vindictive sentences inflicted upon them and the injustice of the entire trial can only have the effect of strengthening the libertarian and Anarchist movement in America.

Their imprisonment is likely to accomplish even more for the No-Conscription movement and for antimilitarism than their agitation. The very fact that they are behind the bars ought to make clear to even the dullest mind that the Prussianism that America has set out to combat, by force of arms, is already enthroned in this country.

The crime of Emma Goldman and Berkman was that they fought for liberty.

Their heroism consists in their willingness to make what even the militarists admit is the supreme sacrifice—the sacrifice of their own bodies and of their own freedom.

It is marvelous to think that Alexander Berkman, after serving fourteen years in a Pennsylvania jail with spirit unbroken, is still willing to go to jail again in behalf of the liberties of the people.

The example of Emma Goldman and Berkman is inspiring, and will serve as a beacon light for many a year to come.

BIBLIOGRAPHY

The complete facsimile edition of *Mother Earth* and the *Mother Earth Bulletin*, published in twelve volumes by the Greenwood Reprint Corporation (New York, 1968) with the title *Mother Earth Bulletin*, is long out of print but available in some library collections, as is the microfiche edition. The copy I used in the preparation of this book is in the stacks of Butler Library, Columbia University. The Tamiment Library, New York University, has the microfiche edition of the Greenwood Reprint books, a full set of bound original copies of *Mother Earth*, and an unpublished card-catalog index of the magazine—all of which I made use of, as well as the microfilm edition of *The Emma Goldman Papers*, edited by Candace Falk and Ronald J. Zboray with Daniel Cornford (Cambridge, England, and Alexandria, Virginia: Chadwyck-Healey, 1990), available in the Bobst Library, New York University. Other publications I frequently consulted are listed below. Bibliographical information concerning some earlier and later editions is given in brackets.

Anderson, Margaret. *My Thirty Years' War: The Autobiography, Beginnings and Battles to 1930*. New York: Horizon Press, 1969. [New York: Covici, Friede, 1930.] [New York: Greenwood Press Reprint, 1971.]

Avrich, Paul. *An American Anarchist: The Life of Voltairine de Cleyre*. Princeton: Princeton University Press, 1978.

_____. *Anarchist Portraits*. Princeton: Princeton University Press, 1988.

_____. *Anarchist Voices: An Oral History of Anarchism in America*. Princeton: Princeton University Press, 1995. [Abridged paperback edition, Princeton: Princeton University Press, 1996.]

_____. *The Haymarket Tragedy*. Princeton: Princeton University Press, 1984.

_____. *The Modern School Movement: Anarchism and Education in the United States*. Princeton: Princeton University Press, 1980.

_____. *Sacco and Vanzetti: The Anarchist Background*. Princeton: Princeton University Press, 1991.

Bakunin, Michael. *God and the State*. Translated by Benjamin Tucker, with a new introduction by Paul Avrich. New York: Dover Publications, 1970. [New York: Mother Earth Publishing Association, 1916.]

Berkman, Alexander. *Prison Memoirs of an Anarchist*. New York: Schocken Books, 1970. [New York: Mother Earth Publishing Association, 1912; New York: New York Review Books, 1999.]

Bruns, Roger A. *The Damndest Radical: The Life and World of Ben Reitman, Chicago's Celebrated Social Reformer, Hobo King, and Whorehouse Physician*. Urbana and Chicago: University of Illinois Press, 1987.

Drinnon, Richard. *Rebel in Paradise: A Biography of Emma Goldman*. Boston: Beacon Press, 1970. [Chicago: University of Chicago Press, 1961.]

Falk, Candace. *Love, Anarchy, and Emma Goldman*. Revised edition. New Brunswick, New Jersey, and London: Rutgers University Press, 1990. [First edition, New York: Holt, Rinehart and Winston, 1984.]

Falk, Candace, Stephen Cole, and Sally Thomas, eds. *Emma Goldman: A Guide to Her Life and Documentary Sources*. Cambridge, England, and Alexandria, Virginia: Chadwyck-Healey, 1995.

Gentry, Curt. *Frame-Up: The Incredible Case of Tom Mooney and Warren Billings*. New York: W. W. Norton, 1967.

Goldman, Emma. *Anarchism and Other Essays*. With a new introduction by Richard Drinnon. New York: Dover Publications, 1969. [New York: Mother Earth Publishing Association, 1911.]

_____. *Living My Life*. 2 vols. New York: Dover Publications, 1970. [New York: Alfred A. Knopf, 1931.]

_____. *Red Emma Speaks: Selected Writings and Speeches by Emma Goldman*. Edited by Alix Kates Shulman. New York: Random House, 1972. [New York: Schocken Books, 1983; Amherst, New York: Humanity Books, 1996.]

_____. *The Social Significance of Modern Drama*. Introduction by Harry A. Carlson; preface by Erika Munk. New York: Applause Theatre Book Publishers, 1987. [Boston: Richard A. Badger, 1914.]

Hapgood, Hutchins. *A Victorian in the Modern World*. New York: Harcourt, Brace, 1939. [Seattle: University of Washington Press, 1972.]

Kropotkin, Peter. *The Essential Kropotkin*. Edited by Emile Capouya and Keitha Tompkins. New York: Liveright, 1975.

_____. *Kropotkin's Revolutionary Pamphlets*. Edited with a new introduction by Roger N. Baldwin. New York: Dover Publications, 1970. [New York: Vanguard Press, 1927.]

Luhan, Mabel Dodge. *Movers and Shakers: Volume Three of Intimate Memories*. New York: Harcourt, Brace, 1936.

Murray, Robert K. *Red Scare: A Study in National Hysteria, 1919–1920*. New York: McGraw-Hill, 1964. [Minneapolis: University of Minnesota Press, 1955.]

O'Connor, Richard, and Dale L. Walker. *The Lost Revolutionary: A Biography of John Reed*. New York: Harcourt, Brace & World, 1967.

Painter, Nell Irwin. *Standing at Armageddon: The United States, 1877–1919*. New York and London: W. W. Norton, 1987.

Wexler, Alice. *Emma Goldman in America*. Boston: Beacon Press, 1986. [New York: Pantheon Books, 1984.]

_____. *Emma Goldman in Exile: From the Russian Revolution to the Spanish Civil War*. Boston: Beacon Press, 1989.

Zurier, Rebecca. *Art for The Masses: A Radical Magazine and Its Graphics, 1911–1917*. Philadelphia: Temple University Press, 1988.

INDEX

Some entries include brief identifications and biographical data.